More Praise

*What Every American Should Know
About the Rest of the World*

"Simple. Brilliant. Timely. M. L. Rossi cuts through the jargon and cuts to the quick in her funny, wise analysis of geopolitics. A cheat sh———

———————————————————————————————— re

"M. L. R——————————————————————————————rt-
ful missi——————————————————————————————ut
the Res——————————————————————————————t-
ten into-——————————————————————————————e
when C——————————————————————————————ld
to the si——————————————————————————————a
proper s——————————————————————————————el
writing a——————————————————————————————

———————————————————————————————— go

M. L. R——————————————————————————————s
penned ————————————————————————————,
Newsda————————————————————————————
server.————

What Every
AMERICAN
Should Know About
the Rest of the
WORLD

**Your Guide to Today's Hot Spots,
Hot Shots and Incendiary Issues**

M. L. Rossi

A PLUME BOOK

PLUME
Published by the Penguin Group
Penguin Putnam Inc., 375 Hudson Street, New York, New York 10014, U.S.A.
Penguin Books Ltd, 80 Strand, London WC2R 0RL, England
Penguin Books Australia Ltd, 250 Camberwell Road,
Camberwell, Victoria 3124, Australia
Penguin Books Canada Ltd, 10 Alcorn Avenue, Toronto, Ontario, Canada M4V 3B2
Penguin Books (N.Z.) Ltd, Cnr Rosedale and Airborne Roads, Albany, Auckland 1310,
New Zealand

Penguin Books Ltd, Registered Offices: Harmondsworth, Middlesex, England

First published by Plume, a member of Penguin Group (USA) Inc.

First Printing, April 2003
10   9   8   7   6   5

Ⓟ REGISTERED TRADEMARK—MARCA REGISTRADA

LIBRARY OF CONGRESS CATALOGING-IN-PUBLICATION DATA
Rossi, M. L. (Melissa L.), 1965–
    What every American should know about the rest of the world : your guide to today's hot
spots, hot shots and incendiary issues / M.L. Rossi.
        p.   cm.
    Includes bibliographical references and index.
    ISBN 0-452-28405-8
        1. World politics—20th century. 2. World politics—21st century. 3. Intervention
(International law) 4. International relations. 5. National security. 6. Low intensity
conflicts (Military science) I. Title.

D840.R57 2003
909.83—dc21

                                                                          2003040578

Printed in the United States of America
Set in Helvetica

To Justin Kumpf,
the original armchair diplomat

Acknowledgments

Thanks to my family, who let me overrun their living rooms, expecially my mom, forced to vacuum around the towering books; Katherine Dunn the most evolved person I know; Anne Pramaggiore for making me laugh; artist Karl Abramovic for living my hell; my editor Gary Brozek for putting the pieces of this puzzle together; the amazingly detail-oriented Jenny Good for fantastic research; my agent Joe Regal for cheering me on; Trena Keating for giving me a chance; Jeff Freiert and Norina Frabotta for marshaling this through all phases of production; Laura Blumenthal for perpetual helpfulness; graphic artist Heidi Good for late-night mapmaking; Ruth Mandel for digging up photos; everyone who worked on this hair-puller in Plume's production, art and editing departments; Professor Toby Miller for pointing me in the right direction; Anne "Ling-ling" Millereau for translations; the Dutch artists Alien Oosting and Jeroem Bergen for general help; Keith Bellows and Jayne Wise for sending me to Romania; Marius Dragomir for opening my eyes; Jason Rieff for chronic brightness; Stephen Knipp for chronic insight; Max and Marina for showing up; Pat Talbot for life-changing walks; Bea Harris for being; Catherine and Sam Couplan for adopting me in Bruxelles; Professor Jaime Kooser for showing the real-life application of geography; the late Pete Glennon for his wry observations; and all the generous, kind, tuned in, humorous and wonderful people in assorted countries I've met along the way.

Contents

What Every
AMERICAN
Should Know About
the Rest of the
WORLD

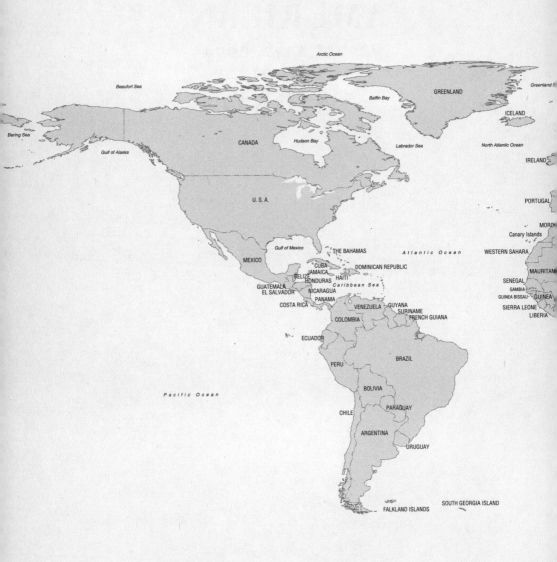

SWEDEN
FINLAND
ESTONIA
LITHUANIA
LATVIA
RMANY POLAND
CZECH BYELARUS
AUSTRIA SLOVAKIA UKRAINE
SLOVENIA HUNGARY
BOSNIA CROATIA ROMANIA MOLDOVA
ALY YUGOSLAVIA BULGARIA Black Sea
MACEDONIA
ALBANIA GEORGIA
GREECE ARMENIA
MALTA TURKEY AZERBAIJAN
TUNISIA CYPRUS
LEBANON SYRIA
ISRAEL
JORDAN IRAQ
LIBYA EGYPT KUWAIT
BAHRAIN
Red QATAR
Sea U.A.E.
SAUDI ARABIA
GER CHAD SUDAN ERITREA OMAN
YEMEN
DJIBOUTI
CENTRAL AFRICAN ETHIOPIA
REPUBLIC
MEROON
A ZAIRE UGANDA KENYA
CONGO RWANDA
BURUNDI
TANZANIA

RUSSIA

Sea of Okhotsk

KAZAKHSTAN

MONGOLIA

Caspian
Sea
UZBEKISTAN KYRGYZSTAN
TURKMENISTAN TAJIKISTAN

Sea of
Japan
NORTH KOREA
CHINA
SOUTH KOREA JAPAN

AFGHANISTAN

PAKISTAN
NEPAL BHUTAN

INDIA
BANGLADESH
MYANMAR
LAOS
Bay of Bengal
South
China Sea
THAILAND
SRI LANKA
VIETNAM
KAMPUCHEA

TAIWAN

Philippine Sea

PHILIPPINES

BRUNEI

MALAYSIA

Pacific Ocean

SOMALIA

Indian Ocean

INDONESIA
PAPUA NEW GUINEA

ANGOLA
ZAMBIA
MALAWI
NAMIBIA ZIMBABWE
BOTSWANA MOZAMBIQUE
SWAZILAND
SOUTH LESOTHO
AFRICA

MADAGASCAR

MAURITIUS
Reunion

Timor Sea

Arafura Sea

Coral Sea

FIJI

NEW CALEDONIA

AUSTRALIA

Great Australian Bight

Tasman Sea

NEW ZEALAND

Introduction

Just call me a cultural romantic. I love to explore other worlds. I love to live where the history is unfamiliar; the architecture thrills me; the language, the food, the rituals are altogether exotic. I love being immersed in the entirely foreign, being in a place where I have to learn about life there from scratch. Travel, in fact, was initially the impetus for this book, if only because in the past decade as I've moved about Europe—Romania to Spain, Croatia to Denmark, Italy to Belgium—I've discovered two crucial things:

1. To understand where you are in the world, you need a map, and
2. Life's a lot easier if you know the language.

That's what this book aims to provide you with: a contextual mapping of the world's geopolitical hot spots and a familiarity with the names, terms and ideas you need to know to decipher global events.

The importance of those simple concepts—maps and vocabulary—struck me when I was in New York during those jittery, stomach-churning weeks after September 11. Like most Americans, I was overwhelmed—not just at the surreal tragedy, but at how the world no longer felt like familiar turf. Overnight the planet, or at least our awareness of it, had ballooned, and Afghanistan, Pakistan, Uzbekistan, Saudi Arabia, Egypt, Sudan, Somalia, Yemen and Indonesia suddenly marched across the TV screen every night. The week before the attack, the media had asked little more than that we knew the general location of Hollywood and Wall Street: now not only were we required to know the whereabouts of half the world, we needed to understand how "they" felt about "us."

Not only were we struggling to keep these countries straight in our mental maps—a task made all the more difficult since we don't study geography extensively in our schools—but our global vocabulary had expanded as well. Previously our world vocab had consisted of little more than "OPEC" and "adios"; now, foreign terms like burka, jihad, madrassa and mujahideen popped up in nearly every news report, and names such as Barak, Chirac, Sharon, Abu Sayyaf, Abu Dhabi, Dubai, Musharraf, Mubarak and Mullah Omar flew nightly from the TV screen. Like many Americans, I felt pummeled by information, and hopelessly lost, feeling like I'd woken up not in a foreign country but on a distant planet. I desperately wanted to learn the new global lingo and to refresh my memory about where these places were, and what was happening there, simply to keep up.

I did what I always do when trying to learn an unknown tongue, be it Russian, Italian, Dutch, Spanish or French: I wrote up a list of words. Instead of jotting down the verb forms for "to eat" and "to be" and phrases like "Excuse me please, where's the loo," I scrawled words such as "Wahhabi," "mufti" and "Pashtun" and other words I picked up from the news. The lists soon turned into flash cards that contained names such as "Ibn Saud: founder of Saudi Arabia," "Hosni Mubarak: president of Egypt" and "King Abdullah II: young monarch of Jordan known for disguises." I started adding quick facts about countries: "Most of world's Muslims live in Indonesia" and "Pakistan's secret service trained the mujahideen." The flash cards grew so bulky that I assembled them into a loose book, adding bits of history that seemed crucial to understanding the present such as "Sykes-Picot: British and French agreement that hacked up Middle East after World War I."

But the world wasn't just about Afghanistan and the Middle East: Kashmir— that volatile region between India and Pakistan—was also snagging headlines as a possible site of nuclear war. The billions the U.S. was giving Colombia no longer concerned only cocaine and left-wing rebels, but also an American oil pipeline there. American troops were heading to the Philippines to help battle the kidnapping terrorist group Abu Sayyaf; American warships were patrolling off Yemen and Somalia. The media spotlight and the world's crucial events wouldn't stay put, and this project just kept growing and gathering momentum of its own, expanding from Asia to Africa, Europe and Latin America and overtaking my life with its intriguing vastness.

Before long, I was imprisoned by towers of books, the printer was clacking all day and all night, I couldn't stay off the Internet and the phone, and spent days and nights reading or writing and calling reporters from Egypt, nurses from Riyadh, UN workers from Serbia, embassies, professors, experts, diplomats, journalists, people I saw on TV, anyone who had insights into global affairs. I forgot to sleep, I forgot to eat, I forgot my friends as I delved deeper and deeper into the puzzle of the world, while simultaneously seeking to answer that question that echoed across our country: "Why do they hate us?" Or more specifically, what are we doing that is so upsetting some members of the global community and making life increasingly dangerous? Or is it just them? Are they just hateful, jealous and deranged?

I found some answers, and I found more questions, more answers, more questions, and through it all, I kept digging. But the more I plunged into my global survey, the more comforting the world became as I began seeing common themes. What emerged wasn't a feeling of doom and terror about madmen overtaking the planet, but instead an understanding that the struggles we're currently witnessing are really nothing new: they've been unfolding for decades or centuries or sometimes millennia.

Take, for example, Al Qaeda. Behind their violent acts, venomous anger and ongoing threats are two basic, related ideas:

1. They want the U.S. to stay out of Muslim countries, and
2. They want to see religious governments installed in Muslim countries.

Though Al Qaeda's techniques are horrifyingly new, their message isn't novel at all. Militant Muslims who want to install Islamic governments and kick out the West have been active in Egypt since the 1930s when their enemy was Britain. Some religious Arabs have been ticked off ever since the Brits and Americans first showed up on their holy soil in the early twentieth century looking for oil; many Arabs, including Al Qaeda's headmen, are furious that the U.S. has maintained a high-profile military presence in the Middle East since 1991's Desert Storm. Further fueling the ire are the U.S.' gifts of billions of dollars of military equipment each year to Egypt and Israel, which ironically, we give because the two agreed to peace in 1978.

Almost all the issues underlying global conflicts are similarly rooted in the past. Some stem from historical inequalities or conflicts that have never been effectively worked out. Take for instance Latin America: the Spanish and Portuguese who colonized South and Central America did more than introduce their languages and religion; still in effect is the racism they inflicted. Now the powerful and rich Latin Americans are almost exclusively of white European descent—with 10 percent holding over 40 percent of the land and the wealth; the Amerindians, the once-powerful Aztecs and Mayans, for example, are peasants. And throughout Latin America—from Mexico to Brazil—the native groups and other peasants are rising up demanding farmland as well as the arrival of running water and electricity to the remote regions where they've been shoved.

Europe is antsy about the number of immigrants—particularly Arab Muslims—who have settled there, but the truth is many European countries invited them in during "guest worker programs" in the 1970s, when the foreigners were assigned low-paying menial tasks. The jobs may have dried up, but the foreigners stayed.

Against this backdrop of old issues resurfacing, there are new developments complicating the picture. Of number one importance, as I see it, is that the world is more heavily armed than ever before, largely because the U.S.—along with Britain, Russia and France—financially profits from selling arms, explosives and military equipment, a racket that is the world's biggest money-maker, generating $700 billion, or more, every year. The world's arsenals contain deadlier weapons than ever before, thanks to scientific leaps made during World War II and the mind game of the Cold War, during which research into chemical warfare and bioweaponry soared. Even more frightening, some of the toxic compounds used to make these weapons are simply missing. As I write this, the world is wondering what substance the Russian government used to free hostages held by Chechen extremists, resulting in the death of more than one hundred hostages.

Despite such fiascos as Chernobyl and Three Mile Island, we still embrace nuclear power that poses grave new terrorist threats, particularly since we still have no idea how to safely store its deadly waste filled with radioactive isotopes that have half-lives longer than the length of time humans have been on Earth. In addition, more people occupy the planet now than ever in history, and the 6 billion population of today will rise to 9 billion by 2050, leading to more conflicts for space and resources. Half of the population lives in poverty, 20 percent don't have clean drinking water, aquifers are drying up, and we may soon see water wars. Millions of people died from famine in the past decade, even though there is plenty of food in the world; now the same number of people—over 1 billion—suffer from being underweight as suffer from being overweight. While women are showing up more in the political arena, millions of women still are considered second-class citizens and are subjected to disgusting indignities, from slavery to rape camps. Since the Soviet Union broke up, the world has only one superpower—the U.S.—and we're accused of being a bully and a self-serving unilateralist that wants to dominate the world, not share it. Oil has become more valuable than ever, and the U.S. is willing to go to war to ensure that we can inexpensively feed our cars. In the same way that many Americans turned to God after September 11—and flags began hanging in churches—Muslims too are more strongly embracing their religion: as incomes drop in Islamic countries while populations and unemployment levels rise, more and more people want hard-core religious governments, believing they will solve their problems and allow them to go back to the past and shut out the West. Ironically, at the same time that some are calling for isolation, the world—economically, politically and information-wise—is more connected than ever before. I'll deal more specifically with these issues in the Big Picture section.

What's happened before our eyes is that this has become one tightly linked global society—and one in which U.S. citizens play an increasingly important role. Americans make the most money, we use the most resources, we theoretically have more power than any other people on the planet. Quite often we throw that power away by not staying informed, by not writing letters, not discussing issues with friends or seeking alternative views, not making phone calls, not voicing our support or opposition to our elected representatives, and by shrugging off the rest of the world and becoming complacent, believing that there is nothing that we can do.

I believe that's beginning to change and that people are tuning in to the global picture. I think that people are thirsty to learn and that they want to have a say in the U.S.' role in the world. I hope this book gives readers the basics they need to feel confident putting together the pieces of the world puzzle and that it whets their appetites to learn much, much more. I pray that this book makes people feel like global citizens and that it makes them want to pick up their pens and their phones and turn to their keyboards to communicate about what is happening on this planet. My experience isn't that people are "out to get us." To the contrary, many people in other countries like Americans: they think we're friendly and kind, but alarmingly ignorant about the world. I hope this book helps erase the term "Stupid American" from the global vocabulary.

In writing this book, I've tried to simplify information and offer the Berlitz approach to geopolitics: you may not get the fine points, but it will hopefully make you conversational. I've thrown in humor whenever possible to try and lighten this up. I've included some controversial information and at points I've been extremely critical, although you will note that I'm an equal opportunity critic. I've included some unflattering views on the U.S., simply because I believe those views help answer the question of why the U.S. is sometimes a political target. Although my intentions were to write a simple, objective book, my opinions have slipped in, most obviously under the heading "Armchair Diplomat Says." (If you want my bias on the Israeli-Palestinian question, it's this: I am very disappointed with all sides, which is also my feeling toward Kashmir, as well as Colombia.)

I've organized this by countries, according, more or less, to their relevancy in the world picture as of late 2002; however, just because a country is listed later or not listed at all doesn't mean it's not relevant, just that it didn't fit in. The first section—"Tickers"—are time bombs where something is going to change and quickly. "Slow Tickers" are countries where the situations are shifting but are not as volatile as "Tickers." "Talkers" are countries that people are talking about— or that are headed by loquacious leaders. In some cases, rather than talk about individual countries, I've discussed regions.

In each section, I've tried to break up the information—so you can read parts of it on the subway, on a break or when you're on hold. In each country profile, you'll find "Fast Facts"—the vital stats on a country; you'll also find "Hot Spots" and "Hot Shots," which are the geographical flash points and names to know. In "Tickers" and "Slow Tickers" you'll also find more analysis in "Background Briefing." After the country profiles, there's another section called "The Big Picture": it gives a brief overview of continental issues. In the very back of the book, there is a glossary broken up into two sections: "Terms of War, Peace, Religion and Geography" and "Power Players and Elitist Groups"—essentially things and people.

As for how to read this, it doesn't have to be read in any particular order, but I'd recommend taking it in somewhat slowly. Whatever you do, do not try to plow through this whole book over a weekend: you'll be overwhelmed and you'll get a huge headache and you'll forget everything by Monday. Whatever your opinions about this book, I hope only that it makes you think, that it makes you care and that it helps you to become a citizen of the world. Because if there's one thing the twenty-first century has taught us already, it's that we're all in this boat together.

— M. L. Rossi
October 27, 2002

Iraq . . . Israel and Palestine . . .
Indonesia . . . Kashmir/India/
Pakistan **PART ONE** . . . North
Korea . . . Colombia . . . Colombia . . .
Iraq . . . Israel and Palestine . . .
Indonesia . . . Kashmir/India/

Tickers . . . . .

. . . Palestine . . . Indonesia
. . . Kashmir/India/Pakistan . . . North
Korea . . . Colombia . . . Iraq . . . Israel
and Palestine . . . Indonesia . . .
Kashmir/India/Pakistan . . . North
Korea . . . Colombia . . . Iraq . . . Israel
and Palestine . . . Indonesia. . .
Kashmir/India/Pakistan . . . North
Korea . . . Colombia . . . Iraq . . . Israel
and Palestine . . . Indonesia . . .
Kashmir/India/Pakistan . . . North
Korea . . . Colombia . . . Iraq . . . Israel
and Palestine . . . Indonesia . . .
Kashmir/India/Pakistan . . . North

IRAQ

Standout Qualities

Broken: U.S. and U.K. broke Saddam's spell
Broken: different ethnic/religious groups vie for power
Broken: Iraq owes billions—can it pay?

Résumé

Home of the world's second largest oil reserves, Iraq was the site of a debilitating U.S.-led attack in March 2003. Saddam Hussein is gone—and law and order—now the U.S. and U.K. are baby-sitting until some government can be stitched together. The weapons of mass destruction that prompted the controversial war haven't been found, nor have Saddam and sons, but the oil (that some believe triggered the war) is flowing, and sanctions are lifting.

Quick Tour

It may be hard to imagine now, with its radioactive soil, its chronic looting, battling ethnic/religious factions, endless gunfire and protests against the occupying U.S., but Iraq—or Mesopotamia as it was known pre-twentieth-century—has often represented the crowning pinnacle of human progress.

Believed to be home of the Garden of Eden and later ark-builder Noah, the land of the Tigris and Euphrates Rivers spawned the first civilizations in 4000 B.C.: here in Sumer the earliest writing—cuneiform—was scratched into clay tablets with fashioned reeds, seeds were poked into the silted soil and different tribes learned to get along—creating cities, markets, agriculture and international trade in between inventing the wheel and the plow. Formerly home of Babylon with its hanging gardens of tropical plants tumbling from high towers, Mesopotamia was also site of the Muslim world's precious jewel—Baghdad. From the eighth century through the thirteenth, the capital of the Abbasid dynasty was a center of learning, art and luxury, where scribes translated Ptolemy and Plato, medicine and science flourished, calculus and algebra were born and *The Arabian Nights* was penned, while Europe stumbled through the Dark Ages.

LAND O' CHAOS

The latest war in Iraq started March 20, 2003, with the U.S.-U.K. invasion; the nastiest fighting was over in a month. But Iraq is still a mess: chronic water shortages and contamination are a source of both strife and cholera epidemics, gunfire crackles day and night, street kids roam alleys, work is at a standstill for many, U.S. distribution of food and money causes chaos, most everything has been looted from hospitals and palaces, orphanages and museums.

Of particular concern: although oil fields were secured, the coalition initially forgot to guard laboratories and other sites where radioactive materials were stored. Who knows how much cesium-137 or other materials for making "dirty bombs" were snatched by the mobs?

Later part of the Ottoman Empire—which was carved up after World War I—most of Mesopotamia became Iraq in 1920. The country never really grew as a united entity, largely because the British drew self-serving boundaries officially roping in three groups that have never gotten along: the Kurds, the Sunnis and the Shiites. Initially presided over by British-backed Hashemite King Faisal and his heirs, the ethnically diverse and disunited country—which had experienced twenty-three coups since 1920—was overtaken by the Ba'ath party in 1968. There wasn't a successful uprising since 1979, when Saddam grabbed the reins and began running acid baths for his foes.

NO NUKES! 'CEPT OURS!

In 1981, Israel bombed Iraq's only nuclear plant, fearing that Saddam would make weapons of mass destruction. Israel is still the only country in the Middle East that is known to have nuclear bombs—and plenty of 'em.

Historically, the country has been segmented—Shiite Muslims occupy the sandy south, ethnic Kurds live in the mountainous north, and a Sunni Muslim majority lives in the central area around Baghdad. Iraq has become more partitioned after 1991's Desert Storm: to protect Shiites and Kurds from Saddam's wrath, the U.S. and U.K. established "no-fly zones," which prevented Saddam's military from bombing them.

DOWNWARD BOUND

Under Saddam, national debt shot into the multibillions, the value of the dinar sank, and, once economic sanctions were slapped on in 1990, unemployment hit 50 percent, some 80 percent lived in poverty and street kids became a chronic problem.

The descent of the not long ago affluent country—which holds the world's second largest oil reserves—was brought on by its megalomaniac dictator, Saddam Hussein, who has been dragging Iraq into costly and purposeless wars since about the minute he blasted his way to the top of the Ba'ath party

pyramid in 1979—murdering and torturing his enemies all the way. Or rather
what pushed the country to this nadir was Saddam's bizarre relationship with
the U.S., especially its two Presidents Bush.

KURDISTAN

The Kurds, a non-Arab ethnic group in northern Iraq and Turkey, had been
promised their own country by the British, who ran Iraq after World War I. They
didn't get it then, but Saddam's massacres of them—and resultant U.S.-U.K.
"no-fly zones" in the 1990s—inadvertently created the long-sought Kurdistan
in northern Iraq. Its postwar status is shaky; violence with Arab Iraqis is growing; Turkey fears Kurds will seal off oil-rich areas Kirkuk and Mosul.

Saddam Hussein wasn't always portrayed by the U.S. government as a modern-
day Hitler: when he launched his first pointless war in 1980—against ayatollah-
happy Iran—the Reagan administration was cheering him on, and reportedly
supplying him with aid and arms. After all, Iran had taken Americans hostage and
Saddam Hussein was initially pushing his country in a forward direction: he offered
free education and encouraged females to become doctors and lawyers; modern
health care was suddenly available, roads were paved and new housing shot up.

THE ROOTS

Saddam launched the Iran-Iraq War over access to the Shatt al-Arab waterway,
but he also invoked historical Arabic battles with Persians (aka Iranians).

The war with Iran, which Saddam thought would be breezy, instead sucked
Iraq into a downward spiral: it dragged on for eight bloody years—during which
a million died and Saddam borrowed $50 billion from Saudi Arabia and Kuwait.
By the time the UN forced the war's end in 1988, Iraq was strapped and hadn't
lassoed even a millimeter of land. As the scale of Saddam's failure became obvious, the Kurds in the north rebelled, hoping he was weak. The Iraqi leader
sent in his beleagured army, who destroyed four thousand Kurd villages and
killed some 180,000, many by sarin and mustard gases.

CHEMICAL WARFARE

Iraq first introduced chemical warfare in the final phases of the Iran-Iraq War.
Even after the lung-scorching gases were turned "on his own people," the U.S.,

then under President George Bush, Sr., continued to support Saddam and supply Iraq with aid, food and "dual use" equipment that could be used for producing weapons of mass destruction. Assorted forms of U.S. aid continued until
the U.S. slapped on an embargo after Saddam fixed his covetous gaze on
Kuwait in August 1990.

By 1990, the wealthy Kuwaiti Emir Jabir al-Sabah was heavily breathing down
Saddam's back to repay Iraq's hefty loans; the already difficult demand was all
the more so since Kuwait was "slant drilling" into Iraqi oil fields, flooding the oil
market with surplus oil and lowering the world prices. Invoking an old territorial
dispute and claiming that Kuwait was part of Iraq, Saddam sent his troops rolling
in to overtake the small and poorly guarded Kuwaiti kingdom in August, a feat that
didn't take long. Seizing the country, making it part of Iraq and kicking out its royal
family wasn't enough for sadistic Saddam: his soldiers rounded up at least twenty
thousand Kuwaitis, tortured them with any of Iraq's notorious 107 methods of
pain infliction and slaughtered them in front of their families for dramatic effect.

MIXED SIGNALS OR GREEN LIGHT?

Saddam was no doubt confused when the U.S. began snarling over the
Kuwaiti invasion. In a July 25, 1990, meeting with April Glaspie, U.S. ambassador to Iraq, Saddam asked her opinion of an Iraqi invasion on Kuwait. She
reportedly said, "We have no opinion on your Arab-Arab conflicts . . . the
Kuwait issue is not associated with America." Saddam had no idea what he
would face when eight days later his army blasted into Kuwait.

From the moment Iraq grabbed Kuwait, Saddam became an official enemy
of Uncle Sam. Of particular concern to the Bush Sr. administration was the
proximity of Saudi Arabian oil fields.

WAS HE OR WASN'T HE?

Although his greed can't be questioned, it's unclear whether Saddam ever
planned on attacking Saudi Arabia—which was the biggest factor in the U.S.
sending 430,000 troops to the Middle East in preparation for war. Some in the
know doubt it. And there's also a school that believed that photos the U.S.
showed to Saudi's King Fahd—showing Iraqi troops heading for the Saudi
Arabian border—were doctored.

After demanding that Iraq pull out from Kuwait, a U.S.-led coalition of Western and Arab armies launched Desert Storm in January 1991 and pushed the Iraqi forces out in a shower of bombs and missiles that had a new tank-penetrating twist: depleted uranium tips.

IRAQI MEMENTOS

Fleeing back toward the borders, the Iraqi army set hundreds of Kuwait oil fields ablaze, exploding oil wells along the way and fires belched oily smoke for months. A river of petro-goo flooded into the Persian Gulf, causing the worst environmental debacle and biggest oil slick known to the region.

Then on February 28, 1991, the bombardment stopped. Coalition members debated the right to kill Saddam and worried what factions would step in if he died. And ever since the coalition pulled back, the U.S. has been kicking itself that it didn't finish off Saddam way back then when it could have.

In early 1991, President Bush, Sr., encouraged the Kurds in the north and the Shiites in the south to rise up against Saddam, implying the U.S. would back them. The U.S.-inspired freedom fighters, believing that the allied coalition was following from behind, rose up all right—particularly the Kurds who "liberated" cities across the north. Their freedom didn't last for long: as soon as his soldiers returned from Kuwait, Saddam sent his army out to recapture the cities. His soldiers slaughtered some 250,000 and sent the "freedom fighters" running to the mountains and escaping into Iran. The now reluctant Kurds haven't forgotten that despite promises the U.S. wasn't there to back them up.

NUKES LITE

Armor-piercing depleted uranium, used to tip missiles and bombs, has only 70 percent as much radioactivity as natural uranium. But radioactive it is, deadly when inhaled and toxic when it seeps into groundwater as well. The U.S. Defense Department is tripping over itself trying to deny that depleted uranium has any detrimental effects. Among those who think otherwise: Iraqi doctors who say that thousands of Iraqi children are dying from leukemia and assorted cancers and that the rates of the diseases are up to seven times higher than before Desert Storm. Some researchers in the international medical community are also now wondering if "Gulf War Syndrome" is actually radiation sickness from exposure to DU weapons. Except for Britain, the EU countries won't use it and NATO has issued a moratorium on DU weapons.

Although Saddam survived, the international community whittled away at his power: Saddam-controlled Iraq was a third of its former size, ever since the UN imposed borders designed to protect Kurds and Shiites from future massacres. The UN also forced Iraq to undergo inspections of its nonconventional weapons, the vast majority of which were destroyed by 1998. Inspectors believed that Iraq was not showing its full hand, however—and in December of that year, U.S. and British planes bombed Iraq for four consecutive nights. By the end of it, Saddam banned the UN inspectors from returning.

AFTERTHOUGHTS

Saddam's massacre of Shiites and Kurds forced the international community to do something: the U.S. and Britain drew up "no fly zones"—where Iraqi planes and military were not allowed to enter—in April 1991. Although not officially UN-approved, they're patrolled by U.S. and British warplanes, which frequently bomb Iraqi military installations. Civilians too have frequently been hit, including the Shiites and Kurds whom the no fly zones are meant to protect.

From 1990 to 2003, Iraq was under heavy international sanctions cuffed on by the UN Security Council and designed to prevent Saddam from building up his military or death arsenal. Controversial from the start, sanctions created a black market where a few thrived, while the commoner typically lived in poverty, unable to get medical supplies and living in a stagnant, inflated world where at least 50 percent were unemployed and hawked their heirlooms to survive. Despite an "oil for food" program that allowed Iraq to essentially trade its crude for food and supplies, Iraq says over a million people perished as a result of the sanctions. Some dispute the numbers; no one argues the disastrous effects.

SANCTIONED STUPIDITY?

Not only did sanctions backfire as a method to strangle Saddam, they gave him new reasons to gripe about the U.S. Arab countries loudly protested the economic handcuffs, and many countries ignored them altogether, with the money from the cheap oil they bought mostly going straight to Saddam's piggy bank. U.S.-secured sanctions on Iraq were also one of the stated reasons Osama bin Laden launched his attack on Americans.

While his people suffered, Saddam built himself new palaces with painted tiles, brocade curtains, marble steps and glassy pools. Black market money also built his grandiose new "mother of all wars" mosque, and as the man exhibited an opposite Midas touch on Iraq, tried to convince his people he was not a world-class failure.

Then, President George W. Bush strolled into office, plotting to topple Saddam from the start. The UN Security Council demanded that Iraq turn over its WMD, but wouldn't back an invasion. In March 2003, the U.S. led a thin coalition—mostly the U.K.—in a very controversial war supported by 70 percent of U.S. residents. Major fighting lasted twenty-six days, but Iraq is neither stable nor secure; the WMD that prompted the war have yet to be uncovered. Despite the questioned methods to do so, at least creepy Saddam is gone.

Future Forecast

Chaos and mayhem. Iraqis wanted Saddam out, but many don't want the U.S. calling the shots. Some want a theocracy, work is at a standstill, money and clean water are hard to find, violence and looting are everywhere. Until the country is stabilized—could take years—Iraq is a mess.

TALLYING UP THE COST OF WAR

According to *The Independent* newspaper of London, as of May 1, 2003:

- Dead: 2,500 Iraqi civilians; 10,000 Iraqi fighters; 105 U.S. soldiers
- Depending: 17 million Iraqis rely on food aid
- Spent: $55 billion by U.S. to fight war
- Spending: $100 billion estimated cost to rebuild Iraq

Background Briefing

With all the well-known "War on Iraq" hawks that President George W. Bush surrounded himself with from his first day in office, you'd think somebody would have figured out who would replace Saddam after he's toppled. Dr. Paul Wolfowitz, deputy secretary of defense, stands behind the Iraqi National Congress, a group of Sunni, Shiite and Kurd businessmen that was literally cobbled together by the CIA and an advertising firm who gave the group its catchy name. Maybe INC needs a snappy jingle too, because they seem to lack popular support in Iraq. Since Saddam was tossed, so many factions are battling for power it's mind-boggling: Baathists (of Saddam's party), Royalists (who want the Hashemite monarchy back on the scene), Kurds (who want their autonomy),

Saddam Hussein: the real Saddam or one of his doubles? (Source: Associated Press)

Shia (some of whom want a religious government), Sunni (some of whom want a theocracy), returned exiles, Assyrians, communists, and even Iran are all pushing forth their agenda, with Turkey calling its demands from the sidelines.

The U.S. wants to establish an interim government, but prospects are so daunting that in May 2003, the government announced it was postponing plans until summer, at earliest. Meanwhile, Al Qaeda attacks in Saudi Arabia and Morocco add to the edginess in the Middle East.

Hot Spots

Tuwaitha: This nuclear research lab outside of Baghdad was looted by Iraqis, who made off with assorted radioactive materials (uranium and cesium-137 among them)—perfect for dirty bombs. Now heavily guarded.

Kirkuk: Located in the north, this oil-bubbling area was Arab-run under Saddam. Now there are lots of conflicts between Kurds and Arabs, and Turkey is worried that Kurds will claim as their own.

Mosul: Oil-rich area in the north, its subterranean wealth explains why the British—who thought they could control King Faisal—put the northern area on the map under "Iraq."

Basra: Area in the Shiite south near battlefields where many depleted uranium missiles were fired. Iraqi physicians say cancer rates are abnormally high—as are birth defects. So many U.S.-U.K. bombs were dropped here to protect Shia in the 1990s that its main drag was called the Road of Death.

Baghdad: Dotted with some magnificent palaces, it's mostly a pit, with seventies-style communist housing and dilapidated slums. Crime now sky-high, libraries and palaces trashed, the masses protesting. A powder keg.

Kurdistan: This chunk of farmland in Iraq's north and east folds into mountains and holds four million Kurds who now call the unofficially autonomous region "Kurdistan," even though it is often divided between rival Kurd factions. Sanctions helped Kurdistan in a big way: Kurds taxed the trucks roaring through with illegal Iraqi oil. Look for major turf wars here among Kurds, Arabs, Turks.

Hot Shots

Saddam Hussein: Iraqi president from 1979 to 2003, aka "The Butcher of Baghdad," this torture-freak dictator was responsible for the death of millions— Iranians, Kurds, Shiites, Kuwaitis, even his two formerly favorite sons-in-law. Saddam makes everyone fearful that they're next to go in one of the many gruesome ways he's devised. He has a gentle side: a reputed former lover says he's sweet in the sack (and takes Viagra), adores dancing to "Strangers in the Night" and loves to don a cowboy hat and watch videos of his foes being tortured. Yikes. Out of power and in hiding.

AND TALENTED TOO!

While being essentially under "country arrest," Saddam reportedly kept busy by penning a romance novel that, so far, has been released only in Iraq. Called *Zabibah and the King,* it's the symbol-laden tale of a king (Saddam) who falls in love with a commoner (Iraq) who has been raped by villains (the U.S.). He's said to be working on a follow-up. Better rush it.

The Hussein Boys: Qusay and Uday: Younger Qusay, the family security man, was being groomed for the dictatorship, even though he messed up royally in 1996, when an explosion injured Saddam and maimed sibling Uday. Formerly the heir apparent and head of the nasty secret police, Uday was best known for his forthright pickup style: "See girl, rape her." After he beat Saddam's favorite bodyguard to death with a bat, Uday was tossed in jail for months at Pappy's request. Disappeared with billions in cash.

Iraqi National Congress: Opposition party that dared not meet in Iraq, they've been plotting a takeover for years and may soon get the chance to sit in the driver's seat for at least a quick spin.

UNMOVIC: United Nations Monitoring and Inspection Committee, this team was sent into Iraq in late 2002 to uncover Saddam's weapons of mass destruction. Headed by Dr. Hans Blix.

Ahmad Chalabi: Head of the Iraqi National Congress, he's been lobbying DC for years. Persistence may pay off.

Massoud Barzani: Head of the Kurdistan Democratic Party and one of the Kurds' two main leaders, he foolishly asked Saddam's army to come in to fight his rival Talibani. Shortly thereafter he SOS-ed the international community to help get Saddam's boys out.

Jalal Talabani: Head of the Patriotic Union of Kurdistan, he and Barzani aren't fighting—this week. Future friction between the two Kurdish power players in Northern Iraq seems inevitable; they've been at it for years. Kurdish media reports Talabani has offered to shelter Saddam's family—or at least the daughters.

UNITED STATES: MIDEAST BRANCH?

In early January 2003, President George W. Bush unveiled tentative plans for a post-Saddam Iraq. Bush envisions that the U.S. will occupy the country for at least eighteen months, perhaps hostilely. The first thing to be "secured": Iraqi oil fields.

UNFORESEEN COMPLICATIONS

When the U.S.-U.K. forces decided to invade Iraq—with some token nods from assorted governments and downright condemnation from others—the international community was shaken: the UN Security Council (which wasn't consulted about the attack) was emasculated, France and Germany were scorned by the U.S., the European Union split on the matter, and world relations became their testiest since World War II. Initially, the U.S. didn't want the UN weapons inspectors back in. However, with news that radioactive materials were snagged from Iraqi labs, the U.S. is welcoming UNMOVIC back. Although the American media may not tell you, there is still a lot of anger at the U.S. about the move that many perceived as being all about oil and real estate.

ISRAEL AND PALESTINE

FAST FACTS ISRAEL

Country:	State of Israel
Capital:	Tel Aviv; Jerusalem (claimed)
Government:	parliamentary democracy
Independence:	created 14 May 1948, from British mandate over Palestine
Population:	6,300,000
Leader:	Prime Minister Ariel Sharon (March 2001)
Ethnicity:	80% Jewish; 20% non-Jewish (mostly Arab)
Religion:	80% Jewish; 15% Sunni Muslim; 2% Christian
Language:	Hebrew, Arabic
Literacy:	98%
Exports:	machinery, software, cut diamonds, food
Per capita GDP:	$18,900 (2000)
Unemployment:	9% (2000 estimate)
Percentage living in poverty:	some estimates put at 20%
Known for:	intense history

FAST FACTS PALESTINE

Country:	Not a country; divided into West Bank and Gaza Strip
Capital:	Jerusalem (declared)
Government:	transitional
Independence:	N/A
Population:	West Bank: 2,163,667 (2002 estimate; includes 182,000 Jewish settlers in West Bank and 176,000 Jewish settlers in East Jerusalem) Gaza Strip: 1,178,200 (2001 estimate)
Leader:	Prime Minister Mahmoud Abbas
Ethnicity:	West Bank: 83% Palestinian and other Arab; 17% Jewish Gaza Strip: 99% Palestinian and other Arab

Religion:	West Bank: 75% Sunni Muslim; 17% Jewish
	Gaza Strip: Sunni Muslim
Language:	Arabic, Hebrew
Literacy:	N/A
Exports:	olives, fruit, limestone
Per capita GDP:	$1,000
Unemployment:	26% both West Bank and Gaza Strip (2001)
Percentage living in poverty:	50% or more
Known for:	suicide bombers

Standout Qualities

Squished: 6 million Israelis and 3 million Palestinians living too close together
Expansive: Israeli settlements, war grabs enlarge Israel, decrease Palestine
Armed: all Israeli men and women well trained in modern, state-of-the-art
army; no Palestinian army but plenty of suicide bombers

WHERE IS PALESTINE?

The land that the British called Palestine after World War I was segmented
into Transjordan (now Jordan) in 1921 and Israel in 1948. What remains of
Palestine at this point is the West Bank and Gaza Strip, the two areas where
many Palestinians live, although the West Bank, which includes East Jerusalem and Bethlehem, is occupied by Israeli settlers—a point of major violent
contention.

WHY WERE THE BRITISH IN PALESTINE?

After the fall of the Ottoman Empire in 1918, the League of Nations granted
Britain and France "mandates" to oversee the Middle East and hack it up as
they wished, installing whatever governments they felt were appropriate.

ARMS FOR PEACE

The U.S. out-and-out gives Israel more than $3 billion annually for participating
in the 1978 Camp David Accords and keeping peace with Egypt. That financial
carrot is also dangled before Egypt, which receives $2.2 billion annually from
the U.S. Both countries must use the bulk of the money to purchase U.S. arms
and military equipment.

Imbalance of Power: Another big issue: Israel has nuclear bombs and the neighbors don't, yet. Iran, however, is bringing nuclear plants on line, much to Israel's dismay.

Résumé

Israel hasn't really known a day of peace since it was unveiled in 1948 as the long-sought homeland for Jews: three major wars and assorted peace powwows later, serene coexistence is still a distant dream, broken by the blasts of Palestinian suicide bombers and made more unlikely by the bulldozing of Palestinian houses by Israeli tanks.

BOTTOM LINES

The underlying issues of Mideast problems: land and water. Over the years, Israel has vastly increased holdings of both. Most of Israel's water now comes from territories it illegally occupies: Syria's Golan Heights and Palestine's West Bank.

Nation-Making: Typically countries are born through wars, empire expansions and/ or colonization. Israel is the only country that was created by the UN.

Quick Tour

From Old Jerusalem's Wailing Wall—stuffed with notes to God—to the collective farms near the Mediterranean coast that grow avocados, lemons and thyme, Israel may be at its most precarious hour. Venomous

anger spews forth from all surrounding countries and Israeli nightclubs, buses, and stores are under siege from suicide bombers who with the pull of a cord erase their own lives and dozens of others in a shower of blood and nails.

ORGANIZATION

Competing political parties—such as right-wing Likud and more moderate Labor—often butt heads, but Israel is highly organized and presents a united front. Palestinians are entirely fragmented: they haven't had cohesive leadership, government, credo, goals, military factions or methods—ever.

Then again, Israel's fifty-five years have been filled with nothing but precarious hours. From the minute in November 1947 that the UN proposed that Palestine—or what was left of it after British pens had hacked it up—be split into a homeland for Jews and a Palestinian state, the Arab world has been screaming its loud objection.

ZIONIST RENAISSANCE

Subject to expulsions, persecution and pogroms for millenia, the Jewish diaspora was spread across the world by the nineteenth century. Writer Theodor Herzl—who'd never been to Palestine—replanted the idea of a country for the Jews in the late 1800s. His ideas, captured in his book *The Jewish State*, became the guiding light for a revival of Zionism—the idea that Jews should live in Palestine, where the acts of their religious history unfolded.

Palestinians refused to endorse the splitting of this holy real estate into a state for Jews and a state for Arabs. Even before the UN—which had inherited the Palestine problem from the British—began studying the issue in the 1940s, the Jews and the Arabs were already grating on each other's nerves: fighting had broken out numerous times since the 1890s when Jewish Zionists had begun streaming in and buying property in the Holy Land.

BRITISH DESIGNS

The creation of countries in the Middle East is tightly linked to the British, who've been mucking about there since the early twentieth century. In 1917, the British presented the Balfour Declaration—an amazing piece of diplomatic double

talk, which the Zionists interpreted as ensuring the creation of a Jewish homeland and the Palestinians interpreted as meaning exactly the opposite. In control of Palestine after 1920 thanks to the League of Nations and deals with the
French, the British immediately lopped off 80 percent of Palestine and gave it
to the Hashemite clan. That land became Jordan. As Zionists poured into the
20 percent that was left of Palestine, Arab-Jewish violence erupted. The British
curtailed Jewish immigration during World War II, seen as particularly cruel since
some who arrived were sent right back to Germany. Befuddled about what to
do about creating a country for Jews after the war, the British tossed the hot
potato to the newly formed UN in 1947 and hightailed it out.

The Jews who'd come from all over the world to start this new country didn't
much care what the Palestinians thought about the 1947 UN Partition Plan:
traumatized from the fresh horrors of the Nazi campaign to destroy them, Jews
wanted their own turf more than ever. Given their history of living in Jerusalem—
a city given them by King David in the tenth century B.C., they also believed they
deserved "the promised land." On May 14, 1948, Prime Minister David Ben-
Gurion proclaimed the birth of the new state of Israel. On May 15, 1948, Israel
woke up to explosions and gunfire. The Welcome Wagon it wasn't: armies from
Egypt, Syria and Jordan rose together to take down the fledgling country in a
war that raged for the next eleven months.

BLOODY HISTORY

Highlights of major Arab-Israeli Wars:

1948 War of Independence: Israel attacked by Egypt, Syria, Jordan,
Lebanon and Iraq. RESULTS: Jordan takes West Bank and East Jerusalem; Israel takes West Jerusalem, extends into Palestinian area and increases Israeli land by one third. Eight hundred thousand Palestinians are
displaced, many fleeing to Jordan.

1956 Suez Operation: Israel, Britain and France attack Egypt when
Nasser nationalizes Suez Canal. RESULTS: U.S. and UN force the invaders to pull out.

1967 Six Day War: Israel launches preemptive strikes against Egyptian,
Syrian and Jordanian troops at its border. RESULTS: Israel takes East Jerusalem, parts of West Bank, Syria's Golan Heights and Egypt's Sinai and
quadruples land holdings. (Sinai was returned in 1982 after 1978 Camp
David Accords).

1973 Yom Kippur War: Egypt and Syria attack Israel during holy day. RESULTS: Syria gets sliver of Golan Heights back; Arab countries launch oil embargo against U.S. for rushing arms to Israel.

The fledgling nation clamped onto its land in the first Arab-Israeli War of 1948–1949. In fact, as with the Six Day War of 1967, the Israelis latched on to more. Between war gains and illegal settlements in Palestine, Israel now spreads over 80 percent of the land drawn in the original UN map. And with each expansion, Palestinians are further pushed out of what was originally supposed to be Palestinian land. Palestine is now a patchwork of districts in the West Bank and Gaza, broken up by Israeli settlements and dotted by checkpoints; Palestinian residents are often under curfews from the Israeli government, and when another suicide bomb goes off, Israeli tanks roll in and crush Palestinian houses.

THE SIX DAY WAR

Of all the Arab-Israeli wars, the 1967 war was the most significant land grab into Palestine. Many peace proposals—such as the 2002 Saudi Peace Plan—hinge upon Israelis pulling back to pre-1967 boundaries: that would require that Israel give up East Jerusalem, the Golan Heights and parts of the West Bank and Gaza Strip seized during the Six Day War. UN Resolutions 242 (of 1967) and 338 (of 1973) call for Israel to pull out of "occupied territories." So did Jimmy Carter accepting the Nobel Peace Prize in 2002.

Unlike Israel, Palestine has never had an army; for that matter Palestine has never been an organized country, but rather a group of people historically functioning without an umbrella government and often running small family businesses curing olives and making soap.

Many Palestinians don't even live in Palestine anymore: as Israel claimed swatches of Palestinian territory through the years, millions fled to Jordan, Lebanon and other parts of the Middle East. The closest thing Palestine now has to a government is the Palestinian Authority: created in 1993—as part of the Oslo Accords—this loose, weak and ineffective political arrangement theoretically oversees what is left of Palestine—the West Bank and Gaza—and is headed by Yasser Arafat, its elected president. The Palestinian Authority also includes a legislative council and some semblance of a police force. Flimsy and poorly organized from the start, the PA is now barely functioning: in retaliation for suicide bombings during 2001 and 2002 Israel froze Palestinian accounts, ravaged Arafat's compound, and considerably weakened the police force. President Arafat looked entirely impotent when Israeli tanks trampled houses. And when the Israeli Army pulled males out of refugee camps, looking for Palestinian terrorists, Arafat could do nothing, including at times, leave his compound.

Even without the Israeli actions, the PA wasn't exactly effective: it's believed that at least 40 percent of the authority's international aid has been squandered. In fact, much of the social services—welfare, medical aid and scholarships—in Palestine are provided not by the government but by Hamas. Started by the Muslim Brotherhood in 1987, Hamas is also known for its gung-ho militants and is a main force behind suicide bombers. Not only does Hamas hate Israel—its destruction is one of their stated goals—they also despise Yasser Arafat. When Arafat makes a promise to halt suicide bombing, Hamas has two reasons to break it. Bomb-happy Islamic Jihad are making life bloodier too.

FRACTIONED FACTIONS

Over the decades, some Palestinians put together militant factions, many of which don't get along. The Palestine Liberation Organization (PLO) was formed by the Arab League; factionalized guerrillas who leaned toward banditry and killing civilians, the PLO was chased out of Jordan (by the king), then out of Lebanon (by the Israelis), and have settled more or less in the West Bank and Gaza. Yasser Arafat, a leader of PLO branch Fatah, emerged as the main power broker in 1974 when he swaggered into the UN wearing a holster complete with gun. The PLO has other branches, such as Popular Front for the Liberation of Palestine; like Hamas, some factions abhor Arafat.

Without a military to declare war, Palestinians have nevertheless engaged in violence: guerrillas have attacked Israeli civilians since the 1960s, and in 1972 a group of Palestinian militants killed eleven Israeli athletes at the Munich Olympics. Palestinians have also put together citizen uprisings against Israelis—intifadas—violent episodes of civilian warfare, which apparently can drag on for years. In the second intifada that started in September 2000 when Ariel Sharon appeared at Jerusalem's Temple on the Mount—along with one thousand soldiers and guards—Palestinians have strayed from the stone-throwing and occasional car bombs that had typified their urban battles before. The new twist is for young Palestinians to transform themselves into lethal weapons—strapping on explosives and blowing themselves up in hopeless acts of martyrdom, viewed by many Palestinians as a rite, complete with farewell videotapes. Saddam Hussein is only one source reportedly writing hefty checks to the martyrs' families. The intifadas are more symbolic of Palestinian rage and helplessness than strategic weapons: far more Palestinians have died during the intifadas, in which violent Palestinian acts are answered by the Israeli Army. The ratio of dead Palestinians to Israelis is about three to one.

Armchair Diplomat Says: Do like the Dutch: Make more land. The process called poldering is used in the Netherlands to create new living communities by filling in the coastline. Environmentally incorrect, it nevertheless would offer more breathing room.

The basic conflict is this: Israel—U.S.-armed, highly organized, militaristic, affluent, cohesive and fighting bac k against centuries of persecution for the land it believes has been promised by God—has spread into territory that was originally designed by the UN 1947 division to be the land of the Palestinians— unorganized, largely unarmed, fragmented, angry, threatening, ineffective and increasingly poor and homeless. Layers of other issues are now piled on top: securing water in this parched region is a big one.

Capitalizing: In September 2002, the U.S. Congress voted to controversially recognize Jerusalem, not Tel Aviv, as Israel's capital. Yasser Arafat subsequently claimed Jerusalem as the capital of Palestine.

Another major to-do: Jerusalem, originally meant to be a shared "international city," is now claimed entirely by Israel as its capital. Israeli settlements into outlying territories in the West Bank of Palestine and Syria are a major source of friction, and international condemnation. The right of Palestinians to return to lands taken by Israel is a sticking point as well. The assassination of Hamas leaders and others involved in armed pro-Palestinian factions, by Israeli military and their crafty secret agents in Mossad, is only amping up the discord, as are the continuing Palestinian human bombs. But the most important issue may be Israel's right to exist. Despite three peace agreements—with Egypt, the PLO and Jordan—in many Arab minds, that issue has never been fully resolved.

Future Forecast

Increasing violence: If indeed Israelis and Palestinians really want peace, they'll have to bring in new leaders. The new Palestinian prime minister, Mahmoud Abbas, gives some hope, as does a heavily pushed U.S. plan for peace called "The Roadmap," which calls for a Palestinian state in 2005. Optimists are joyous, but may be driven off the road any minute.

Background Briefing

The U.S. has a reputation for always backing Israel. For good reason: the U.S. almost always does back Israel.

THE TEFLON BULLDOG

In October 2002, much of Prime Minister Ariel Sharon's Labor Party cabinet, including his Foreign Minister Shimon Peres, walked out over Sharon's plans for additional funding for West Bank settlements. Despite being as effective in achieving peace as Arafat—which is to say not at all—Sharon won reelection in 2003. Hard to imagine him as peacemaker.

Condemning Words?: When Ariel Sharon ordered yet another demolition of Arafat's Ramallah compound in 2002, President Bush chastised the move as "not helpful." Whoa!

Not only does the U.S. supply the Israeli Army with state-of-the-art weaponry, tanks and war planes free of charge, it also sells them more, and loans Israel billions. When the Palestinians try to arm themselves, the U.S. condemns them. The U.S. and Israel typically vote together in the UN, and the U.S. looks the other way when Israel ignores UN resolutions to pull out of Palestinian territories. The U.S. knows that Israel has nuclear weapons, but when Iran buys nuclear plants—theoretically to tap "the peaceful use of the atom"—the U.S. has a fit. The U.S. is also Israel's number one trading partner.

ICIEST DAY

When President George W. Bush said in 2001 that he supported the creation of a Palestinian state, Israeli Prime Minister Ariel Sharon went through the roof. "Israel will not be your Czechoslovakia," he bellowed, creating the frostiest moment in U.S.-Israeli history. The reference was to the days leading up to World War II—when Czechoslovakia was handed over to Hitler in the hopes of containing him. Bush and Sharon have since made up.

Despite the obvious bias toward Israel, the U.S. is constantly called upon to broker peace in the area. Assorted U.S. leaders and VIPs have certainly tried—and between mysterious "confidence building exercises" (the Tenet Process and the Mitchell Plan) and weeks of conferences at Camp David there's been the occasional semblance of progress. Land for peace deals—wherein Israel will give back taken territory if a country recognizes Israel's right to exist—have held the most promise. This was the case in the 1978 Egyptian-Israeli Camp David Accords (which also had billions tossed in to sweeten the deal).

President Clinton pushed for peace harder than any U.S. president since Jimmy Carter, bringing together Israel's Prime Minister Ehud Barak and the Palestinian Authority's President Yasser Arafat in 2000. It was a no go. Barak's offers were generous, but they didn't address Arafat's concerns about settlement and the status of Jerusalem. Barak looked like a fool to the Israeli Parliament (Knesset) for not making peace, and was replaced with aggressive Prime Minister Ariel Sharon. Arafat looked like a fool to the Western world. Never mind that wasted opportunity: Arafat was barely in control then, and he's been losing his grip ever since. Gaining momentum: Hamas, with whom striking a peace deal appears even less likely since they want to annihilate Israel.

In this dark corner of political futility, religious strife and constant warring, there are nevertheless flickers of hope. Shimon Peres is more diplomacy-inclined than Ariel Sharon; Palestinian legislative councilwoman Hanan Ashrawi may be the best bet in Palestine. Her organization MIFTAH (the Palestinian Initiative for the Promotion of Global Dialogue and Democracy), is open for intelligent discussion; Israel's Peace Now movement wants Israel to pull out of settlements on the West Bank. And while the world keeps relying on the U.S. to figure out the solution, perhaps it's best to look for guidance from the European Union, which isn't as heavily invested in one side or the other. But whatever happens, just pray that the British aren't put in charge of the maps.

PEACE AGREEMENTS

Egyptian-Israeli: 1978 Camp David Accords
PLO-Israeli: 1993 and 1995 Oslo Accords
Jordan-Israel: 1994 Peace Agreement

Hot Spots

Jerusalem: Holy blood-soaked land, this symbolic piece of real estate is the number one holiest spot for Jews and holds the number three holiest spot for Muslims. The UN thought it could be shared, but Jordan took the east half in 1948 and Israel took the west half the same year. Israel took the east half as well in 1967, and now claims it as Israel's capital, though most countries do not recognize it as such. Arabs claim that Jerusalem is "occupied." However, the Muslim holy sites here—such as Al Aqsa Mosque—while controlled by Israel, are maintained by Palestinians.

HOLY, HOLY, HOLY

Jerusalem is brimming with holy sites for Judaism, Islam and Christianity. Among the holiest:

The Temple Mount/Haram al-Sharif: Thirty-five acres sacred to both Jews and Muslims, this compound contains the Al-Aqsa Mosque—third holiest place for Muslims and Dome of the Rock—where Muhammad is believed to have ascended. Jews say the Temple Mount was the site of their first two temples, which were razed, and fundamentalists believe this is where ascension will occur when the Messiah arrives. The Western Wall of the compound is also a holy site for Jews.

The Church of the Holy Sepulcher: A few miles west of the Temple Mount is the site where Christ is believed to have risen. Constantine's mother had a vision that it was so.

West Bank: Fifty miles along the Jordan River, the West Bank holds Bethlehem, Nablus and East Jerusalem. Residents live under curfew amid road blocks and Israeli tanks. Being fenced in by Israeli security wall.

Gaza Strip: This tiny section of southern Palestine hugging the Mediterranean and Egypt is more densely populated than the West Bank and surrounded by desert. Almost entirely fenced in by Israel.

Golan Heights: Strategic corner of Syria now mostly occupied by Israeli settlers. Much of Israel's water now comes from here.

Lebanon border: Israel occupied southern Lebanon in 1982 and pretty much set up camp there until 2000; already planning to pull back, Israelis were chased out by Hezbollah. Now Hezbollah is setting up military equipment at the borders. Another point of contention: the Hasbani River, which Lebanon is threatening to cut off.

Hot Shots

Ariel Sharon: Israeli prime minister since 2001, former general with a history of bullying and disregarding orders, Sharon caught hell back in 1982, for standing by and allowing the Lebanese massacre at Sabra and Shatila to take place. Hot-tempered, aggressive and blamed by Palestinians for triggering the last intifada when he strolled across the Temple of the Mount—with a thousand soldiers and guards at his side—he has responded to waves of suicide bombers by unleashing tanks into Palestinian communities and holding Arafat personally responsible. Clearly a hawk, the widower apparently has a nonwar side: he reportedly cooed about Condoleezza Rice's distractingly lovely legs. One can only hope that when he retires, he doesn't start a school for diplomacy.

Half of the Equation: During the summer of 2002, President Bush repeatedly called for Yasser Arafat to step down. He forgot to request that Sharon take a bow and get off the stage too.

Benjamin Netanyahu: Israeli Prime Minister from 1993–1994, Netanyahu is handsome, intellectual and a hardline right-winger. A member of the Likud party, he favors Israeli settlements in the West Bank and is opposed to the creation of an official Palestinian state. If he returns to power, which many believe is likely, he may prove a serious impediment to the peace process, as he values security over negotiations with Palestinians.

Shimon Peres: Israeli statesman who's been prime minister twice and was hand-tied foreign minister under Ariel Sharon (November 2001–October 2002), Peres shared the 1994 Nobel Peace Prize with Israel Prime Minister Yitzhah Rabin and the PLO chairman Yasser Arafat for his work on the Oslo Accords the previous year. Appears sincerely dedicated to negotiating peace with Palestinians.

Yasser Arafat: Former Chairman of the PLO (1969–1996), current president of the Palestinian Authority, since 1996. Of all the Middle East figures who have gathered around the "Mideast Peace Table," the image of Yasser Arafat—red-checked kallifah, coffee-bean eyes and pitted olive skin—has been the most memorable, if only because the Palestinian has far outlasted his Israeli counterparts. Since the 1970s Arafat has do-si-doed with Israeli leaders from Rabin and Netanyahu to Barak and Peres, changing his titles along the way (from chairman of the Palestine Liberation Organization to president of the Palestine National Authority) and fluctuating wildly in the popularity and power he actually wields. He nearly lost all Palestinian backing in 1982, but somehow retained it; in 1990, when he backed Saddam Hussein in the Persian Gulf War, he nearly lost all credibility, but somehow regained it. The meetings between the squat Palestinian and Israel's leaders have produced more stalls and rejections than linear progress, but every so often an agreement gets signed: in 1988, the then PLO chairman formally recognized Israel's "right to exist," work on the Oslo Accords garnered the 1994 Nobel Peace Prize that Arafat shared with Israel's Shimon Peres and Prime Minister Yitzhak Rabin. And like most every other agreement through the years, that one is crumbling to dust. Sick with Parkinson's Disease and unable to control his people, there's only one place for Arafat to head: out the door.

WHAT IS A PALESTINIAN?

The definitions are vague, but generally a Palestinian is someone who lives or lived in Palestine, which once stretched from the Mediterranean to what is now Iraq. Many Palestinians are Arabs and Muslim.

Mahmoud Abbas (aka Abu Mazen): Palestinian authority prime minister since spring 2003. Abbas is smart, articulate, and more dedicated to peace than Arafat. A book he wrote in 1984, questioning that six million Jews died in World War II, however, is a handicap. We'll see.

THE THREE THORNS

In every peace talk, three issues emerge:

1. The right of return for Palestinians displaced since 1948
2. Israeli settlements in the West Bank and Gaza
3. The status of Jerusalem, which Israel claims as all its own

Hamas: Militant anti-Israeli group started by Egypt's Muslim Brotherhood in 1987, Hamas also provides social services in Palestine, hate Arafat and have training camps all over the world.

INDONESIA

FAST FACTS

Country:	Republic of Indonesia
Capital:	Jakarta
Government:	Republic
Independence:	August 1945 (Japan); Dutch didn't leave until 1949
Population:	228 million (most live on Java, Sumatra, Bali)
Leaders:	Megawati Sukarnoputri; Hamzah Haz
Ethnicity:	more than three hundred ethnic groups and tribes (45% Javanese; 14% Sundanese; 41% other)
Religion:	88% Muslim; also Hindu, Buddhist, Christian, animist
Language:	Bahasa Indonesia (official) plus some 300 more
Literacy:	84% (90% men; 78% women)
Exports:	oil, gas, plywood, rubber
Per capita GDP:	$2,900 (2000 estimate)
Unemployment:	20%
Percentage living in poverty:	20%
Known for:	coffee, tourist paradise Bali, massacre in East Timor

Standout Qualities

Record-making: country with most Muslim citizens
Badly shaken: after Asian Financial Crisis, heads rolled, literally
Political quaking: on fourth leader in four years; her power is shaky

Thailand

Vietnam

Philippines

Philippine Sea

North
Pacific
Ocean

South China Sea

Celebes
Sea

Sumatra

Malaysia

Kalimantan
(Borneo)

Sulawesi
(Celebes)

Jakarta

Indian Ocean

East Timor

Arafura
Sea

Timor Sea

INDONESIA

Australia

Résumé

The stunning tropical isles of the world's largest archipelago are crackling and hissing with anger; secessionists and Muslim militants are stoking the fires and targeting foreigners as they try to shake off and shake up Indonesia's government.

Quick Tour

Never mind its beguiling beauty—the spine of cloud-tangled volcanoes peering over mood-ring lakes, the jungles home to tigers, tree-sized flowers and lost-in-time tribes, the hills thick with coffee, and the tropical breezes heavy with the scent of nutmeg. Resource-blessed Indonesia is rife with religious-ethnic-separatist problems that threaten to unravel the necklace of more than seventeen thousand islands that drape from Southeast Asia to Australia and are home to three hundred ethnic groups. Mostly bound by location, the islanders share a common tongue—Bahasa Indonesia—and 90 percent of the population is Muslim, making the island chain the world's largest stronghold for the religion. Never tightly woven, the social fabric has been fraying since the country was ripped apart by the Asian Financial Crisis—an event from which Indonesia has not fully recovered and that unleashed the discord evident today.

ISLAND GROWN

Java, Sumatra and Sulawesi are famous for their premium coffee beans.

Starting in May 1997—when Indonesia's currency began its downward spiral, ultimately plunging in value 80 percent—a deathly chain reaction blasted across the country. Riots broke out, dictator Suharto was tossed, and a frenzied violence swept across the islands: Muslims and Christians torched each other's homes on the Spice Islands and in Sulawesi; on beautiful Borneo, the Dayak hacked up—and ate—their enemies the Madurese. Even on relatively modernized Java, villagers decapitated each other, fearing that sorcerers had brought a black magic curse to the country.

As if the place wasn't falling apart already, in 1999 East Timor, the long-abused island where some two hundred thousand had died during its quarter century of forced annexation, won its freedom, inspiring other separatist movements. Both ends of the island chain wanted to break free: the most western region of Aceh demanded independence, as did West Papua, the most eastern.

BALI BLAST

The October 2002 bomb that killed over 180 in a tourist disco on Bali was more than an attack on foreigners and the lucrative tourist industry. Believed to be the work of militant Muslim group Jemaah Islamiah, the act was as much directed at President Megawati Sukarnoputri, whom Muslim fundamentalists want to boot for two reasons: she's a woman and she is ignoring their wish to change Indonesia's government from secular to religious. After surveying the damage and denouncing the attack, passive Megawati disappeared and didn't let out another official peep for days.

Ineffective President Megawati Sukarnoputri, democratically elected in 2001, has her hands full simply keeping the country—where the inhabitants range from technology-savvy city dwellers to jungle tribes—knitted together, while the U.S. pressures her to actively clamp down on terrorists if she wants continued U.S. military aid. Meanwhile, fringe Muslim groups are fueling riots and killing tourists to underscore their demands that Indonesia become an Islamic government complete with Shariah law. Ta-ta tourism that typically brings in $5 billion a year.

Future Forecast

Seemingly dim-witted, Megawati may soon permanently flicker out.

Indonesia President Megawati Sukarnoputri (right) often appears to be out to lunch. (Source: Associated Press)

Background Briefing

Big surprise that the place isn't holding together: seventeen thousand islands are a lot to contend with, especially since their inhabitants are mostly different ethnicities, most have different agendas and many don't even appear to be living in the same era. Besides, the islands—not long ago thousands of individual kingdoms, tribal villages and sultanates—have been together as a country for a shorter period than some couples have been married, which is to say fifty-four years.

Oddly, it wasn't until the Japanese occupied the then Dutch East Indies during World World II that the islands were given the chance to unite: when the Japanese were pushed out in 1945, they handed the government to a nationalist radical who went by only one name—Sukarno. When Sukarno declared the archipelago an independent country, the Dutch, who'd been running much of the place as their colony for three centuries, didn't hear—and a war broke out for four years. After the international community stepped in, the Dutch stomped out, and the many islands were bound by the national motto "Unity in Diversity." Its new leader, Sukarno, wooed the country with an idea of democracy, then a less free "guided democracy," then just a plain old dictatorship while he drove the economy into the ground.

Some of the islands already wanted a divorce, but that became even less a possibility when Sukarno told the U.S. "to hell with your foreign aid!" and began flirting with the Soviet Union and China. The U.S. backed his 1966 overthrow by his soundalike general, Suharto, who began his dictatorship with a horrendous purge: while the world looked the other way, the new military-savvy president ordered the killing of an estimated 750,000 suspected communists, many of them ethnic Chinese. Suharto immediately threw open the country to American business interests and other Western corporations, which quickly moved in to tap the many resources from petroleum and wood to cheap labor.

OOPS!

A U.S. State Department history book detailing the American government's support for, and involvement in, the 1966 Indonesian massacre was quickly snatched back from bookshelves when it briefly appeared in 2001. The government explained that the document had been accidentally sent to the Government Printing Office.

Not happy with merely seventeen thousand islands, Suharto snatched other outlying independent isles: his ships pulled up to lasso West Papua in 1969 and East Timor in 1976. He stamped out restiveness everywhere by unleashing the army into any dissident areas: hundreds of thousands of Indonesians were massacred or starved to death. The case was particularly grim in rebellious East Timor, where tens of thousands died annually protesting their forced inclusion in the Indonesian chain. Despite chronic cronyism and corruption, Suharto did rev up the country economically; when the 1997 Asian Financial Crisis rocked the country, however, the dictator of thirty-two years went flying.

SEMI-SLAVE LABOR?

Western corporations still thrive in Indonesia by paying extremely low wages: Gap clothing factories, for instance, reportedly pay $1 for 36-hour workdays, during which bathroom breaks are rarely given.

Three years and two more ejected leaders later, the soft-spoken, publicity-shy daughter of Indonesia's founder Sukarno was elected as the country's leader. Some criticize Megawati Sukarnoputri's lack of experience and foggy grasp of issues, but perhaps all the country wants right now is a sweet-faced grandmother who leads mostly by talking softly and holding its hand. Nevertheless, in the continuing aftershocks of the financial crisis and the ethnic-religious-separatist fires that blaze since Suharto's heavy foot stopped stomping them out, she appears but a temporary fix.

TIMBER!

Indonesia's luscious forests—home to tiger, rhino and orangutan—are getting hacked at alarming rates: scientists say that most of the lowland woods could vanish by 2010. The reason: vicious logging gangs, who bribe and murder as they illegally fell trees. More depressing: two of the biggest uses for Indonesian wood are making paper and matches.

Hot Spots

Aceh (AW-chay): Stretching out from the northwest corner of the Indonesian island chain as though trying to escape, resource-rich Aceh has been yearning for independence from Indonesia for five decades. Since the 1970s, the secessionist fire has been fueled by the Free Aceh Movement (GAM) and in 1989 Dictator-President Suharto loosed his military for eight years. Their violence—torching villages and killing an estimated five thousand—only increased the longing to break up with Jakarta. Freedom won't come easy: oil wells line the coasts, which explains why the Indonesian government is clamped on to Aceh like a leech. Peace treaty signed in late 2002.

East Timor: The first country of the twenty-first century, East Timor came into the world in May 2002 entirely broke and with many of its buildings still scorched from the brutal battles waged for its independence. A Portuguese colony for four centuries, East Timor shook off Portugal in 1975, but that freedom lasted but a few weeks: Indonesia promptly marched in to claim this eastern half of the island Timor. The mostly Catholic population demanded independence from Muslim Indonesia, with which it shared neither history nor common tongue. The Indonesian Army steamrolled uprisings, and some two hundred thousand Timorese died.

WAKE-UP CALL

World attention focused on the little known area in 1996, when two East Timor activists—Bishop Carlos Belo and resistance leader José Ramos Horta—shared the Nobel Peace Prize for blowing the whistle on Indonesia's ongoing slaughter and abuse.

Pressured by the UN, Indonesia finally allowed East Timor to vote in 1999—and three-quarters voted to secede. More violence flared as pro-secession and anti-secession factions battled it out, until the UN finally stepped in to protect the fledgling nation during its precarious transition to statehood.

NOT WITH OUR GUNS!

The Indonesian Army so ravaged East Timor in retaliation that the sheepish U.S. stopped supplying arms to Indonesia from 1999 to 2002.

President Xanana Gusmao will be forced to develop the area's natural gas resources to prevent graffiti left by the retreating Indonesian army—"A free East Timor will eat rocks!"—from becoming the reality.

Kalimantan: This southern half of the fabled island of Borneo—the northern half is Malaysia and the tiny oil-rich country of Brunei—is being eaten by oil refineries, massive logging operations, timber mills and mineral mining. Even if they're not aware of the environmental consequences of hacking down Indonesia's tropical rain forest, which is second only to Brazil's, the Dayak—the friendly natives pictured on tourist brochures—have reason to be ticked off as the jungle that was their home disappears. They have mostly vented their anger on the wealthier Madurese tribe, eating entire families alive—but saving their heads as magic charms. There goes the tourism.

The Moluccas (aka Maluku): The fabled Spice Islands that sailors could find by scent alone now frequently smell of burning villages and corpses. Since the Asian Financial Crisis, these islands have been the site of brutal fighting and raids between Muslims and Christians, particularly in the capital city, Ambon. The high-strung group called Lashkar Jihad—Muslim fundamentalists who hop around from Java—have stormed in to add more fire to the already hellish conflict, and the uninvited rabble-rousers have called for the Moluccas to become an independent Muslim state. The Indonesian government began aggressively rounding up the group in spring 2002, but these guys get around, hurling their anger; the emotional infernos they stir up usually burn long after they leave.

West Papua (aka Irian Jaya): The western half of the island of New Guinea—the eastern half is Papua New Guinea—was forcefully roped into Indonesia in 1969 and stripped of its history right down to its name, which became—by government order—Irian Jaya. The locals rose up immediately with the "Free Papua Movement," which was quashed by Suharto's repressive army. Originally home to many of Indonesia's most isolated tribes, the region is the destination of many Javanese sent there to settle in government-sponsored "repatriation programs." The result: a big knot of ethnic and religious tensions. The development of a huge gold and copper mining operation in the midst of tribal lands has done little to endear Jakarta to the area, which some fear may go the violent separatist way of East Timor.

Hot Shots

Megawati Sukarnoputri: President of Indonesia since 2001, she is called "The Housewife," though Megawati Sukarnoputri is also sometimes likened to a princess, due to her nearly royal upbringing as daughter of Indonesia's founder, Sukarno. Introverted, plumpish and politically passive, the fifth president of Indonesia (and first female to hold the position) was initially strong enough to succeed thus far in keeping the country together in its most tumultuous time. Since the bombing in Bali, she is losing her grip. During national emergencies she tends to head to the movies or hide in her garden.

Suharto: President of Indonesia from 1966 to 1998, Indonesia's second dictator, former General Suharto never was a pacifist: during his tight-reined rule that united the country, albeit largely in fear, his heavy-handed army blazed a foul trail of rape, torture, razing and execution, directly or indirectly killing more than a million people. Suharto also stands out for turning Indonesia into a prosperous, developing nation where chainsaws ripped through jungles, oil rigs dotted the coast, cities modernized and bustled, and cronyism and corruption ran unchecked. Suharto's family, who run many of Indonesia's largest enterprises, are still in the news: his son Tommy was convicted in 2002 of murdering a judge.

Sukarno: Founder of Indonesia and president from 1949 to 1966, a nationalist leader who cut ties with the Dutch and roped together the diverse islands, Sukarno started out with a constitution and an idea for democracy, but by the late 1950s, he'd tossed such silly notions aside and just became an unorganized dictator. Sukarno's greatest achievements: uniting the many islands politically, educating the people in one official language and producing a daughter who would lead the country some thirty-five years after he had tumbled.

Hamzah Haz: Vice president of Indonesia since 2001, fundamentalist Haz is bound to make a grab for the number one power seat. If he snags it, he could turn Indonesia's secular government into a much more religious one.

Abu Bakar Bashir: Leader of Jemaah Islamiah, the sixty-four-year-old Muslim cleric insists that the militant Islamist group that he allegedly heads doesn't actually exist. A hardcore fundamentalist who adores Osama bin Laden, wants a religious government, and believes women shouldn't hold power, Bashir says the 2002 bombing of a Bali club was carried out by the U.S. Nevertheless, the dreamer was arrested on suspicion of being behind that bombing and others.

Jemaah Islamiah, Lashkar Jihad and Islamic Defense Front: Most Indonesians are moderate Muslims, but these three militant groups are filled with radicals who want less West, more Islam. Pushing for religious rule, they're stirring up trouble anywhere they can as well as threatening Westerners and Western interests. Jemaah Islamiah, which has a grand plan for linking Indonesia, Malaysia and the Philippines into one Muslim nation, was believed responsible for the 2002 Bali bombing, but we'll be hearing more from all three.

KASHMIR/INDIA/ PAKISTAN

Kashmir Standout Qualities

Really high: most altitudinous battleground in world
Really cold: more die from weather than violence
Really unfair: India and Pakistan's psychoses play out here

Kashmir Résumé

Ever since India and Pakistan split up in 1947—a messy divorce during which a million died—the Himalayan-edged region of Kashmir has been ripped apart like a child in a painful custody battle. Now that its wanna-be parents are brandishing nuclear weapons, the seething anger between them is even more unnerving. Selfishly, neither allows Kashmir to live on its own.

Kashmir Quick Tour

With a million troops amassed at its borders, grenade-tossing militants running amok through its towns and tens of thousands fleeing their homes, you'd never guess that Kashmir—"The Happy Valley"—was once the epitome of peace. With snow-dusted mountains, market-lined canals and towns of houseboats on crystalline lakes, it was the vacation jewel of the north, luring the wealthy to its clean, cool air and tranquil beauty. That changed fifty-six years ago, when the Brits hastily pulled out from colonial "British India" and the subcontinent was divided into a smaller Hindu-dominated India and Pakistan, a new nation of Muslims.

The fate of Kashmir was laid before the prince of the mountainous land, Ma-

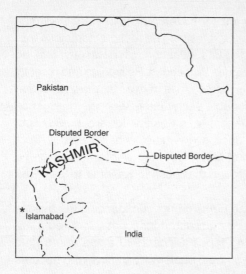

haraja Hari Singh. The maharaja was Hindu, most of his subjects were Muslim, and his land was caught smack-dab between the freshly ripped apart countries. While he pondered what to do, his kingdom was attacked by Pakistani tribes. The prince called for India's help. Requesting military protection, he signed a temporary agreement giving India limited powers over Kashmir; as part of the agreement, the Kashmiri people were to vote on which country to align with in the future, but fifty-six years later that vote has not yet taken place.

NOW, WHAT'S THE PROBLEM?

Pakistan believes that Kashmiris should be given the vote promised in 1947, because they believe Muslim-majority Kashmir will join up with Pakistan; India points to the maharaja's agreement, believes the vote is unnecessary, doesn't want international interference and claims Kashmir as part of multicultural Mother India. Lost in the scuffle: the desire of most Kashmiris to shake loose of both of them. Even if Kashmiris are given the vote promised decades ago, independence is currently not one of the options. And it should be.

Attempting to preserve Kashmiri autonomy, the maharaja inadvertently ensured that this pristine land would become a symbol worth fighting for—and it did: war started before the ink dried on the Indian accession papers. After a ceasefire between Pakistan and India in 1949, Kashmir was divided—with the northwestern third of it taken by Pakistan (Azad or "Free" Kashmir) and two-thirds claimed by India (the state of Jammu and Kashmir), which is where most of the action takes place. Division didn't end the hostility, and the region of glaciers and glassy waters is a mirror for India and Pakistan's tempestuous relations: whenever things get testy, they play out here—as they did with two more major wars in 1965 and 1971.

Factoid: The candy maker Cadbury infuriated the Indian government when they pictured a tempting chocolate bar on a map of Indian-controlled Kashmir with the tagline "Too Good to Share."

Although an independence movement stirred the region, in 1989 the whole Kashmir cricket match became far more explosive. The reason: homeless mujahideen—Muslim warriors—who blasted into India-controlled Kashmir looking for new battles to fight after the Soviet-Afghan War ended. Revved up and recently trained in guerrilla warfare, the righteous mercenaries from as far away as Sudan had been sent in by Pakistan's questionable secret Inter-Services Intelligence (ISI) to spread discord and push Indian-controlled Kashmir toward the Pakistan cause. The mujahideen splashed violence everywhere, chasing Hindus from their homes, tossing acid in the faces of Muslim women who weren't wearing burkas and forming militant Islamic groups that pushed Kashmir to join Pakistan or become an Islamic state.

India has been just as brutal: human rights groups, denouncing the actions of both sides, allege Indian forces have massacred innocents, tortured thousands and frequently engaged in gang rapes. Since 1989 alone, more than thirty-five thousand have died—many of them hapless Kashmiris who became victims of the battle for an elusive icon.

A NUCLEAR SPRING

India started it. On the eleventh of May, 1998, India blasted three nuclear missiles in the Pokhran desert, three hundred miles southeast of New Delhi. Two days later, they shot off two more. Gleefully announcing the success of the nuclear tests, India threw the world into a tiz. President Clinton grabbed the phone and demanded that Pakistani Prime Minister Sharif not respond. Clinton was dreaming. On May 28, Pakistan blasted a nuclear device in their desert, then another, then another, and another, ultimately answering India's five nuclear tests with Pakistan's six.

If the world wasn't fully paying attention, it snapped to in May 1998, when first India, then Pakistan tested their nuclear weapons in a series of underground blasts. When the radioactive dust cleared from their nerve-wracking nuclear pissing match, more than 150 countries had condemned the acts and both countries were slapped with stiff economic sanctions. The international community began sending in many a diplomat—President Clinton was but one—to try to soothe tensions in what is dubbed "The Most Dangerous Place in the World."

IF INDIA AND PAKISTAN NUKE IT OUT

Estimated number killed: 12 million on the first day of fighting
Estimated number injured: 7 million

Meanwhile, most Pakistanis and Indians remain blissfully ignorant of the nuclear hazards their governments' arsenals present; most appear to favor military action in Kashmir even if it turns nuclear.

The "War on Terror" has only inflamed the situation further by giving Pakistan preeminence, while Pakistani militants attack Indian and Kashmiri legislatures and military camps. In May 2002 a major showdown, perhaps nuclear, seemed so likely that the U.S. warned Americans to flee both countries.

Kashmir Future Forecast

Come on, guys, give it up. Someday Kashmiris will be handed the vote—including the choice to become independent. Of course with its land mine–dotted roads, bombed-out houses, restive factions that won't willingly leave and mental scars from decades of violence, it may never get back to the sedate tourist getaway it used to be.

UV INDEX

Ray of hope: Some experts believe that despite the inherent dangers, the nuclear weapons that both India and Pakistan possess have in fact stabilized the region. Their logic: since they both have capabilities of mutually assured destruction, neither is likely to start a nuclear war.
Clouded ray of hope: India's new President, Dr. A. P. J. Abdul Kalam, is a nominal Muslim, who might ease Hindu-Muslim tensions, but he was also the man who developed India's nuclear missile program.

Kashmir Background Briefing

The key to grasping Kashmir is to understand the hissing spitfire dance between India and Pakistan, who've been furious with each other for nearly six decades. India, which highly values its multicultural makeup, is still livid that

Pakistan was ever hacked off from what was once India's western frontier; as far as India is concerned, Pakistan is still a renegade. That the U.S. identified Pakistan, which has let loose its hellion rebels on its neighbor to the east, as a leading partner in the "War on Terror" was absolutely appalling to Mother India—and it only stirred up the always-simmering rivalry.

Angry underdog Pakistan, whose army is vastly outnumbered by Indian troops, is still fuming that in 1971 India militarily backed an independence movement in what was once East Pakistan and is now Bangladesh. When India developed nuclear capabilities—in part to protect against China, which invaded India in 1962—Pakistan followed a decade later to even the score. India outshines dismally lagging Pakistan economically and technologically, but Pakistan has stronger links to the walleted West.

HYDROPOLITICS

Three major rivers—the Indus, Jhelam and Chenab—flow through Kashmir to Pakistan and supply the latter's agricultural sector. India occasionally makes noises about damming the heck out of them and leaving Pakistan with a trickle.

Maybe the two countries should spend more time looking in their own backyards: while they're busy hating each other, their domestic situations are self-destructing. That is the most tragic part of the problem: both India's Prime Minister

Pakistan's President General Musharraf and India's Prime Minister Vajpayee are divided on the Kashmir issue. (Source: Associated Press)

Atel Behari Vajpayee and Pakistan's President General Pervez Musharraf might be willing to work out the Kashmir problem in better times. Both, however, suffer eroding power, and to give up the Kashmir conflict—a popular cause for many Indians and Pakistanis—could lead to their ousting. In fact, many believe that the Kashmir problem flares up simply because political leaders need to bolster popular support.

THE MUJAHIDEEN PROBLEM

When you look at this one you have to say, "Um, what were you thinking?" When the Soviets invaded Afghanistan in 1979, the U.S., Saudi Arabia and Pakistan conspired to create an army of militant Muslims—gathered from Africa, South Asia and the Middle East—to battle Soviets back. By arming, training and funding these militants, the boys made the world a much more violent place. Kashmir, Afghanistan, Pakistan, Chechnya and the Philippines are but a few places mujahideen have shown up for showdowns. Understandably, their own countries don't want the hothead rabble-rousers back.

Kashmir Hot Spots

Line of Control: 460-mile border that delineates the tug-of-war over Kashmir between India and Pakistan. To the north and northwest of the line of control is Pakistan's Azad Kashmir; most of the rest is India's Jammu and Kashmir. One small corner belongs to China.

Kashmir Hot Shots

Harakat ul-Mujahideen, Lashkar-e-Taiba, Jaish-e-Muhammad: Militant Islamists from all over the world who poured into Kashmir when Soviets pulled out of Afghanistan and they had nobody to fight. Some of these former mujahideen want Kashmir to become an independent Islamic state, some want it to hook up with Pakistan, most are aided by Pakistan's ISI. Not a lovable bunch.

Jammu-Kashmir Liberation Front: Kashmiri independence group whose leader was killed in 2002.

Factoid: Almost as many Muslims live in India as in Pakistan. More Muslims live in South Asia than in the entire Middle East.

COUNTRIES WITH MOST MUSLIMS

1. Indonesia (201 million)
2. Pakistan (145 million)
3. India (124 million)
4. Bangladesh (109 million)
5. Turkey (67 million)
6. Egypt (66 million)
7. Iran (66 million)

India/Pakistan Background Briefing

India's Mahatma Gandhi and Pakistan's Mohammed Ali Jinnah—too bad both of these men kicked (Gandhi was assassinated, Jinnah died of cancer) about the second their countries split, because maybe Gandhi and Jinnah could have worked out the problems that they started. Mahatma Gandhi triggered India's independence movement with peaceful protests but never did understand why Muhammed Ali Jinnah felt so strongly that Muslims should have a nation of their own. Gandhi so despised the thought of India—even more gigantic back then—losing its land and its people—that he suggested that Jinnah lead India, just to get him to keep the country intact. Jinnah had other ideas. He felt Muslims could never live as number two to Hindus, and in the confusion that arose from the upcoming independence, his Muslim League pulled a swift legislative power play: they created a new nation for India's minority Muslims in 1947. Many Indians have never forgiven Jinnah and his upstart country for so suddenly bidding adieu.

Factoid: *The mass migration of Hindus and Muslims during 1947 was the largest single movement of people in history. Twelve million switched from one boundary to the other—and 500,000 died in violence along the way.*

The surgical division of "British India" into Hindu-majority India and Muslim-dominant Pakistan was performed in five weeks by Sir Cyril Radcliffe, a British bureaucrat who was utterly unfamiliar with the country he was carving up. Working with scanty, outdated information about the foreign land, he inadvertently split villages in two and divided farmers from their crops, as he nervously separated what he hoped were majority Muslim areas from the Motherland. Fearing assassination, he fled before the boundary divisions were announced, never talking about the matter again and never returning to the land that he had redrawn.

PAKISTAN V. BANGLADESH

Originally Pakistan was actually two inconveniently located Pakistans: East and West Pakistan were separated by one thousand miles of India. When East Pakistan rebelled against West in 1971, India backed them in the civil war against their western half. East Pakistan ultimately became independent Bangladesh, a breach for which Pakistan (formerly West Pakistan) has never entirely forgiven its former eastern branch. Besides, West Pakistan never rated a George Harrison song.

India's secret fear: China, Pakistan's ally, invades again like it did in 1962.
Pakistan's secret fear: A two-front war battling India to the east and from the south.
U.S.' secret fear: Either country's nukes grabbed by radicals.

India

FAST FACTS

Country:	Republic of India
Capital:	New Delhi
Government:	federal republic
Independence:	15 August 1947 (from U.K.)
Population:	1,029,992,000 (2001 estimate)
Leaders:	Atel Behari Vajpayee; Dr. A. P. J. Abdul Kalam
Ethnicity:	72% Indo-Aryan; 25% Dravidian; 3% Mongol
Religion:	82% Hindu; 12% Muslim; also Christian, Sikh, Buddhist and others
Language:	Hindi, Bengali, twenty-two others
Literacy:	65% (76% men; 54% women)
Exports:	textiles, gems, jewelry, engineering goods
Per capita GDP:	$2,200 (2000 estimate)
Unemployment:	N/A
Percentage living in poverty:	29% (2000 estimate)
Known for:	Bollywood, Bhopal, assorted assassinated Gandhis

India Résumé

The planet's biggest democracy and number two most populous country, India is also the world's biggest religious melting pot, with Hindus, Muslims, Sikhs, Buddhists, Confucians and Christians part of the complex cultural tapestry that celebrates "unity in diversity." Well, that's the idea—lately Hindu nationalism is threatening the underpinnings of the country, and Muslims are just one faction that isn't liking their rewriting of history and stitching together of religion and politics.

India Quick Tour

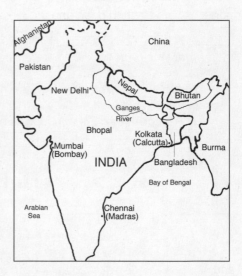

Layered with ancient history, culture and mystery, India—where tinkling handbells and chanting of mantra mixes with the sounds of loudly squawking crows and constant horns—has never been accused of being a simple country. From its mountain cave homes of hermits to its incense-filled temples layered in gold, it's hard to make generalizations beyond it's big, its cities are jam-packed and there are sure lots of cows wandering around.

HERE'S THE BEEF

Muslims, who believe in only one god and hold that icons are evil, are surrounded with deity pluralism and millions of icons in India; Hindus, who believe in many gods, are subjected to Muslim calls of "There is but one god . . ." five times a day from mosques. Muslims don't get why cows wander freely through India's streets; Hindus don't understand how Muslims can eat the sacred beings. In fact, in 2002, amid the Gujarat violence, Hindus issued a formal statement to Muslims insisting their conflict won't be resolved until Muslims stop chomping beef.

The variety of India's architecture and the complexity of its past are as much sources of pride for the country as the diversity of its people, who for much of their country's fifty-six-year history have more or less gotten along. That's changed recently as Hindu nationalism has swept the land just as Muslim fervor was spilling over the Kashmiri border. Hard-core Hindu political parties, including the Bharatiya Janata Party (BJP) of Prime Minister Vajpayee, rose to power and religious tensions coiled ever more tightly through the 1990s, with violence levels hitting record highs: when radical Hindus ripped down a mosque (with their hands) in Ayodhya in 1992, the ensuing riots killed three thousand, most of them Muslim. In February 2002, when Muslims torched a train carrying chanting Hindu nationalists, killing 58, the hatred spilled into grisly mass mayhem in the Gujarat region: more than two thousand Muslims were killed by Hindu hard-cores, many victims doused with gas and set on fire; pregnant women reportedly were slashed open and their fetuses ripped out.

SACRED GROUND

Like Kashmir, Ayodhya too is a shared symbol: considered the birthplace of the Hindu god Rama, it was believed to have been home to a Hindu temple, which legend has it a Muslim Mughal ripped down to build a mosque in 1528. Although the mosque had fallen into disuse, Hindu Nationalists seized the bit of folklore and used it to pump up the masses to rip the structure down. Now Hindu nationalists want to rebulld a temple in the same spot— and the issue sparks high-tempered conflicts. Predictably, the god theoretically born there— Rama—is the Hindu god of war.

India has experienced religious violence before—friction between Hindus and Sikhs led to the 1984 assassination of Prime Minister Indira Gandhi by her Sikh bodyguard—and some view sectarian tensions as going with the territory in such a diverse society. However, the ever-growing Hindu Nationalism and its rigid schools—Hinduism's answer to Muslim madrassas—have country-watchers predicting more violence ahead unless more moderate Hindus step to the forefront.

Factoid: Peaceful Gandhi was assassinated by a Hindu Nationalist in 1948.

The country does have a remarkable knack for turning situations around: chronic famine was theoretically "solved" by the Green Revolution in agriculture; the country's economy is diverse and vibrant and now open to world business; the country's achievers gain international recognition in fields from technology and medicine to literature, and India's film industry—Bollywood—puts out more movies than Hollywood.

Bollywood has fueled the rise in radical Hinduism, releasing plenty of propagandistic films that glorify Hindus and portray Muslims in a less flattering light. Meanwhile Indian documentaries about the dangers of the nuclear buildup have been banned.

For all its potential and abundant talent, India must soon deal with its problems, which include the fastest growing world population, a high poverty rate, alarming 46 percent illiteracy for women, child labor abuses, a large discrepancy between Hindu and Muslim education and income levels and an inability to forgive Pakistan for anything, including existing.

BHOPAL

It was just another pesticide factory until December 3, 1984, when a colorless, odorless cloud escaped from the Union Carbide chemical plant in Bhopal, killing at least sixteen thousand people downwind who inhaled the gas that chemically scorched their lungs; some one hundred thousand were injured. Union Carbide, never brought to trial, paid the Indian government $470 million in 1989, which amounted to several hundred dollars per claimant. Most victims never received competent medical treatment and many suffer from respiratory diseases and cancers. Nearly two decades later, the now-shutdown factory is still a toxic dump where tons of chemicals seep into the ground and poison water supplies.

Hide-n-Seek: Former Union Carbide CEO Warren Anderson has been hiding ever since that fateful night. The U.S. pushed India to lessen the charges against him from "culpable homicide" to "rash negligence" so he can come out from the underground and avoid extradition, but in August 2002, a Bhopal magistrate reaffirmed the "culpable homicide" charge and called for the start of Anderson's extradition proceedings.

INDIA TERMS TO KNOW

Hindutva ("Hinduness"): A term tossed around by Hindu Nationalists who seek to gain power and erase the effects of the Muslim culture on India.
The Raj: What started as the British-operated East India Company in the 1600s ultimately became the full-time Raj, which ran India as a pretty

little colony from 1858 to 1947. During those years—known as the British Raj—Britain performed many notable acts, including pulling the rug out from under India's textile markets and using "the colony" to grow opium to hook China. Most memorable: they changed the social dynamics by knocking the Muslims out of power after a four-century rule, and brought Hindus back to the forefront of the power game. On a kinder note: the British contributed to the concept of Indian democracy.

Deobandism: Similar to Wahhabism of Saudi Arabia, Deobandism instills very traditional Islam with a very anti-Western twist. Started in 1866, this Islamic school of thought was a reaction to colonialization and the British execution of hundreds of Muslim clerics who started a mutiny in 1857. Its font is the esteemed Islamic university—Darul Uloom—in the Indian town of Deoband; many of its alumnae teach their hellfire brand of Islam in Pakistani religious schools. Among the students: the Taliban of Afghanistan fame.

India Hot Spots

Jammu and Kashmir: Indian-controlled Kashmir is a simmering heap of grenade-tossing, land mine–exploding anger; much violence erupts near the placid lakes of Srinigal, where Brits once took summer lodgings on houseboats and Muslim, Hindu, Confucian and Buddhist all got along.

Ayodhya: Bloody holy spot for both Hindu and Muslim where thousands have died in recent years over which house of worship should stand there.

Gujarat region: This western state on the Pakistan border is a hotbed for Hindu Nationalists, violence-prone and the site of vicious attacks on Muslims, while police stand by watching people being ripped apart.

India Hot Shots

Atel Behari Vajpayee: Prime minister since 1998, poet, gourmet cook and Hindu Nationalist of the BJP, heady Vajpayee was glowering when the U.S. befriended Pakistan's General Musharraf. He's had to tone down his own party's fervent Hinduist line—temporarily banning the temple building at Ayodhya for one—to deal with the growing religious conflict. Like Musharraf, he can't stay in power if he caves in on Kashmir.

Dr. A. P. J. Abdul Kalam: Indian president since 2002, poet, engineer and Muslim (at least in name), this popular leader—India's third Muslim president—is seen as a moderating force who might cool down religious fires.

Mohandas "Mahatma" Gandhi (1869–1949): "Don't fight, just don't eat" was the message of this Hindu, whose effective hunger strikes, sit-ins and marches to the sea finally prompted the British to skedaddle.

Arundhati Roy: Winner of the prestigious 1997 Booker Prize for her novel *The God of Small Things,* Roy was tossed in jail for protesting the building of India's Narmada Dam.

Pakistan

FAST FACTS

Country:	The Islamic Republic of Pakistan
Capital:	Islamabad
Government:	Federal Republic
Independence:	15 August 1947 (from Britain)
Population:	144,617,000 (2001 estimate)
Leader:	President General Pervez Musharraf
Ethnicity:	Punjabi, Sindhi, Pashtun and more
Religion:	77% Sunni Muslim; 20% Shia Muslim
Language:	58% Punjabi and variants; 12% Sindhi; 8% Pastu (only 8% speak official language Urdu)
Literacy:	42.7% (55.3% men; 29% women) (1998 estimate)
Exports:	textiles, garments, yarn
Per capita GDP:	$2,000 (2000 estimate)
Unemployment:	6%
Percentage living in poverty:	40% (2000 estimate)
Known for:	fierce secret service, militants, decapitated heads

Pakistan Résumé

In the first country created specifically for Muslims, democracy alternates with military dictatorship and all leaders are ousted, executed, assassinated or die un-

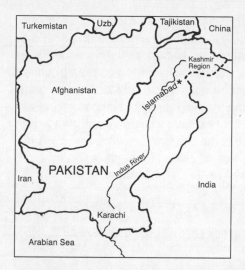

der mysterious circumstances. Training spots for mujahideen warriors fighting Soviets in Afghanistan, since 1989 Pakistan's border cities have degenerated into militant cesspools.

These days a chronic tension hangs across this land of mountains, overcrowded cities and historic ruins that is home to many a gun-toting mujahideen, Pashtun tribe member and Afghan refugee. Despite the ecstatic joy many Muslims experienced when they crossed over to a Hindu-free land in 1947, hastily created, poorly planned Pakistan simply hasn't kept up with founder Mohammed Ali Jinnah's dream for a Muslim paradise. Nearly half of Pakistanis can't read, the public school system barely functions, and in cities, where poverty and opium addiction run unchecked, social services consist mostly of amateurs who yank teeth in city parks.

Although founder Jinnah created a secular state, much of the underlying bristling stems from militants who want Pakistan to become entirely Islamic, with religious government, laws and schools. So far they've at least seen two-thirds of their dream realized—Shariah courts dominate in some parts, and religious madrassas teach eight-year-olds how to shoot Kalashnikovs in between reciting the Koran. Some corners, particularly the "Northwest Territories" that hug Afghanistan, are entirely lawless societies where one can buy anything from bombs and guns to toxic radioactive materials and poison gases. Along Afghan borders tribal elders mete out such gruesome punishments as gang rape for perceived transgressions.

FUNDAMENTALISM RISING

Typically, religious hard-cores receive only 5 percent or so of votes in national elections. In 2002, however, they snagged a whopping 25 percent of the vote.

While the country's Muslims are mostly moderate and there is an educated elite, most of it living in capital Islamabad, Pakistan is mostly an uneducated backwater that has succeeded only in three areas: creating a well-trained military, developing a state-of-the-art nuclear program and forming a fierce intelligence agency, the ISI, considered "a state within a state" that no leader can fully control.

It was the ISI who, with help from the CIA and Saudi Arabia, created much of the violence that runs unabated here, where churches are often bomb sites and kidnappers are particularly loathsome, as evidenced by the treatment of American journalist Daniel Pearl, who was decapitated in 2002. With funding from Saudis and the U.S., the intelligence agency trained Muslim warriors to fight Soviets in neighboring Afghanistan, running guerrilla war camps in Pakistan through the 1980s. Although the fighters had initially flown in from across the Arab and Muslim worlds, after the war the charged-up, weapons-savvy militants spilled back over the Pakistan borders, looking for another jihad.

BE QUIET, YOUR UNCLE SAM IS BUSY NOW

The U.S., after helping create the mujahideen forces to battle Soviets in the 1980s, utterly ignored Pakistan's pleas to help them deal with mujahideen taking over their border cities.

The ISI shoved many off to Kashmir, which unleashed another round of violence, while some fighters simply spewed their militant views in the border towns, which over the course of a few months went from sleepy to highly armed and seething. Meanwhile Pakistan's politics have been precarious: the sanctions suffered after its 1998 nuclear tests further rattled its shaky economy; few leaders finish out terms in what is theoretically a democracy, and some, such as Musharraf, in charge since 1999, take power in military coups.

General Musharraf, at least initially a kinder, more liberal dictator than most, raised Pakistan—at least in the eyes of the West—from the pariah status stamped on it in 1998 by signing up with the U.S. anti-terror coalition in 2001.

The Pakistan payoff: a billion dollars from the U.S., though much of it came in the form of forgiven debts. Internally, the move is controversial: Musharraf—called "Busharraf" by some—is under attack by both militants and, increasingly, the moderate middle class, for his close bonds with the U.S., which like India is demanding that he crack down on militant Muslims. Easier said than done: while the general has banned five groups and arrested thousands, he has limited control over militants, who are his worst enemies too. A virulent bunch, many of whom were educated in Pakistan's fiery madrassas, they've pushed relations with India to the brink with their attacks and they haven't welcomed the international business community either with their issued death threats to all visiting Westerners. Diplomats would rather be stationed in deep Africa than in testy Pakistan, where they might end up like Daniel Pearl. Meanwhile Al Qaeda has snuck over from the

Afghan border—perhaps with the help of the Islamist-leaning ISI, which may be secretly sheltering Osama bin Laden.

Future Forecast

Whether with militants or the hard-core ISI, a power struggle will threaten Musharraf's hold on his nukes. If the Pakistani army can't put out the fires, the U.S. will go in.

What Pakistan Needs: U.S. markets for its textiles. Southern legislators, however, are blocking those moves.

Pakistan Hot Spots

Peshawar and Karachi: Warrior-filled border towns where the number of drug addicts exceeds the number of college graduates.

Pakistan Hot Shots

General Pervez Musharraf: Chief executive since October 1999, president (self-appointed) since June 2001 and head commander under Prime Minister Nawaz Sharif, Musharraf was flying back to Islamabad in 1999 when he discovered he'd been fired. Worse, Sharif, fearing that the ISI would install Musharraf, would not let the plane land, even when the pilot informed him they were nearly out of fuel. The plane landed anyway, Musharraf bloodlessly took power (with the ISI's aid) and charged Sharif with attempted murder. The international community was up in arms—President Clinton had just convinced Sharif to pull his forces out of Kashmir, a move that probably led to Sharif's downfall. Once vilified by the world press, Musharraf emerged as their new 2001 hero when he said he'd help the U.S., disavowed the Taliban and let American troops fly from Pakistani bases. Although he immediately fired the head of the ISI, he's got to worry about what the Taliban-connected crew is plotting these days. Just as worrisome: with Kashmir such a battle-worthy cause to the ISI, militants and many of the masses, Musharraf can't fully back off. One more stress: his popularity is plummeting.

ISI (Inter-Services Intelligence Agency): Who knows what really gives with this secretive bunch, who trained Muslim warriors, loved the Taliban, and promote the Kashmiri cause, but some think they could be helping out their former ally Osama bin Laden. That may explain why they haven't tossed Musharraf yet: they don't want more attention on their clandestine activities.

Mohammed Ali Jinnah (1876–1948): Quaid-I-Azam, or Great Leader, Jinnah created the world's first country for Muslims, dying a few months after being installed as Pakistan's first president. Without his guiding vision, the country has suffered.

CAN'T STAY AWAY

What was already a strange do-si-do between former Pakistani Prime Ministers Nawaz Sharif and Benazir Bhutto—who pushed each other out of office during each of their collective four terms—has gotten stranger. Nawaz Sharif was charged with attempted murder (of President Musharraf) and exiled to Saudi Arabia, and Benazir Bhutto, previously found guilty of corruption and bribery, was exiled as well. But both want to return and run in elections; Musharraf was slammed when he passed a law slamming the door on their plans.

NORTH KOREA

FAST FACTS

Country:	Democratic People's Republic of Korea (North Korea)
Capital:	Pyongyang
Government:	authoritarian socialist one-man dictatorship
Independence:	August 1945 (from Japan)
Population:	21,968,000 (2001 estimate)
Leaders:	Kim Jong-il and his dead dad
Ethnicity:	almost entirely Korean
Religion:	Confucianism
Language:	Korean
Literacy:	99% both sexes (claimed)
Exports:	illegal: recreational drugs, bottled diseases, medium-range missiles, counterfeit $100 bills
Per capita GDP:	$1,000 (South Korea: $12,600)
Unemployment:	N/A
Percentage living in poverty:	N/A
Known for:	selling anything to anybody

BUZZWORDS

The Agreed Framework: A 1994 agreement that South Korea, Japan and the U.S. would give North Korea fuel oil and two light-water nuclear reactors if North Korea stopped developing nuclear weapons and shut its gas-graphite nuke plants, which made far more plutonium. Pricetag: $5 billion. The Framework unhinged since Kim has admitted he didn't halt his nuclear weapons program.

Sunshine Policy: "If you can't beat 'em, at least talk to 'em" was the idea behind this South Korean diplomatic behavior toward the rogue in the North. Warmed relations considerably, but the lands remained divided.

NUCLEAR ALARMS

The October 2002 news that North Korea had a nuclear program was old news to those following the country: what was new was that Kim finally admitted to it, apparently trying to reshape his image as an honest leader. The move backfired: the U.S. now refuses to back the 1994 Agreed Framework to help North Korea acquire light-water nuclear reactors, Kim booted inspectors in December, revved up a closed nuke plant and began bellowing about war.

Standout Qualities

Military muscle: huge army, sophisticated arsenal, nukes
Skeletal bodies: millions have starved, millions malnourished
Warped brain: Dear Leader operates out of suspicious fear, between (supposedly) writing operas and chasing babes; now threatens war with the U.S.

Résumé

Long before North Korea snagged a spot on President Bush's "Axis of Evil," the mountainous country that pokes out from China was regarded as the world's most closed, mysterious and paranoid society. Plutonium stockpiles, long-range missiles that could blast Seattle, and a skirt-chasing leader who lets his people eat grass give just a hint of what's worrisome about the "Hermit Kingdom."

GEOGRAPHICAL CONFUSION: NORTH KOREA V. KOREA

After the Korean War (1950–1953), Korea was cleaved into two countries: communist North Korea and more Western-leaning South Korea. Although its military is impressive, North Korea has economically floundered and is diplomatically isolated. South Korea, while not exactly paradise—the country has suffered dictatorships, corruption and first instituted a five-day workweek in 2002—is relatively affluent, diplomatically connected and under the protection of the U.S. military; thirty-seven thousand troops are stationed there, but many South Koreans want them to leave. Korea used to mean the whole Korean peninsula; it now refers only to South Korea.

Quick Tour

With its choreographed facade of order—the frighteningly stiff army marching by with nonhuman precision, the stadiums of synchronized card holders whose placards collectively form designs of tanks—North Korea is surreal, a land that lifts fantasy to a national lifestyle. Reports of miracles, double rainbows and the latest aggressions of imperialist devils dominate the news in this last Stalin-style society, where radios are preset to government stations (lest North Koreans hear that their noncommunist relatives in South Korea are not starving like they are), anthems like "My Country Is the Best" continually blare from loudspeakers, and the man officially listed as "Eternal President" is actually stone-cold dead. From its shiny modern capital, Pyongyang—devoid of the poor, pregnant or elderly—to the misnamed Demilitarized Zone that splits Korea into north and south with barbed wire and a million heavily armed guards on each side, you'd think this is a place only Hollywood could have created. In fact, North Korea's leading man Kim Jong-il is a major movie junkie who's mad about *Gone with the Wind,* James Bond and Daffy Duck. So flick-crazy is the pasty-faced sixty-something that he ordered the kidnapping of his favorite South Korean actress and her director ex-husband. "Dear Leader," as Kim Jong-il is known, kept them busy and captive for eight years.

LANGUAGE LESSON

As is the case in many Asian countries, the first name is the family name—e.g., both Kim Jong-il and his father, Kim il-Sung, are referred to as "Mr. Kim."

Dear Leader, who eventually stumbled into power after the 1994 death of his dictator daddy, "Great Leader" Kim il-Sung, needs tips on directing all right—as in how to stop directing his country in the downward direction. North Korea's economy has been a shambles since the Soviet Union fell and stopped propping it up. Dear Leader may be stripping off the socialist straitjacket and pushing toward an open, free market economy, but his ideas are often batty: his pet projects include ostrich farms, which he envisions as a soon-to-be thriving industry

supplying the world demand for ostrich steaks, feathers and leather.
When trying to solve mundane problems such as famine, Dear Leader
grows bored, More than 2 million
North Koreans have starved since
1995, while he swirls $600-a-bottle
cognac and plays Rock, Paper, Scis-
sors with scantily clad maidens. Do-
nated food goes mostly to his army—
the third largest on the planet. "If the
U.S. imperialists know that we do not
have rice for our military then they
would immediately invade us," Dear
Leader has explained.

North Korea's "Dear Leader" Kim Jong-il
(lower left): possesses lethal weapons.
(Source: Associated Press)

Kim Jong-il's greatest talent: ter-
rifying the international community,
which shudders at the idea that North
Korea possesses nuclear bombs. Dumping most of the country's little money
into his military-chemical-biological arsenal, Kim is known for selling anything,
including missiles, to anyone who can pay—Egypt, Syria and Iran are said to
be customers. Unknown is how much plutonium North Korea's nuclear reactors
have produced or how many nuclear bombs have been made, though many
believe Dear Leader has at least two, and more on the way.

EXPENSIVE KNEE JERK

Even though Pyongyang's 1998 multistage Taepo Dong II missile test was utterly unsuccessful, that single event pushed through the U.S.' super-pricey
"Missile Shield Defense" program.

When the U.S. pulled the plug on two promised nuclear plants—and
stopped delivering food and oil to North Korea in late 2002—Kim threatened to
build more nuclear bombs and start fighting.

In the land where the Cold War still chills, one thing rankles North Korea
most: the showy U.S., which vows to protect South Korea and stations thirty-
seven thousand troops near the Demilitarized Zone. The flashy "Team Spirit"
war games that the U.S. and South Korea taunt Pyongyang with annually—
when 200,000 troops simulate battles with the North for a week—are one big
factor in keeping Dear Leader permanently wacked: he views them as declara-

tions of war. He wasn't pleased about Bush's "Axis of Evil" remark either, and a leaked 2002 U.S. government report listing North Korea as a target in possible nuclear scenarios merely confirmed what Dear Leader feared all along.

CONTENTS OF KIM'S BOX O' DANGERS

Smallpox virus   Plutonium
Sarin gas   Missiles for sale
Plague germs

Future Forecast

Cut! Whether from covert forces, gung-ho military, envious relatives or just another hard night of boozing, Kim Jong-il will soon fall. With communist hard-liners growing old, Dear Leader's departure might spell a wrap to the isolated, desperate society that's being forced to redefine its world role. More than ever, South Korea will have to tend to its atrophied twin.

SUNNY SKIES?

Ray of Hope: Diplomacy   After fifty years of mutual hatred, South Korea and North Korea finally sat down and talked in 2000—after Seoul extended a "Sunshine Policy" of engagement to Pyongyang; some families reunited, the two Koreas launched joint business ventures, and a commercial airline now flies between their capitals, though ordinary folk can't ride it.

Partly Clouded Ray of Hope: Talks with U.S.   Previously, Kim had been happy to negotiate with any American VIPs who dropped by; early re-marks and actions of the Bush II administration dimmed that possibility, but with Kim screaming about war, they may resume.

Distant Ray of Hope: Hollywood   Kim Jong-il always longed to be a director or movie critic: Hollywood could swoop in and save the day by of-fering the man a new job. He may be the answer Disney's been looking for.

More Rays   In September 2002 Japan's Prime Minister Koizumi flew in to meet with Kim—an earth-shakingly hopeful move since leaders from the two countries have never met in North Korea's fifty-three-year history. Koizumi apologized for Japan's brutal treatment of Koreans up to and dur-ing World War II; Kim apologized for kidnapping Japanese and promptly returned some of them. Kim also dropped his demands that Japan pay for occupying Korea previously, and instead accepted Japanese financial aid.

Background Briefing

Think North Korea, think extreme paranoia: they've been suffering a nasty case of it for over fifty years. They've had reasons: for four of those five decades, the U.S. had nuclear missiles pointed at them from the Demilitarized Zone and on several occasions (starting with Eisenhower) seriously threatened to use them. Even after nukes were dismantled in 1991, the DMZ remained the number one most militarized and volatile border on the globe.

It's amazing that since 1953 no major battles have ignited here because there have been plenty of sparks. "Great Leader" Kim il-Sung, who led the country for forty-six years, successfully created a society hateful of American imperialists, frightened of being eaten alive by American soldiers and believing that North Korea was under chronic threat of U.S. attack. There were certainly "incidents" under his forty-six-year rule—the 1976 Tree Chopping Debacle for one, when two American soldiers hacked down some North Korean poplars and were themselves hacked to death—but it was when Great Leader's son Kim Jong-il got near the control board that the international community became nail-bitingly jittery. Among Dear Leader's alleged accomplishments: ordering a 1983 bombing in Rangoon that killed 17 South Korean ministers, and arranging the 1987 downing of a South Korean commercial plane that killed 115. Junior may lack his father's charisma, but he ain't stupid: when he pumped up North Korea's nuclear and missile programs, he gave the country its only international clout.

HISTORY REFRESHER:
THE KOREAN WAR (AKA "THE FORGOTTEN WAR")
1950–1953

When Japan, which had occupied Korea since 1911, was forced to hand it over after World War II, the U.S. oversaw evacuation in the south and Russia supervised it from the north. Postwar relations were already so tense between the two superpowers that a temporary demarcation line was imposed at the thirty-eighth parallel. Russia installed communist Kim il-Sung as head of North Korea, encouraging him to communize the North and militarily convince South Korea to go the same way.

After Kim il-Sung's troops marched into the South in 1950, a U.S.-led UN team ultimately drove them back north, to the 38th parallel. When the Chinese Army suddenly showed up to bolster North Korea's security, UN forces backed down, the Demilitarized Zone boundary stayed up, and North Korea remained communist, while its southern half leaned more to the West. No official peace treaty was signed to end the three-year war that claimed more than 3 million lives: all that keeps peace in place is a weak 1953 armistice signed by North Korea, China and the UN—and not by South Korea or the U.S.

Factoid: North Korea's "Super K" notes were such convincing counter-feits of American one-hundred-dollar bills that the U.S. was forced to re-design the Franklins.

NEIGHBORLY RELATIONS

South Korea: The situation is decidedly warmer between Korea's two halves, but they remain disunited. Kim Jong-il's schizophrenic on-again, off-again behavior was best illustrated in June 2002: on the same day North Korea sent a letter congratulating South Korea for its World Cup performance, the North Korean military attacked a South Korean boat. South Korea nevertheless doles out aid for its enfeebled sibling.

Japan: Years of North Korea's spy subs in Japanese water chilled rela-tions, as have Kim's missiles pointed at U.S. bases on Japan. Warmer since the Koizumi-Kim 2002 meeting, North Korea dropped demands for ten billion dollars in reparations for crimes committed during Japanese oc-cupation, in exchange for hefty aid.

China: North Korea's only ally, China gets international flack for ship-ping back escaped North Koreans who will be sent to concentration camps. After China opened its former closed communist economy, North Korea feels pressure to follow.

Hot Spots

Demilitarized Zone (DMZ): The 150-mile, 2.5-mile-wide demarcation line at the 38th parallel—where 2 million soldiers stand guard, loudspeakers blast propaganda and billboards satirize the other side's government—is the most heavily militarized place on earth, making it a perfect photo op for vis-iting presidents.

Yongbyon: The site of two nuclear plants that caused a huge ruckus and were closed down under the 1994 Agreed Framework. Kim Jong-il starts worldwide panics when he won't allow international atomic energy inspec-tors in for a peek at its plutonium.

Pyongyang: Creepy capital city where only hard-line Communist party types can live.

Hot Shots

Kim Jong-il ("Dear Leader," "Peerless Leader"): He was born in 1942, the son of Kim il-Sung, and became Communist Party chairman in 1997, chairman of the National Defense Committee in 1998. South Korean intelligence says he's bonkers, the world press portrays him as a googly-eyed playboy, he's fanatical about germs, his stepmother abused him, and his last wife ran off to less-than-cheery Russia to be treated for depression. His "official bio" says he was born under a double rainbow and is an architect and opera composer, but he'll go down in the archives for allowing so many to starve and for militarily boosting North Korea's world presence.

Kim il-Sung ("Great Leader," "Eternal President"): President from 1948 to 1994, eternal president from 1994 to the present and a guerrilla fighter back when Korea was one country occupied by the Japanese, Kim il-Sung rallied support from Soviets after he turned communist and led an attack on the South. Though his philosophy centered on *juche*—self-reliance—he never achieved it, but he did transform the society into a brainwashed personality cult forced to follow him even though he's dead.

Kim Dae Jung: President of South Korea from 1998 to 2002, South Korea's first democratically elected leader, Kim Dae Jung was a diplomat who first tried to open doors to the North with his "Sunshine Policy."

COLOMBIA

FAST FACTS

Country:	Colombia
Capital:	Bogotá
Government:	republic
Independence:	20 July 1810 (from Spain)
Population:	40,350,000 (2001 estimate)
Leader:	President Álvaro Uribe Velez (August 2002)
Ethnicity:	58% mestizo; 20% white; 14% mulatto; 4% black; 3% black-Amerindian; 1% Amerindian
Religion:	90% Roman Catholic
Language:	Spanish
Literacy:	91.3% (91.2% men; 91.4% women)
Exports:	coffee, oil, emeralds (illegal: cocaine, heroin)
Per capita GDP:	$6,200 (2000 estimate)
Unemployment:	20%
Percentage living in poverty:	55% (1999 estimate)
Known for:	coffee, cocaine, kidnapping

Standout Qualities

Danger! A murder rate thirteen times higher than the U.S.'!
Suspense! How many politicians will live to see Election Day?
Mystery! How many sides can a civil war have?

Résumé

Colombia used to mean coffee—"mountain grown, it's the richest kind"—but a more jittery mountain-grown stimulant, coca, is the cash cow today. Ever since cocaine blasted into the underground economy, Colombia has become the Western Hemisphere's most dangerous place and the kidnapping capital of the world.

MEET THE FIGHTERS

Three main groups are behind the violence in Colombia:

Left-Wing Rebels (FARC, ELN and Others): Originally supporting the peasant farmers, these groups now kidnap, tax the cocaine trade and blow up pipelines.

Right-Wing Paramilitaries (AUC and Others): Originally security guards for the rich, they formed their own armies that roam the countryside massacring anyone they believe is affiliated with the left-wing rebels.

Colombian Army: Historically not as well-trained as the left-wing rebels, their forces are being bolstered under Uribe.

Quick Tour

The most spectacular place you'd never want to visit, magical Colombia is intoxicating, from its jagged mountain ranges crisscrossing the land, to its lush rain forests, valleys thick with fluttering butterflies and secluded beaches spreading out along sapphire blue waters. Brilliant color is splashed everywhere, from buses to villages, in this deeply folded land of coffee, cocaine, emeralds and oil, where the people are known for singing, dancing and supernatural beliefs and the cities are dripping with ornate Catholic icons and gold. Alas, Colombia is also littered with gun-happy militants, who ensure that blood red is also a dominant part of the national color scheme. You can call them left-wing guerrillas, right-wing paramilitaries or the Colombian Army, but whatever you call them they're guilty of turning dreamy Colombia into a violence-wracked nightmare fraught with heinous human rights abuses, massacres, assassinations, kidnapping, torture and sabotage that kills 3,500 a year.

BY THE NUMBERS

Killed since 1990: 40,000 (mostly civilians)
Kidnapped since 1990: 38,000
Number in poverty: 22,000,000
Number holding half the money: 4,000,000
Number of attacks on pipeline: 1,000
Number of barrels of crude oil leaked: 2.9 million

Granted, Colombia has been South America's winner of the "Just Can't Get Along" prize since the 1940s, when their nasty civil war "La Violencia" sputtered into a low-grade conflict fought ever since by several guerrilla groups against the government. But when cocaine became the country's most valuable export in the 1980s, new money, new crimes and new groups emerged to make the place even bloodier. The U.S. began pumping hundreds of millions into the country in the 1990s to battle the cocaine destined for North American nostrils; by 1999, the country had become the third largest recipient of U.S. military aid. The reason: Plan Colombia—a $7.5 billion program Colombian President Andres Pastrana devised to eradicate coca at its roots, by fumigating the heck out of the jungles (and inadvertently poisoning the villagers in the process.) Critics say Pastrana knew that a war on cocaine would play well in the U.S., and it has played—to the tune of $2 billion since 1999.

Colombian President Álvaro Uribe and wife (right) with former president Pastrana and family: one failed with peace, the other may fail with force. (Source: Associated Press)

The objective changed in 2002: planes still swoop down spraying Monsanto herbicides, but much of the money is now used to battle left-wing guerrillas FARC, who (like every other powerful group there) snag a piece of the drug money. FARC isn't demure: kidnapping, assassinations, hijacking, mortar attacks and murders are among the tricks this group that controls nearly half the country uses. They also demand taxes on every stage of the drug trade, from farming to runways. U.S. tax dollars, however, funnel into paramilitary groups, who are even more violence-prone and known for slaughtering entire villages limb by limb with machetes and chain saws—singing merrily all the way.

The ravaging of Colombia may only get worse with new President Álvaro Uribe at the helm. He's building up the army and creating a million-strong band of citizen spies to help battle left-wing guerrillas; initially armed with radios, the citizens will probably be offered arms in the future. Meanwhile, the real objective of the U.S. is beyond extending the "War on Terror" and the "War on Drugs": rebels are attacking an American-operated oil pipeline, Occidental Petroleum's Caño Limón, and over $98 million is earmarked simply to protect that infrastructure.

Future Forecast

The Great War of the Andes may be playing soon at a country near you.

RUMORS

The Brazilian press reports that a plan is under way for a UN-led force to invade Colombia in 2004, using South American and U.S. troops to aid the Colombian Army.

Background Briefing

Confused about Colombia? No wonder: the saga of discord has more characters and subplots than a Gabriel García Márquez novel. But like the surreal writing of the Nobel Prize–winning Colombian, the tale is worth unraveling: with the billions the U.S. is pouring in, Colombia may be our next Vietnam.

What now has spread out into a complex tapestry of violence has its origins in two things: farmers' rights and a pyramidal power base where the wealthiest 10 percent control the vast majority of land and money. Discontent brewed up on coffee plantations back in the 1930s, when peasant farmers armed themselves to protect against brutality.

LA VIOLENCIA

What started mostly as a power struggle between Liberals (who wanted separation between church and state) and Conservatives (who did not), came to
a head in 1947 when a peasants rights' activist (and Liberal candidate) was
shot. The assassination catapulted the country into a vile eleven-year civil war
that killed some three hundred thousand. "La Violencia," as it was called, officially ended in 1958 when Liberals and Conservatives formed the National
Front party. Fighting never really stopped, largely because most Colombians
remained economically wounded and politically splintered, and were never
fully integrated into the new government.

After the country's civil war in the 1940s and 1950s, realizing that they still
didn't have a voice in the new government, many peasants trekked into mountainous jungles to set up agricultural villages there. As wealthy plantation owners expanded their lands, these peasant-claimed tracts too became the sites of
violence and army attacks. In the name of protecting the indigent farmers, several guerrilla groups sprang up—including FARC and ELN—who demanded
agricultural reform and more rights to the people. Not only did guerrillas attack
government targets, they brutalized each other as they sought to gain turf.

Already messy, the situation went entirely awry in the 1980s. When cocaine
shoved its way into the economy, anyone with a gun sought a piece of the
multibillion-dollar industry. Drug lords became the nouveau riche landowners,
and guerrillas took to kidnapping first them, then anyone with money, for ransom. Potential kidnap targets hired security guards—many former army men—
who banded together in paramilitary groups. Taking such cheery names as
"Death to Kidnappers," they set out massacring anyone possibly affiliated with
guerrillas. These right-wing paramilitaries also assassinated members of newly
formed left-wing political parties. FARC's political wing was nearly blasted out
of existence—with more than one thousand of their politicians killed over several years, until they closed up headquarters in 1990s, headed back to the jungle and began a more brutal campaign. Meanwhile, the country opened up to
international oil development, including ventures of California's Occidental Petroleum, and guerrillas began kidnapping oil execs as well as attacking their
pipelines. When the economy took a downturn and unemployment shot up to
20 percent, always impoverished villagers began swelling the ranks of FARC,
which pays far better than the military, and even larger swaths of land came under FARC rebels' control—complete with taxation for "security."

PITY THE PEASANT

Who pays the heaviest price: peasant farmers, economically forced to grow coca, taxed by FARC, killed by paramilitary and fumigated by the government.

The never lily-white government at least has made numerous attempts at peace talks with guerrilla rebels, but the right-wing paramilitaries—who are affiliated with the army—have helped to blast those dreams to smithereens.

PASTRANA'S PEACE EXPERIMENT

In 1998 the hopeful eyes of the country were on FARC, when President Pastrana handed them a Switzerland-sized territory to lure them into talking peace. Instead they mostly amped up their attacks, assassinations and abductions and turned the territory into a military training camp/execution center. The last straw: when FARC hijacked a commercial plane in February 2002 simply to kidnap a senator on board.

Sickened by the constant violence, in 2002 the people elected yuppie lawyer Álvaro Uribe, who promised to restore law and order—with the aid of the U.S. Linked to paramilitary groups, Uribe may initiate an all-out war to wipe out left-wing rebels. FARC celebrated his inauguration by launching a mortar attack in Bogotá that killed thirteen. Within five days of taking office, Uribe had declared emergency law, initiated a civilian army of a million spies and slapped big business with war taxes to help build the military and police forces.

It's so hard to figure out who is a "white hat" around here that even residents can't keep track of who is kidnapping/torturing/killing whom, much less why. Many just want to get out, and since the 1980s there's been an exodus, with villagers swelling into Bogotá's slums and millions of the educated upper classes grabbing their visas and fleeing South America entirely. Meanwhile, the issues that started the whole bloody shebang—land ownership, inequality of wealth and needed agricultural reform—are lost in the dust.

JUST ANOTHER 48 HOURS

A typical two days in Colombia brings:

16 kidnappings
20 politically motivated murders

assorted car bombs, grenade attacks, road blockades
blackouts from electric grid sabotage
a bombing of the Caño Limón pipeline

Ray of Hope: *As violent as Colombia is today, it's better than it was during the nineteenth century, when the chaotic country experienced eight civil wars.*

Factoid: *Colombia is sometimes known as "Locombia"—land of the crazy.*

Hot Shots

Left-wing guerrillas (aka rebels, insurgents):

FARC (Fuerzas Armadas Revolucianariás de Colombia or The Revolutionary Armed Forces of Colombia): An unprovoked army attack on farmers in 1964 led to this armed "peasant rights" Marxist movement that pushed for land reform and also offered seeds, medicine, electricity and "protection" to Indigent farmers neglected by the government. Led by Mañuel Marulanda, the jungle guerrillas entered politics in the mid-1980s but changed course after most of their politicians were offed. Now numbering eighteen thousand—and growing by the day—this heavily armed, camouflage-wearing group of poor villagers is best known for high-profile kidnapping, sabotage, murder, taxing the coca trade and making a joke of peace talks. Now spilling into Peru.

FARC'S BAD PR

Never popular with the urban masses, FARC's popularity plummeted in 2002 when they refused to release a military man whose twelve-year-old son, dying of cancer, pleaded from the television screen nightly to meet briefly with his father. Not only did FARC shrug off the boy's wishes, they went on to murder his dad.

ELN (El Ejército de Liberación Nacional or Army for National Liberation): Urban intellectuals who had just returned from a field trip to Cuba started up this left-wing Maoist outfit that, like FARC, espouses agrarian reform. Now numbering two thousand or so, ELN specializes in kidnapping and sabotage—particularly against oil companies, whom they believe exploit the country's poor.

BLOODY OIL

With both ELN and FARC attacking, the Caño Limón pipeline, partly owned by U.S. oil giant Occidental, is shut down half of the year and since 1986 has leaked eleven times more crude oil than the *Exxon Valdez*. Both groups tap the pipeline too, and create a powerful "underground oil industry."

Right Wingers (aka paramilitaries, private security forces):

AUC (Autodefensas Unidas de Colombia or The United Self-Defense Forces of Colombia): These overzealous, overarmed private guards rose to power during the 1980s kidnapping craze, when they began protecting the new multimillionaire drug lords and other rich families. Now numbering nine thousand and growing (they pay far better than ELN and FARC), the thugs are organized in the United Self-Defense Forces of Colombia (AUC). Headed by brothers Carlos and Fidel Castaño, these right-wing paramilitaries, alleged to be linked to the military and to take a cut of the drug money, terrorize the country, purifying it of anyone they imagine may be guerrilla-linked. These guys take the brutality cake: whether with machine guns, machetes or chain saws, they make a gruesome mess wherever they go; human rights groups say AUC commits the majority of massacres and most heartless crimes.

Occidental: Since 1986, when the L.A.-based oil company set up in Colombia, its employees have been routinely kidnapped and occasionally murdered, mostly by ELN, which also targets its pipeline. Just as problematic: the U'wa Indians, who have threatened mass suicide if Occidental digs up their jungle home. Critics of Plan Colombia fault this company, which heavily lobbied Congress to authorize funding.

Andres Pastrana: President of Colombia from 1998 to 2002, Pastrana left office in 2002 with *huevo* on his face for his failed peace experiments with FARC. He was more persuasive with the U.S. government—whom he convinced to commit over $2 billion to Plan Colombia—with much more coming—most of which was earmarked for helicopters, crop dusting chemicals, transport equipment and state-of-the-art arms.

Álvaro Uribe Velez: President of Colombia since 2002, educated at Harvard and Cambridge, lawyer Álvaro Uribe looks like he could be working Wall Street. Instead he's attempting to pound law and order into a system that's gone haywire. To succeed where others have failed, Uribe is relying heavily on his military—whose power is beefed up thanks to arms, helicopters and money from Uncle Sam. But will the man who wants to arm civilians as a front line of defense also call out the macho right-wing paramilitaries to help? Dodging death threats throughout his campaign—and a mortar attack the night of his inauguration—Uribe is sure to make Colombia even bloodier.

BUZZWORD

Plan Colombia: Ka-ching! The Colombian government and army are the great benefactors of this controversial operation that officially aims to slash cocaine production in half by 2005 and unofficially protects U.S. oil interests. The U.S. began by handing over a hefty $1.3 billion in 1999 for a six-year military-heavy fumigation operation that targets coca production (and now targets left-leaning FARC rebels as well). The plan is a public relations nightmare as it poisons drinking water, deadens the ground and sickens villagers who may or may not be planting coca. Detractors also note that in the first year of intensive fumigation the coca crop actually increased and Colombia's cocaine production shot up 11 percent. The pipeline still attacked, too.

DIVVYING UP THE CASH

Eighty percent of U.S. funding is earmarked for the military, while a mere 8 percent is funneled toward "crop substitution"—i.e., educating the peasant farmers and giving them new crops to plant. Meanwhile, $2 million is simply missing.

Hot Spots

Putumayo region: A FARC stronghold and site of intensive coca planting.

Caño Limón Pipeline: A 480-mile rebel target.

DADDY DEAREST:
LEADERS WHOSE FATHERS WERE KILLED

President Álvaro Uribe: father killed by rebels
AUC's Carlos Castaño: father killed by FARC
FARC's Mañuel Marulanda: father killed by army

Russia . . . Saudi Arabia . . . Egypt
. . . Iran . . . China . . . Taiwan . . .
Sudan   **PART TWO**   Afghan-
istan . . . Somalia . . . Japan . . . Russia
. . . Saudi Arabia . . . Egypt . . . Iran . . .
China . . . Taiwan

Slow Tickers . . .

. . . Saudi Arabia . . . Egypt
. . . Iran . . . China . . . Taiwan . . .
Sudan . . . Afghanistan . . . Somalia
. . . Japan . . .Russia . . . Saudi Arabia
Egypt . . . Iran . . . China . . . Taiwan
. . . Sudan . . . Afghanistan . . . Somalia
Japan . . .Russia . . . Saudi Arabia . . .
Egypt . . . Iran . . . China . . . Taiwan
. . . Sudan . . . Afghanistan . . . Somalia
. . . Japan . . .Russia . . . Saudi Arabia
Egypt . . . Iran . . . China . . . Taiwan
. . . Sudan . . . Saudi Arabia . . . Egypt
Iran . . . China . . . Taiwan . . .
Sudan . . . Afghanistan . . . Somalia

RUSSIA

FAST FACTS

Country:	Russian Federation
Capital:	Moscow
Government:	federation
Independence:	24 September 1991 (from Soviet Union)
Population:	144,979,000 (2002 estimate)
Leaders:	President Vladimir Putin; Prime Minister Mikhail Kasyanov
Ethnicity:	82% Russian; 4% Tatar; 3% Ukrainian and others
Religion:	Russian Orthodox, Muslim
Language:	Russian
Literacy:	98% both sexes (1989 estimate)
Exports:	petroleum, gas, wood
Per capita GDP:	$8,300 (2001 estimate)
Unemployment:	10.5% (2000 estimate)
Percentage living in poverty:	40% (1999 estimate)
Known for:	Chernobyl, the Cold War, scientists for sale

Standout Qualities

Cold winds: chiseled the Russian persona
Cold War: world's most expensive mind game
Warm-up: 9/11 prompted a hasty thaw

Résumé

Formerly occupying the number one spot on Uncle Sam's hate list, Russia is now the U.S.' antiterrorist pardner and good pal. Well, sort of.

GEOGRAPHICAL GIANT

Even after the Soviet Union officially split into fifteen republics in 1991, Russia remains the world's largest country in terms of land mass.

Quick Tour

Russia is massive, grabbing eleven time zones as it pulls nearly half of Asia and part of Europe into its cumbersome embrace. But wherever one stands along this arctic-capped expanse of steppe, mountain, rivers and tundra—whether gazing at the tiled swirls of the Kremlin or the gleaming Winter Palace of St. Petersburg—Russia is rarely a lighthearted place where one skips down the streets, plucking daisies and singing about the good life.

Broken Machine: *The post-communist economy is still traumatized: one-third of Russians live on less than $1 a day.*

There are reasons: among them, the cruel Russian winter. A brutalizing, cold-to-the-bone, trudging-through-waist-high-drifts kind of winter, when blasts of Arctic wind slap your face and knock you over, the Russian weather has stopped the unstoppable and beat the unbeatable, turning back armies from Napoleon's to the Nazis, hundreds of thousands of once-hearty men finally surrendering not to the enemy but to the stinging cold.

LANGUAGE LESSON

Is it the hardship of moving in subzero weather that makes the Russian language so detailed in its "verbs of motion"? There isn't one infinitive "to go" in Russian—there are dozens. Each different verb signifies with one little word whether the trip is on foot, on horse or via machine, and whether it's a round trip or one-way, not to mention if you're just starting off or going through, under or over something, or make the journey frequently. Such concerns are paramount only when it's very nasty outside.

Winters like that drive one to knocking back straight shots of vodka with black bread and pickles; they instill a wind-blasted intensity, survival skills and a resigned acceptance of the hardship of life. Further weathered by centuries of oppression from tsars and feudal lords, the Russian mentality was ideal for communism, or rather the propagandistic Soviet style of "war communism" and its clunky, misfiring Marxist machine that was born in 1917, when the Tsar Nicholas II and his family were pushed out and brutally killed the following year.

PRICEY CHILL

The Cold War that emerged between the U.S. and the Soviet Union after World War II was the defining political mind-set of the second half of the twentieth century. Although never meeting each other head-on in war, both countries spent trillions of dollars preparing to do so: the edgy time witnessed the development and proliferation of the most sophisticated weaponry—nuclear, conventional, chemical and biological—as well as a "race for space" and a rapid increase in espionage and peeping technologies. The period that saw the birth of the CIA and KGB also gave rise to important alliances—NATO among them—and a chess game of power plays wherein both countries sought to win friends by opening their wallets, providing economic backing as well as food supplies, energy resources and military equipment. The Cold War also led to a number of "hot wars"— including the Korean War and the Vietnam War, which the U.S. entered to battle communism—and the close call of the Cuban Missile Crisis. The U.S. also helped create the mujahideen to fight the communist Soviets when they invaded Afghanistan in 1979. The era also gave birth to such unlikely concepts as communist "containment," "mutually assured self-destruction" and the "peaceful use of the atom."

Stalin, who took over in 1924, cobbled together a much larger "empire" after World War II, as he roped first East Germany, then most of Eastern Europe into the Soviet Union. The Cold War essentially began in 1948 when Stalin blocked Western food shipments to East Berlin, prompting the dangerous "Berlin Food Airlift" into the blockaded territory. As country by country fell to the Soviets, the Allies ultimately created NATO in 1949 and other alliances to ward off the expansionist Soviet threat.

Though so much of the Soviet Union and its output was inept, inefficient and misguided, the early Soviet powers—Lenin, Stalin and Khrushchev—nevertheless succeeded in building a communist powerhouse based on research, development and heavy industry. Competitive by nature and all the more so during the Cold War, the Russians shot to space first, were the second to develop nuclear weapons and ran chemical and biological test programs every bit as extensive as those in the U.S.

DIVIDED WE FALL

A key ingredient in the Soviet success formula was keeping elements divided: when Stalin drew up the Central Asian Republics (aka "the 'Stans"), he often moved in not just one ethnic group, but their ethnic rivals as well, to keep the residents fighting among themselves. Type Triple A competitiveness in Soviet schools drove a wedge between friends, and the omnipresent KGB and its citizen spies also ensured an edginess that kept the masses from effectively uniting against Moscow.

The massively inefficient and sloppy Soviet machine was already in need of repair—as evidenced by the Chernobyl explosion in 1986—when the Soviets rolled into Afghanistan in 1979, not knowing that they'd stay for ten years before giving up and finally putting the tanks in reverse.

NUCLEAR NIGHTMARE

When one of the reactors at the Chernobyl plant failed, causing a power surge and a chain reaction of chemical explosions—the biggest nuclear disaster in history—the surrounding countryside was blasted with radioactivity: 41 died, at least 2,000 now have thyroid cancer, 8,000 died from radiation sickness and food is still regularly checked for radioactivity. Mushrooms and berries are likely to blip on the Geiger counter. Twenty-three percent of Belarus is contaminated.

That expensive humiliation, known as "Russia's Vietnam," along with nationalist uprisings in republics such as Kazakhstan, Armenia and Azerbaijan, led President Mikhail Gorbachev to declare a "perestroika," or restructuring of Soviet communism. Instead of being restructured, the communist empire fell apart. In December 1991, the Soviet Union was officially dissolved. Russia and fourteen other independent republics stood in its place.

DIFFERENT KIND OF WAR

Afghanistan's mountainous terrain, best suited for battles with spears and horses, wasn't made for the tank, Soviets had never fought guerrilla-style warfare, and the mujahideen were fierce warriors. But what killed thousands of Soviets wasn't the war itself: it was the diseases they caught from bad water in the 1979–1989 Soviet-Afghan War.

Russia initially floundered with the transformation of the state-run communist economy to a free market democratic state: the banking system nearly collapsed, the ruble plummeted in value, and the scary Russian Mafia emerged from the shadows. But what Russia has that almost everybody wants: oil and lots of it. By 2001, Russia was the second biggest petroleum exporter in the world, behind only Saudi Arabia, and the U.S. is pushing to buy much more of its oil.

OIL TWITCHINGS

Currently the world's number two oil producer, Russia, like oil exporters Mexico and Norway, does not belong to the Organization of Petroleum Exporting Countries (OPEC), and has the capacity to offset the OPEC cartel, by acting independently and flooding the market, thus lowering the prices cartel members try to set. Russia makes Saudi Arabia very nervous.

Portly and towering Boris Yeltsin may have best embodied the look of the Russian bear when he ran the show in the 1990s, but between his boozing and his health he was not having an easy go of it. After firing four prime ministers in seventeen months and canning his entire cabinet, Yeltsin yanked former KGB Lieutenant-Colonel Vladimir Putin to the top rung. In 1999, Yeltsin—in another bad mood—surprised everyone and stomped out, naming Putin as acting prime minister. The young leader won presidential elections the next year.

HOSTAGE HORROR

For months the Russian government had assured its people that the three-year war with Chechnya was almost over and that Russian troops had the upper hand. The dubiousness of those assertions was illustrated in October 2002, when 42 Chechen rebels, including women wired with bombs, held over 700 hostages in a Moscow theatre demanding that Russian troops pull out of their homeland. The end of the three-day ordeal was just as horrifying as the act itself: after attempts to negotiate failed, Russian forces filled the theater with a hallucinogenic nerve gas. The gas killed most of the Chechens, and also snuffed out more than 115 of the hostages.

The inexperienced politician immediately faced a tragedy: the nuclear submarine *Kursk* sank in the Barents Sea in August 2000. All 118 on board died as the government dawdled in rescuing the sunken sub. Blame was heaped on President Putin, who had been on vacation and didn't immediately return to face the ordeal. His subsequent defensiveness only worsened the problem, as did the fact that the corpse-filled submarine sat underwater for a year until a Dutch firm pulled it up.

To deflect criticism, Putin clamped down on the media and intensified war efforts in Chechnya—typically a popular Russian cause.

THE CHECHNYA CONFLICT

The problems between ethnic Russians and ethnic Chechens—who are often Muslim—goes back for centuries, but Stalin helped it along. Accusing the Chechen mountain people of collaborating with Nazis, he rounded them up during World War II and sent them to barren Kazakhstan in Central Asia, where they had no way to make a living and little food. Most of them starved. Some say while there the already fierce bunch became even more hardened and prone to criminal activities. It wasn't until 1957 that they were given permission by Khrushchev to return to their home—in the mountains of southwestern Russia between the Black and Caspian Seas.

Since communism fell, Chechens have continually demanded their independence, and Russia doesn't want to give it—in part because there's oil in Chechnya. Yeltsin sent in his troops in 1994 to squelch their independence idea; two years later, Chechen guerrilla fighters had sent the Russian Army packing. Chechnya was essentially independent for three years—until 1999, when Russia blamed a Moscow apartment bombing that killed nearly three hundred people on Chechen rebels, as well as a dirty bomb discovered in a city park.

Cynics say Chechnya may have had nothing to do with either, but in any case Russia rolled back in to try to conquer the mountain-grown secessionists. Three years later the fighting continues, tens of thousands have died and more than three hundred thousand refugees have fled—many over the hills to Georgia. Capital Grozny is a wasteland, torture is as common as vodka, village men and boys are frequently rounded up, many are killed and some are imprisoned for months in holes in the ground in this never-ending conflict in which both sides have acted entirely savage. Some say the war continues because it's too popular to give up: an oil and arms black market has emerged that's profitable for both sides, Putin can distract his poor people with the war against terrorists, while constant battling gives unemployed Chechen youth something to do.

The U.S. previously had jumped on Russia's case about the vicious war in Chechnya, but the deck was reshuffled after 9/11. Reports from the collapsing World Trade Center were still streaming in, when a call from Moscow beeped through to the office of National Security Council advisor Condoleeza Rice. On the line: a shaken President Vladimir Putin. Of all the world's leaders, Russia's president was the first to express his deep sorrow at the tragedy of September 11, and was quick to voice his support for the subsequent "War on Terror."

PUTIN'S THAW

The Russian president's September 11 phone gesture was significant: while not exactly frosty, relations between Putin and Bush had been a bit cool. In March 2001 each president had quietly booted out fifty of each other's diplomats, suspecting them of being spies.

Before long he was flying out to the Bush ranch, dancing the "Cotton-eyed Joe" and conducting call-in interviews with the American people on National Public Radio. To celebrate the moment, President Bush made a special announcement: the U.S. would be reducing its arsenal of nuclear weapons from seven thousand to two thousand. So what if the U.S. had planned on doing that anyway: with U.S.-Russian relations looking almost affectionate, it seemed the right time.

The historic November 2001 summit in Crawford, Texas, between Putin and Bush seems to have cemented an unlikely friendship between the two leaders, who quickly took to back-slapping, telling jokes and assuring American audiences that while they might not see eye to eye on all issues they were resolved to work out any problems. One such problem: Bush wants to amend the previous Anti-Ballistic Missile Treaty with Russia and put up an anti-ballistic missile shield in the U.S.; Putin doesn't support the missile shield, having signed an agreement with China in July 2000 to oppose just such a thing.

It's ironic that the acts of Osama bin Laden sparked something resembling true warmth between the U.S. and Russia: in the 1980s the U.S. brought the new enemy (Osama) to power when they set him loose to battle the old enemy (the Soviet Union) in Afghanistan. Nevertheless, Russia-U.S. relations are at an all-time high, and these days Russia even has some say in NATO, the military alliance that five decades ago sprung up to defy it. But there are still differences to work out before one brings out the Stolichnaya and caviar and kicks up a Russian-style celebration. Among them: Russia still sells arms and nuclear technology all over the place, including to China and Iran. And Russia doesn't want the U.S. to proceed with a national missile shield, which will merely continue an international arms race.

Future Forecast

Russia will continue to embrace the West, which it desperately needs to help its economy. But it probably will still peddle arms and who knows what else on the side.

NEWS BLACKOUT

Since becoming president in 2000, Putin continually shuts down the media, and at least once tossed a TV station owner in jail. The Russian press is now almost entirely censored from within.

Background Briefing

While the U.S. nuclear and biochemical warfare industries boast a less than shining record, their Soviet counterparts are worse: toxic wastelands dot the former Soviet Union especially in Kazakhstan, where Western scientists are working with Russians to clean up the poisoned land. Nuclear waste from other countries, such as Yugoslavia, is also being sent to Russia for safekeeping, although that may be a joke: the Russians have never been particularly good at keeping tabs on their arsenals, from which several "suitcase nukes" and other deadly weapons are missing.

DEATH TECHIES

When the Soviet Union collapsed, warfare scientists were among those who were suddenly unemployed. It's feared that Soviet scientists may have helped develop weapons programs everywhere from North Korea to Iraq.

Another area to watch: pipelines. Gas and oil from the 'Stans typically is pumped through Russian pipes to ports, but American companies are getting into the action. Russia appears to be giving a nod, but we'll see how long that lasts.

Hot Spots

Chechnya: The current round of fighting, started in 1999, shows little sign of ending: Muslim Chechens want their freedom; Russia doesn't want to grant it. Capital Grozny is ruined, refugees are running, tens of thousands are dead. The October 2002 hostage incident in Moscow only underscored how desperate and determined Chechens are to win independence.

Georgia: It's no longer a Soviet Republic, but Russia is threatening to send in troops if the Georgians don't clamp down on Chechen rebels who are spilling over the border.

Caspian Sea: Rights to oil and pipelines along the Caspian are still being hotly worked out. Among the players: Russia, Azerbaijan, Kazakhstan, Turkmenistan and Iran. This could get very tricky.

Hot Shots

Vladimir Putin: Acting prime minister since 1999 and elected president since 2000, young, athletic and kinda cute, the former KGB man is far more likeable than his predecessors, especially when he's wearing a cowboy hat. His considerable diplomatic skills aside, he's still trying to assert Russia as hegemon—the country still bosses former republics around and is trampling Chechnya—and his way of dealing with criticism is to shut down the press.

Igor Ivanov and Sergei Ivanov: Foreign minister and defense minister respectively, Putin usually makes them lodge criticisms of the U.S.

Josef Stalin: Soviet dictator from 1924 to 1953, power-loving autocrat Stalin acted all chummy to the Brits' Prime Minister Winston Churchill and the Americans' President Franklin D. Roosevelt during World War II when Russia joined up with the Allies to fight Germany and Japan, but Stalin's warmth was a ruse. As became evident after the Yalta Conference—when Germany's holdings were divvied up for supervision between the Allies— Stalin simply wanted Hitler's land for himself. Like the führer, Stalin also rounded up ethnic minorities, be they Jewish, Chechen, Turkoman or Uzbek. By the time Stalin bid a final *dosvidanya* in 1953, he was responsible for over 50 million deaths.

Mikhail Gorbachev: President from 1989 to 1991, he accidentally triggered the downfall with Glasnost (openness) and Perestroika (restructuring) and millions love him for it. Recipient of the 1990 Nobel Peace Prize, "Gorby" now heads his own humanitarian foundation.

Commonwealth of Independent States: After the crumbling of the Soviet Union in 1991, twelve former Soviet republics banded together the same year in this loose-knit economic, political and military organization. Not terribly effective, it will probably eventually go the same way as its Soviet Ma.

TIT FOR TAT?

In fall 2002 Russia backed the U.S. by voting yes on UN Security Council Resolution 1441, calling for Iraq to disarm its weapons of mass destruction. As a result, it lost an Iraqi oil contract worth billions. Weeks later, Russia dismissed all Peace Corps workers, saying the Americans were spies.

SAUDI ARABIA

Standout Qualities

Keys: Koran penned, Muhammad born here
Fill 'er up: world's biggest petroleum exporter
Tinted windows: secretive society

Résumé

To Muslims, Saudi Arabia is home to the world's two holiest places. To Americans, Saudi Arabia is home to the world's biggest gas pump. It's the precarious juggling of those two roles that induces schizophrenia in the Middle East's enigmatic giant—and explains why fifteen of the nineteen September 11 hijackers came from here.

ISLAMIC HOLY SPOTS

1. Mecca, in southwest Saudi Arabia, birthplace of Prophet Muhammad, where Muslims face when praying
2. Medina, in central Saudi Arabia, where Muhammad led followers after being booted from Mecca, also where he is buried
3. Al-Aqsa Mosque, where Muhammad ascended in Jerusalem

Quick Tour

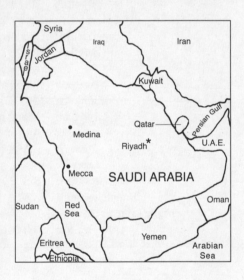

The most powerful monarchy on the planet, Saudi Arabia presents a bizarre world of contrasts to Westerners, starting with the white-gowned men and black-cloaked women, who look like walking tents with beautiful eyes. The worldly and the spiritual subtly spite each other here in the land of Bedouin deserts broken by gleaming cities of spellbinding architecture, where college education is free, people live tax free and whip-brandishing religious police shove the masses to mosques five times a day, in between checking that women are suitably covered and in possession of the requisite "OK-to-be-out" note from their husbands.

UNVEILED

Powers of the religious police, officially known as the Committee for the Promotion of Virtue and the Prevention of Vice or Mutawwa'in, are being reined in, after a 2002 fire in a girls' school. The police pushed girls who escaped back into the flames because they'd run out without veils; fifteen schoolgirls died and many more were injured.

Sure, there are the flashy malls (where women dare not shop unchaperoned) and neon bars (where you can't drink) and restaurants (where men and women, as at home, dine separately); but besides camel races the biggest entertainment is the weekly beheadings at Riyadh's "Chop-Chop Square." Shariah law is in full force here, and schools indoctrinate students with a rigid form of Islam that regards Westerners, who are intricately tied up in the petroleum economy, as heathen infidels who should not step on holy Saudi soil.

FRIDAY FUN

Thousands turn out to witness public punishments dictated by Shariah law: floggings for boozers, hand choppings for thieves, beheadings for murderers, car bombers and pot smokers. Foreigners who wander in are pushed forward for front-row views.

The largest dichotomy, however, is that while royalty expects mass conformity to the repressive religion, some princes blatantly ignore its dictates while living lavish lifestyles, throwing big boozy soirees with wanton women and reportedly even running illegal bootlegging outfits. There's no money available to fix run-down hospital wings, but there's plenty to buy new palaces and new racehorses, even though gambling is forbidden. Those royal peccadilloes might have been more easily overlooked in better times.

AVERAGE PER CAPITA INCOME FOR SAUDIS
1980: $26,000
2000: $7,000

Now, with oil prices and salaries way down, unemployment way up and two-thirds of the population under twenty-five, the blatant hypocrisy—and the notorious royal waste—is causing plenty of grumbling. So is the government's relationship with the U.S., which has been breathing down the Saudi's back since September 11 and pressuring this secretive bunch to cough up information and crack down on extremists. Not the sort for loud protests, some Saudis show displeasure with American troops—who have remained on Saudi bases twelve years after the Persian Gulf War—by bombing cars and living quarters of Westerners. Whether the radical fringes have enough gumption or power to eject the House of Saud is a frequent topic of intellectual debate, but one thing is agreed: throughout the kingdom ill feelings are festering.

Factoid: The eighteenth-century founder of the state religion, Muhammed al-Wahhab, preached it was a duty to overthrow leaders who strayed from the faith; bin Laden and other radicals stress the point.

Future Forecast

Continued sporadic attacks until U.S. troops leave. An American invasion of Iraq might hit an emotional gusher and be perceived as a further U.S. attempt to dominate the region. Skyrocketing oil prices could be just the beginning.

TAKE THAT, HEATHEN

Assorted attacks:

1995: car bomb at American National Guard office, 7 killed, 60 injured
1996: car bomb at Khobar Towers, 19 Americans die, 547 injured
2000–2002: car bombs, grenades target Americans and Brits

SAUDI GRIPES

Don't want nonbelievers around
Mad that U.S. backs Israel
Blame West for modernity

SCANDAL!: Protests are few in the country that doesn't encourage free-dom of expression. In 1990 however, 47 feisty Saudi women booted their drivers, grabbed the wheels and drove around a Safeway parking lot for a wild ten minutes until they were arrested. Charges were later dropped.

Background Briefing

Whether you're talking about the glittering glass cities rising from the red-gold sands, the gem-encrusted airports, the pooled palaces or the McDon-alds', the Starbucks and Osama bin Laden, what made Saudi Arabia what it is today is the car. Not only does the four-wheeled beast whisk across the now-ribboned desert on high-speed journeys that took the camel long dusty weeks, the car catapulted Saudi Arabia into a world force, turning the Muslim world's sacred sandbox into the Western world's most valuable treasure trove.

Factoid: Saudi Arabia has 25 percent of all known oil reserves—the most oil in the world.

Without the hungry car—and American demands for the gas to feed it—pumps wouldn't creak in the desert, tankers wouldn't leak off Jidda, warships wouldn't be parked in the Gulf, American soldiers wouldn't be stationed at desert bases, modernity would have been kept at bay and the subterranean snake of riches would have just laid there quietly under the shifting dunes as it had for millennia. In other words, Saudi Arabia would have remained precisely as the religious half of the kingdom had wanted it to stay back in 1933 when King Ibn Saud welcomed the first team of geologists to his new land in the sand.

Factoid: Ibn Saud actually wanted the geologists to look for water.

CONQUERING A DESERT

In 1902, when Ibn Saud set out to conquer Arabia, a land that had slipped through his family's hands twice before (1804–1818 and 1843–1891), he did so with a holy man who preached a hellfire, tradition-loving form of Islam—Wahhabism. Over thirty years of fierce trekking, the king and his mesmerizing sidekick delivered a one-two punch: the preacher converted the masses with his divine words; the warrior followed with fighters, ensuring all were true Wahhabi. Piece by piece, tribe by tribe, convert warrior by convert warrior, they stitched together the patchwork kingdom, officially united in 1932: the new Saud king, who stamped his family name on Arabia, shared power with the holy man, whose family became the religious gurus.

Factoid: Dashing Ibn Saud personally bonded with conquered fiefdoms by plucking a young maiden to join his harem, and becoming king and kin to some forty tribes.

Even back in 1933 the supreme Muslim leader—the grand mufti—didn't want Westerners and their modern ways tramping around the sacred, history-steeped soil; the king, however, liked the foreigners' radios and their non-camel transport, and besides, he needed the money they were tossing his way for exploration rights.

When experts concluded that a sea of oil ran under their feet, a deal was struck between king and mufti: the monarchy would take care of business and finances and the religious elite would shut up and tend to mosques, courts, laws, schools, social protocol and fashion. Oil wealth would also pump the rigid state religion of Wahhabism across the Muslim world through schools, missions and social aid. The compromise between worldly and spiritual leaders continued, little questioned, for almost fifty years, though it did produce a fragmented society where seventh-century tradition lives on in the twenty-first century.

POWER SWITCH

Saudi Arabia was oil rich, but it was not wealthy until the royal family bought into the main oil company, the formerly U.S.-dominated Aramco, beginning in the 1970s, and took full control in 1980. KA-CHING!

Two events, however, tossed substantial power back to the religious elite:

1. Ibn Saud's son, King Faisal, was assassinated in 1975 by his nephew, a royal prince, who was widely believed to have gone mad due to exposure to the influences of the West.
2. Religious fanatics overtook the Grand Mosque in Mecca in November 1979 and held hostages for two weeks. It took 127 deaths and nerve gas to get them out; the ordeal made the monarchy look utterly weak and ineffective and like poor custodians of Islam's holiest place.

By 1990, post-boom income was slip sliding down the slope of falling oil prices, discord was slithering through the mosques, and clandestine tapes of radical imams were circulating, when roly-poly King Fahd made a decision that still rattles and rankles the kingdom today. On August 3, 1990, when King Fahd looked to the north, where Saddam's tanks rolled into Kuwait, and to the east, where his oil fields lay, and at satellite photos the U.S. had given him showing Iraqi forces amassed at the Saudi border, he called in the West. Little did the king or the U.S. president know that when King Fahd accepted the American offer to protect

King Fahd said no to bin Laden and yes to the U.S., inadvertently planting the seed for Al Qaeda. (Source: Associated Press)

his country, the monarch had infuriated a Muslim warrior named Osama bin Laden, who had wanted to take on Iraq, with one hundred thousand mujahideen. When King Fahd instead brought in American forces, he ensured not only that bin Laden's wrath would be unleashed on the U.S., but that the Muslim fighter would do all in his power to topple the monarchy.

Factoid: *Twelve of the September 11 hijackers came from the southwest of Saudi Arabia—the Asir region, where tribal loyalties are stronger than ties to the House of Saud. The CIA believes bin Laden is trying to rile up formerly powerful tribes to toss the royals.*

Rumors: *Some American investigators say the photo the U.S. showed Fahd was doctored and that Saddam never planned on invading Saudi Arabia as implied.*

INFIDELITY

The grand mufti, under pressure, gave his official okay on what would become "Desert Storm," but the appearance of six hundred thousand nonbelievers on sacred soil was highly controversial; despite promises the Americans would soon leave, the "infidels" as Saudi school books call non-Muslims—or at least six thousand of them—stayed.

Factoid: *Saudi Arabia and Kuwait bankrolled much of the American participation in Desert Storm; the Saudis also have picked up the tab for continued U.S. troops in the kingdom.*

BIN LADEN'S SMASHED DREAMS

Osama bin Laden was once pals with the royal set: the al-Saud backed bin Laden's 1980s dream of a righteous Muslim army taking on the atheist Soviets in Afghanistan. The problem ten years later: what to do with the war hero after he returned all fired up. The royals politely dismissed bin Laden's 1990 patriotic offer of going after Iraq with his mujahideen: instead they offered him a lucrative renovation project of the Grand Mosque in Mecca. His male ego wounded, bin Laden, once gracious, transformed into a loud bad-mouthing machine. So vitriolic were his diatribes against the ruling family that in 1992 he was asked to leave the country. Even from Sudan, his antimonarchy stance was so provocative that he was stripped of Saudi nationality in 1994.

ARAB-ISRAELI MATTERS

Increasingly, Saudis are upset about American backing of Israel. Crown Prince Abdullah was so discouraged that he sent President George W. Bush a "Dear John" letter in August 2001, expressing outrage over American backing of Israel's Ariel Sharon and requesting that U.S. forces leave Saudi bases. The president promptly responded, promising more attention to Middle East peace. The prince unveiled his own peace plan in spring 2002. Endorsed by the Arab League, it called for "normalized relations with Israel" if Israel would pull back to its pre-1967 borders.

Factoid: Saudi Arabia's 1973 oil embargo was a reaction to the U.S. military aid to Israel during that year's Arab-Israeli War.

VOCABULARY BUILDER

khalifa: head scarf worn by men
djellaba: flowing gown worn by men
abaya: body cloak worn by women

THE SAUDI BLACK HOLE

How can such a rich country be losing money—so much that it recently was forced to take out a multibillion-dollar loan? Pricey arms and military equipment: since 1990, Saudi Arabia has been the number one arms buyer in the world. Who's been raking in billions from the sales? The U.S.

Hot Spots

Prince Sultan Base: The U.S. loves this state-of-the-art facility, headquarters for six thousand American troops. The Saudis refuse to let the U.S. use it for sorties on Afghanistan and don't want it involved in invasion of Iraq, or so they sometimes say. A possible site for anti-American attacks.

Asir: The southwestern area around this mountain range breeds religious extremism and royal distrust. Last area to be roped into kingdom, most likely to rebel. Most of 9/11 hijackers from here.

Crown Prince Abdullah (left) pushed for Arab-Israeli peace but failed. (Source: Associated Press)

Language Lesson: *"Bin" means "son of." A full Saudi name tells the family tree.*

Hot Shots

Ibn Saud: Founder of the religious monarchy, Ibn Saud changed the course of history when he let oilmen drill. He fathered at least 44 sons and 125 daughters; all government high rollers are his descendents.

King Fahd: Out of operation since a 1995 stroke, King Fahd called in the Americans to protect the kingdom from Iraq.

Crown Prince Abdullah: Minding the store since Fahd checked out, Crown Prince Abdullah is less Western-oriented, but more thoughtful and religious. Cracked down on corruption in the family; didn't win popularity contests for cutting off stipends to thousands of royals used to a $10,000 monthly income since birth. Greatly concerned about Arab-Israeli situation, unveiled peace plan in 2002.

Prince Turki al-Faisal: Head of Saudi intelligence until August 2001, Turki funded Osama bin Laden's mujahideen army in Afghanistan and set up the Taliban for takeover in Afghanistan in 1994, giving trucks, oil, money. He has since tried to negotiate with bin Laden, but failed. Named in class-action suit brought by families of 9/11 victims.

Prince Bandar bin Sultan al-Saud: Saudi ambassador to U.S.

Prince Sultan bin Abdul Aziz al-Saud: Saudi foreign defense minister who rejected bin Laden's offer to fight Iraq. May be eyeing throne.

ALMOST LAST SUPPER

The French press and others report recurring rumors that Riyadh mayor Prince Salman bin Abdul-Aziz hired an assassin to kill Osama bin Laden. The would-have-been killer supposedly poisoned bin Laden's dinner in November 1998. While the dose apparently wasn't lethal, bin Laden may have severe kidney problems as a result.

Princess Haifa bint Faisal: Wife of Bandar, sis of Turki, she triggered a scandal: donations she made to a sick Jordanian woman may have ended up funding two 9/11 hijackers.

SHAKY HOLD

A suicide bombing attack that killed dozens in May 2003 signals clearly that all is not well in the kingdom, and that Al Qaeda and/or fundamentalists want to oust the monarchy. Ironically, the attack on a compound that houses Westerners came only days after the U.S.—wisely—announced that it would be pulling its remaining six thousand troops out of the country.

EGYPT

FAST FACTS

Country:	Arab Republic of Egypt
Capital:	Cairo
Government:	republic (theoretically)
Independence:	February 28, 1922 from U.K.—nominally
Population:	69,537,000 (the Arab world's most populous)
Leader:	Hosni Mubarak
Ethnicity:	99% East Hamitic (Egyptian, Bedouin, Berber)
Religion:	94% Sunni Muslim; 6% Coptic Christian and others
Language:	Arabic
Literacy:	51.4% (63% men; 39% women)
Exports:	crude oil, cotton
Per capita GDP:	$3,600 (2000 estimate)
Unemployment:	officially 11.5% (2000 estimate); unofficially 20% plus
Percentage living in Poverty:	23% (1995 estimate)
Known for:	pyramids, pharoahs, Islamists

Standout Qualities

Brains: Al Qaeda's thinkers come from Cairo
Bros: Muslim Brotherhood still influential after seventy-five years
Billions: U.S. has given $40 billion in arms since 1979

Résumé

Land o' pyramids, the formerly flooding Nile and the Suez Canal, Egypt didn't have an Egyptian-born leader from the death of Pharaoh Nectanebo in

332 B.C. to the mid-twentieth century. Since then, three powerful "presidents" (read: lifetime dictators) have performed an uneasy, often violent, dance with militant Muslims who demand an Islamic government. Among the dissidents: the master strategists of Al Qaeda.

SPEAKING UP

When prominent sociologist Sa'ad Ibrahim dared question Egypt's very questionable political process, he was smacked with a seven-year prison sentence in 2002 for "tarnishing" the name of Egypt. The U.S., which often keeps silent on such matters, is furious about the sentencing and is raising Cain with Egypt about it. Ibrahim has many a high-profile American friend, including Tom Brokaw.

Quick Tour

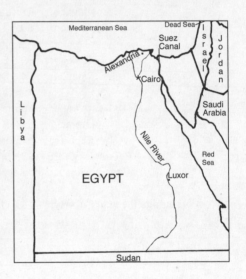

You may not notice it in the wildly zigzagging traffic of Cairo—where a green light means go and a red light means go faster—or in the spice markets' cinnamon breezes or in thick smoke-clouded cafes where turban-wrapped men play dominoes around bubbling hookahs, but Egypt, long the Arab world's leader and its most populous country, is slowly falling apart, despite efforts of the army, police and government to make it appear cohesive, U.S.-leaning and, above all, tourist-friendly.

You can see it on college campuses, where young women don the veils that their mothers ripped off. You can see it in censorship protests, where they're not protesting that some books and movies *are* banned, they're upset that they're *not*. And you can see it in the boycotts of American goods and the fiery demonstrations against Israel and the U.S. This typically moderate Muslim country, is shifting to the tradition-hugging, Western-loathing Islamic right. What's fueling it: discontent with the nonreligious, supposedly democratic government, where elections are rigged and presidential opponents can't run, where dissenters are jailed and hung, and the army keeps vigilant watch—all with a thumbs-up from the U.S.

BEHIND THE REAPPEARING VEIL

Egypt's first powerful president, Gamal Abdel Nasser, emphasizing the secular nature of his new Egypt, pushed for women to modernize and drop the veil. Putting the veil back on is not only a sign of returning to traditional Islam, it's a way of protesting governmental authority. It's also a modern woman's statement about equality. Explained one young Egyptian woman, "Female students don't want the men looking at them just as sex symbols."

The Western world has encroached with its movies and fast food, but even more with its influence: the U.S. government forks over $1.3 billion each year in military aid, a gift for which Egypt is expected to back American military moves and political postures and join U.S.-led coalitions. Increasingly, in the mosques and in the universities, Egyptians—notoriously passive—are loudly whispering that they don't want the pocketbook friendship anymore. Militant types have been more than vocal. Their most brutal display of dissatisfaction: a 1997 massacre at the Temple of Hatsheput near Luxor, when AK-47–wielding militants sprayed bullets into fifty-eight cowering tourists, mostly European and Japanese, then hacked them up with swords. The note shoved in the mouth of one—"No to tourists in Egypt!"—might as well have said, "Stay away, U.S.!" The group's inspirational leader, after all, was the "Blind Sheik" Omar Abdel-Rahman, found guilty of conspiring in the 1993 bombing of the World Trade Center.

WE'LL JUST GO TO DISNEY WORLD, THEN

The Luxor attack slammed Egypt's $4 billion annual tourist economy: tourism dropped by 70 percent over the next year.

It's no coincidence that many of Al Qaeda's power players—from Osama's right-hand man Ayman al-Zawahiri to 9/11 ringleader Mohammad Atta—cut their teeth in the dusty streets of Cairo, in well-to-do sections. Both Al Qaeda operatives had been embraced by the Muslim Brotherhood, a secret society of Egyptian physicians and scholars who for seven decades have plotted two goals: (1) installing an Islamic government (a lá that in Iran) and (2) severing ties with the Western non-Islamic world—a force seen as immoral, infectious, corrupting, self-serving and entirely too modern.

VOCABULARY BUILDER

Islam: the monotheist religion "popularized" by Muhammad in seventh century A.D.

Muslim: a person who practices Islam, be it the Sunni or Shiite branch

Islamist: a Muslim who believes that his government should be religion-based, not secular, and free from Western influence; not all Islamists are militant, but almost all militant Muslims are Islamists

What's new: increasingly, students and many moderates are sharing the militants' views, if not their methods. More and more of the restless masses want to break the Egyptian-Israeli peace treaty for which Egypt is rewarded with its hefty annual U.S. check. President Hosni Mubarak is juggling—forced to cave to Western pressures to fund his all-important army, which is the Middle East's most powerful, he must also placate a populace that wants to toss out his secular government and install Shariah (Islamic) law in full force. Soaring unemployment—especially among educated youth—a shaky economy and a rocketing population that grows by 1.5 million each year are just a few more elements heating up discord like a slow-burning harissa.

GEE, WHAT POPULAR LEADERS!

Egyptian presidents can count on being reelected with landslide victories, sometimes lassoing as much as 97 percent of the vote. It's not necessarily that they're so beloved: rather, no one can run against the incumbent leader. Dissidents are jailed during elections, and besides, 75 percent of Egyptians, knowing the outcome, don't bother to vote. Despite the great odds for success, President Mubarak has been accused of rigging his elections.

BALANCING ACT

President Hosni Mubarak has been forced to master the art of talking out of both sides of his mouth. A few examples:

• Says he supports Bush's Palestinian peace plan; doesn't back ouster of Arafat
• Keeps Muslim Brotherhood banned; lets brothers run for parliamentary office
• Holds "Democratic" elections; bans presidential opponents, jails critics of electoral sham such as Sa'ad Ibrahim
• Allows shariah courts to operate; reverses their verdicts

Future Forecast

Egypt will slip out of the Western lasso once Mubarak is gone, or perhaps sooner. Despite the deaths and exiling of thousands of Egypt's feistiest hard-liners, Islamists pushing religious rule may still have their day—but not if the U.S. can prevent it, because thanks to U.S. gifts, Egypt is armed to the hilt.

GRATING RELATIONS

Israel doesn't get good press in Egypt. A few of the unbelievable rumors:

- Israel gave Palestinian children radioactive candy
- Israeli shampoo is toxic
- Israeli bubble gum makes chewers oversexed/infertile
- Israel is sending sexy spies to spread AIDS
- Israel is injecting AIDS virus into oranges
- Israel sends secret messages via lingerie sprayed with invisible ink

CHANGING HISTORY: THE CAMP DAVID ACCORDS

History-making, groundbreaking, earthshaking peace treaty between Egypt's Anwar Sadat and Israel's Menachem Begin, the Camp David Accords called for Israel to return the Sinai Peninsula (taken during the 1967 Arab-Israeli War) to Egypt in exchange for Egypt recognizing Israel's "right to exist." The 1978 agreement, brokered by President Jimmy Carter, also included provisions to address the plight of Palestinians, but this part got shoved aside. The Camp David Accords marked the first time that an Arab country had formally acknowledged Israel as a legitimate nation, and Sadat and Begin shared a 1978 Nobel Peace Prize for their work. An added incentive: the U.S. offered to pay over $3 billion annually to the two countries to play nicey-nice.

Background Briefing

To understand what's happening in Egypt, and why, look no further than the Muslim Brotherhood. These intellectual Islamists have been outlawed, jailed, tortured, killed and forced underground by the Egyptian government but no-body can make them shut up, despite seventy years of efforts. In fact, their influence has grown in recent decades (as has membership in the more violent organizations they've spawned): although no one knows the exact numbers for these shadowy groups, it's believed that those who support them and their

The world's most expensive handshake: Sadat, Carter, Begin celebrate pricey Egyptian-Israeli peace and promised billions of U.S. military aid. (Source: Associated Press)

dream of an Islamic government for Egypt number high in the millions. Some say that if Egyptians actually had the power to vote for presidential candidates they wanted, the Muslim Brotherhood would be in the power seat; seventeen members serve in Egypt's Parliament, even though the Bros are banned.

That the Brotherhood (and their ideas) are not more influential is one of their historical gripes. After all, it was the Muslim Brotherhood who ushered Egypt's existing government to power in 1952 when they linked arms with the Free Officers Movement—a revolutionary group of Army VIPs—to topple King Farouk, an Algerian remnant from the days of the Ottoman Empire. Of course back then, when they aided in the coup, the Brothers thought all parties shared the same vision for a religious government. President Gamal Abdel Nasser didn't. When he pushed the new, free-from-foreign-influence Egypt in the worldly direction, the Brothers felt betrayed. When Nasser aligned with atheistic communists, the Muslim Bros. took aim for his head. For that assassination attempt, they were banned, some were executed, and some four thousand were marched to prisons and concentration camps in the sand.

EGYPTIAN VIOLENCE

1930s: Muslim Brotherhood bombs theaters showing Western films
1948: Muslim brother assassinates prime minister
1954: assassination attempt on President Nasser

1981: al-Jihad kills President Sadat
1995: Gama'a Islamiya attempts assassination of President Mubarak
1995: al-Jihad blows up Egyptian embassy in Pakistan
1997: Gama'a Islamiya Luxor attacks

Remaining members crept underground, forming hundreds of secret chapters and subgroups. They infiltrated Egypt's military, schools and labor unions—subtly pushing their agenda to rid the country of Western influence and install religious rule. Some left to become teachers in Saudi Arabia; some headed for Jordan, Syria and Sudan to spread the word there. Extremely influential, the Brethren evolved into the most powerful international force for spreading Islamist thought. During the 1970s, when released from prison by Nasser's successor, President Anwar Sadat, the Brothers and their offshoot groups moved into social services, setting up low-cost clinics, unemployment centers and ambulance services—all of which actively illustrated the Muslim goal of charity and were compelling instruments of PR. When Sadat, despite promises, did not institute Shariah law and then did the unimaginable by making peace with Israel in 1978, his days were numbered. Two years after he signed the Camp David Accords, Sadat was gunned down by Egyptian al-Jihad, one of the Brotherhood's younger offshoots. Again, Islamists were rounded up by the thousands—this time by President Hosni Mubarak. In recent years, however, the Brotherhood, while technically banned, has surfaced in mainstream society, as Mubarak realizes that the more he represses the group—which is moderate compared to its offspring—the more momentum it gains for government change.

Although they've had their violent moments, the Brothers aren't hard-core militants; they just want to see an Islamic government and Islamic law in Egypt. However, the dedicated idealists have planted their philosophies across the Middle East, and spawned such assassination-happy groups as Egypt's al-Jihad and Gama'a Islamiya, not to mention the Palestinian militia Hamas.

THIS WON'T HURT A BIT!

If they want to marry, and most do, Egyptian females are expected to have undergone surgery beforehand. Female genital mutilation—a clitoris-snipping operation—is sometimes performed by the local barber. Although illegal, painful and hazardous, "FGM" is a rite of passage, and some 97 percent of Egyptian women have undergone it.

Factoid: In apparent response to a 1995 UN Conference on Population in Cairo, the Grand Mufti of al-Azhar University issued a fatwa mandating FGM as a Muslim woman's duty.

SHAKING LOYALTIES

The true test of power is how a government stands up during an earthquake. President Mubarak's didn't fare well during the 1992 temblor that killed four hundred fifty and trapped thousands. Mubarak, in China at the time, sent out emergency teams—two days after the quake. Who helped the victims when they needed it? The Muslim Brotherhood, which sent out rescue teams.

Hot Spots

Al-Azhar University: Islam's most esteemed place to study and headquarters of Egypt's most powerful religious circles; now under close government scrutiny, the university alumna include the Blind Sheik Omar Abdel-Rahman.

Cairo University: Another site of anti-Israeli, anti-U.S. protests. Al Qaeda brains Ayman al-Zawahiri graduated here as a doctor.

Hot Shots

Gamal Abdel Nasser: Egyptian president from 1954 to 1970, Nasser brought Egypt to the tip of the Arab power pyramid: he told the West to shove off when he nationalized Egypt's Suez Canal (causing an attack from Israel, Britain and France in the process) and got chummy with the Soviets; he tried to unite the Arab world, and in 1958 created the United Arab Republic with Syria (400 miles away) that lasted three years; he initiated the 1967 war against Israel and was sorely defeated—and promptly resigned. He stepped back into power a few hours later.

Anwar al-Sadat: Egyptian president from 1970 to 1981, Nasser's vice president took power upon his death, and became a study of reversals: he started off buddy-buddy with communist Russia then cut those ties; he alternately released, then jailed, members of the Muslim Brotherhood and other Islamists; he tried to restore Egyptian pride by ordering a 1973 attack on Israel; then he made peace with the former foe, for which he paid dearly. After he signed the Camp David Accords in 1979, Egypt was shunned by the Arab world (who cut all financial aid and kicked it out of the powerful Arab League), and Sadat was killed by a still-simmering dissident two years later.

Hosni Mubarak: Egyptian president from 1981 to the present, Sadat's former vice president took the power seat during chaos, and has dodged bullets, cracked down on militants with a heavy hand and tried to openly support the U.S. despite a public that is more and more anti-American. But he's had to contend with an increasingly conservative populace: Islamic courts now operate along civil ones, many of his people want to send the Egyptian-Israeli peace agreement to the recycling bin, and were it not for his beloved army, Mubarak might not be in power.

Gamal Mubarak: The president's business-savvy son is believed to be a likely successor. The thirty-eight-year-old is definitely more worldly and flexible than his pa and even some of his father's opponents may give him the thumbs-up.

The Muslim Brotherhood (aka Ikhwan): Formed in 1922, the group's original members are gone or have gone batty, but its influence carries on—molding the thoughts of twenty-first-century Islamists across the Muslim world, including Al Qaeda masterminds, such as Mohamad Atta, Ayman al-Zawahiri and Mohammed Atef. Still simmering over a broken political promise to make Egypt an Islamic, not secular state, the group has quietly worked mostly against the government it helped install five decades ago. This is the godfather of nearly all Islamists movements in the Middle East, whose reach extends from Malaysia to New Jersey.

al-Jihad: A younger, more violence-prone group that likes to work stealthily: like a social virus, they infiltrate the organizations they hoped to bring down. Allegedly behind the assassination of Anwar Sadat, they've also assassinated diplomats and they blew up the Egyptian embassy in Pakistan. Headed by Al Qaeda power boy Ayman al-Zawahiri.

Gama'a Islamiya: Mostly country boys, these guys were never subtle: they were the ones behind the bloody Luxor attack. Their leader is now advocating peace from his prison cell, and has penned a book—*The Initiative of Stopping Violence.* Hasn't hit the best-seller list.

Coptic Christians: A minority religious group within Egypt, the Copts and their gold stores are frequent targets of militant Muslims.

IRAN

FAST FACTS

Country:	Islamic Republic of Iran; Persia until 1935
Capital:	Tehran
Government:	Islamic republic
Independence:	1979 (Islamic republic proclaimed)
Population:	66 million
Leaders:	Religious Leader Ayatollah Khamenei; President Mohammad Khatami
Ethnicity:	51% Persian; 24% Azeri; 7% Kurd; 3% Arab
Religion:	89% Shia Muslims; 10% Sunni Muslims
Language:	Farsi, Azari, Kurdish, Arabic, Turkic
Literacy:	72% (78% men; 66% women)
Exports:	oil, gas, carpets
Per capita GDP:	$6,300 (2001 estimate)
Unemployment:	14% (1999 estimate)
Percentage living in poverty:	53% (1996 estimate)
Known for:	ayatollahs, rogues, rugs

Standout Qualities

Sounded the call: first twentieth-century Islamic revolution
Soundalike leaders: Khomeini, Khamenei, Khatami
Sounds of repression: dissidents often killed

Résumé

The land that introduced the terms "shah," "ayatollah," and "Great Satan" to the Western vocabulary, Iran is the true loner of the Middle East—and the site of the first Islamic revolution in centuries. Now a power struggle between the entrenched religious establishment and reformist president illustrates that nobody is quite sure how to disembark from the social experiment where the ayatollah is perma-glued to the helm.

IRANIAN PLOT?

Is it a scheme to confound simple Western minds? What other reason can explain the confusing names of Iran's most powerful leaders? Ayatollah Khomeini (ho-may-NEE) started the religious government and is dead; Ayatollah Khamenei (ha-meh-NAY) is trying to prevent the religious government from dying; and reformist President Khatami (ha-ta-MEE) is pushing democracy so hard (well, for Iran) that it's amazing he's still living.

Quick Tour

Resting on the Persian Gulf and the Caspian Sea, Iran is a study of brilliant contrast. Three mountain ranges roll across the land, dividing two deserts that sweep around ruins. Green hills tumble toward the sea, while lone minarets perch over valleys of stone. The architecture—a dizzying study of dome, honeycomb, arch and line—dazzles, from villages of flat-roofed mud shacks to the intricate blue mosaics that swirl across mosques. The conflict of style is best seen in Tehran, where ancient onion-shaped domes rise along sharply angled modern architectural marvels in a stew of polluted air.

IT'S LONELY OVER HERE

Iran is a sore thumb in Persian Gulf country. At the northeastern fringes of the Middle East, Iran is "different": most Iranians are ethnically Persian, not Arab, a very important ethnic distinction over there. And though Iran is a Muslim country, Iranians are "Shiite" not "Sunni"— two branches of Islam that have been at it for over twelve centuries.

Despite its beauty and history as centerpiece of both Persian and Islamic cultures, Iran hasn't exactly been teeming with Western tourists since 1979, when the biggest uprising in modern Islamic history exploded in the middle of capital Tehran. Bazaaris—wealthy merchants who sell rugs and gold in bazaars—teamed up with students to shove out Shah Mohammad Reza Pahlavi, the faux-royal dictator regarded as a weapon-loving American puppet (he was), who spent most of his money on war toys (he did) and relied on his secret service, SAVAK, to extinguish the sparks of rebellion (ditto).

Secret Slaughter: *Number of Savak-related deaths in last six months of 1978: 3,000.*

In his place, they installed craggy-faced, coal-eyed, scraggly bearded Ayatollah Khomeini. He'd been coaxing and guiding this Islamic revolution via smuggled tapes and radio while in exile for fifteen years.

ALL PRESS IS GOOD PRESS?

In 1978, the exiled Khomeini's popularity was surging, and the shah's was nose-diving—due in part to religious clerics irate that their lands had been seized during one of Pahlavi's social reform movements. Desperate, his people planted a false story about Khomeni's communist ties in a leading Iranian newspaper. The exiled ayatollah's followers blew up at the deceit and the shah soon fled in January 1979.

The place quickly slipped back in time, as the secular government became a religious one (after being put to a vote) and everyday life fell under Islamic law: veils were pulled on, stereos were switched off, beards grew back, booze was poured out and whips started lashing as Iran tried to shut its door to the rest of the world.

MORE RIGHTS THAN SAUDIS

Women in Iran still drive, still vote, can hold parliamentary seats and are not forced to cover their entire face, just hair and body.

What was at first incomprehensible quickly became highly disturbing: in November 1979, Islamic students scaled security walls and overtook the Ameri-

can embassy. They rounded up fifty-two hostages, most of them American—
and ultimately kept most for 444 days.

The students demanded that the shah return to face trial. Initially in the U.S.
for cancer treatment, the shah refused to go back, even though he was termi-
nally ill, had six months to live and the hostages would have been released.

Costly Error: In 1988, the U.S.S. Vincennes *accidentally fired at a commercial Iranian jet flying over the Persian Gulf. All 290 passengers were
killed. Two decades later, Iran is still steamed about it, saying the U.S.
never adequately apologized and even promoted the officer who made the
erroneous call. Some believe that incident prompted Iran to hire Libya
and avenge the death with the 1988 Lockerbie bombing that killed 270.*

Sensing Iran was vulnerable, neighborhood vulture Saddam Hussein chose
the moment to send his Iraqi troops rolling in.

*Rumors: Some Iranians believe that in 1980 the U.S. actually sent Iraq
in to weaken Iran. Some Americans agree.*

If Iraq's president thought the fighting would be quick and dirty, he was wrong: the
Iran-Iraq war dragged on for eight excruciatingly bloody and expensive years,
making it the longest conventional war of the twentieth century. Memorable highlights: Iraq used chemical weapons on Iran; Iran showed how devout its martyrs were by unleashing human waves of children across mine-riddled fields.

TAKING SIDES

Since Iran was Shiite, Persian and revolutionary, most Sunni Arab countries
backed Iraq, which was also Arab and Sunni. The U.S. and Russia even agreed
on something: both supported Iraq and supplied Saddam with money and
arms. Only Syria and Lebanon backed Iran.

When the UN finally foisted a peace agreement on the two countries in 1988,
a million were dead, billions of dollars had been wasted, nobody had really won
and both countries slunk back with their economies entirely devastated. Iran had
a new problem: a population boom was well under way thanks to the ayatollah,
who'd encouraged the birth of new Islamic warriors. Meanwhile, the price of oil—
Iran's main export—had bottomed out.

WHAT A YEAR!

Despite the bad music—"Y.M.C.A." was a chart topper—1979 was a memorable year: not only did Iran start an Islamic government and take Americans hostages, the Camp David Agreement was signed and the Soviets invaded Afghanistan, where they would fight the newly created mujahideen forces for the next decade. Radicals also overtook the Great Mosque in Mecca, holding hostages in the Saudi holy place for two weeks. Billy Carter went on a few drunks, further damaging Jimmy's career.

If politics was governed by public opinion polls, the religious government idea might have been tossed out right then: between the economy and heavy war tolls, many Iranians were not pleased with this new social-religious experiment. The ayatollah stoked the fires by issuing a 1989 fatwa calling for the death of Salman Rushdie, whose offense was writing a novel called *The Satanic Verses.* Since the ayatollah died without removing his edict, the death order can't be removed.

HORRORS!

During Khomeini's 1989 funeral, ardent fans, who tore his shroud and tried to kiss the dead man, knocked the scantily clad corpse out of the coffin and it flipped into the crowd, bare feet and all. Some mourners threw themselves into his grave. At funeral's end, the ayatollah had plenty of company: at least eight were dead—many from trampling—and more than ten thousand injured.

Ever since Khomeini kicked, the country has been slowly unraveling. The religious establishment boosted a new grand ayatollah—Khamenei—to the power seat, but despite the similarities in names, the second religious leader lacked the charisma of the first. For the past decade, the relevance of the once-fervent Islamic agenda has faded as the country's many problems—massive heroin addiction, widespread prostitution and rocketing unemployment among them—loom with no solution in sight. Besides, half of the population is under twenty-five and can't remember why the revolution was such a big deal in the first place; all they know is the repression they've grown up with is not the lifestyle of most of the Western world.

GREEN LIGHT FOR RED LIGHTS?

The government, or rather unnamed factions within it, is considering running legal "chastity houses"—aka brothels—to help control the rapid spread of AIDS. It's estimated that more than three hundred thousand chastity gals work Tehran alone.

Nothing revealed the simmering discontent more than the landslide victory of reformist President Mohammad Khatami in 1997, whom the young and the women brought to power. Reelected in 2001—again with more than 75 percent of the vote—Khatami rattles the traditional religious establishment that runs the show. Ayatollah Khamenei and his cronies frequently squelch Khatami's moves to guide the country toward democracy and open its economy to the West.

MARRIAGE BY THE HOUR

After Khomeini's death, the government tried to defuse youthful "tensions" by allowing young people to be married under the "sigheh" system. Requiring no paperwork, witnesses, froufrou dresses or flowers, these contracts were invoked simply by saying a few phrases from the Koran. Before marrying, however, the couple had to stipulate the length of their bonds: a marriage could be scheduled to last a few seconds or centuries. Once the minimal ceremony was completed, they were legally and religiously free to embark on the "honeymoon."

Nevertheless, the signs of change are everywhere: It's visible on the TV when Khatami, eyes flashing under black turban, speaks about a "dialogue between nations" in a new century; it's there in the newspaper when typically unyielding Ayatollah Khamenei did not counter Khatami's offer to rescue U.S. soldiers in need during the Afghanistan war; it's most obvious at the soccer games when the boys crank up their radios and the girls take off their scarves and for a few hours all rules are forgotten and some people actually dance. Student protests are getting louder, housewives are spilling their guts on the Internet, and a government-sponsored exhibit at the former American embassy, rife with U.S. bashing and slams, was shut down after a few weeks because so few showed up.

Some protestors are complaining not only that they don't want the ayatollah, but that Khatami is working too slowly.

But for every lurch toward democracy or the West, Ayatollah Khamenei tries to block it. Students are routinely rounded up and jailed—sometimes killed—for threatening to overthrow the Islamic government. Magazines and newspapers by the dozens are being shut down. Political opponents are hung. The government is once again cracking down on satellite TVs.

Khatami pushes on—demanding more power and that the people have more say—and students, the group that once helped bring in a hard-core Islamist government, are increasingly adamant about pushing it out. For all the religious government's show of force, Khamenei knows that his power is slipping and his prayer rug is about to be pulled out from under him. Whether he'll introduce needed change or let Khatami lead a counterrevolution remains to be seen.

Future Forecast

If Khatami isn't killed, he'll slowly lead the country to a more open, less repressed society and renew bonds with the U.S. If Khatami is killed, a revolution will kick up. Either way, the death knoll rings for the hard-core Islamist government. And when Khamenei dies, nobody will jump into his grave.

Religion vs. democracy: Supreme Ayatollah Khamenei and reformist President Khatami. (Source: Associated Press)

Background Briefing

President Khatami is well aware that Ayatollah Khamenei hates him. But throughout 2002, it appeared that President George W. Bush felt the same way. Ignoring the obvious changes taking place in Iran, where at sports events cleric-led chants of "Down with the

USA!" were met increasingly with "We love the USA!" Bush listed Iran on the "Axis of Evil." This pronouncement gave the fiery religious government reason for more anti-U.S. rhetoric and propaganda blazing. Diplomats, already uncomfortable with the Axis of Evil concept, rushed to Iran's defense; U.S. citizens wrote to Khatami trying to ease the sting.

A few months later, President Bush did it again: he brushed off President Khatami's slow but steady efforts, and said the Iranian wasn't working hard enough. Instead Bush appealed to the people, which again backfired: not only was Khatami winded again, the people largely thought Bush was arrogant.

TEA FOR TWO OR BULLHORN FOR ONE?

Khatami continually notes that Iran is offended by the Bush administration's pushy and belligerent commands. After all, the Iranian president has called (and is still calling for) "a dialogue" between nations, not a monologue blasted at Led Zeppelin levels.

Despite the rhetoric, the Bush administration has a point if they're trying to say that Iran is developing "weapons of mass destruction." Despite an abundance of oil and natural gas, nuclear plants have popped up all over the earthquake-prone land, thanks to Russia, which is under U.S. pressure to quit supplying them with the coveted technology. Always ready for cash, North Korea has also tossed them long-distance missiles.

POINTING FINGERS?

Israel is most alarmed at the thought that Iran may someday possess nukes. After all, Israel is the only nuclear power in the region. Another issue: Iran financially backs Hezbollah and provides Palestinian arms.

Meanwhile, Iran is getting very antsy at the increasing American presence around them. Ayatollah Khamenei thinks much of the political posturing and war mongering since September 11 is based in a desire to control the area around the Caspian Sea, where billions of gallons of oil and gas are now pumped from the 'Stans. Alas, Khamenei may be right.

Hot Spots

Borders: Drugs, refugees and militants slip in from Afghanistan and Pakistan; Iraq sends in anti-Iran groups; and Russia and the 'Stans are increasingly dominating commerce on the Caspian Sea.

Qom: The most strict and religious outpost is site of the "Spider Murders," with dozens of prostitutes strangled with their veils during 2002.

Tehran: The pulsating center, where plenty of protests are taking place and riots could break out, is one of the most polluted places on earth.

Hot Shots

President Mohammad Khatami: Flowery, persuasive and kind, the former head librarian for the National Library was also a censor: continually got in hot water for approving too many reformist magazines and books. Has written two books of his own. Students say not pushing hard enough.

Grand Ayatollah Khamenei: The second, and probably final, religious leader of the Islamic Republic of Iran. Killing dissidents madly.

Grand Ayatollah Ruholla Khomeini: Proof that you don't have to be beautiful to be powerful, Khomeini started mouthing off back in the 1960s. He was exiled (first to Turkey, then France) for criticizing the shah's policy of not holding American military responsible for any crimes in Iran.

Shah Mohammad Reza Pahlavi: Leader 1941–1979, the son of the first shah—a military man who was pushed out by the Allies because he sided with Nazis—the shah couldn't get enough guns. Even the U.S. government, typically happy to supply arms to nearly anyone, noted that the shah had "an insatiable appetite for more and newer military equipment." Tried the "White Revolution," which among other things gave women the right to vote and seized land from mosques. Died in Egypt after being kicked out of the U.S., where his presence had triggered the taking of fifty-two American hostages.

Students: Growing angrier by the minute, the force that once put the Islamic government in power may be the only way to get it out.

CHINA

FAST FACTS

Country:	People's Republic of China
Capital:	Beijing
Government:	communist state
Independence:	People's Republic of China proclaimed in 1949
Population:	1,273,111,000 (July 2001 estimate)
Leader:	President Hu Jintao
Ethinicity:	92% Han Chinese; also Zhuang, Uighur, Hu, Yi, Tibetan, others
Religion:	3% Taoist, Buddhist; 1% Christian; 3% Muslim
Language:	Mandarin Chinese, Cantonese, others
Literacy:	81.5% (89.9% men; 72.7% women)
Exports:	machinery, textiles, clothes, shoes, toys
Per capita GDP:	$4,300 (2001 estimate)
Unemployment:	10% urban; higher rural
Percentage living in poverty:	10% (1999 estimate)
Known for:	pandas, Ping-Pong, secrecy

Standout Qualities

Wallflower: shy to strangers
Wallbanger: represses dissidents
Wall Street: financial green light

Résumé

Whoa Nellie! After a century of being financially out to pasture, newly energized and market-reformed China is galloping toward economic superpower status with the world's second largest economy. Politically, the stifling Commu-

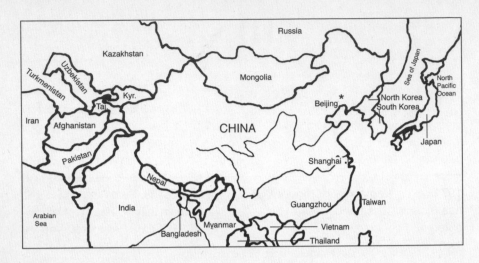

nist Party keeps cracking the whip and is skittish as ever about the U.S. No hard feelings: behind the fake smiles, the U.S. doesn't trust China either.

Quick Tour

With its pagodas, flowery scrolls and really long walls, its culture that values introspection, inwardness and order, its revolutions of intellectuals and straw hat–wearing peasants and its four-thousand-year written history, China is the epitome of foreign to the U.S. The written word of artistic scrawls is read right to left, the spoken languages are based on tonal nuances lost on American ears, and the style of life—with its chopsticks, bean curd and ancient medicine that uses poked needles and powdered batwings—baffles the West. Politically the Chinese are puzzling as well—they jumped from millennia of emperors and dynasties to decades of communism under Chairman Mao, whose guiding hand killed millions upon millions of his people. Some died by execution, many more from the famines that accompanied his many starry-eyed ideas on reform, despite the fact that he'd rarely picked up a hoe.

THE CHAIRMAN V. THE FÜHRER

Depending on whose statistics you're quoting, Chairman Mao was directly and indirectly responsible for more deaths than Hitler, making him the number one killer of the twentieth century. Mao: 44 million to 72 million.

Hitler: 45 million to 60 million.

History Review: In the Korean War, newly communist China backed North Korea, while the U.S.-led UN force fought for the South. In retaliation, the U.S. made a point of militarily and economically helping Taiwan, which Mainland China regarded as a renegade.

For most of the Mao years (1949 to 1976), in China the U.S. was widely considered a "capitalist, imperialistic pig"— largely due to its warm relations with Taiwan, the island where the nationalists who'd been running China fled after communists won the Chinese civil war. U.S.-Sino relations changed with Henry Kissinger and Richard Nixon, who thawed the mainland ice beginning in 1971 and diplomatically dropped Taiwan in the process. Since then the U.S. has more or less bonded with Mainland China, which insists that all of its disputed and controversial territories—Taiwan, Tibet and the Muslim Xinjiang region among them—are all part of "One China," headquartered in Beijing.

The Magic Words Behind U.S.-Sino Relations: There is only one China, and Taiwan is part of it. There is only one China, and Taiwan is part of it . . .

SHAKY U.S.-SINO MOMENTS

1989: Tiananmen Square—police quash student pro-democracy protest, hundreds, some say more than 1,000, were killed; world uproar makes Chinese human rights an international issue; China denies any deaths occurred

1996: China struts its naval might in Taiwan Strait and launches two missiles toward Taiwan just to let Taiwanese know what it thinks of their democratic elections; President Clinton sends in two warships to baby-sit

1999: Chinese embassy in Belgrade, Yugoslavia, accidentally bombed by U.S.-led NATO team; 3 killed, 27 injured; U.S. pays $4.5 million to victims' families, but that doesn't buy Chinese forgiveness; China says U.S. acted like it was no big deal

2001: Crashed plane: daredevil Chinese pilot dies after midair collision with U.S. Navy reconnaissance plane, forced to land on Chinese island; since plane was spying over its waters, China demanded an apology, while holding crew for days

2002: Twenty-seven secret listening devices found on President Jiang Zemin's jet, which had been retrofitted by Boeing; U.S. government and Boeing scratch heads over how bugs got there

---

The two vastly different countries, however, remain highly suspicious "friends": China balks when the U.S. talks of its "internal" human rights problems and loathes the increasing U.S. military presence encircling China from Kyrgyzstan to the Philippines. The U.S. is torn between policy makers who want to continue engaging the world's most populous country and those who still eye the communist country as forever "Red." In the meantime, both shamelessly spy on each other and sell arms to each other's enemies; the U.S., in particular, while saying out of one side of its mouth that it recognizes only China, peddles mountains of military equipment to Taiwan.

COMMUNIQUÉ-TION

China and the U.S. seems to get along best with formal written agreements—even those that "agree to disagree." Three "communiqués" have guided U.S.-Sino relations:

> *1972:* the Shanghai Communiqué: Nixon groundbreaker/ice thawer
> *1979:* the Joint Communiqué on Normalization of Relations: Carter's formal transfer of diplomatic recognition from Taiwan to Mainland China, specifically Beijing
> *1982:* the Joint Communiqué on Arms Sales to Taiwan: Reagan's promise that the U.S. would gradually stop supplying so much weaponry to Taiwan

That's a Joke: Despite the 1982 communiqué and promises to reduce arms sales, subsequent presidents sold even more military equipment to Taiwan.

Future Forecast

When "little emperors"— the pampered boys in one-child families—grow up, they'll push the now "kinda-communist" country into full consumer-capitalist mode. In the meantime, U.S.-China relations will turn real ugly real fast if Taiwan takes an independence hike.

POPULATION CONTROL

China has led the world's population for over a millennium, but India may soon surpass it. The reason: China's innovative "child tax" system wherein couples pay high taxes for having more than one child. While the system, put in place in 1979, dramatically slowed population growth, it had an unintended result: infanticide—especially of baby girls. Besides being a source of status, boy children in China are far more likely to serve as "social security" and support their aging parents.

Re: Arms: Israel is China's number two arms supplier, and the U.S. fears that the sophisticated equipment and designs it sells to Israel end up here.

KISSING COMRADES

China and the Soviet Union slashed most ideological-political unions in 1959. After Soviet leader Khrushchev toured the Chinese countryside and saw what a mess Mao's Great Leap Forward was making, he pulled out Soviet advisors and cut aid. The two countries warmed up again in 1982, and today Russia is China's number one arms dealer.

People Power: China's People's Liberation Army, with 2.5 million, is world's largest

CHINA'S WORRY LIST

U.S. military surrounding China since 9/11
U.S. growing closer militarily with India
U.S. dropping Anti-Ballistic Missile Treaty
U.S. building National Missile Shield Defense
U.S. keeps releasing reports saying China a threat
U.S. said it will protect Taiwan if China attacks
U.S. listed China as a nuclear target
U.S. considering Asian Missile Shield Defense

U.S. WORRY LIST

China could kick America's tush and become world economic leader by 2012.

Putting Their Money Where Their Mao Was: China GDP 1978: $1.4 trillion; China GDP 2001: $5.56 trillion

Background Briefing

China is decidedly xenophobic, and really who can blame them? The British tried to get the Chinese addicted to opium to even out the balance of trade, western European countries claimed chunks of Chinese land during the nineteenth and twentieth centuries, and the Japanese brutally invaded during World War II. The People's Republic of China has been trying to put itself geographically back together for decades.

British-run Hong Kong was returned in 1997, Portuguese-administered Macau followed in 1999, and China has bullied its way into de facto ownership of the disputed Spratly Islands, as well as the Paracel Islands off of Vietnam. The Chinese government is likewise holding tight to its western lands, including Tibet, where it has been accused of killing millions and trying to wipe out the culture. And China persists in claiming Taiwan as its own, despite the fact the two function pretty much independent of each other. China has threatened to militarily keep Taiwan part of its territory if necessary. Despite its efforts at keeping everything neatly tied together, China is coming undone and most of its republics function independently.

> *REPRESS-ATHON?* China will be hosting the 2008 Olympics, a move some human rights groups fear will just lead to more "tidying up" of dissidents.

Meanwhile, China is trying to battle its general distrust of foreigners as it opens up its market to foreign investments, which along with free-market reforms have helped its GDP quadruple since 1980. Its 2001 acceptance into the World Trade Organization should only spur its remarkable economic growth. Whether that leads to a more liberal political atmosphere remains to be seen: China is still brutal with dissenters—and the group currently topping its internal enemy list is Falun Gong, a spiritual movement whose practitioners often demonstrate in Tiananmen Square, where they are typically arrested. Human rights groups say China's violations across the land include torture, labor camps and forced detentions in psychiatric hospitals. On a cheerier note, experts say there are probably fewer abuses now than under Mao.

> *Factoid:* The Chinese government says no one was killed during the Tiananmen uprising in 1989. Witnesses and the world media strongly disagree—putting the number of pro-democracy protesters killed there between five hundred and five thousand.

Hot Spots

Xinjiang: Western region, home to Turkish-speaking Muslim Uighurs, is constant target of government suppression, with more than ten thousand rounded up since 1990. Joining "War on Terror" gives China more legitimacy to clamp down on area, where government says Al Qaeda operates; three thousand picked up since 9/11. Given the oil underground, China is even less likely to listen to any calls for Xinjiang independence.

Tibet: Sacred land of Tantric Buddhists, this mountainous western expanse, where temples are built into cliffs and magic lakes are believed to evoke spiritual visions, is China's most controversial holding. More than a million Tibetans died when Chinese forces invaded in 1949 and overtook this Himalayan-edged land, trashing thousands of history-rich temples in the process; Chinese are still accused of torturing and jailing monks and nuns, as well as attempting "cultural genocide." Tibetan spiritual leader the Dalai Lama is exiled.

FREE TIBET?

Although the Dalai Lama is not pushing for full Tibetan independence—just more cultural autonomy—his followers are. The Free Tibet Movement is a cause célèbre with Richard Gere, Brad Pitt and Steven Segal among those pushing for Tibetan independence from China.

Spratly Islands: Boring but potentially oil-rich islands in South China Sea to which China, Vietnam, Taiwan, Malaysia and Brunei all lay claim.

Hong Kong: The former British colony retains substantial autonomy and, unlike the rest of China, freedom of the press.

FAUX PAS DEUX

President George W. Bush horrified the Chinese government in October 2001 when he flew to Shanghai for an economic summit and brought up Chinese human rights abuses to the press. Chip off the old block: his father horrified the Chinese government when he invited dissidents to a state dinner in Beijing, where authorities forcefully held one back from attending.

FASHION REVENGE?

Maybe that's why the Chinese insisted Bush Jr. wear a traditional silk jacket of royal blue with gold polka dots at the 2001 summit. While beautiful, the jacket wasn't his style, seemed several sizes too small and made him look like a dork.

Hot Shots

Jiang Zemin: What title didn't the man hold? Communist Party general secretary until 2002, he's expected to pass on the presidency to Hu Jintao in 2003, but will retain his role as military leader until 2007. Came to power during Tiananmen Square turmoil in 1989 and became president in 1993.

Deng Xiaoping: Western-embracing (well, for China) leader and reformist who opened up economy in 1980s.

Hu Jintao: Reserved vice president since 1998, Hu is due to take over reins in 2003. Some say he may open up China further, although others report the incoming prez was involved in Tibetan massacres in the 1980s.

Mao Zedong: Chairman of the Communist party from 1949 to 1976, Mao adapted Marxist communism to agricultural China, beat the Nationalists and proceeded to lead his country through land reforms, technological leaps, cultural revolutions, massacres and famines. His actions (and his Little Red Book) directly or indirectly killed over 42 million or more.

The Dalai Lama: Believed to be the fourteenth incarnation of a Dalai Lama, the 1989 Nobel Peace Prize winner and spiritual leader travels the world spreading the word of Tibet. The Chinese government tries to shut him up, pressuring world leaders not to meet with the enlightened one, Tenzin Gyatso.

TROUBLESOME MEMORIES

Ever since the Dalai Lama singled out a six-year-old boy as the reincarnation of a Tibetan holy man in 1995, the Chinese government has kept the child incarcerated. The child reportedly could identify personal items that previously belonged to the Panchen Lama and is thus considered the latest incarnation of the second highest spiritual leader of Tibetan Buddhism.

Pandahuggers: *Term bandied about by conservatives to characterize politicians seen as too warm toward China.*

Falun Gong: Considered China's number one internal threat, this spiritual movement, based on meditation and ritualized exercise, is not a political organization, but gets treated like one. They've been officially banned ever since ten thousand practitioners showed up one morning in 1999 outside the government compound in Beijing; they were quickly rounded up, many are still in jail, some have been reprogrammed and some reports say more than one thousand have been executed. Chinese officials consider the practice, similar to Tai Chi, "an evil cult"—and want its founder, Li Hongzhi, now living in New York, to be arrested. The man and his practices are unusual: he teaches followers how to create a swirling swastika of energy in their bellies, which among other miracles can cure disease, say believers.

Fiery Extremists: Five demonstrators, believed to be Falun Gong practitioners, set themselves on fire in Tiananmen Square in 2001 and one died. Falun Gong says the incident was a government setup.

LEADERSHIP VIA INTERNET

From his computer in Queens, Li Hongzhi urges Falun Gong followers to head to Tiananmen Square, where they are always arrested and subjected to whatever the police see fit. Their numbers have dwindled since the Chinese government began enforcing "public responsibility." Now when a demonstrator turns up, his family, coworkers, bosses, neighbors and local police are all held accountable and may be severely punished.

Dr. Wan Yanhal: Chinese AIDS activist who started first AIDS hotline in China, Wan was tossed in jail for a month in 2002 for criticizing the government's closed approach to the problem. The UN predicts China may have 10 million HIV cases by 2010.

TAIWAN

FAST FACTS

Country:	The Republic of China/Taiwan (formerly Formosa)
Capital:	Taipei
Government:	multiparty democratic regime headed by popularly elected president
Independence:	still part of China officially
Population:	22,548,000 (2002 estimate)
Leaders:	President Chen Shui-Bian; Prime Minister Yu Shyi-Kun
Ethnicity:	84% Taiwanese (including Hakka); 14% Mainland Chinese
Religion:	93% Buddhist, Confucian, Taoist blend; 4.5% Christian
Language:	Mandarin Chinese (official), also Taiwanese and Hakka dialects
Literacy:	94% both sexes (1998 estimate)
Exports:	machinery, electrical equipment, metals, textiles
Per capita GDP:	$17,200 (2001 estimate)
Unemployment:	3% (2000 estimate)
Percentage living in poverty:	1% (1999 estimate)
Known for:	making independence noises

Standout Qualities

Small but powerful: heavily armed
Small but rich: an Asian tiger
Small but connected: U.S. has said it will defend

Résumé

For decades, Taiwan pretended it was part of "One China" to avoid being forcefully roped to the mainland. Emboldened by its vibrant economy, youthful democracy and heaps of shiny military equipment from the U.S., the pretty little island could trigger World War III if its president continues to point out the inherent "One China" lie and to call for independence.

Quick Tour

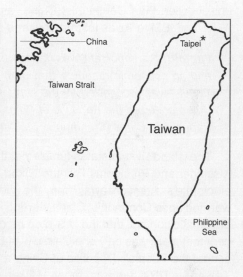

Forest-thick, resource-rich, mountainous and thoroughly modern, the tear-shaped isle that lies a hundred miles off China's east coast might as well be a hundred light-years away from the land to which it is politically handcuffed. Granted, Taiwan's inhabitants speak Mandarin Chinese, and millions of Taiwanese came from the mainland in 1949, when the wealthy industrialists fled the communist takeover. But itsy-bitsy Taiwan just isn't the same as great big China, the country that insists Taiwan maintain political loyalty and keep bowing to the "One China" farce, conveniently ignoring the fact that the two political systems and societies are entirely different and that for fifty years the two "countries" have run independently. So important is maintaining the fantasy of eventual reunification—and preventing Taiwan from membership in world organizations—that China has loudly threatened to militarily tie the knot should Taiwan try to slip out on its own.

General Twitchiness: Hundreds of China's missiles point at Taiwan; Taiwan has madly armed itself through the 1990s.

Taiwan may have endured a dictatorship and one-party system when China's Civil War loser Chiang Kai-shek and his Kuomintang nationalists fled there in 1949, but communism never took root there, nor were Taiwanese forced to undergo Mao Zedong's social experiments, such as the Great Leap Forward or Cultural Revolution that killed upward of 50 million on the mainland.

Factoid: Chiang had a dream of reunifying with the mainland all right—
with the nationalists in charge. He died in 1975, along with the idea of
his fantasied reconquest.

Taiwan's role as a noncommunist island in the shadow of the Red Giant
caught the eye of the U.S. Starting in the 1950s, the U.S. offered protection,
moved its troops onto island bases, and doled out plenty of economic and military aid. American money steered family business–oriented Taiwan in a different direction than Communist China, as did the American companies (from
AT&T and IBM to Texas Instruments and Microsoft) that swept across the land.

Factoid: So important was Taiwan both as an anticommunist symbol
and an economic resource that until the 1970s the island's capital—
Taipei—was recognized as the capital of China in a diplomatic charade
that recognized the Republic of China (Taiwan) but ignored the People's
Republic of China (Communist Mainland China).

The island's world status tumbled at the hands of Secretary of State Henry
Kissinger and Presidents Richard Nixon and Jimmy Carter. Trying to shift the
electorate's attention away from the Vietnam debacle, Kissinger and Nixon
warmed up to Communist China starting in 1971. Among China's conditions for
diplomatic contact: that the U.S. stop recognizing the renegade Taiwan and accept that there was only one China, with Beijing at its head. Kissinger helped to
secure the People's Republic of China a seat at the UN in 1971, while getting
Taiwan—a UN Charter member—kicked out.

WHICH ONE CHINA?

This two-word piece of diplomatic rhetoric is what could trigger a huge military
action. China refuses to recognize Taiwan as anything but an island that is
part of "One China"— a phrase that surfaced in Nixon-Mao dealings and has
rolled off the tongue of Beijing's politicians ever since. Since the 1970s the
U.S. has continually answered that yes, that's right, there is only one China,
and Taiwan is but a part of it, while selling Taiwan arms.

Jimmy Carter sealed the deal: in 1979, the U.S. began officially recognizing
only the mainland's capital as the real capital of China and shut down diplomatic
contact with the island. Taiwan might have been told to get lost, except that so
many American interests operated on the island that Congress immediately
passed the Taiwan Relations Act, which allowed American businesses to continue operating in Taiwan and also approved American arms sales to the island.

Bye-bye Bombs: *Taiwan previously had embarked on a nuclear weapons program, now theoretically kaput.*

The Taiwan Relations Act also includes a clause that says an attack on Taiwan from Mainland China would be a cause for grave concern. Whether that means the U.S. would defend Taiwan in an attack is a matter of interpretation.

IDLE PROMISES?

Both President George W. Bush (in April 2001) and Defense Undersecretary Paul Wolfowitz (in March 2002) have signaled that should Taiwan be attacked, the U.S. will defend it.

Following passage of the Taiwan Relations Act, the schizophrenia that marks U.S.-China-Taiwan relations was now firmly entrenched in the international psyche. Diplomatically, there was no Taiwan—which is not recognized as independent by the U.S., the UN or most powerful nations. Economically and militarily, however, there certainly was a separate Taiwan: the U.S. has raked in billions and billions from selling arms and maintaining Taiwanese businesses.

The situation became more complicated when Taiwan became a multiparty democracy in 1987, lifting the martial law that had been in effect since 1949, allowing a free press and ultimately reforming its constitution. Initially "cross-strait" talks with the mainland blossomed, but as talk of Taiwan being a separate state popped up, China stomped out of the dialogue.

THE ROAD LESS DECIDED

A 2002 public opinion survey showed most Taiwanese just want to maintain the status quo, which is to say keep living the lie. The majority don't want to be bonded with the People's Republic of China, but they don't want to get bombed for independence.

In 1996, on the eve of Taiwan's elections—the first democratic, direct presidential elections ever held in China's history—Beijing showed its displeasure with a Taiwan politician pushing for separation, by launching several missiles off Taiwan's coasts. The Taiwanese elected the controversial politician Lee Teng-hui anyway.

Tensions have skyrocked since 2000 and the election of President Chen Shen-bian of the Democratic Progressive Party, which was formed waving the

President Chen: pushing for Taiwan's independence. (Source: Taipei Economic and Cultural Office)

independence banner. Although Chen initially backed off on his call for sovereignty and tried to open dialogue with the mainland, he was so thoroughly snubbed, that after two years he pulled out all stops. Not only did he publicly call Taiwan "independent," he also called for the people to vote on whether to officially separate from the People's Republic of China. Though he's since backpedaled a bit, dem is fighting words to Beijing.

Future Forecast

Taiwan will keep pushing the independence button until China either caves in or closes in with warships. Chen has been led to believe the U.S. will militarily back him, but sorry, Charlie—don't bank on it this week.

BEIJING BLOW-OFF

Since Chen came to office in 2000, Beijing has

- Blocked Taiwan from becoming a member of the World Health Organization
- Attempted to block diplomatic relations between Taiwan and every country from the U.S. to Indonesia
- Refused to use Chen's name
- Begrudgingly accepted Taiwan's entry into the World Trade Organization

Oops!: In November 2001, President George W. Bush made a major gaffe when he welcomed both Taiwan and Mainland China to the WTO: he referred to them as two different countries! His office secretly let Beijing know that the president had simply been confused, and the One-China policy was still intact.

Background Briefing

The intricate "One China" masquerade—and all the passive-aggressive acts that have accompanied it—has really only benefited two parties: Russia and the U.S. Russia has sold billions in military equipment to Mainland China, while the U.S. has sold billions to Taiwan, which buys even more whenever the Defense Department issues another report that China is ahead in the arms race. The fear of a possible blockade from China that would cut off energy imports also has prompted earthquake-active Taiwan to purchase nuclear reactors from General Electric. Controversy swirls around a planned fourth nuclear power plant. Approved by the nationalist regime, it was canceled by Chen, but put back on the drawing board when it was pointed out that Taiwan would have to pay GE and other parties as much to cancel the project as to continue it.

Hot Spots

Taiwan Strait: This stretch of the South China Sea between Taiwan and the mainland is so hot it should be boiling. A key sea lane, its blockage could rearrange Asian geopolitics.

Hot Shots

Chen Shen-bian: Taiwan president since 2000, a former lawyer and Taiwan's leading renegade, Chen is trying to establish a greater international presence for Taiwan and keeps mouthing off to Beijing. U.S. wishes he'd shut up and quit almost dragging them into a major conflict.

Annette Lu: Taiwan vice president since 2000, a Harvard-educated scholar who spent five years in prison during the Chiang dictatorship for giving a twenty-minute speech on human rights, in 1979, Lu met Chen when he was her lawyer. She is the first non-royal female VIP in the history of China.

SUDAN

Standout Qualities

Large: Africa's most expansive country
Tired: Africa's most protracted civil war
Extreme: world's most powerful radical magnet

Résumé

Refuge of Osama bin Laden during the 1990s, Sudan gave birth to Al Qaeda and nurtured grandiose Islamist plots. The catalyst: wizened religious guru

Hassan al-Turabi, who threw international anti-West fests here where the White Nile meets the Blue.

Quick Tour

Whether you're in dusty capital Khartoum—a pitifully poor city of dirt roads, minarets and ugly box buildings, where women are whipped for showing a strand of hair, political prisoners are tortured in "ghost houses" and street kids are rounded up to forcefully donate their kidneys—or in the verdant Nuba Mountains—where villages are routinely torched, ground is scorched, schools are bombed and women are snatched by northerners as sex slaves—it's hard to think of Sudan's many, many problems and not want to pour yourself a really stiff drink. Of course doing so would be dangerous in the parched Arab north, where alcohol-prohibiting Shariah law has rained on the parade for the past decade, years when militant Muslims crowded the streets. But that could be changing. In fact, everything, including the brutal civil war, could be changing in this land that has been entirely screwed up since it pushed off from British-Egyptian rule and became suicidally independent from Britain in 1956.

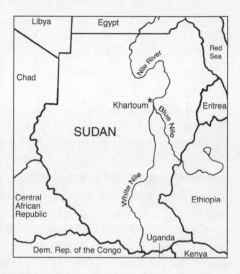

MAKE THAT A TRIPLE: EFFECTS OF THE UNCIVIL WAR

Famine: 2 million starved
Kid soldiers: a million or more
Slave trade: up to 200,000
Refugees/street kids: 4.5 million
War-related death toll since 1984: 2 million

One reason why the country has been at its own throat for thirty-six years: somebody drew the map too big. Instead of two countries—an Arab Muslim north and a black tribal animist south—there exists one oversized country that has never gotten along and probably never will.

THE PROB

Different religions, races and cultures laid the backdrop, but two factors accelerated the civil war:

The north tried to impose Islamic law on the non-Muslim south.
The south has the oil that is the only economic hope for this sorry land.

The raging conflict turned more sinister after oil companies, such as Canada's Talisman, moved in. The north—which hoards all the oil revenue—has taken to clearing the land for the foreigners, eliminating villages near oil fields, burning crops and crucifying Christians, among other atrocities—and the rebels in the south, who, like those in the north, rely on child soldiers, have been nearly as nasty. The southerners also target the pipelines that propel the north's military machine.

Or at least that's how it's been since 1984, when after a lovely decade of silenced guns called "The Last Peace," the civil war between the north and south broke out yet again—killing over 2 million (through attacks and war-related famine) and making refugees of some four million more. In the summer of 2002, however, U.S. Special Envoy John Danforth produced a small miracle when he got the two sides—the Arab army and militias of the north and the rebels of the south—to agree to peace, doled out with six month-renewable truces.

The Bush administration sent in former Senator Danforth after getting heat from two groups: American oil companies, who wanted sanctions lifted so they could explore in Sudan, and American church groups, horrified by the slaughter of southern Christians, some of whom were attacked to eliminate interference with oil companies' plans.

Meanwhile the radical Islamic government headed by military President Lieutenant-General Omar al-Bashir, under substantial pressure from the U.S., has turned over a new, more moderate leaf. Anxious to have economic sanctions dropped, and to avoid being the next Afghanistan, Bashir and his government have coughed up valuable information about Osama bin Laden, Al Qaeda and other militant Muslim groups.

Talking for Dollars: Economic sanctions, slapped on Sudan in 1995, were yanked in September 2001 when Bashir started yapping.

Future Forecast

Unless north and south face up to the facts and finally break up, the 2002 truce is just a dreamy siesta. Peace will last long enough, however, for American oil companies to swoop in and tap the petroleum resources that had been off-limits.

Hassan al-Turabi: Islamic guru shaped Al Qaeda. (Source: Associated Press)

Background Briefing

President Bashir, who bashed through the presidential gates in a 1989 coup, had plenty of beans to spill to the U.S.: not only did Osama bin Laden run here (buying houses and setting up businesses) when he was kicked out of Saudi Arabia in 1992, but for much of the past decade, Khartoum has served as head-quarters of the world's most violent and extreme Islamic militants. The magnet: religious scholar and Parliament leader Hassan al-Turabi, who until 2000 was running the place, welcoming extremists from all corners of the globe. Hamas, Hezbollah, Egyptian Jihad, Gama'a Islamiya, Algerian Islamic Jihad, and some fifteen thousand mujahideen were but a few of those he extended an invite to plant roots in the country where he'd imposed Shariah law at its harshest (only to faint at the sight of the first public amputation). Everyone who was anyone in Islamist circles made an appearance at Turabi's annual Popular Arab and Islamic Conference, where the Big Boys plotted terrorist acts and forged powerful alliances.

INVITATION LIST

A few countries unofficially represented at Turabi's conferences: Egypt, Algeria, Yemen, Iran, Saudi Arabia, Lebanon, Syria, Pakistan.

Charismatic and turbaned Turabi was a networking genius: not only did he introduce bin Laden to the brains of Egypt's al-Jihad—creating the group that is America's number one enemy—he even got the Sunnis and the Shiites, two branches of Muslims who've hated each other for centuries, to come together and plot the demise of their common enemy: the West.

TURABI'S ALLERGY TO THE WEST

A Muslim brother who spent time in Egypt, Turabi was never a huge fan of the modern Western world. He was less so after a trip in 1992. In London, where he expected to be greeted by cheering masses, his arrival was met with loud protests. In the U.S. Senate, he was rotisseried by angry politicians grilling him on Sudan's human rights abuses. In Ottawa, he was beat up by an expat Sudanese, a martial arts champion, who left him for dead on the street. When Turabi awoke several days later from a coma, he hastily departed for Sudan, and directed followers even more ardently to vent their rage at the oppressive West. He insists the Ottawa incident was a CIA plot.

Some Islamists will use force to establish religious governments for their individual countries, but Turabi was even more extreme: he envisioned a united Muslim theocracy that took down the West and was the major force in the world. His rantings were effective: Sudan was fingered in a number of terrorist crimes, including the 1998 American embassy bombings in Tanzania and Kenya—events that prompted the U.S. to bomb a Sudanese pharmaceutical plant that was believed to be making nerve gas, although that may not have been the case.

HEADLINE NEWS

1989: Bashir heads military coup; brings in Turabi
1991: Harshest Shariah law introduced
1991–1999: Turabi's annual Popular Arab and Islamic Congresses

1993: Sudan put on rogue list, when its diplomats were linked to 1993 WTC bombing

1995: Assassination attempts on Egypt's President Mubarak; he points finger at Sudan; U.S. and UN slap sanctions

1996: Sudan pressured to push out bin Laden

Rumor: Some reports says Sudan offered bin Laden to U.S. and Saudi Arabia, but neither country wanted to take him

1998: Embassy bombings in Tanzania and Kenya, 224 die; U.S. bombs Sudanese pharmaceutical plant

1999: Bashir shuts down Parliament (and Turabi)

2001: Bashir orders Turabi arrested

After years of being pushed to the sidelines, Bashir pulled the plug on Turabi—who was further hacking away at presidential power—in December 1999, when he shut down Parliament. He had Turabi arrested in 2001 for plotting to overthrow the government. The annual hoedowns for hard-core Islamists are no longer held in Sudan, Turabi is now shut off from the outside world, and the militants in his coterie have scattered. But the little guru with the wily smile stirred up and united Muslim revolutionaries like few before him—and those riled-up Islamists are putting into effect the plans they conceived in Khartoum.

Triple Irony: Turabi, after signing a peace agreement with southern rebels, was reportedly shipped off to one of the torture-filled "ghost houses" he helped establish. Human rights groups are protesting that Turabi should be released.

Hot Spots

Ghost houses: Secret torture chambers, run by Sudanese security forces, where untold thousands are believed to have suffered and died.

Khartoum: Capital of slums, dust, refugees and militants.

Nuba Mountains: Even though villages are smoldering, roads are mined and little kid soldiers tote guns, some still hope that the land of goat herders and subsistence farmers in the south becomes a tourist destination.

Hot Shots

Hassan al-Turabi: Head of Parliament until 2000, wizened mystic, Muslim scholar, holder of a Sorbonne Ph.D., multilingual Hassan al-Turabi was spiritual and terrorist inspiration guru for thousands of Islamist militants, including Osama bin Laden (an active part of Turabi's coterie until 1996). A member of the Muslim Brotherhood, he started his own Islamic party, the National Islamic Front, and rode into power on Bashir's coattails.

Omar al-Bashir: Leader-dictator from 1989 and president since 1993 to the present, this army man has more staying power than anyone imagined. Without Turabi, he's somewhat more palatable.

Sudanese People's Liberation Army: The main rebel unit of the south, headed by John Durang, who is reportedly as vicious as his northern counterpart.

Lords Resistance Army: So what is a Ugandan rebel group, known for kidnapping six-year-olds and arming them, doing in southern Sudan? Khartoum invited them to raise some southern hell. Now they won't go away.

Dinkas: Tribe from Sudan's south that is most often kidnapped for slavery; sometimes forced to move north, where they work for slave wages.

PERSONAL TO OIL COMPANIES

Look to the north for your next fields, or this country may never split up. And it needs to.

AFGHANISTAN

Standout Qualities

Warring factions: Pashtun, Tajik, Uzbek, Hazara hate each other
Soviet-Afghan War: U.S. helped create mujahideen to fight commies
U.S.-Afghan War: U.S. fought mujahideen it helped create

Résumé

Former home of Osama bin Laden and training pen for Al Qaeda, Afghanistan has known nothing but hell for the past twenty-eight years. The U.S.-led anti-terror coalition team may have pried the Taliban loose in 2001, but that doesn't mean Afghans will get along.

PIPELINE SCOOP?

Until 1998, American oil giant Unocal dreamed of a pipeline running from Turkmenistan through Afghanistan to Pakistan. They flew the Taliban out to Texas to wow them, conducted feasibility studies, lobbied and trained Afghans in pipeline construction. Also wooed by Argentinian oil giant Bridas, the Taliban never signed on. Now a pipeline—funded partly by money from the international community—is in the works, but Unocal says it has nothing to do with it. Nevertheless they have an "in": President Hamid Karzai is a former Unocal employee, as is U.S. special envoy Zalmay Khalilzad.

Quick Tour

Whether you're talking about the average life span (forty-eight years), the literacy rate (31 percent) or the three wars that have ravaged Afghanistan for the past twenty-four years, this country wedged between Iran, Pakistan and the 'Stans is still one utterly dysfunctional place. Oh, it's better now: the Taliban are gone, hands no longer get whacked off in public squares, hanging corpses don't rot from poles, burkas aren't requisite fashion, kites can fly, music can play, schools are open, women are working and white flags don't flutter to mark the homes of virgins to be plucked by soldiers for forced marriage. For the first time in twenty-four years some semblance of a government is functioning, but headed by dashing interim President Hamid Karzai with old King Shah hanging around for show, the new Afghan government, however, isn't exactly a stable affair. The vice president was killed within a few weeks of stepping into office, as was a cabinet minister; Karzai is dodging bullets, and car bombs keep exploding as warlords show their lack of support.

LANGUAGE LESSON

Dari (Afghan Persian) and Pashtu are the two most common languages, but many rival tribes speak their own tongue. Maybe that's why they have such a history of fights: it's hard to have civilized discussions when the two parties have no idea what each other is saying.

IMPORTANT DATES

1979: Soviet invasion to keep communist puppet in power

1980s: New mujahideen force created; guerrilla training camps built in Afghanistan and Pakistan with U.S., Saudi money; Osama bin Laden a star

1989: Soviet pullout; mujahideen still in fighting mood

1989–1995: Civil war with leftover weapons; Unocal wants pipeline

1995: Taliban takeover—funded by Saudi Prince Turki, supported by U.S.

1996–2001: Osama bin Laden returns from Sudan, runs Al Qaeda training camps

1998: In retaliation for embassy bombings in Tanzania and Kenya, U.S. drops bombs on Osama bin Laden's training camps; Unocal drops pipeline plan

2001: September 11 attack on New York and Washington DC kills nearly 2,000; Taliban won't turn over Osama bin Laden; in November U.S.-led "War on Terror" coalition begins extensive bombing campaign/food drop

2002: In June, Hamid Karzai officially voted in as interim president; in August, accidental U.S. bombing of civilians at wedding party kills 42

This extraterrestrial land of craggy mountains, jagged crevices and labyrinthine caves needs a major overhaul if it is to ever be civilized: the place stands out most for its astonishing lack of cohesion. Its many tribes are united in little but hatred that goes back centuries.

The fierce tribes have rallied together to conquer invaders, however: Genghis Khan was driven out, as were the nineteenth-century Brits, who rode in on elephants, complete with attendant slaves carrying boxes of cigars and booze, and never rode out: the one survivor of the first Anglo-Afghan war, or so the legend goes, survived an ax to the head simply because under his hat he'd stuffed a thick book.

Cities are few in this rugged terrain crossed by few roads and no train, where mules limp along dusty trails past tents and mud shacks. Famine still sweeps the drought-plagued land, where thousands in remote mountain areas starve because food supplies can't reach them. Removal efforts are ongoing, but the earth is still studded with millions of land mines, mementos from the Soviet-Afghan

War. And the opium-producing poppies that the Taliban wiped out are once again being harvested: 2001 was a bumper crop.

PUBLIC WORKS

The Karzai government hopes that a pipeline will give thousands of Afghans jobs, starting with constructing it. Alas, the pipeline will probably be subject to attacks, as is the case in Colombia. Perhaps some of the international funds can be used to pay Afghans to build roads in this poorly connected country.

But it's better, really. Aid groups are returning, the international community is tossing over billions and Kabul at least is almost a normal city again: *Newsweek* named it as a new hot spot for filmmakers. And maybe this time the Western world—which ignored it after the Soviet-Afghan War ended in 1989—won't turn its back.

Future Forecast

Bad news: warlords will launch another civil war.

Background Briefing

Muslim-fought, Pakistani-taught, American- and Saudi-bought, the Soviet-Afghan War (1979–1989) is where the September 11 attack had its roots. When the Soviets rolled in their tanks to keep a communist puppet in power, a religious call of jihad went out, and wanna-be Muslim warriors flew in from all corners to fight atheist communists. Bringing together Muslims and teaching them to be guerillas seemed like a good idea at the time. No one had guessed that they were creating an international militant Muslim university and that these same warriors would direct their wrath at the West.

MUJAHIDEEN FACTORY

The snowball got rolling with Islamic religious man Sheik Abdullah Azzam, who let out a loud call for a holy war in Afghanistan when communists arrived in 1979. Osama bin Laden jumped in on recruitment efforts: flying in young Muslims from the Middle East, he also built housing and training camps, and convinced the Saudi royal family to fund the mujahideen cause. The U.S. also backed it: providing funding, arms and CIA expertise. Guerrillas received most instruction, however, from Pakistan's secret service, the ISI.

Thirty thousand ready-for-training militants flew into Pakistan, where dozens of training camps taught the arts of mountain fighting, grenade tossing and automatic weaponry. The mujahideen battled fiercely, but mostly the Soviets were just ill-prepared. Their tanks were laughable in the unforgiving terrain best fought on horseback. Their clothes weren't right for 130-degree days and 20-degree nights, their shoes weren't made for mountain climbing, they got sick from the water. The Soviets slinked away in 1989, defeated. But the Americans, Saudis and Pakistanis had created a volatile situation that wouldn't go away: the heavily armed, overzealous mujahideen wanted to continue the fighting, as did tribes who now had plenty of grenades, guns, and missile launchers.

Civil war broke out immediately, and wasn't contained until the Koran-thumping Taliban installed harsh rule on the masses, making public displays of their enemies to show they were serious.

TURKI SHOOTS

Prince Turki, the former Saudi minister of intelligence who backed Osama bin Laden during the Soviet-Afghan War, almost singlehandedly put the Taliban in power several years later. Meeting Mullah Omar and the gang during a hunting spree in 1994, Turki believed that the highly religious Taliban could end Aghanistan's civil war—something Saudi Arabia and the U.S. both wanted to see—so that the Unocal pipeline, in which the Saudis were also invested, could go through. The prince supplied them with money, oil, arms and the pickup trucks that soon became the symbol of Afghan oppression. Also in support of the Taliban takeover: President Clinton and, of course, Unocal.

Osama bin Laden had returned a hero to Saudi Arabia in 1990, only to be enraged that the Saudi royal family wouldn't let his mujahideen take on Saddam Hussein and instead called in the Americans. Asked to leave Saudi Arabia because of his persistent bad-mouthing, he flew to Sudan, where he hooked up with like-minded militant Muslims and formed Al Qaeda. Forced to leave Sudan in 1996, after the U.S. blew up when he called for the death of U.S. military men, bin Laden returned to his former stomping grounds in Afghanistan and set up an even bigger guerrilla training operation. This time, however, the mujahideen enemy wasn't the Soviet Union. This time they wanted to take on the U.S., as well as the Saudi and Egyptian governments. The Taliban didn't mind: Osama was paying good money to rent his caves.

RETURN OF TURKI

In 1998, the Saudi prince flew to Afghanistan with a second private luxury plane in tow. The reason: to bring back Osama bin Laden, accused of plotting that year's U.S. embassy bombings, to Saudi Arabia. Mullah Omar became so apoplectic at the demand of turning over bin Laden that he instructed his servant to douse him with cold water. Turki returned to Saudi Arabia alone.

After September 11, the U.S. warned the Taliban to kick out their guest or else. They played coy until November 2001, when the first storm of bombs dropped on Kabul. Some Taliban and Al Qaeda forces were killed, some were flown to a U.S. prison in Cuba, many fled over the Pakistani border. Still missing: Taliban leader Mullah Omar and the man who started it all, Osama bin Laden.

A MESSY WAR

The U.S. had hoped it would be quick and surgical, but the 2001 campaign in Afghanistan dragged on for a year and got messy. Civilian deaths climbed into the thousands and when a bomb accidentally dropped on a wedding party in July 2002 killing forty, even President Karzai asked the U.S. to back out. More than five thousand international troops remain as of October 2002.

Hot Spots

Hindu Kush: The mountain range that divides the country into north and south and is often a zone of heavy fighting.

Tora Bora: Multistoried mountain cave complex near Pakistan border that was pummeled in December 2001. Hundreds killed, but Osama bin Laden escaped.

Herat: Region on the western border near Iran. Run by warlord Ismail Khan, who like the rest of the warlords doesn't support the interim government. The point of entry from Iran and Turkmenistan.

TA-TA TALIBAN

What made President Clinton and Unocal turn cool toward the Taliban? Mavis Leno—who kicked up public protests against their treatment of Afghan women.

Hot Shots

Osama bin Laden: See Al Qaeda in Glossary.

Hamid Karzai: Former Unocal employee, previous foreign minister during the Soviet-Afghan war, he's now dodging bullets as interim president until 2004. Support weakening, and his best move may be to quit and become a hat model.

King Shah: Ruled Afghanistan during its golden years—1933–1973, which abruptly ended when he left for surgery in Italy. Shacked up in Rome until recently, the eighty-eight-year-old king is back mostly as a unifying figurehead.

Loya Jirga: The grand assembly of tribal leaders that makes important decisions such as approving a president.

Taliban: Afghanistan's ruling party from 1995 to 2001, their name literally means "religious students." This group of Deobandi devotees came to power thanks to Saudi Prince Turki, who backed them to calm the civil war that erupted in the wake of the Soviet-Afghan war. Instituting rigid Islamic law, the religious bunch blew up millennia-old Buddhas; forced women to don burkas and men to grow beards; closed schools; raped, tortured and killed thousands—in the name of purifying the country.

Mullah Omar: Taliban leader from 1995 to 2001, missing an eye from his mujahideen battles in the 1980s, mysterious Mullah Omar believed he had mystical powers and apparently others agreed. Sometimes seen waving a piece of cloth, said to be Muhammad's, the rarely photographed Muslim leader disappeared in fall 2001. No word on what happened to his holy rag.

Mujahideen: A term for Muslim warriors through the ages, mujahideen now usually refers to the guys who answered the call for jihad and showed in Pakistan and Afghanistan during the 1980s to battle Soviets. Typically devout, poorly educated and unemployed, the wanna-be fighters swooped in from Saudi Arabia, Egypt, Syria, Lebanon, Yemen and beyond to fight in a country that days earlier they couldn't find on a map. Ever since their guerrilla war training, most haven't stopped fighting, and many joined Al Qaeda or other splinter groups.

EENY MEENY MINEY MO

Who will be the next leader of Afghanistan? A few warlord possibilities:

Burhanuddin Rabbani: Former Afghan president and a Tajik, Rabbani was shut out of the interim government. Rumored to be plotting overthrow with his Jamat-e-Islami warriors.

Gulbuddin Hekmatyar: Pashtun and former mujahideen leader who wants foreign armies out, and is threatening to call a jihad. Said to be behind assassination attempts.

Ismail Khan: Tajik and self-proclaimed governor of Herat, makes millions from road taxes.

Abdul Rashid Dostum: General and warlord whose troops sometimes fight Rabbani's, despite the fact they were formerly united in the Northern Alliance.

Abdullah Sayyaf: Former mujahideen leader, who inspired the Philippine group Abu Sayyaf.

BUY BACK

After heavily arming mujahideen and Afghans with guns and land-to-air missile launchers, the U.S. a decade later tried to buy the weapons back. Very few were returned.

SOMALIA

FAST FACTS

Country:	Somalia Democratic Republic
Capital:	Mogadishu
Government:	theoretically a democratic republic
Independence:	1960 (from Italy and Britain)
Population:	7,488,000
Leaders:	Transitional: President Abdukasim Salat Hassan; Prime Minister Hassan Abshir Farrah
Ethnicity:	85% Somali (also Bantu and Arab)
Religion:	Sunni Muslim
Language:	Somali, Arabic, Italian, English
Literacy rate:	24% (36% men; 14% women)
Exports:	livestock, bananas
Per capita GDP:	$550 (2001 estimate)
Unemployment:	N/A
Percentage living in poverty:	N/A, but high
Known for:	mayhem and misery, novelist Nuruddin Farah

Standout Qualities

Everybody related!
Everybody fights for their clan!
Nobody can figure out who should lead the ripped-apart land!

Résumé

Chronic famine, hideous epidemics and a raging decade-long civil war that devours cities are a few woes, but Somalia is etched in Western memories for one thing: the death of eighteen Americans during the incident dubbed "Black Hawk Down."

Quick Tour

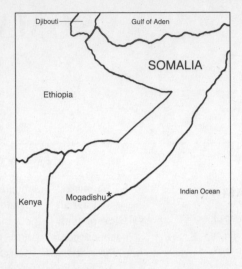

Stretching like a boomerang along the eastern "horn of Africa," militia-filled Somalia is an anarchists' paradise: its scrubby land—upon which more than three hundred thousand have starved since 1990—is slashed into warlord territories, its main airport runway is booby-trapped, its harbors are gang-controlled, tanks roll down the main streets, food shipments are blocked and the country is dotted with millions of land mines. Piracy of ships and kidnapping of aid workers are the newest problems plaguing this nation that hasn't had laws or fully functioning government since 1991, when its nasty dictator Siad Barre was tossed out—after using food aid to bomb his own people. Alas, there hasn't been a man who could unify the clan-divided land since, including transitional president Abdulkassim Salat Hassan, who controls but a few patches of the Texas-sized country and is not recognized by warlords.

Islamic groups have stepped in to provide social services since aid workers are fleeing in response to the new epidemic of hostage-taking. The festering country's potential attractiveness to Islamic militants has prompted the U.S. to reinvolve itself despite the nightmare of a decade before when eighteen army rangers were killed in a shoot-out with Mogadishu warlords. American warships patrol Somalia's waters and planes monitor from overhead. Recently, the U.S. financially clamped down and closed Al-Barakaat, the country's main employer and Internet supplier, believing it was funneling money to Al Qaeda. These allegations remain unproven.

American diplomats have arrived for the first time in almost a decade to make a stab at stabilizing this shaky land, and along with UN diplomats, were greeted by cheering masses. Surprisingly, amid the mayhem of shoot-outs, some businesses survive, and some Shariah law courts still make judgments in this Muslim country. But millions of Somalis cope by chewing khat—a stimulating leaf that further fuels the chaos.

Factoid: Somalis chew $300,000 worth of khat every day. When Kenya cut off deliveries—as a means to get warlords to the peace table—the country went berserk.

Future Forecast

Nobody wants to run back into such a depressing scenario, but international agencies have to organize this unruly mess. Perhaps start by pushing down on the main warlord—Hussein Aideed—who lived in California, holds a U.S. passport and was first sent to Somalia as a U.S. Marine. Maybe his former commanding officer could have a word?

THE DAY THAT CHANGED AMERICAN AID

"Operation Rescue Hope" was supposed to be a food delivery mission. The goal: to get the food trucks past warlords who'd set up blockades in every direction. Mogadishu's main warlord, Mohammed Aideed, was a particularly gnarly thorn to contend with, so much so that a secret mission of Delta Force operatives set out to "borrow" two of his lieutenants to serve as human hostages to facilitate food deliveries. What really happened on October 3, 1993, is riddled with uncertainty: some say Al Qaeda's lieutenant Mohammed Atef tipped Aideed off, but then again the warlord's son was right there—as a marine supposedly helping out the U.S. with translation. Whatever the cause, forty Delta troops—who successfully nabbed the warlord's men—became trapped in the city of mobbing masses and roadblocks. When four Black Hawk helicopters arrived to help the Delta force escape the chaos, they were greeted with automatic gun fire and land-to-air missiles a shoot-out that dragged on for fifteen nerve-wracking hours and downed two helicopters. By the end, eighteen Americans were dead, as were hundreds of Somalis. The image of a dead Marine being dragged through dusty streets like war booty prompted President Clinton to call the boys back.

Factoid: *Many believe that the ordeal left such a foul taste in Clinton's mouth that he never sent peacekeepers in to Rwanda and dragged his feet in deploying troops to Kosovo.*

RAY OF HOPE: SOMALILAND

While Somalia has been busy disintegrating, the northwestern corner—once part of British Somaliland—snuck off and seceded to become relatively peaceful Somaliland. Founded by Mohamed Egal, Somalia's foreign minister back when it was a democracy, Somaliland is entirely unrecognized by anybody. That should change: agencies need to look at this place for guidance because Somaliland's people generally aren't starving and the interclan problem is down to a dull roar. Around here, that's quite an accomplishment. Egal's death in 2002, however, makes the future iffy.

Background Briefing

Just call Somalia the "Land of the Feuding Cousins": legend holds that all Somalis are descended from a common ancestor—Sam—thus all Somalis are ethnically alike and from the same tribe. But clans and subclans Somalia has aplenty—more than three hundred of 'em—and branches of the dysfunctional family tree don't agree on much besides Sam being their great-great ancestor. They've been fighting for centuries over whose camels watered where as the nomads crossed this parched land, but when Western Europe's pens redrew the territories in the 1880s—dividing them into Ethiopia, northern British Somaliland and southern Italian Somaliland—things got more stressful: clans were split, watering holes were inaccessible, and there's been a push to reunite into one Greater Somalia ever since.

Two of the areas—British Somaliland and Italian Somaliland—were united in 1960, and for the next nine years Somalia was ruled by a functioning democratic government. There were problems: the northern Somalis largely were educated, the southerners largely were not, and besides that old clan problem raised up its divisive head.

MORE BRITISH PEN PROBS

For centuries, Ethiopia and Somalia never have gotten along, but the situation worsened in 1953 when the British lopped off part of Somalia and gave it to Ethiopia to atone for British war crimes. To the Brits it may have been worthless land—most of it was desert—but the handing over of Ogaden separated Somali families and clans, and they've been screaming to get the territory back ever since. The two countries have militarily slugged it out over Ogaden at least seven times since, with two of the episodes turning into major wars. Even when not actively warring, the two countries fund each other's insurgents and many believe that Ethiopia is financially backing Somalia's main warlords. Somalis say that Ethiopia feeds the U.S. false info about Islamic militants.

In 1969, when President Abdel-Rashid Ali Shermarke was assassinated, army commander Siad Barre barged in with promises of "scientific socialism" and putting a stop to clan warring. He instead promoted his clan, and turned to

Soviets to help fund his dream to reunite "Greater Somalia" complete with the Ethiopian sections. After seven years, the Soviets got sick of him, and began backing the newly socialist Ethiopians—and the battle to take back the Ethiopian region of Ogaden grew bloodier and then futile.

HEY, MR. WARLORD, WHERE'D YA GET THAT GUN?

One of Somalia's main problems is too much weaponry floating around—from automatic rifles to land-to-air missile launchers. Millions of dollars in arms flooded into the country starting in the 1970s—first from the Soviets, then compliments of the U.S.

Barre's acts became more heinous when the residents in north Somalia rebelled against him: he used food aid money to bomb them, killing some fifty thousand, and going on to order the poisoning of their wells and chopping down of the frankincense trees valuable to their economy. His despotism finally prompted the rivaling warlords to overcome their mutual hatred and band together to boot him out in 1991. Although assorted warlords claimed leadership, none has retained power. A transitional government finally was agreed upon in 2000, but predictably Mogadishu's main man—Hussein Aideed—and other important warlords boycotted the meeting and don't recognize the new government. One problem: the

Mogadishu's warlords Hussein Aideed (right) and Ali Mahdi keep Somalia divided. (Source: Associated Press)

new president was a minister in Siad Barre's government, which the warlords ousted.

Factoid: By 1991, when Siad Barre was tossed, his regime had been credited with killing or starving 10 percent of Somalia's entire population.

THE ONLY GOOD THING ABOUT BARRE

The self-appointed dictator ordered the creation of the written Somali language, until then only spoken. He also hired linguists to teach the masses to read. So much for that: only one in four Somalis have mastered the written language.

Factoid: Until September 11, when someone realized that Somalia could be a terrorist hatching ground, the U.S. gave the self-destructive country its frostiest shoulder.

WILL THE REAL RADIO MOGADISHU PLEASE STAND UP?

In Somalia, warlords have taken to the airwaves: their most valuable holdings are radio stations. Hopefully their programming is more innovative than their names: three warlords use the name "Radio Mogadishu."

Hot Spots

Ogaden: The British gave this part of Somaliland to Ethiopia in 1953, and Somalis have longed for it ever since.

Mogadishu: Factionalized capital, where somehow things sort of hold together. Transitional government "shares" power with warlords.

Ethiopia: Somalia's longtime foe is—unbelievably—supposed to be in charge of reunification efforts, while being accused of funding Somali rebels.

Puntland: The other unrecognized independent republic is best known for being pirating central, making these waters the world's most dangerous.

Hot Shots

Mohammed Aideed: Now dead, he was Mogadishu's leading warlord, whose militia was most active in blocking food dispersal during a famine that killed three hundred thousand. His men were the targets of the infamous botched U.S. raid.

Hussein Aideed: In a word: traitor! The new big man on Mogadishu's campus is American and was actually sent to Somalia as a Marine because he spoke Somali. Perhaps nobody knew that his father was the biggest and baddest of the warlords in Mogadishu. He returned in 1995 to become "president" warlord upon his father's death and has been just as troublesome as his pa. In 2001, however, he urged the U.S. to return to battle Islamic militants. Political motives suspected.

Transitional National Government: Even less powerful than it sounds, this thirteenth attempt at national government in a decade was created at a 2000 conference in Djibouti that was boycotted by the biggest Somali players. Initially not recognized by the U.S., but now they at least serve as somebody to talk to.

Abdulkasim Salat Hassan: Interim president since 2000, he speaks plenty o' languages, including Russian, but he can't get out the right words to make the country unite under him. Perhaps one reason: he was a VIP minister under brutal Siad Barre. Warlords won't give him time of day.

Siad Barre: Dictator from 1969 to 1991, this pilfering egomaniac was so annoying that even the Soviets gave him the heave-ho; he then turned to Italy and the U.S.—supposedly for food aid, but instead used the money for his vicious attack on northern secessionists.

Al-Itihaad al-Islamiyya: Islamists that the U.S. named as a terrorist group and believed were linked to Al Qaeda. Ethiopia doesn't like them either, ever since they made a raid. Nevertheless, they provide social services, including clinics in this land where aid workers fear for their lives.

Queen of Sheba: This, it's said, was her land.

INCREASED PATROLS

Somalia's anarchy—and its possible links to the 2002 bombing of a hotel in Kenya—is bringing it under closer scrutiny from the U.S. Neighboring Djibouti is serving as base for cranked-up naval patrols.

OIL AGAIN?

Although President George Bush, Sr., swore it was solely a peacekeeping effort, the 1993 food delivery mission may have been prompted by the several U.S. companies that were in Somalia looking for more black gold.

JAPAN

FAST FACTS

Country:	Japan
Capital:	Tokyo
Government:	constitutional monarchy with a parliamentary government
Independence:	660 B.C. (traditional founding by Emperor Jimmu)
Population:	126,975,000 (July 2002 estimate)
Leaders:	Emperor Akihito; Prime Minister Junichiro Koizumi
Ethnicity:	99% Japanese (2000 estimate)
Religion:	84% observant of both Shintotism and Buddhism
Language:	Japanese
Literacy:	99% both sexes (1970 estimate)
Exports:	cars, electronics, tools
Per capita GDP:	$27,200 (2001 estimate)
Unemployment:	5.5% (2002 estimate)
Percentage living in poverty:	N/A
Known for:	cars, competitiveness, suicides

Standout Qualities

Shaky ground: more than one thousand seismic events annually
Shaky relations: Asian neighbors await apologies
Shaky future: only the tea leaves know what lies ahead

Résumé

For decades Japan pumped all its energy into its car-driven economy, transforming into a wildly consumerist society in the process. With its finances now precarious, its economy stalled and its world role questionable, the society is slowly regrouping—and perhaps coming to terms with its history as it ponders what lies ahead.

Quick Tour

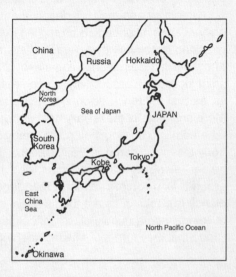

When gazing at sedate Mt. Fuji rising over Tokyo, or passing under the graceful, pi-shaped wood gate to a Shinto shrine hidden deep in the woods, or silently witnessing that first flutter of icy snowflakes swirling across a rice field, you might not sense the shadow that hangs over Japan. Summer festivals, when flower-splashed kimono are once again slipped on and paper lanterns illuminate the way for ghosts journeying back to ancestral homelands, can likewise induce forgetfulness. So, of course, can a few thimbles of high-octane sake, even in the neon-flashing heart of the capital that for so long epitomized the country's embrace of the corporate, consumerist West. Immerse yourself in a meditative tea ritual, carefully pinching precious green tea from red lacquer boxes while offering thanks, or concentrate on the twisting lines of ikabachi flower arrangement, and the concerns are likewise pressed away like troublesome creases, snipped off like price tags you don't want your father to see.

THE WAY: MICHI

Traditional garb is now reserved for special occasions, and increasingly Japanese are trading tatami mats and floor-level meals for Western chairs and tables, but ritual lives on, with everyday life guided by elaborate procedures. Bowing, still Japan's answer to handshakes, follows specific rules—the lower the bow, the deeper the respect—as does handing over a business card. Bathing, making tea, arranging stone gardens, dipping brush into ink—all are guided by procedures known as "the way."

But strip away all the layers of delicacy in this land that has elevated denial to an art form, and everyone knows that this isn't Japan's shining hour. Tokyo still pulses, the bullet train still races, towers still gleam with glassy expectation, and the Japanese still surround themselves with photo-snapping Internet phones and the latest technological gadgetry. But the former financial superstar won't be claiming the twenty-first century as its own, as experts not long ago predicted and the U.S. deeply feared. Japan's wobbly economy, once the envy of all its neighbors, is crumpling like a fragile rice-paper house in a nerve-wracking temblor. With its financial system weakened by billions in bad loans and a stalled demand for Japanese cars, the country whose whole postwar spirit focused on productivity, corporate families and GDP is in a silent malaise, its eternal affluence no longer guaranteed, its future relevance questioned. More and more of the "salarymen" once promised lifelong employment are now "shamed" into quitting their posts, many slinking off to join the ranks of the new homeless who camp in train stations. The number of divorces is soaring— helped along by paid seducers who trick philanderers and document the grounds for divorce; as a result, many young people aren't bothering to wed. Violence is climbing, as are the numbers of those flinging themselves off of high buildings; some middle-class schoolgirls are so addicted to their Gucci and Prada that they turn tricks just to keep up with the fashion trends.

GIRLS

Young women, the country's biggest consumers, are shooting off into a myriad of social directions. While some embrace cutesy, heart-happy pink fashions and sugary-voiced pop stars, others are forming fashion "tribes" with prescribed glam-rock or goth looks adopted by cliques, or grabbing guitars and turning into punk rockers. Meanwhile at least 4 percent of schoolgirls "date" middle-aged men, who pay them for sexual favors.

With all the economic and social waves rippling through their society, the Japanese are turning inward. Touchy issues, pushed down for decades, are reemerging, albeit in a variety of ways. Right-wing nationalists are spinning new explanations for Japan's involvement in World War II. A revisionist history that casts Japans as a freedom-giver and glosses over massacres is now put forth in textbooks, causing loud outbursts from Japan's once-occupied neighbors, in particular China and Korea. Even some schools refuse to use the government-approved but controversial history guides.

CHECKBOOK APOLOGIES

Japan may not have issued a broad apology for its brutal actions, but it has tossed over billions in grants and aid to Asian countries. In fact, for the past decade Japan has been the number one most generous donor worldwide, typically doling out $9 billion or more a year.

On the other hand, the apologies long awaited by China, the Philippines, Indonesia, as well as North and South Korea for brutal Japanese occupations until 1945 are slowly coming after fifty-eight years. Long after Germany copped to its war crimes, Japan is beginning to confess to the sex slaves, labor camps and even the devious tactics used battling its neighbors and taking their land. Prime Minister Koizumi shocked the world when he met with North Korea's Kim Jong-il in September 2002; both leaders confessed to their countries prior misdeeds in the first-ever meeting between the two nations.

BURIED TRUTH

Japan long denied that it used chemical weapons during its attacks on China in the 1930s. However, in 2002, the Japanese government conceded that it had used chemical agents on the Chinese—and it sent toxic specialists to China to dig up and remove the buried poisons.

The acknowledgment of past violent acts is nothing short of radical in the easternmost stretches of Asia, where the cloak of denial has brewed up simmering resentment among neighbors who mistrust Japan and often demand compensation for such incursions as the Rape of Nanking, where the Chinese say three hundred thousand were killed. Also up for review in this regrouping period: Japan's postwar constitution, written by the U.S. during its occupation. Most controversial: Article 9, which prevents Japan from ever engaging in military attacks. Among those urging the change: the U.S., who wants the Japanese military to be available to jump into international struggles, including defending Taiwan in the case of Chinese attack. Japan's longtime antinuclear stance is also looking shaky: nuclear plants now power 15 percent of the country's energy output and some think that the resulting plutonium is used to secretly make nuclear bombs.

SPEAKING OF APOLOGIES

The U.S. has never formally apologized for the 1945 dropping of atomic bombs on Japan, which killed 80,000 and injured 120,000 more in Hiroshima, and another 75,000 killed in Nagasaki, and from which an estimated 70,000 suffered radiation sickness. Japan has never formally apologized for attacking Pearl Harbor, which killed 2,300, and launched the U.S. into World War II.

Future Forecast

Japan will drop Article 9, boost its military further and will rally for the U.S. in case of terrorist attacks or blocked oil shipments. As for fully investing in Theater Missile Defense or helping the U.S. defend Taiwan: we'll see.

SHRINES AND TEMPLES

The Shinto religion has no religious text and no prescribed morals. Shrines, be they small cliff-top boxes or simple wood rooms wedged between skyscrapers, are set up to worship nature and the gods and supernatural spirits of sun, mountains and rocks. While Shinto affirms that humans are basically good, it abhors death. For that reason, most Japanese practice both Shinto and Buddhism: baptized and married in Shinto shrines, they have their death rites in Buddhist temples.

Background Briefing

Talk about talking out of both sides of the mouth: the U.S. wrote Japan's antimilitary clause, but ever since has been pressuring Japan to delete it from the constitution. The situation grew more intense after the 1991 Persian Gulf War, when Article 9 prevented the Japanese from sending troops for Desert Storm; nevertheless, the country was persuaded to toss $10 billion to the coalition cause. The U.S. also wants Japan to triple its military spending, which is already substantial: Japan bought a hefty $22 billion of U.S. arms during the 1990s, making it the number two purchaser of American military supplies.

SELF-DEFENSE FORCES

The "Ground Self-defense Force"— a euphemism for Japan's army—is mightily well armed, although it's supposed to be mostly an emergency response team. With a total armed forces availability of 30 million (and 236,000 active troops), it has more ships than the entire American fleet that patrols the Pacific. Its performance in emergencies is questionable: when a 7.2 earthquake rattled Kobe and killed over five thousand in 1995, the self-defense forces were woefully slow to respond.

In 1993, the U.S. first invited Japan to invest in its ongoing scheme for Theater Missile Defense—a multibillion-dollar ground, sea and air-defense system for Asia that would protect overseas American military bases and American-friendly countries. The theory: satellites and planes loaded with sensitive technology would detect any incoming enemy missiles, thus enabling intercept missiles on land and sea to be fired to destroy them before they reached their targets. Japan has anted up modest amounts for research but is noncommittal. For good reason: not only is the plan terrifically pricey, the technology has never been shown to fully work. Nevertheless, if the U.S. puts in a domestic missile shield defense, and China responds by increasing its war arsenal, Japan may be forced to pay up for the "Star Wars"–style defense.

TENSE MOMENTS

In 2001, a U.S. nuclear submarine surfaced below a Japanese trawler, the Ehime Maru, in the waters off Hawaii. The collision killed 9. Also problematic: the 1995 rape of a twelve-year-old girl by three Marines stationed at the U.S. base in Okinawa. Ever since, Okinawa has been trying to whisk the U.S. military off the island.

Hot Spots

Yasukuni Shrine: This controversial Shinto shrine honors 2.5 million Japanese who died serving their country, whose spirits are believed to live in the simple wood hut. It's the fourteen World War II war criminals who are honored at the shrine that cause China and both Koreas to go ballistic if a Japanese prime minister officially pays respects here.

No-Nos: *Public nose blowing is offensive in Japanese society, as is wearing shoes into houses. Other impolite acts: crossing one's arms, exposing the bottoms of one's feet and wearing the provided "bathroom" slippers outside the bathroom.*

Hot Shots

Junichiro Koizumi: Prime minister since 2001, initially the country's most popular postwar leader, Koizumi was appointed after promising economic reform but he hasn't accomplished much in that field. He has stirred up controversy with his visits to Yasukuni and by stoking a nationalistic fever. However, he also has expressed regret for Japan's previous militaristic actions, and reopened doors of negotiation with problematic North Korea.

Emperor Akihito: Emperor since 1989, Akihito plays soft second fiddle to the prime minister. The emperor shocked the country by admitting he is of Korean ancestry, since Koreans have long been considered inferior.

Aum Shinri Kyo: Cult that unleashed Sarin gas in Tokyo subway in 1995, killing twelve and injuring thousands.

Factoid: Over 30,000 Japanese have killed themselves every year since 1998. Suicide is considered an honorable way to end one's life, and books talking about the best methods and sites for suicide have become bestsellers.

Alberto Fujimori: Peru's former president, born in Peru of Japanese parents, fled here to avoid corruption charges. Peru wants him back, but Japan won't extradite him. In Japan, he's quite a V.I.P.

THE GRAYING OF JAPAN

The high cost of living in Japan has worked as a contraceptive device: the birth rate is falling, while many of the green tea–swilling Japanese live into their eighties. By 2015 at least a quarter of the country's population will be sixty years or older, which gives economists more reason to worry about how the economy will keep up.

Turkey . . . Caucasus Combo . . . The 'Stans . . . Philippines . . . Syria . . . Lebanon **PART THREE** Spain . . . Jordan . . . Mideast Medley . . . Balkan Bunch . . . United Kingdom . . . Western Europe . . . *Talkers* . . . . Libya . . . Venezuela . . . Mexico . . . Nigeria . . . African Assortment . . . Southeast Asia Sampler . . . Canada . . . Turkey . . . Caucasus Combo . . . The 'Stans . . . Philippines . . . Syria Lebanon . . . Spain . . . Jordan . . . Mideast Medley . . . Balkan Bunch United Kingdom . . . Western Europe . . . Rwanda . . . Thailand . . . Latin American Medley . . . Cuba . . . Libya . . . Venezuela . . . Mexico . . . Nigeria African Assortment . . . Turkey . . . Caucasus Combo . . . The 'Stans . . . Philippines . . . Syria . . . Lebanon

TURKEY

FAST FACTS

Country:	Republic of Turkey
Capital:	Ankara
Government:	republican parliamentary democracy
Independence:	29 October 1923 (from Ottoman Empire)
Population:	67,309,000
Leaders:	Prime Minister Recep Tayyip Erdogan (since March 2003); Deputy Prime Minister Abdullah Gul
Ethnicity:	80% Turkish, 20% Kurdish
Religion:	99.8% Muslim (mostly Sunni)
Language:	Turkish (official), Kurdish, Arabic, Greek
Literacy:	85% (94% men, 77% women; 2000 estimate)
Exports:	apparel, food, textiles
Per capita GDP:	$6,700 (2001 estimate)
Unemployment:	11% (2001 estimate)
Percentage living in poverty:	N/A
Known for:	letting U.S. use its airbases, not being allowed into EU, not letting U.S. use airbases

Standout Qualities

Whirling: dervishes twirl into ecstasy
Swirling: endless trail of dinner plates
Dizzying: future unsure

Résumé

Is it Europe or is it Asia? Is it secular or is it Islamic? Is it a democracy or a military government enforcing what it thinks is democracy? This land bridge between two worlds has a rich history aligned with the Islamic Middle East; but it's looking to the West for its future.

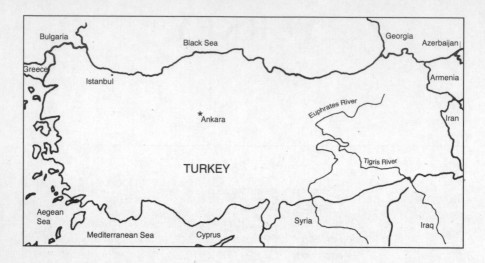

Quick Tour

Napoleon never ruled Turkey, neither did Stalin or Hitler. Just about every other Western power monger since the beginning of time, however, left an imprint here. Turkey, once called Anatolia, occupies mountainous, river-threaded land that spreads like a geologic accordion. The first civilization sprang up here—at the headwaters of the Tigris and Euphrates, Alexander the Great marched through and claimed it, Roman emperor Diocletian had a palace here, and it was this land that created beauty Helen of Troy and where the calming hills served as retirement home for the Virgin Mary. Entry point to the East for wanderer Marco Polo, Turkey was once coveted by the British, who managed to snag much of the rest of the region from the Ottoman Empire when it folded after World War I.

WATER WAR

The twenty-first century will be the century of water, say experts, who predict water wars will start here. Turkey is rolling in water, a resource more valuable than oil in the parched Middle East. The country's controversial $32 billion Southeast Anatolian Project—a hydropower complex of nineteen power stations and twenty-two dams—is under way: valleys of ancient civilations are now lakes, and Syria and Iraq are already screaming, since the project cuts into their downriver water supply. The project was viewed as so destabilizing to the Middle East that the World Bank refused to fund it.

Future Forecast

If the European Union keeps rejecting Turkey much longer, all reforms thus far will be null and void, and Islamists will gain power. The U.S. will do everything in its power to prevent that.

Background Briefing

Turkey's eternal appeal hasn't been oil but the strategic location of the land. Turkey has one arm in Asia and the other reaching toward Europe, not to mention sheer beauty and cultural riches. Its dramatic terrain—soft hills that settle around inland seas like a shawl, jagged mountains where civilizations chipped their way in, wind-blasted plateaus and terraces that peer onto springs and calm pools—is dotted with jeweled cities of domes encircled by missile-like minarets and tangles of steeply angled back streets that spill into spice markets. Turkish culture is just as intense as the land: here a dinner spreads out over hours as small plates of egglant and lamb pass by at a dizzying pace. Belly dancing may have originated in Egypt, but plenty of shimmying gals entertain pillow-reclining audiences in Istanbul, while mystical dervishes spin themselves into Sufi ecstasy, and appear to ascend into the air.

MIDDLE OF IT ALL

Turkey's strategic location is why it was rushed into NATO in 1952. Its military bases are instrumental for sweeps into the Middle East. Israel sells Turkey sophisticated arms; in return Turkey pipes it water.

The Ottoman Empire put what is modern-day Turkey on the power map, as administrative headquarters that was dripping in opulence and marked by unusual hats—some cylinders that rose two feet from the head, some bent at right angles, some billowing bundles topped by an emerald. Embracing a variety of cultures—from those of the forested Balkans to the souks in Morocco to the palaces of Baghdad—the empire that peaked under Süleyman the Magnificent in the sixteenth century was puttering out by the early twentieth, when it was dubbed "The Sick Poor Man of Europe."

Factoid: The Ottoman Empire was once known as the Sublime Porte or "Great Door." Ottoman governors—called pashas—were sent to oversee foreign lands.

Having made the fatal decision to side with Germany in World War I, the Ottoman Empire crumbled after a British-led Arab revolt, where Lawrence of Arabia fought with the Hashemite Clan against Turks. The British planned on snagging the land, but their plans were shoved aside by a former Ottoman officer Mustafa Kemal, who took the name of Atatürk. After a three-year civil war, he emerged as victor and marched the country into a modern, secular mode. Men were banned from wearing the trademark fez, women were freed from their veils, and the government—in this country where 99 percent are Muslims—was designed to be free of religion.

NOAM WINS

Turkey, where the media is not free to report on religion, military matters or Kurds, frequently tries (and convicts) publishers if they print books with the word "Kurdistan" in them, or which mention Turkey's poor treatment of Kurds or its denied massacre of a million Armenians. When Fatih Tas, the publisher of Noam Chomsky's book *American Interventionism,* was tried because of the chapters on anti-Kurd brutality, Chomsky himself showed up in the courtroom. Wary of the publicity, the Turkish government dropped the case.

The only problem is religion keeps creeping back in, as the people vote for Islamist parties—often more helpful than the government in providing food and aid to the poor—to serve in parliament. Three times since the 1970s, the ever-watchful military has escorted religious-leaning governments out.

They may have to do it again after the November 2002 elections. Some worry that the Justice and Development (AK) Party, which has a decided Islamist bent, will emerge victorious. The religious issue is only one facing Turkey, where 70 percent want the country to join forces with the European Union. The EU offers economic stability to the country whose financial scene is recession-prone, but to fully join on, Turkey has to jump through many a hoop.

SHIFTING RELATIONS

Ever since 1832, when Greece violently shook off the Ottoman Empire, relations between the two countries have alternated between bitter and rancorous. Turkey's invasion of Cyprus in 1974, and Greece's constant blocking of Turkey's bid to enter the European Union are but a few factors that nearly pushed the two to all-out war several times. That all changed on August 17, 1999, when the ground under Izmir in northwestern Turkey rocked with a 7.2-magnitude earth-quake that killed seventeen thousand and knocked buildings to the ground. First to arrive on the scene: Greek doctors and emergency teams, bearing med-icine, food and blankets, and digging out their former enemies. When Greece was shaken by a quake several weeks later, Turkey returned the favor. Ever since the 1999 Izmir earthquake, Greece has supported Turkey's admission into the EU and the two are getting along much better. Still being debated: the future of Cyprus: part of the lovely isle is claimed by Turkey.

The EU views harshly the human rights abuses in the country that has tried to physically and culturally eradicate the Kurds. In a show of "Look, we're re-forming!" Turkey banned its death penalty (which Kurd leader Abdullah Ocalan faced) and allowed the Kurdish language to be legally spoken for the first time in eight centuries. Now if Turkey could just sort out its "Cyprus Problem" with Greece: since Turkey invaded in 1974, the Mediterranean island has been hos-tilely divided between Greeks and Turks.

Hot Spots

Istanbul: Geologists say it's due for a big rattler that could level this stunning city that overlooks the Bosphorus.

East Turkey/Kurdistan: Populated by religious peasants, the east is also home to many Kurds, who have a history of attacking pipelines. Battles be-tween Kurds and the government have killed over thirty thousand since 1984, but relations are somewhat improved.

Bone-chilling evidence: The Turks still deny the Ottoman slaughter of more than 1 million Armenians in 1915, but skeletons in northeastern Turkey keep rising to the surface. Armenians are furious that Turks won't cop to the truth. But even Armenia sent people to help after the 1999 earth-quake.

Cyprus: Since 1974, the independent isle has been uneasily split by "the green line": Greeks run the southern two-thirds, and Turkey occupies the northern third, which the world doesn't recognize as Turkey's territory. Greek Cyprus is now "new EU"; Turkish Cyprus isn't.

Hot Shots

Kemal Atatürk: President from 1923 to 1938, when he died. Founder of modern Turkey, who insisted it be secular and Western-leaning, he changed Arabic script to the Latin alphabet form, banned polygamy and gave women the right to vote. Marched Turkey in the forward direction, modernizing its businesses and infrastructure, but didn't recognize the Kurds.

Recep Tayyip Erdogan: Leader of Turkey's Justice and Development Party (AK), charming Prime Minister Erdogan has been leading the country since the November 2002 elections, when his party took over 36 percent of the vote. Some are wary of the party's strong religious ties, but Erdogan has promised that he will not transform Turkey's secular government into an Islamic one. The Turkish government tried to keep him out of the prime minister's seat, but he snagged it in March 2003.

AK Party: Islamic party that rose to power in 2002 with promise to address headscarf issue: women have been banned from wearing scarves in school; many want to. Some Kurdish members.

Abdullah Ocalan: Leader of PKK (Kurdish People's Party) and an icon to Kurds, whom he led in guerrilla attacks of the Turkish government since 1984—even when he was out of the country. Ocalan was rounded up in 1999, prompting even more violence. He ultimately appealed to Kurds to stop their violence, even when his appeal to toss out his death sentence was ignored. Reforms mandated by the European Union—abolishing the death penalty is one—have thus far saved him from eating his last supper.

SLAM-O-RAMA

While secular, Turkey's Islamic population has raised eyebrows in the entirely Christian EU. In 2002, Giscard d'Estaing, former president of France, speculated that allowing Turkey to join would mark "the end of the European Union."

UNBRIBEABLE

The U.S. offered $6 billion to Turkey to use its airbases during the 2003 Iraq War, but the legislature turned it down. Look for future snubs from U.S. to IMF retaliation.

CAUCASUS COMBO: AZERBAIJAN, GEORGIA, ARMENIA

Standout Qualities

Off the map: Americans don't know where they are
On the map: U.S. oil companies sure can find them now
On the way: a crucial link to get energy to market

CASPIAN CONSIDERATIONS

What makes this region so important is its location directly west of the energy-rich, landlocked Caspian Sea, where five countries are butting heads over how to divide water rights and the offshore riches. What's more, oil and gas from the 'Stans often cross through this potentially turbulent territory.

It's horribly misleading that a majestic mountain range that cleaves Europe and Asia and rises up between the strategic Caspian and Black Seas has such a lackluster name. The Caucasus sounds like the snooziest part of a political convention. The countries that spill down from this icy spine of jagged rock are certainly not dull: as if political shakeups, religious brouhahas, ethnic seething, assassinations and war weren't enough—oil and natural gas are gushing and pipelines are snaking all over the place.

Literary Love: *The astounding beauty of the area is praised in works of Tolstoy and Pushkin.*

To the north of Iraq and Iran, the Caucasus region (particularly Azerbaijan, along with the nearby 'Stans) is so petrol-rich it's sometimes called the new Middle East. That may be an exaggeration, but what's for sure is the countries that lie south of the snow-sprinkled mountains are a power corridor. Their lands are the crucial energy doorway to get newly tapped resources to the West.

GEOGRAPHICAL CONFUSION

The term "The Caucasus," while actually the name of the mountain range, is used to define the region: sometimes "The Caucasus" refers solely to the southern gateway countries—Azerbaijan, Georgia and Armenia. Sometimes "The Caucasus" includes the countries to the north of the mountains, which is where Chechnya, Dagestan and other sections of Russia are situated and separatist battles are raging.

Big money is being pumped in here—U.S. oil giants are sinking billions and billions—in hopes that big oil will be pumping out. With a tangle of pipelines in the works and five countries—Azerbaijan, Kazakhstan, Russia, Turkmenistan and Iran—competing over the rights to the Caspian Sea, expect to see fireworks, wild power plays and huge land grabs around here.

UNSPOKEN ANGST

Azerbaijan, Georgia and Armenia—once part of the Soviet Union—are now theoretically independent, but Mother Russia remains in their picture. Still leaning on Russia economically, the countries often take orders from Moscow, and their new importance in the energy world gives reason to wonder if the world's biggest country won't pull them back into its oppressive bear hug.

Future Forecast

This will be the new place to watch: could emerge wealthy and as the new travel destination, could be pulled back into Russia, could be rearranged in aftermath of a U.S. war in Iraq.

Azerbaijan (ah-zair-bye-YAWN)

FAST FACTS

Country:	Republic of Azerbaijan
Capital:	Baku
Government:	republic
Independence:	30 August 1991 (from Soviet Union)
Population:	7,798,000 (2002 estimate)
Leader:	President Heydar Aliyev (was president under Soviets too)
Ethnicity:	90% Azeri; 3% Dagestani; 2.3% Armenian; 2.5% Russian
Religion:	93% Shia Muslim; 2.3% Armenian Orthodox; 2.5% Russian Orthodox
Language:	Azerbaijaini (also Russian, Armenian)
Literacy:	97% (99% men, 96% women; 1989 estimate)
Exports:	oil and gas; also cotton, machinery
Per capita GDP:	$3,100 (2000 estimate)
Unemployment:	20% (1999 estimate)
Percentage living in poverty:	64%
Known for:	oil, pipeline node, being forgotten

Snuggled up next to the Caspian Sea, this oil-oozing country was nearly forgotten until recently. At the beginning of the twentieth century, however, it was big news: Azerbaijan was the first place big oil was pumped—in the 1840s—and by the early 1900s almost half the world's petroleum was shipped out of its capital, Baku. The Rockefellers and Nobel Brothers (of Nobel Prize fame) made a killing here.

EARLY LIGHT

The country has a strange history with fire. Legend holds that Prometheus brought his stolen flames here and gave them to humans. Azerbaijan was also where the mystical religion Zoroastrianism burst to life in the seventh century B.C.: mesmerized by fire, the mystical group built temples over self-flaming gas vents in the earth's crust that kept the holy places perpetually illuminated.

The Russians initially pumped the heck out of this resource-rich gem, and then pretty much dropped it. However, the country's independence in 1991, coupled with new petroleum and gas field discoveries in the area, lured the Western world to come in and dust it off. Even if it didn't have energy resources of its own, the country is geographically key: it lies between the 'Stans and the Mediterranean ports. With rigs pumping away in the Caspian and a half dozen pipelines in the works, Baku—already booming—might become the next Houston.

BAKU A-GO-GO

Until Russia grabbed it in 1828, Azerbaijan was part of the Persian Empire, and most Azerbaijaini are Shia Muslims. In its capital, Baku, playground for politicians' kids and visiting oilmen, you might not guess that it has a deeply religious history: until the president recently blew his top and demanded nightlife wrap up at midnight, many bars never shut down, and in between the tango and the disco some offered "red-light specials" in back.

Unemployment causes riots and Azerbaijan suffers ethnic hatred and land tension too: in 1988, Armenians who lived in the Azeri region called Nagorno-Karabakh proclaimed it independent. A civil war dragged on for six years over that parcel that Azeris say is the prettiest part.

MUSICAL SHOTS

Famous Azeri cellist Mstislav Rostropovich recently returned to Baku bearing $1 million worth of hepatitis B vaccines. The liver-eating disease affects upward of 7 percent of population.

Although both parties in Azerbaijan agreed to a cease-fire in 1994, the people are still hopping mad and some eight hundred thousand Azeris are displaced. Not only do they refuse to do business with the Armenia-occupied Nagorno-Karabakh, they've also locked sanctions on Armenia, which is now entirely blocked off from Azerbaijan. To get there now, one must detour six hours through Georgia.

PIPELINE POWER

A few of the biggies in the works:

Baku-Ceyhan: "Main Export Pipeline," $3 billion pipe to bring Azerbaijan's fossil fuels via Georgia to Turkey's Ceyhan Mediterranean port.

Caspian Pipeline Consortium Pipeline (CPC): $4 billion pipe from Kazakhstan via Azerbaijan and Georgia to Russia's Black Sea port of Novorossiisk.

Trans-Caspian Gas Pipeline (TCGP): $3 billion pipeline for Turkmenistan's gas to cross Azerbaijan and Georgia and hook up with Turkey's pipelines.

Georgia

FAST FACTS

Country:	Georgia
Capital:	Tbilisi
Government:	republic
Independence:	1991 (from Soviet Union)
Population:	4,961,000 (2002 estimate)
Leader:	President Eduard Shevardnadze
Ethnicity:	70% Georgian; 8% Armenian; 6% Russian; 6% Azeri, others
Religion:	65% Georgian Orthodox; 11% Shia Muslim; 10% Russian Orthodox; 8% Armenian Apostolic
Language:	Georgian (also Russian, Armenian, Azeri; 1998 estimate)
Literacy:	99% both sexes
Exports:	citrus fruits, tea, wine
Per capita GDP:	$3,100 (2001 estimate)
Unemployment:	17% (2001 estimate)
Percentage living in poverty:	54% (2001 estimate)
Known for:	beauty, Pankisi Gorge

With lush pine forests, wind-blasted gorges and ancient hilltop villages, one can imagine the hills overflowing with tourists. Like Armenia and Azerbaijan, this country that tumbles down from the mountain and skirts the Black Sea was once a major vacation destination for Russians, back when they had money. Most visitors to Georgia now, however, are refugees, who hike over the mountains from war-ravaged Chechnya, and set up in tents in Pankisi Gorge. It's the Chechen rebels who also hide in the lawless valley that have both the U.S. (who see an Al Qaeda link) and the Russians (who see Chechens as the enemy) all hot and bothered. Since spring 2002, the U.S. military has been training Georgian police in how to nab terrorists; since fall of 2002, Russia has been threatening to invade and clean up Pankisi Gorge itself.

SICKENING WARMTH

Hunters in western Georgia recently discovered a new heating device in the woods; the strange canisters stayed warm on their own. Having cuddled next to them as they camped out that night, the hunters became horribly ill the next day—with radiation sickness as it turned out. The canisters were "lost" nuclear batteries from the Soviet era.

President Eduard Shevardnadze's worry list doesn't end there: the resource-scarce and poor country is behind on its energy bills, and it's hard to keep on the lights; blackouts are common. That might change with new pipelines going through that will provide the country with "transit tariffs" and also access to more natural gas to keep electricity plants humming. Georgia has territorial problems too. The regions of Abkhazia and South Ossetia have proclaimed independence, and military-weak Georgia can do little but shrug and go along.

FESTIVE RELIGION

Like Georgia, breakaway region Abkhazia has a bad rep for corruption and Mafia mind-sets, but until recently it held high the tenets of "Kebzeh," a religious philosophy based on respect toward women and elders. One of the practice's requirements: frequent dancing, which disciplines sexual energy.

Armenia

FAST FACTS

Country:	Republic of Armenia
Capital:	Yerevan
Government:	republic
Independence:	1991 (from Soviet Union)
Population:	3,330,000 (2002 estimate)
Leader:	Prime Minister Andranik Markaryan (since May 2000)
Ethnicity:	93% Armenian; 2% Russian; 2% Kurds
Religion:	94% Armenian Apostolic
Language:	Armenian, Russian
Literacy:	99% both sexes (1989 estimate)
Exports:	diamonds, metal, brandy
Per capita GDP:	$3,350 (2001 estimate)
Unemployment:	20% (2001 estimate)
Percentage living in poverty:	80% (2002 estimate)
Known for:	strong lobby in U.S., massacre by Turks

Of all the stunning countries in the area, Armenia may have the most problems: with the percentage of those living in poverty hitting the 80 percent mark, young people are leaving and violence sometimes rages. In 1999, a protester broke into the Parliament and gunned down the prime minister and several other ministers, saying that the country's dire straits drove him to the desperate move. A manufacturing center under the Soviets, Armenia is now reliant on small-scale agriculture and its economy is struggling. The sanctions that Azerbaijan and Turkey clamped on it after Armenia took over Nagorno-Karabakh aren't helping matters any. Armenia got even: the Armenian lobby convinced the U.S. to slap a trade embargo on Azerbaijan.

Armenian history is filled with woe: a Christian country, it's wedged between Muslim-majority Turkey and Azerbaijan. The Turks massacred more than a million Armenians in 1915, and the Armenians say they were persecuted by the Azeris when the Soviets moved them to the Nagorno-Karabakh enclave decades ago.

Despite its strategic location, no new pipelines are going through Armenia: threats originating from factions here, to blow up existing pipelines, have made the place undesirable in the new energy plans. Nevertheless, if things calm down and the Armenians and Azeris ever make up, this place could be a travel paradise.

FEUDS

Christian Armenians and Muslim Azeris have loathed each other since the nineteenth century when the tsar, say the Azeris, favored the Armenians, whom he'd located in Azerbaijan. They both suffered later under the Soviets, but the Armenians say they were mistreated by the Azeris who dominated their settlement in Nagorno-Karabakh. Their hatred now plays out in the marketplace. After the Armenians claimed Nagorno-Karabakh, the Azeris convinced Turkey to quit trading with Armenia; in retaliation, the Armenians convinced the U.S. to ban trade with Azerbaijan. President Bush lifted that clause, supposedly rewarding Azerbaijan's attitude in the "War on Terror," but it may have more to do with the oil there.

REGISTRATION WEIGHT

When the U.S. began its controversial registration for foreign-born residents in December 2002, Armenians were on the list alongside Iranians, Iraqis and others from Arab or Muslim countries. The Armenian lobby quickly worked its magic, and Armenians were deleted from the list.

THE 'STANS

Standout Qualities

Old comrades: all former Soviet republics
New comrades: all suffer same autocrats they had under communism
New capitalists: all opening doors to West

Résumé

Winners of "The You've Got to Be Joking, We'll Never Remember Those Names!" awards are the so-called 'Stans. Known for their poverty, president-dictators and human rights abuses, these former Soviet republics make oil and mineral companies go all googly-eyed, and not just from the intoxicating radioactivity and nasty chemicals everywhere.

Closed Clan: Also known as "The CARS" or Central Asian Republics, the so-called Stans do not include the better-known Pakistan or Afghanistan.

Quick Tour

Whether you're curving along on the hair-raising mountain passes in Tajikistan, where the gushing rivers that thread across the jagged land are toxic, or you're gazing at the marooned ships poking out from the sands where the Aral Sea used to be, you can sum up the 'Stans in one word: wasteland. The 'Stans—Kazakh-, Tajiki-, Uzbeki-, Turkmeni- and Kyrgyz- —served as Moscow's clandestine test laboratory/toxic trash can.

At least that's what much of this chunk of Central Asia was deemed when it was under control of the Soviets, who used these backwaters as places to ship

off "undesirables," conduct hazardous
military experiments and grow cotton.
It's debatable which use had the fur-
thest reaching ill effects: rival tribes,
intentionally located in the same territories, ensured that countries would
never unite against Moscow; radioactivity from numerous nuclear tests
blasted cancer rates sky high; and
the heavy pesticides and irrigation
required for cotton dried up and thoroughly poisoned rivers and lakes. In
fact, the region is teeming with so
many dangers—particularly Uzbekistan, where anthrax was precariously

buried in the ground, and Kazakhstan, where military labs brewed up smallpox
and plague germs—that they're getting plenty of American help in decommis-
sioning its most hazardous areas.

Thirsty Lands: *Due to pollution, drinking water shortages plague the
region; even some hospitals don't have running water.*

It's ironic that the area best known during communist days for its "white
gold"—cotton—is best known in its new capitalist phase for its black gold.
There's plenty of petroleum and natural gas bubbling up in these parts, especially in Kazakhstan, Turkmenistan and Uzbekistan, where eager corporations
are moving in with their drills and pumps.

Pipe Dream: *Some writers say the oil riches of Kazakhstan were a factor in the 2001 Afghan war, since the U.S. needed to stabilize Afghanistan to get a pipeline from the 'Stans to Pakistani ports.*

One can only hope that with the wealth that lies ahead for the region, some
of the money makes it to the people: in each of these countries between 25 and
80 percent live in poverty. Alas, these newly independent republics—which are
all still headed by the same crooked communists who ran them before—are
widely corrupt: elections are rigged, and kickbacks and sticky fingers abound,
while torture and jailing of dissidents (especially in Uzbekistan) run rampant.

Future Forecast

This could be the new Middle East, and pipelines are being constructed in every direction. U.S. military presence is increasing as well.

Meet the Stan Clan

"Stan" means "land." Kazakh, Uzbek, Tajik, Turkmen, etc., refer to the dominant ethnic tribe in the area. So in Kazakhstan, land of the Kazakh tribe, you'll find most of the population is Kazakh.

Kazakhstan ("The Big, Oil-Rich One"): The biggest, oiliest, potentially richest (and most radioactive) of the republics, Kazakhstan is the world's ninth biggest country. It is also home to some of the world's highest cancer and birth defect rates. Maybe that has something to do with the nearly five hundred nuclear tests conducted there between 1949 and 1989, and the chemical labs that concocted such vast quantities of deadly mixtures that Russia could have killed every inhabitant of the world ten times over. Kazakhstan is believed to hold at least 1.5 percent of the world's known oil reserves.

FASTER FACTS

Country:	Republic of Kazakhstan
Capital:	Astana
Leader:	Nursultan Nazarbayev
Population:	16.7 million (2001 estimate)
Ethnicity:	50% Kazakh; 35% Russian
Religion:	47% Muslim; 44% Russian Orthodox
Percentage living in poverty:	33%
Per capita GDP:	$5,000 (2000 estimate)

Uzbekistan ("The Crowded Oppressor"): Uzbekistan has the largest population, the biggest military and the most clout, thanks to zealot "President" Islam Karimov, who was the first to allow the U.S. to use military bases for the Afghan mission. The most oppressive leader of this heavy-handed bunch, he's keen to stamp out the militant Islamic movement of Uzbekistan, which one day in 1999 set off six car bombs in Tashkent. Karimov may have gone overboard: he's rounded up some seven thousand Muslims, some merely for sporting a beard. Anthrax is just one of the toxic treasures buried in these lands.

FASTER FACTS

Country:	Republic of Uzbekistan
Capital:	Tashkent
Leader:	Islam Karimov
Population:	25,155,000
Ethnicity:	80% Uzbek; 14% Russian
Religion:	88% Islam; 9% Eastern Orthodox
Percentage living in poverty:	50%
Per capita GDP:	$2,400 (2000 estimate)

What a race!: *Karimov, who typically receives 99.5 percent in presidential votes, wanted to illustrate he could win if he allowed someone to run against him. He rounded up a soft-spoken philosopher as the opposition candidate; even the anxious philosopher cast his vote for Karimov.*

Turkmenistan ("The Gas Problem"): Headed by a self-aggrandizing nut—Saparmurat Niyazov—who likens himself to a prophet, then proclaims himself spiritual "Turkmenbashi" (leader of all Turkomans) and then, at the behest of his foot-kissing cabinet, announced that he is "president for life," Turkmenistan has a little gas problem: it can't get it out (and antacids won't help). The republic must wait for a rich multinational to construct a pipeline, but that should happen soon enough. The Turkomans are sitting on 2 percent of world gas reserves.

FASTER FACTS

Country:	Turkmenistan
Capital:	Ashkhabad
Leader:	Saparmurat Niyazov
Population:	4.6 million
Ethnicity:	72% Turkoman; 6.7% Russian; 9.2% Uzbek
Religion:	89% Muslim; 9% Eastern Orthodox
Percentage living in poverty:	58%
Per capita GDP:	$4,300 (2000 estimate)

Tajikistan ("Mountainous Divides"): Eye-pleasing mountains aren't all that divide this land: it's ethnic and religious groups duked it out in a civil war in 1992, when 50,000 died and a million relocated, some 250,000 fleeing the country. The source of most of the 'Stans' militant Islamists—Uzbekistan has lined the border with landmines to deter their arrival—lovely Tajikistan is best known for being the poorest of the bunch.

FASTER FACTS

Country:	Republic of Tajikistan
Capital:	Dushanbe
Leader:	Emomali Rakhmanov
Population:	6,579,000 (2001 estimate)
Ethnicity:	65% Tajik; 25% Uzbek
Religion:	85% Muslim (mostly Sunni)
Percentage living in poverty:	80%
Per capita GDP:	$1,140 (2000 estimate)

Kyrgyzstan ("Pleasant, pretty liberal."): Kyrgyzstan may not have oil riches, but it boasts stunning, jagged scenery and the closest thing to democracy in these parts, with a liberal thinker as its head. Even the press is free, well, for the 'Stans.

FASTER FACTS

Country:	Kyrgyz Republic
Capital:	Bishkek
Leader:	Askar Akayev
Population:	4,753,000 (2001 estimate)
Ethnicity:	52% Kyrgyz; 18% Russian; 13% Uzbek
Religion:	75% Muslim; 20% Russian Orthdox
Percentage living in poverty:	50%
Per capita GDP:	$2,700 (2000 estimate)

PHILIPPINES

FAST FACTS

Country:	Republic of the Philippines
Capital:	Manila
Government:	republic
Independence:	4 July 1946 (from U.S.)
Population:	84,526,000 (2002 estimate)
Leader:	President Gloria Macapagal-Arroyo
Ethnicity:	92% Christian Malay; 4% Muslim Malay
Religion:	83% Roman Catholic; 9% Protestant; 5% Muslim
Language:	Filipino, English, Tagalog
Literacy:	95% (both sexes)
Exports:	electronics, machinery, garments
Per capita GDP:	$3,800 (2000 estimate)
Unemployment:	10%
Percentage living in poverty:	40% (2001 estimate)
Known for:	"People Power" that pushed out Marcos

Standout Qualities

Prim: President Arroyo embodies the word
Proper: politely accepts need for outside help
Precarious: from "trashslides" to fringe groups, not balanced

Résumé

The U.S. extended its "War on Terror" in early 2002 when it flew troops into the Philippines to advise on fighting vicious jungle thugs Abu Sayyaf. Ever since, things have gotten worse, and now Manila is being bombed, as well as the south.

Quick Tour

Filipinos seem to thrive on drama. Theatrics naturally flourish in the tropical island chain, home to active volcanoes and so many floods, typhoons, earthquakes and even landfill slides that it's been called the world's "most disaster-prone country." But the shakeups and disasters extend beyond the physical environment: the political arena is just as unstable, with players such as dictator Ferdinand Marcos and drunk actor Joseph Estrada allegedly draining the coffers, alternating with sensible women such as Corazon Aquino and Gloria Arroyo, who try to put the place back in order again.

BREEDING GROUNDS

Two percent of the population owns a third of the land. One-third of the population lives in poverty. Ideal proportions for communist guerrillas, a chronic threat to the government.

President Arroyo no doubt thought that was what she was doing when she accepted the U.S. offer to enter into the latest act of political theater. This one was played out in the farthest southern reaches of the island chain, Mindanao, an area traditionally held by Muslim sultanates. It's also an area where the Filipino government is trying to actively relocate Christians. The problem: rabid Abu Sayyaf. A six-hundred-strong mutant offshoot of Muslim extremists, the Uzi-toting youth had tossed aside any religious motivation and taken to simply nabbing tourists, missionaries, children and businessmen and holding them for exorbitant ransoms, while keeping them chained to trees. Arroyo had tried refusing their orders for money, only to have hostages' heads chopped off; she'd sent in the military with the same results. In January 2002, U.S. special units arrived to train Filipinos in more effectively rounding up the enemy.

INVITING TROUBLE?

Arroyo's move was a gamble: the Filipino government had ordered the U.S. military off the islands' bases in 1991; protests immediately flared up across Manila at the 2002 return of American troops.

Six months later—after a dramatic attempted rescue of the most prominent American hostages (missionaries Gracia and Martin Burnham) that resulted in one hostage being wounded but escaping (Gracia) and two being killed in the process—and after several shoot-outs that slightly diminished Abu Sayyaf's numbers, the mission was hailed a success and the U.S. shoved off, with promises to return for more exercises. Immediately the kidnapping started up again, as did the decapitation of hostages. Worse, other groups jumped into the fray— including the local communist guerrilla group, who attacked power lines, killed police and promised to become more active in local warfare. Within three weeks of the U.S. military's departure, the situation appeared to be far worse than when they had stepped in.

Factoid: A July 2002 survey showed 90 percent of Filipinos approved of the American military presence. The only reason: the Americans stimulated the local economy.

Who knows exactly what triggered the bloody rampage that saw dozens killed, several decapitated and at least eight kidnapped during a few days in August. Was this chain reaction a historical backlash to the century before, when the Americans, who'd helped Filipinos oust the Spanish in 1898, instead bought the Philippines for $20 million and moved in for the next fifty years?

Factoid: Mark Twain was infuriated about the U.S. occupation of the Philippines in 1898 and became an outspoken critic.

Was it memories of the U.S. wiping out the islands' insurgents, who fought them with rusty guns and magic charms, and the two hundred thousand, many civilians, who died from war or famine? Was it the recollection that the Americans had "subdued" Muslim sultanates, socialist guerrillas and revolting peasants while running the country like a colony?

Or was it simply that, with fresh reports in from the Filipino field, the U.S.

(which is viewed as either a savior or heavily armed bully) had put another group on its terror list—this time the New People's Army, the fighting arm of the Communist Party? Perhaps it was simply the smell of blood in the air that unconsciously activated the call to kill.

Whatever caused the unleashing of even more drama-laden killings across the island, it will only serve to heighten American military presence, the very thing that many Filipinos—especially nationalists—don't want.

Future Forecast

Dust off those bases! Bring back the babes! Get those cash registers oiled because you can count on it—the Yanks will be returning! While fighting insurgents—be they Muslim or communist—they'll definitely be monitoring what the Chinese are doing over in the nearby and disputed waters of Mischief Reef.

Hot Spots

Mindanao and Jolo Island: One's huge, the other's small, but both jungled islands in the south are sites of numerous conflicts between Muslims, who've lived there for centuries, and Christians, who are relocating there as part of government programs.

Hot Shots

Gloria Arroyo: Philippine president since 2001, winner of the Best Dressed President Award—absolutely no one looks better in cotton-candy pink suits—Arroyo is articulate and smart too. Daughter of a former prez, she's seen violence escalate.

Joseph Estrada: President from 2000 to 2001, hard-drinking, hard-gambling former actor Estrada was kicked out of office for alleged "plunder." Swears he'll be back for an encore.

Imelda Marcos: With her husband dead, why bother parading around in all those shoes? Instead Marcos opened a shoe museum outside Manila.

Abu Sayyaf: Blood-loving twenty-somethings who've taken names such as Commander Robot, these guys—mostly Muslims from Jolo—seem to get a big kick out of their work, whether it's rolling grenades down aisles of packed churches, massacring Christians, torching villages, raiding hospitals, grabbing children as gunfire shields or lopping the heads off of nurses and missionaries. They grossed over $25 million last year from kidnapping and expanded their arsenals of state-of-the-art arms and high-speed boats. U.S. says they're linked to Al Qaeda, but Arroyo has denied it. In any case, their leader was trained in an Afghan camp.

On a happy note: Abu Sayyaf may have inadvertently prevented a devastating airline attack in 1995. While in Manila, where Ramzi Yousef was teaching them how to make bombs, the neophytes set his apartment on fire. Yousef fled the Philippines, leaving behind his notes on plans for a midair disaster wherein eleven planes were to be bombed over the Pacific.

Moro National Liberation Front/Moro Islamic Liberation Front: Both groups have been fighting for decades, for autonomy of Muslim parts of Mindanao, and occasionally signing peace agreements. The Moro Islamic Liberation Front split off, feeling the former group wasn't militant enough—and are now twelve thousand strong. They spawned the little darlings known as Abu Sayyaf.

New People's Army: These communists, sometimes combined with peasant forces, have been battling with the government since the 1940s, but in the past three decades their guerrilla campaigns have become even more violent, leaving some forty thousand dead. Their enrollment numbers are climbing—current figures of twelve thousand or so are double what they were five years ago. Now targeting the power grids and telephone systems, the group is also calling for all Muslim insurgents to join their cause.

Road to Nowhere: Notoriously corrupt, the government is under heavy fire for bribe-taking and building pricey roads to nowhere. Arroyo is giving up: she won't run in 2004.

SYRIA

Standout Qualities

Shifty: Hey, whose side are they on?
Struggling: Hey, who's in charge there?
Stuck: Hey, Syria, wake up! Lebanon is not Syria anymore!

Résumé

Syria, an anorexic wisp of its former "Greater Syria" self, kept shrinking through the twentieth century. The geographical disappearing act it's endured helps explain why the country has ferociously sunk its teeth into Lebanon—which the French officially sawed off from Syria in 1920—and why it won't stop backing anti-Israeli groups until Israel returns the Golan Heights—seized in 1967.

> *Factoid: Greater Syria included today's Lebanon, Jordan and Israel. The region was carved up under the controversial 1916 Sykes-Picot Agreement that gave the French supervisory control.*

Quick Tour

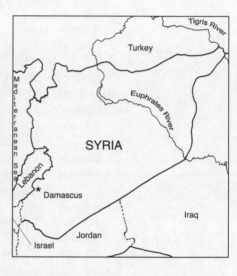

You want to know what's going on with Syria, look at Bashar al-Assad. The thirty-seven-year-old president almost always wears an expression like "Help! Get me out of this place!" which is understandable since he is usually surrounded by a bunch of rigid geezers, leftovers from his father's humorless, autocratic regime. Besides Bashar is in charge of a country that was once a star in the Arab world and now distinguishes itself by clinging to memories of the days when it mattered. For decades now, Syria has stood out mostly for whom it's militarily siding with that week, not for anything it's actually done, unless you count the occasional massacre.

> *Factoid: In 1958, Syria hooked up with Egypt as part of the "United Arab Republic" even though Egypt was 400 miles away. That political experiment ended in 1961.*

Stunning, secretive Syria lives in the past: antique cars sputter down streets, millennia-old "dead cities" dot the land of desert treasures, and its former prestigious role as the center of the Islamic world during the seventh and eighth centuries is referenced like it was yesterday; classroom textbooks still show a century-old map, when Syria was double its current size, and portray it as a major Arab shaker, which it hasn't been for at least forty years.

WHY FRENCH IS A DIRTY WORD

The French routinely emasculated once powerful Syria. Among their deeds:

1920: Tossed out Hashemite King Faisal, approved by the Syrian Congress

1920–1946: Stripped Syria of independence, ran as French colony

1920: Formally created state of greater Lebanon, snatching part of Syria's beloved coast, and went on to give part of Aleppo region to Turkey

The country's obsession with the good old days also plays out in Lebanon. Syria is in deep denial about this independent country. For the past quarter century, it has been running as though it's still Syria's coast (which it hasn't been for eighty-three years), with Syria's government and very present armed forces calling the shots.

Overstaying the Welcome: Syrian troops were invited in to help maintain calm during Lebanon's 1976 civil war. Twenty-six years later, twenty thousand troops remain and everything that happens in the country is "Syria-approved."

And while it's apparently okay for Syria to occupy Lebanon, the Syrians are furious about the Israelis who occupy the Golan Heights, the disputed crescent of land that lies in Syria's southwest. For thirty-six years, it's been a national preoccupation to snatch back the water-rich area.

WATER MAIN

After taking the militarily strategic Golan Heights during the 1967 Arab-Israeli War, Israel transformed the mountainous outcrop of springs into one of its main sources of water. Israeli settlers moved into the "disputed territory" where at least twenty thousand of them now live, ignoring UN Resolution 242.

Factoid: Syria is also in disputes with Turkey and Iraq over water from the Euphrates.

Politically, too, Syria is defined by the past: the country seems unsure what direction it's heading since the death of its fierce, white-knuckled Dictator-President Hafez al-Assad. Starting in 1970, when he assumed leadership of the Ba'ath party after his gang of armed goons overtook a political meeting, al-Assad instilled thirty years of fear. A member of the unpopular, minority Alawite sect—which draws on both Shiite and Christian beliefs—Assad was defensive from the start. The Muslim Brotherhood accentuated that quality with its staged rebellions and attempted assassinations in his early years of rule.

Following the Money Trail: Politically shifty, Assad's regime was bank-rolled by Soviets until the 1990s, when Syria became more Saudi-dependent and Western-leaning; during "Desert Storm" Syria signed on with the U.S., for which it was rewarded handsomely with a bundle of cash from the Sauds.

Few dared defy Assad, whose name means "The Lion," after the 1982 massacre in Hama, when his army, led by his gung-ho brother Rifaat, steam-rolled the town, killing at least ten thousand Syrians in seventy-two hours. The remaining Muslim Brotherhood members slipped out of Syria, and other Islamists never attempted an overthrow again.

Although Syria has long condemned Israel, against whom it has battled in four wars—in 1948, 1967, 1973 and 1982—peace with Israel briefly looked possible in 1999. Alas, Israel's Prime Minister Ehud Barak, who was offering return of most of the Golan Heights, was ejected and, several months later, Assad died.

Ray of Hope: Syria's mysterious beauty could one day make it a tourist hot spot.

Now the task of guiding the country, which has never been a financial powerhouse, falls to Assad's bashful son Bashar, a former eye doctor who inherited not only the presidential seat, but the white-haired powermongers who surround it. The younger Assad is perpetually frustrated as he tries to modernize the country by hooking it up to the Internet and creating a more open political clime; his moves—such as encouraging public debate—are often shot down by the power elite, who round up dissidents who criticize the regime.

Opening Doors: Bashar has released more than three hundred political prisoners since 2000.

Bashar is also facing major heat about Syria's continuing occupation of Lebanon. The international community that looked the other way when the elder Assad crushed an anti-Syrian administration in 1990 (after all Syria was helping out in Desert Storm) appears to have suddenly noticed that Syria is still there, despite promises to pull out in 1992.

In the 2002 Syria Accountability Act, the U.S. also threatens sanctions if Syria doesn't clamp down on Hezbollah, Palestinian Islamic Jihad and other groups who make violent runs into Israel. There's a hitch: while Bashar's administration has turned over plenty of info about Al Qaeda, which it loathes, it views anti-Israeli organizations as legitimate resistance groups. Israel has warned that if Syria continues support of the groups, it may come under military fire—a move the U.S. has approved.

Bashar doesn't like being bullied; the American attempts to change Syria's behavior may backfire and push Syria more to the radical left. Bashar has already warmed up to his father's longtime enemy Saddam Hussein, whose country now illegally supplies Syria with much of its oil.

Future Forecast

Bashar may unshackle Lebanon, but he'll keep funding Hizbollah and other anti-Israel causes unless the Golan Heights is handed back. Skirmishes with Israel are increasingly likely, as is the return of Bashar's nutty, power-hungry Uncle Rifaat.

> **UN Snipery:** *Who needs the soaps? Watch as Syria and Israel verbally duke it out during Syria's two-year stint (2002–2004) on the UN Security Council! From their first day they've been hissing and sniping and calling the other one "terrorists," though it hasn't yet come to blows.*

Hot Spots

Golan Heights: Ten miles wide and forty miles long, this plateau that rises up in Syria's southwest is one of the most hotly contested bits of Middle East real estate. It was claimed by Israel during the 1967 Arab-Israeli War, but Syria snatched a bit back in 1973, and its strategic military placement and water importance make it coveted by both sides. Syria won't make peace without it.

Hama: In 1982, when the army discovered a stash of arms in this Syrian city best known for ancient waterwheels, the Muslim Brotherhood killed ninety soldiers. This led to one of the most heinous massacres in Middle Eastern history when Assad's army stomped out the rebellion, killing between ten and thirty thousand. Neither Assad's anger nor his absolute control was ever questioned again, although it was actually his brother Rifaat who was calling the military's shots.

Hot Shots

Alawites: In Sunni-majority Syria, Alawites make up 11 percent of the population. Although now dominant in Syria's Ba'ath party, Alawites are often seen as heretics.

Ba'ath Party: Never mind religion, specific ethnicity or geographical location. All Arabs everywhere were to be united in this political movement started in the 1940s by a Christian and a Muslim. The socialist-leaning party soon split, and some banded in Iraq, where they brought Saddam Hussein to power. Iraqi and Syrian branches usually don't get along, which is one reason Assad was happy to join the 1991 U.S. coalition against Saddam Hussein.

THE LION KINGDOM: MEET THE ASSADS

Bashar al-Assad: Born in 1966 and Syrian president since 2000, this formerly unassuming eye doctor in London who liked 1980s soft rock and computers got tapped to be the next president when brother Basil died. He has tried to crack down on corruption and open up the society, but who knows how much power he really wields. He looks most uncomfortable with the job, but is reportedly snuggling up with Hezbollah.

President Bashar al-Assad likes Phil Collins. (Source: Associated Press)

Hafez al-Assad: Syrian "President-Dictator" from 1970 to 2000, this bone-crushingly tough despot, whose hate list included Yasser Arafat, Saddam Hussein, the Muslim Brotherhood and Israel, marched Syria into Lebanon and was obsessed with the return of the Golan Heights.

Rifaat al-Assad: When Hafez al-Assad suffered a heart attack in 1983, brother Rifaat—heading the country's military—stepped into his sib's still-warm shoes. When Hafez recovered, he was so livid that their mother had to be called in to sort it out. Rifaat, named vice president, was essentially exiled. Stripped of all titles in 1998, he has been verbally bashing Bashar since Hafez's death and should be showing up shortly to stage a comeback.

Basil al-Assad: Daddy's decided favorite, dashing, daring Basil was groomed to fill Hafez al-Assad's seat, but screwed up plans in 1994 when racing to the airport, his car careened out of control, killing its driver. Like they wouldn't have held the plane.

Farouq Sharaa: Syria's powerful foreign minister, who snags more ink than Bashar.

In late 2002, Syria shocked the world when it voted yes on Resolution 1441, forcing Iraq to disarm and submit to inspections. Syria has been accused of possibly hiding Saddam's weapons while inspectors looked for them in Iraq.

LEBANON

FAST FACTS

Country:	Lebanese Republic
Capital:	Beirut
Population:	3,678,000 (2002 estimate)
Government:	Arabic, French, English
Independence:	1944 (from France)
Leaders:	President Émile Lahoud, Premier Rafiq al-Hariri
Ethnicity:	95% Arab; 4% Armenian
Religion:	70% Muslim (majority Shia); 30% Christian
Literacy:	87% (91% men, 82% women; 1997 estimate)
Exports:	foodstuffs, tobacco, textiles
Per capita GDP:	$5,200 (2001 estimate)
Unemployment:	officially 18%, may be 25%
Percentage living in poverty:	28% (1999 estimate)
Known for:	bombings, massacres, attracting hoods

Standout Qualities

Weak: exhausted from infighting
Stronghold: Hezbollah home base
Strongarm: Syria unofficially annexed Lebanon

Résumé

Once likened to Switzerland and Paris, for its mountains and vibrant cultural scene respectively, former vacation hot spot Lebanon went to pieces in the seventies and hasn't recovered yet.

Quick Tour

Lebanon is still dusting itself off from a 1975–1990 civil war that decimated its economy, flattened capital Beirut, killed a hundred and forty thousand or so and transformed it from an intellectual, artistic gem into a floundering militant magnet. Always a religious hodgepodge of assorted Christians and Muslims, the Mediterranean-nudging country has a ridiculously complicated political system that is supposed to reflect the religious makeup of the population. It doesn't anymore: despite having a Maronite Christian president, the country actually has a Shia Muslim majority these days. Hezbollah, a Shia political group that is trying to destroy Israel (that's one of its stated charter goals) is well entrenched: they have seats in the Parliament as well as radio stations, TV stations, clinics, social services and ambulances. Funded mostly from Iran, the group is so powerful that when the U.S. named Hezbollah a terrorist group, the Lebanese government refused to freeze their assets.

Lebanon's relations with neighbors are stressful: the PLO fled here from Jordan, turning Lebanon into an outlaw post; in 1982, Israel rolled in to chase them out; seventeen thousand were killed. Then General Ariel Sharon, who took over a security zone in the south, was implicated for turning a blind eye to a gruesome massacre at refugee camps Sabra and Shatila; eight hundred were killed, many women and children among them. Upset at Israel's presence, radical Shiites formed Hezbollah that same year. Much to everyone's surprise, Hezbollah pushed Israel out in 2000—the first time Israel has been forced out of any place militarily; now the group and other anti-Israel forces make frequent runs out of Lebanon and into Israel. Meanwhile, Syria lords over the beleaguered place, where education levels are high and 25 percent of the population lacks jobs.

Lebanon stands out to Americans as the site of several bombings during the 1980s when the U.S. came in to calm things down. Probably the works of Hezbollah—particularly master thug Imad Mugniyah—the incidents no doubt shocked militant types as much as they shocked Americans, albeit for different reasons. The Americans couldn't believe it was happening; the militants couldn't believe that the U.S., then under President Reagan, didn't fight back.

Instead the Reagan government demonized Libya's Moammar Qaddafi, while letting Lebanese hellions off free and easy, probably because they were more difficult to find.

Future Forecast

If Hezbollah continues attacks, Israel will be rolling back in.

LEBANON'S ANTI-WEST GESTURES

A few things Qaddafi had nothing to do with, but Hezbollah probably did:

1983: bombing of U.S. embassy kills sixty-three; bombing of Beirut barracks kills 241 U.S. Marines.
1984: bombing of U.S. embassy annex kills twenty-four; kidnapping of CIA station chief William Buckley and thirty others; Buckley killed
1985: hijacking of TWA Flight 847; U.S. Navy diver killed

Hot Shots

President Émile Lahoud: Since 1998 army man Lahoud says Syria's continuing presence is fine and dandy. Yeah right.

Hezbollah ("Party of God"): Officially formed in 1982, some of this Shia resistance group's main players were probably involved in the Iran hostage crisis of 1979. Targeting Israelis and American military, Hezbollah also has international branches: in Argentina, they blew up a Jewish center and the Israeli embassy (killing 114 in total). Funded by Iran.

Prime Minister Rafiq Hariri: Smart, business-savvy billionaire trying to lure foreign investment. Good luck!

SPAIN

FAST FACTS

Country:	Kingdom of Spain
Capital:	Madrid
Government:	parliamentary monarchy
Independence:	Unified 1492
Population:	40,038,000
Leaders:	Ruler: King Juan Carlos I; Prime Minister: José María Aznar
Ethnicity:	mix of Mediterranean and Nordic
Religion:	99% Roman Catholic, not all of them practicing
Language:	74% Castilian Spanish; 17% Catalan; 7% Galician; 2% Basque
Literacy:	97%
Exports:	machinery, cars, food
Per capita GNP:	$18,000 (2000 estimate)
Unemployment:	14% (highest in EU, though many work "under the table")
Known for:	fun, sun, battle-worthy rocks

Standout Qualities

Fiestas: parties for bulls, tomatoes, saints
Siestas: naps needed post-fiestas
Stones: Hey, you, get off of their rocks!

Résumé

Ever since dictator Franco croaked his final adios in 1975, Spain has been throwing a giant party, with arts, culture and business in renaissance mode and

SPAIN

FAST FACTS

Country:	Kingdom of Spain
Capital:	Madrid
Government:	parliamentary monarchy
Independence:	Unified 1492
Population:	40,038,000
Leaders:	Ruler: King Juan Carlos I; Prime Minister: José María Aznar
Ethnicity:	mix of Mediterranean and Nordic
Religion:	99% Roman Catholic, not all of them practicing
Language:	74% Castilian Spanish; 17% Catalan; 7% Galician; 2% Basque
Literacy:	97%
Exports:	machinery, cars, food
Per capita GNP:	$18,000 (2000 estimate)
Unemployment:	14% (highest in EU, though many work "under the table")
Known for:	fun, sun, battle-worthy rocks

Standout Qualities

Fiestas: parties for bulls, tomatoes, saints
Siestas: naps needed post-fiestas
Stones: Hey, you, get off of their rocks!

Résumé

Ever since dictator Franco croaked his final adios in 1975, Spain has been throwing a giant party, with arts, culture and business in renaissance mode and

Spaniards whooping it up until breakfast. Too bad a handful of Basque separatists keep trying to dictate what music is playing: they prefer funeral dirges.

Quick Tour

Viva la diferencia: Nearly three decades have lapsed since the despot General Francisco Franco died, but Spaniards are still wildly celebrating their not-so-newly-found freedom— and the regional dialects, cultures and festivals that were forbidden when the killjoy's shadow loomed over all corners. A zestiness abounds in this liberal and still-affordable country—a parliamentary monarchy headed by King Juan Carlos I—that is dripping with all the requirements for "*la dulce vida*": sun and beaches, mountains and bays, stunning cities, world-class museums, mind-blowing architecture, a cultural blossoming and a nightlife that pulses till morning.

SPAIN'S CULTURAL RICHES

- The Prado (works of Goya, Velázquez, Picasso, Dalí)
- Alhambra (Moorish palace atop Granada)
- Gaudí (his architecture melts in Barcelona)
- Basque cuisine (Spain's finest)
- Castles, castles, castles (some that serve as hotels)

Another factor that lures the 50 million visitors who bring in $33 billion annually: unfathomable diversity. From the Ireland-green hills of Galicia (home to redheaded bagpipers) and the parched white villages tumbling down the hills of Andalucía (still dotted with palaces of Muslim Moors), to the wind-sculpted Mediterranean coast unrolling toward France (where pirates hid their gold in hidden coves), Spain is a patchwork of different histories, personalities and terrains, each corner possessing its own distinct spirit.

Ironically, it's the very regionalism that makes the country so culturally rich, that also poses the land's greatest woes: while all of Spain's seventeen regions enjoy great autonomy, two are more fiercely independent than most. Catalonia, the region that spreads out from Barcelona in the northeast, is most spirited in its talk, but the Basque country is the most violent—and the region that poses the most migraines for Madrid.

It's true that the Basques—who speak their own unique language—were the most suppressed under Franco, who banned the Basque tongue, customs and culture in this mountainous area, one of the regions that fought him hardest during the Spanish Civil War, 1936–1939.

Nazis for Hire: *Picasso's disturbing* Guernica *is his tribute to the town firebombed during the civil war. Franco contracted Nazis for that job.*

The group known as ETA—Euskadi Ta Askatasuna (Basque Homeland and Freedom)—emerged in 1959 to defy Franco's steamrolling and censure of all that was theirs. But even after the dictator kicked, even after Spanish democracy returned—and even after the Basque region gained substantial autonomy and its own police, courts and legislature—the movement didn't subside. In fact, it's grown more violent: more than eight hundred have died since 1975. Now the enemy isn't Franco, it's the central Spanish government that keeps the Basque region chained in; ETA assassinates politicians and explodes car bombs as a means to let everyone know they want to break off.

Breakup Blues: *One-third of Basques want to become independent.*

The government, tired of trying to negotiate with the violent Basque secessionists, is now fed up: in 2002 Madrid—which had long before put ETA on its most wanted list and rounded up much of the gang—simply banned ETA's alleged political arm Herri Batasuna for its supposed links to violence. While the central government in Madrid is hoping that by freezing the party's funds they'll smother Basque violence, the move immediately did just the opposite and only inflamed the separatists' call.

Future Forecast

Increasing car bombs (but not enough to keep tourists from flocking). The government banning of the ETA political arm Herri Batasuna in 2002 will only serve to increase the number of Basque who want a referendum to decide if they should break up.

NOT NOW—WE'RE BUSY RECLAIMING A FEW ROCKS

In 1998, ETA claimed that if the Spanish government would simply put the fate of the Basque country to a vote, they'd abide by the results, be they "stay with Spain" or "shove off." No chance of that vote happening, especially now, when Spain is busy clinging to its every millimeter.

CURRENT TERRITORIAL CONFLICTS INCLUDE

Parsley Island (Isla Parejil): When six Moroccan military men "seized" it, Spanish warships went in to reclaim this smaller-than-a-city-block rock that's three hundred feet off Morocco and home to a few flocks of goats; probable reason: fishing—there's a gold mine of silvery sardines in these waters.

Ceuta and Melilla: Small, prosperous Spanish settlements actually on the African coast, and Morocco wants them back—no way, José.

Rock of Gibraltar: Despite Spanish grumbling and the occasional "invasion," this "rock" that is twelve miles from Africa has been British territory since 1713; the mostly British residents want to keep it that way.

Hot Spots

Catalonia: Home of the gust-twisted Mediterranean coast that inspired Dalí, the swirling buildings of Antonio Gaudí, and "Europe's most sophisticated city," Barcelona, Catalonia is a bit smug. Understandably, perhaps: the hilly northeastern corner that unrolls toward France is the wealthiest of all Spain, and one of the country's big tourist draws. Don't bother with your *español* here. Like the residents of the Basque country, Catalans speak their own dialect—a gruff blend of French, Portuguese and Italian—and it's official: Catalan is the language taught in schools and is used on subways and streets signs and spoken on local TV; even Spanish films are dubbed. Catalonia's independent streak—and the substantial contribution the area makes to the country's coffers in Madrid—has given the region political chips: it's Spain's most autonomous.

Riches: When Salvador Dalí—a native Catalan—left his estate to the government in Madrid, the regional VIPs were livid. At least Catalonia gets his remains: El Mustachioed One lies in the Dalí Museum in Figueres, some say against his final wishes.

Basque Country: Home to glittering San Sebastian, the jagged Pyrenees, cliff-perched towns and the Guggenheim Museum in Bilbao, this verdant region that hugs the sailboat-dotted Bay of Biscay and France is the least attached to the land that lies below it. The home of 2 million and the epicenter of Spain's culinary revolution, the Basque country may only have thirty paid full-time radicals, but its youth are angry and bored, and ETA is teaching them new firebomb tricks. Despite ETA antics, most Basques want to stay firmly attached to Madrid.

Hot Shots

King Juan Carlos I: A Bourbon whose father was ejected from the throne, King Juan Carlos was brought back center stage by General Franco, who took it upon himself to tutor the crown prince. In 1975, when the monarch ascended, he took the future of Spain to the people with a democratic vote: they called for a parliamentary system with the king as head of state and a premier as leading politico. Understanding the regional divides of his land, Juan Carlos gave plenty of power to nineteen autonomous regions. Beloved, as is his queen, Sofía.

King Juan Carlos I and Queen Sofia revived Spain after Franco. (Source: Associated Press)

José Maria Aznar: Prime minister since 1996, conservative Aznar once seemed to guide Spain into its most prosperous hours. Totally messed up starting in 2002: mismanaged handling of *Prestige* and cleanup of nasty oil spill. Aznar infuriated Spaniards—90 percent who opposed the Iraqi war—by signing on with U.S. coalition in 2003. Spain's least popular person.

ETA Euskadi Ta Askatasuna (Homeland and Freedom): An equal opportunity terrorist group that includes women, ETA wants the Basque region in northern Spain to shake off the rest of Spain, having apparently not noticed that Franco—the heavy-handed dictator they rose up against—is no longer around. Best known for assassinating political figures (Franco died naturally), they blast the occasional bomb to underscore their secessionist wishes. Wounded by recent arrests and the formal banning of their political arm, Herri Batasuna, they may limp off into the mountains—or at least so the government hopes. Alas, the government is probably dreaming.

WHEN SPANISH EYES ARE CRYING

ETA bombings used to be what brought Spaniards to the streets in massive protests. The sloppy handling of the *Prestige* also brought out the masses; antiwar protests, however, have prompted the biggest demonstrations in recent history. Many millions showed up in frequent marches against the unpopular U.S.-led Iraqi war.

Loss of Prestige: When the Prestige—*a single-hulled oil tanker—sunk off northwest Spain in November 2002, it coated the pristine coastline of Galicia with over three million gallons of petrol goo. The Spanish government, which first tried to drag the ship to Portuguese waters, has been under fire for not acting quickly to minimize the oil spill.*

JORDAN

FAST FACTS

Country:	Hashemite Kingdom of Jordan (Jordan)
Capital:	Amman
Government:	constitutional hereditary monarchy
Independence:	25 May 1946 (from British administration)
Population:	5,300,000 (2002 estimate)
Leaders:	King Abdullah II; Prime Minister Ali Abul Ragheb
Ethnicity:	98% Arab (of that 65% Palestinian)
Religion:	92% Sunni Muslim; 6% Christian
Language:	Arabic, English
Literacy:	87% (93% men, 80% women; 1995 estimate)
Exports:	phosphates, fertilizers
Per capita GDP:	$3,500 (2000 estimate)
Unemployment:	25–30% (1999 estimate)
Percentage living in poverty:	40%
Known for:	diplomacy, lack of oil, pluck

Standout Qualities

Close calls: king might have ruled entire Middle East
Close connections: uniting force between East and West
Too close for comfort: tension from all sides

Résumé

Recipe for ruin: Take an absolutely stunning land of pinks sands, lost cities and geological wonders. Deprive it of oil. Stick it in the middle of the world's two hottest flash points, wreck its tourist economy, pump unemployment to the 30 percent mark, fill it with refugees from every war in the past half century and there you have it: Jordan—the right place in the wrong time.

Quick Tour

Just call it the Oz of the Middle East: from the Dead Sea and its glistening salt-encrusted boulders to Petra, an intricately designed nine-thousand-year-old city carved into rose-colored cliffs, Jordan is jaw-droppingly beautiful and enchantingly bizarre. The land that awkwardly squats between Israel, Iraq, Saudi Arabia and Syria is studded with cultural and archeological jewels.

Factoid: The lowest place on the planet, the Dead Sea is four hundred meters below sea level, and eight times saltier than typical seawater: no marine life can live in it and here you can't sink, because every body floats.

The place should be swimming with tourists, and until recently the photo-snapping crowd was the country's biggest moneymaker. Even though Jordan is usually peaceful, it lives in a rough neighborhood. But it's more than the effects the neighbors' noisy rows have on Jordan's tourism business that is presenting its leader, King Abdullah II, with an Arabian Peninsula–sized headache. Map-wise, money-wise, power-wise, the kingdom is right in the middle: diplomatically bonded to the U.S., its largest aid donor and number two trading partner, Jordan is tied to Iraq, its number one trading partner and provider of its oil. Given U.S.-Iraqi tensions, the 2002 murder of a U.S. diplomat and rising violence, it's a wonder that the king can sleep at all.

BEWARE OF BRITS BEARING PENS

Until the twentieth century, there was no Jordan per se: it was just part of Palestine. After World War I, the British marked off this chunk—first called Transjordan—and installed the ruling Hashemite clan in 1921, when the territory was under British control. They also (briefly) presented the Hashemites with the throne of Syria (the French had other ideas) and later Iraq. That worked out for a few years, but the monarchy's Iraqi reign ended with a brutal courtyard murder in 1958.

Ever-juggling, trying-to-please-everyone Jordan also has a peace treaty with Israel, but the Arab country is brimming with unhappy Palestinians, many of whom fled here during Israeli land expansion into Palestine in 1948. The unspoken fear in Jordan is that the usually nonviolent residents will actively join in on the Palestinian struggle—and some say this place that is typically extremely laid back is now teeming with spies. The U.S., which awarded Jordan status as a free trade area in 2000, is pressuring it to serve as a wartime base for U.S. fighter jets and sign on as an anti-Saddam ally, but Jordan's leadership is balking: to do so would guarantee a mass backlash, and its young king could be toppled. And nobody wants to see that: forty-one-year-old King Abdullah II is actually America's most valuable Arab ally, the one who best spells out the Middle East to the West—and he does so in English, having been educated at Oxford and spending many of his formative years abroad.

It's ironic that a monarch of the once-powerful Hashemite clan—descendents of the Prophet Muhammad—would find himself in charge of such a strategically important but economically worthless land, where the only power he can give it is through diplomacy and financial ties. His poor country is resource-short, and he's always having to hit up other countries for loans. Consequently, his powerful neighbors can call all the shots, regardless of what Jordan thinks. It just wasn't supposed to be like this: after all, the Brits—specifically Lawrence of Arabia—swore up and down that the Hashemite clan would rule the whole Arab world after World War I.

OTTO OUSTER

Specifically the British wanted the Hashemites to rally assorted Arab tribes to rebel against the Ottoman Empire, which backed Germany in World War I. They did so in 1916 in the Great Arab Revolt. In return, the British promised that the Arab territories of the Ottoman Empire would become independent, and that the Hashemites would govern them.

Instead the British and French signed the secret Sykes-Picot Agreement, carved up the Arab territories and, with an okay from the League of Nations, baby-sat from 1920 until the 1950s. In 1920, the British tried to put Hashemite King Faisal on the throne in Syria, but that ended in a double whammy. First, the French battled the Hashemite king, and ultimately ousted him. At the same time Hashemite warriors were fighting up in Syria, the clan's incredibly valuable territory in Arabia—the Hejaz, which held holy site Mecca—was seized by the marauding warriors of Ibn Saud. Next, the British instead gave King Faisal Iraq, but that too was seized from the Hashemite rulers after a few decades. So the clan that once held huge expanses of petroleum-rich territory ultimately ended up with only a fetching patch of Palestine called Jordan that held nary a teaspoon of oil.

> *On the Other Hand:* At least King Abdullah II has a bright, charismatic and beautiful Palestinian wife—Queen Rania—whom the international press adores.

Back in its early days, under the first Hashemite king—King Abdullah I—the country that rose up on the east of the Jordan River grew by leaps and bounds, literally. During the 1948 Arab-Israeli war, Jordan snatched lands on the other side of the river, namely the West Bank and East Jerusalem—land that was largely designated as Palestinian territory. In the 1967 Arab-Israeli war, Israel knocked out Jordan and claimed the territory as its own. Who was screwed in both cases: the Palestinians.

BULLETPROOF PENDANT

Good for the treasury due to its many pilgrims, Jerusalem wasn't good for the king's health. He was shot down there by a Palestinian radical while entering the city's Al-Aqsa mosque in 1951. At his side was his grandson—then Prince Hussein—who was a target as well, but the bullet that nearly pierced his chest was deflected by a decorative pin; eerily, Abdullah had given it to Hussein only the night before.

King Hussein was the monarch who really put Jordan on the map—and not just because of gorgeous wife Queen Noor, the American Lisa Halaby, whom he married in 1978. Initially taking the throne as a teenager, Hussein was laughed off as unlikely to last, but he did, and with such verve and style that he became known as the "Plucky Little King." An able negotiator who put the issues on the table, he was on good terms with many Israeli leaders, although he didn't formally sign a peace treaty with Israel until 1994.

ADVANCE WARNING

King Hussein warned Israel's Prime Minister Golda Meir that Arabs were planning to attack during Yom Kippur in 1973. She apparently didn't believe him, because Israel was taken by surprise.

Considered just and wise, King Hussein could be forceful too: when Yasser Arafat and his Palestine Liberation Organization tried to oust the king in 1970 he rounded them up and pushed them out during "Black September," when thousands died. Arafat and the remaining PLO hightailed it to Lebanon.

Chummy with the West, King Hussein shocked the world when he backed Saddam's invasion into Kuwait in 1990; Jordan officially maintains it was neutral during the resulting Desert Storm. The move was costly: Saudi Arabia slammed shut its checkbook, as did the U.S. Meanwhile Iraqi refugees flooded the borders, putting more strain on a country that was hideously broke. Saddam provided the only comfort: for a time, he gave Jordan free oil.

INSIGHT

King Hussein was pretty much forced into backing Saddam: his people sided with Iraq, which supplied Jordan's discount oil, Iraq claimed that Kuwait was angling its pipes and draining Iraqi oil fields—which may indeed have been true—and besides, King Hussein didn't much care for Kuwait. When he'd hit up the emir for a million-dollar loan to build a university a few years before, the Kuwaiti had sneered that a poor little country like Jordan didn't deserve luxuries like universities. Relations have been frosty since.

When King Hussein died in 1999, the power and prestige he'd brought to the country through his diplomatic moves was evident: the funeral was attended by nearly every head of state on the planet. Even Saudi Crown Prince Abdullah showed up, despite the iciness since 1990.

ROYAL CHAUFFEUR

King Abdullah II shares his father's charisma and populist touch. He's known for donning disguises and adopting commoner roles—as a taxi driver, a TV reporter or cranky old man at the tax office—just to see what his subjects really think of their country and what government employees are up to.

A last-minute switcheroo—for decades Hussein's brother had been the crown prince—brought Hussein's eldest son, Abdullah II, to power. Well-educated and Western-savvy, King Abdullah II was almost immediately put to a test: the Palestinian intifada broke out in 2000 just over the river in the West Bank. Muslim radicals tried to bomb Jordanian hotels, but authorities broke up the "millennium plot." The Muslim Brotherhood is popping up in politics, the king has already dodged assassination attempts, and Jordan's Palestinians are increasingly restive—all the more so given that the tourism-based economy is doing a nosedive thanks to the war next door. And now Jordan finds itself between Iraq and a hard place, called Israel and Palestine. The king's moderation could leave this country vulnerable to Al Qaeda and fundamentalist attacks.

Future Forecast

Who knows? Maybe King Abdullah II—whose Hashemite relatives sat on Iraq's throne—will end up inheriting Saddam's sad country. In the meantime, the king faces violence and a ruined economy; the U.S. is promising $500 million in damages.

American diplomat Laurence Foley was shot down in Amman in October 2002, the first Western official assassinated in Jordan. The culprit: Al Qaeda.

Hot Spots

Western border with Palestine: All's still fine on this other side of the Jordan River, but how long will it last?

Eastern border with Iraq: All's still fine on this other side of Saddam, but how long will it last?

Dead Sea: It's dying all right—drying right up. Jordan and Israel signed a 2002 agreement to pump whatever research and money it takes into keeping this natural wonder from sinking further.

Maan: Impoverished town in Jordan's south that is a hotbed for Islamist radicals. Could be site of anti-king rebellion and government clamping down, trying to round up weapons. Violence rising.

Hot Shots

King Abdullah II: Jordanian king since 1999, educated at Sandhurst and Oxford, he had to learn Arabic before taking the throne. Tough ride so far, but he'll keep a strong hold.

Queen Rania: Jordanian queen since 1999, feisty, unassuming and gorgeous, the Kuwait-born Palestinian has been known to demonstrate on the streets with her people. Just as charismatic as her hubby, the queen pushes all sorts of programs, from vaccinations to small business for Jordanian women.

King Abdullah II and Queen Rania: bridge between Middle East and West. (Source: Associated Press)

King Hussein: Jordanian king from 1952 to 1999. Beloved Mr. Pluck, he adored piloting his own planes, and survived dozens of assassination attempts in his forty-six years of rule. The Middle East's finest diplomat.

King Abdullah I: On the way to help his brother King Faisal stay in power in Syria back in 1920 (a fruitless effort), Abdullah camped on the east side of the Jordan River, and after the British named him ruler of the entirely undeveloped land, he stayed. He changed the name of Transjordan to Jordan when he snatched the West Bank and East Jerusalem in 1948, a land grab that raised the ire of the Arabic world. The name stuck even after Israel snatched East Jerusalem back in 1967.

SECOND GENERATIONS

King Abdullah II is one of a new wave of young, modern Mideast rulers who inherited the post. Also part of the club: King Mohammed VI of Morocco, President Bashar Assad of Syria.

MIDEAST MEDLEY

There's more to the Middle East than Saudi Arabia, Israel, Palestine, Iran, Iraq, Syria, Lebanon and Egypt. Here's the rest of the varied bunch.

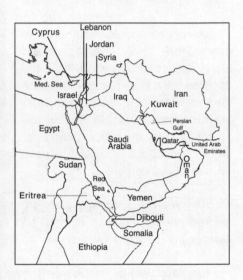

MAP PERSPECTIVE

Ever wonder why the Middle East is called that when it's neither in the middle nor the East? Because the Europeans were the ones drawing the maps. To them, the Near East was Turkey, the Middle East was the Persian Gulf Area and anything much beyond that was the Far East.

Bahrain

FAST FACTS

Country:	State of Bahrain (Bahrain)
Capital:	Manama
Government:	constitutional monarchy
Independence:	August 1971 (from U.K.)
Population:	645,400 (includes 228,000 non-nationals) (2001 estimate)
Leaders:	King Sheikh Hamad bin Isa al Khalifa; Prime Minister Sheikh Khalifabin Salman al Khalifa
Ethnicity:	63% Bahraini; 10% other Arab; 19% South Asian; 8% Iranian

Religion:	70% Shia Muslim, 30% Sunni Muslim
Language:	Arabic and English
Literacy:	85% (89% men, 80% women; 1990 estimate)
Exports:	petroleum, aluminum
Per capita GDP:	$15,900 (2000 estimate)
Unemployment	15% (especially youth) (1998 estimates)
Percentage living in poverty:	N/A
Known for:	U.S. air base, free medical care, education, pensions

Tinier than tiny Qatar—its neighbor on the Persian Gulf—Bahrain is actually a smattering of islands that sometimes serves as military base for U.S. and U.K. endeavors. With less oil reserves than its neighbors, it's delved into aluminum—and now is home to one of the world's biggest smelters. Unemployment is running high among bored youth and there's plenty of friction between Sunni and Shia.

Yemen

FAST FACTS

Country:	Republic of Yemen
Capital:	San'a
Government:	republic
Independence:	May 1990—North and South Yemen unified
Population:	18,079,000 (2001 estimate)
Leaders:	President Field Marshal Ali Abdallah Salih; Prime Minister Abd al-Qadir Ba Jamal
Ethnicity:	mostly Arab
Religion:	Muslim—Sunni and Shia
Language:	Arabic
Literacy:	38% (53% men, 26% women; 1990 estimate)
Exports:	oil, coffee, fish
Per capita GDP:	$820 (2000 estimate)
Unemployment	30% (1995 estimate)
Percentage living in poverty:	19% (1992 estimate)
Known for:	Osama link, ship bombings

Proof that not every country on the Arabian Peninsula is rolling in dough, there's dirt-poor Yemen, the mountainous backwater that was home of Osama bin Laden's progenitors, and where the typical woman has seven kids. Tribes and warlords abound in an extraterrestial setting rather like Afghanistan. When the U.S. sent in a CIA drone that killed an Al Qaeda suspect and five others, the Yemeni government looked the other way; so did the U.S. when Yemen received missiles from North Korea in late 2002. Site of the 2000 attack on the U.S.S. *Cole,* a 2002 attack on a French oil tanker and the 2003 murder of U.S. missionaries, Yemen is more danger-prone than its neighbors.

Kuwait

FAST FACTS

Country:	State of Kuwait (Kuwait)
Capital:	Kuwait City
Government:	nominal constitutional monarchy
Independence:	16 June 1961 (from U.K.)
Population:	2,042,000 (includes 1,160,000 non-nationals) (2001 estimate)
Leaders:	Emir Jabir al-Ahmad al-Sabah; Prime Minister/ Crown Prince Saad Al-Sabah
Ethnicity:	45% Kuwaiti; 35% other Arab; 9% South Asian
Religion:	45% Sunni Muslim; 40% Shia Muslim; 15% other
Language:	Arabic, English
Literacy:	79% (82% men, 75% women; 1995 estimate)
Exports:	oil, fertilizers
Per capita GDP:	$15,200
Unemployment	2% (1996 estimate)
Percentage living in poverty:	N/A
Known for:	Saddam's 1990 annexation, which launched Desert Storm

Oil-rich and super-insular, this tiny kingdom ruled by the al-Sabah clan used to have a reputation for being rather snobby. Now it has a reputation for being emotionally damaged. Ever since 1990, when Iraq brutally annexed Kuwait for seven months—a heinous occupation filled with public torture, mass murders and thick black clouds of oil smoke billowing from blazing wells—the country seems to be suffering a collective case of post-traumatic stress disorder; at least 16 percent of the population suffers psychological ailments from the ordeal. The numbers of drug addicts and suicides are rising. Scarier is the new wave of crime, including sadistic acts by youth who seem to be letting loose the savagery they were once forced to watch. Now under military protection of the U.S., Kuwait often serves as a launchpad for American warplanes in the Middle East. Although a monarchy headed by Emir Jabir al-Ahmad al-Sabah, Kuwait has a parliament, which can overturn his decrees. Currently dominated by Muslim fundamentalists who are pushing for Shariah law, the Parliament recently vetoed the Emir's wish to give women the right to vote; nevertheless women can work and don't have to wear veils, at least for the moment.

A HAPPY IMAGE

A widely viewed shot beamed across the world by CNN shows the liberated Kuwaitis cheering joyously and waving American flags. How did they get those flags? American ad whiz John Rendon—on assignment for the U.S. government—handed them out moments before the camera rolled.

The Kuwaitis' post-war trauma aside, it's an affront to Americans that Kuwait's history books and new Persian Gulf War Museum skim over the fact that Kuwait was liberated in February 1991 by outside forces, specifically a coalition led by the U.S. A new concern: civilian attacks on U.S. military.

Ouch: Kuwait spent $5 billion to repair Iraqi-inflicted damage to oil wells. Bet Saddam never paid them back the billions they loaned him in the eighties either.

United Arab Emirates

FAST FACTS

Country:	United Arab Emirates
Capital:	Abu Dhabi
Government:	federation of monarchies
Independence:	December 1971 (from Britain)

Leaders:	Sheikh Zayid bin Sultan al-Nuhayyan; Prime Minister Maktum bin Rashid al-Maktum
Population:	2,408,000 (2001 estimate)
Ethnicity:	19% Emirati; 23% other Arab and Iranian; 50% South Asian (overseas workers)
Religion:	80% Sunni, 16% Shia
Languages:	Arabic, Persian, others
Literacy:	79% (79% men, 80% women; 1995 estimate)
Exports:	oil, natural gas, dates
Per capita GDP:	$22,800 (2000 estimate)
Unemployment	N/A
Percentage living in poverty:	N/A
Known for:	glitzy Dubai, bank scandals, world's tallest flagpole!

Not long ago a string of sleepy fishing villages stretching out along the Persian Gulf coast, the seven sheikdoms that are collectively the United Arab Emirates were best known for pearl diving during the first half of the twentieth century when they were British protectorates. The discovery of oil in the 1950s, however, changed all that and now one can find skyscraper-dominated modern cities dotting the crescent of land that was once a hotbed of piracy and is now one of the richest countries in the world.

IT PAYS TO MARRY LOCAL

With jumps in the number of UAE males taking foreign brides, Sheik Zayid instituted the "Marriage Fund": local men who marry local women qualify for hefty long-term, low-interest loans. The government also capped the amounts that could be spent on dowries and weddings, formerly notoriously expensive affairs. Those who throw too lavish a matrimonial bash can find themselves honeymooning in jail.

The UAE is generally the most open and Westernized of Arab countries: there's legalized drinking, dancing, yachting, horse racing, world-class golf and coral reefs to be found alongside the Gucci and Armani, the Rolex and the Mercedes Benz. Islam has gone liberal here—at the beach the locals may take a dip in their full veil and garb or they may trot around in thongs. Now transformed into a slick media center, the UAE has long been a financial hub. It has suffered a few banking scandals, however, and money that funded the 9/11 attack may have funneled through here. Also stocking up on U.S. arms.

LOOKEY HERE!

Jetsetter paradise Dubai may get the swanky crowd—Benazir Bhutto likes to hang here—but capital city Abu Dhabi is sure trying to get some attention: it has the world's tallest flagpole, and the world's tallest hotel—not to mention the world's biggest bowl of spaghetti. Tourists should be flocking!

Oman

FAST FACTS

Country:	Sultanate of Oman
Capital:	Muscat
Government:	monarchy
Independence:	1650, when Portuguese expelled
Population:	2,622,000 (includes 527,100 non-nationals; 2001 estimate)
Leader:	Sultan Qaboos bin Said al-Said
Ethnicity:	Arab, Baluchi, South Asian, African
Religion:	75% Ibadhi Muslim; also Sunni, Shia and Hindu
Language:	Arabic, English, Baluchi and more
Literacy:	near 80%
Exports:	petroleum, fish
Per capita GDP:	$7,700 (2000 estimate)
Unemployment:	N/A
Percentage living in poverty:	N/A
Known for:	legendary home of Sinbad the Sailor

Since 1970 when he swept out his alarmingly backward father, elegant Sultan Qaboos bin Said al-Said has led the coast-hugging land that was an eighteenth-century haven of piracy, into the twenty-first century.

Factoid: Frankincense, Oman's traditional treasure, was once worth more than gold.

Literally locked up (for a year) by his pa for his sinfully modern thoughts, Sultan Qaboos quickly unveiled them once he broke out of his palace-prison. He boosted the number of schools from three to almost a thousand; he built new roads and wrote a new constitution including freedom of the press. What's more, once his nutty father was out of the picture, people could start wearing sunglasses again. Taking over a nearly medieval land, Qaboos so revamped the medical system that Oman was recently rated fourth in the world for health care.

IS THAT NEAR LONDON?

Oman was long known for its navigational feats—it was a Portuguese colony until 1650—and its first official ambassador sailed to the U.S. in 1840.

Contemporary though he may be, Qaboos also keeps his roots in tradition: the sultan spends much of the year on the road, traveling from village to village and stopping by for a chat with his people. Visitors don't miss the sultan's love of the old ways: when Secretary of Defense Donald Rumsfeld dropped by in 2001, the American looked hilariously awkward sitting on the floor pillows of the Omani royal tent.

Base-friendly: *U.K. and U.S. military often use Oman's base, and Oman is buying lots of their arms.*

Qatar

FAST FACTS

Country:	State of Qatar
Capital:	Doha
Government:	changing from absolute monarchy to constitutional monarchy
Independence:	1971 from Britain
Population:	793,341 (2002 estimate; only 200,000 are native Qataris, the rest foreign workers)
Leaders:	Emir: Sheik Hamad bin Khalifa al-Thani; Prime Minister Abdullah bin Khalifa
Ethnicity:	40% Arab; 18% Indian; 18% Pakistan; 10% Iranian

Religion:	95% Sunni Muslim
Language:	Arabic
Literacy:	79.5% (79% men, 80% women; 1995 estimate)
Exports:	oil, natural gas, steel, fertilizers
Per capita GDP:	$21,200
Unemployment:	2.7% (2001 estimate)
Percentage living in poverty:	N/A
Known for:	being small but loud

LANGUAGE LESSON

Although popular pronunciation is "ca-TAR," Qatar is actually pronounced "CUT-er."

Résumé

This quiet oil-rich kingdom turned noisy when it plugged in the Al-Jazeera television network, headquarters in capital Doha.

Quick Tour

Sheik Hamad al-Thani: Qatar's maverick modernizer. (Source: Associated Press)

A tiny thumb of land that appears to be hitch-hiking off the Arabian Peninsula, Qatar is ruled by Sheik Hamad al-Thani, who's been stirring up a political storm with his modern, freewheeling ideas ever since he ousted his father from power, bloodlessly, in a 1995 coup. Best known for ripping away state censorship and starting up controversial Al-Jazeera—the TV network that broadcasts Western-style news 24-7 and has infuriated every leader in the Arab world (and possibly every *leader* in the world)—Sheik Hamad also gave women the right to vote, run for office and drive, even though they still are covered head to toe save for eye slits. Guiding the Islamic country toward democracy—the public is to vote for parliament in general elections in 2004—the sheik's goal is to diminish his role as absolute ruler and to transform Qatar into a constitutional monarchy. A 2001 WTO meeting in capital Doha was such a protester-free success that there's talk about holding more there. Also newsworthy: after signing a ten-year military agreement with the Persian gulf country in 2001, the U.S. is hauling much of its equipment and thousands of troops from Saudi Arabia to Qatar's Al-Udeid air base. Unlike Saudi Arabia, the Qatari government won't balk if the U.S. runs planes from there to attack Iraq.

Future Forecast

Their newly tapped gas field may make Qataris the world's richest citizens by 2020.

BALKAN BUNCH

Rising and falling between the Adriatic Sea and the Black Sea are the hauntingly beautiful forested hills known as the Balkans—which roll down from Romania and Moldova in the east to the former Yugoslavia in the west. Renowned for their beauty, islands, wine and wood, the lands have been rounded up by everyone from the Romans and the Ottomans to the Soviets. For much of the twentieth century, their loveliness has known sadness after sadness, from genocide and crazed dictators to brutal regimes and rape camps. Most of

the mad leaders are dead or put away, communist bullies are ousted, the rape camps are closed, the mass graves discovered.

Problems still lurk in the shadows, particularly in the east and the south, where Mafia gangs run the show and blaze a smuggling trail of arms, drugs and young girls. And except for relatively wealthy Slovenia, almost everywhere poverty has descended like a thick impenetrable fog. In the communist days they had money, but little to buy; now they have everything to buy but little money to buy it with. Hope is peeking out nevertheless from this dazzling piece of real estate, and one of the hopes is tourism. Another is cola: Coke and Pepsi are major employers in these parts.

Romania

FAST FACTS

Country:	Romania
Capital:	Bucharest
Government:	republic
Independence:	13 July 1878 (from Turkey)
Population:	22,317,730
Leaders:	Chief of State: President Ion Iliescu (since December 2000); Head of Government: Prime Minister Adrian Nastase (since December 2000)
Ethnicity:	89.5% Romanian; 7.1% Hungarian; 1.8% Roma; 0.5% German; 0.3% Ukrainian; 0.8% other
Religion:	70% Romanian Orthodox; 6% Roman Catholic; 6% Protestant; 18% unaffiliated
Language:	Romanian, Hungarian, German
Literacy:	97% both sexes
Exports:	textiles and footwear, metals and metal products
Per capita GDP:	$6,800
Unemployment:	9.1%
Percentage living in poverty:	44.5%
Known for:	Ceausescu

Think of the most riveting, heart-piercing, soul-shattering violin piece you've ever heard: that's Romania. Gorgeous in a nineteenth-century sort of way, castles peek through the forests, scarved peasants sell dusty apples and hand carved wood chess sets in the last rays of autumn sunlight, herds of sheep and goats meander across the backroads that thread through mountainous Transylvania.

A few hours away via a rickety communist-era train, creepy capital Bucharest—where orphans live under streets sniffing glue—still retains the feeling of Nicolae Ceausescu, the Stalin-like leader who crushed dissent with his brutal secret police, encouraged women to have six or more kids and plucked billions from the treasury. All the while, he was building himself new palaces, as his people starved to death. The dictator is dead—after decades of his hell, his people rose up and killed him in 1989—but corruption and thuggery are so prevalent you can almost smell them. Nevertheless, at least outside of eyesore Bucharest, there's a renaissance of sorts under way, in the country: the new free press is thriving, and pushing the envelope (journalists are sometimes tossed in jail), and a new generation of Type A's is learning every language they can in the hopes of linking up this country with the rest of the world.

SNAPSHOT

"The neighbors couldn't know," Marius told me as I delved into a bowl of wonderful, garlic-rich cream soup, unaware that it was made with tripe. "We listened to the radio in a dark back room, away from the windows." His grandmother used to tune into Radio Free Europe as well, back in the 1940s when the hope-filled broadcast first crackled over Romania's airwaves. "Her generation listened every night and they waited and waited for the Americans to come and save Romania from Russia. Some of them are still resentful because you never came."

I wondered how many Americans had known of Romania's plight after World War II when Russia invaded and turned it communist or how many today could find Romania on a map.

"Other people thought you would help us topple Ceausescu. But we waited and waited and the U.S. never came. So we had to do it ourselves."
—Interview with journalist Marius Dragomir, 1999

Bulgaria

FAST FACTS

Country:	Republic of Bulgaria
Capital:	Sofia
Government:	parliamentary democracy
Independence:	1991 (from Soviet Union)
Population:	7,621,000 (2002 estimate)
Leaders:	Head of Government: President Georgi Parvanov (January 2002); Head of State: Prime Minister (King) Simeon Saxe-Coburg-Gotha (July 2001)
Ethnicity:	84% Bulgarian; 10% Turk; 5% Roma gypsies
Religion:	84% Bulgarian Orthodox; 12% Muslim
Language:	Bulgarian
Literacy:	98% both sexes (1999)
Exports:	clothes, shoes, iron and steel, fuels

Per capita GDP:	$6,200 (2001 estimate)
Unemployment:	17.5% (2001 estimate)
Percentage living in poverty:	35% (2000)
Known for:	being unknown

With a Roman past and a folded terrain much like Romania's, Bulgaria may not have had Ceausescu, but communists successfully pillaged the once-rich land. Now corruption and Mafia gangs are the rule, but that may change someday. King Simeon—who was ousted when communists arrived in 1946—has returned to the heart of it all. Oddly, he's not the monarch—but the prime minister elected in 2001. In this tarnished, broken-down system where many live on $100 a month, who knows how much he can actually accomplish, but the billion-dollar loan from the IMF may help.

The Former Yugoslavia

Part of the Ottoman Empire until the early twentieth century, Yugoslavia was once the kingdom of Serbs, Croats and Slovenes. In 1932 the name Yugoslavia— "Land of the Southern Slavs"—was slapped on the region that extended from Slovenia in the north through Croatia, Bosnia and Serbia to Macedonia in the south. Once Marshal Tito came to power in 1929, the country functioned cohesively and prosperously—for a communist dictatorship—despite the ethnic divisions that had triggered plenty of battles before. It was when Tito died in 1980 and communism died a decade later that the country fell apart, launching the nasty Bosnian War.

Now what was once Yugoslavia is five countries: Slovenia, Croatia, Bosnia-Herzegovina, Macedonia and a country called Serbia and Montenegro—the latest name for the country that contains Serbia, Montenegro and the autonomous area Kosovo.

Slovenia

FAST FACTS	
Country:	Republic of Slovenia
Capital:	Ljubljana
Government:	democratic republic
Independence:	1991 (from Yugoslavia)

Population:	1,933,000 (2002)
Leaders:	Head of Government: President Mil Kucan (April 1990); Head of State: Prime Minister Janez Drnovsek (October 1992)
Ethnicity:	88% Slovene; 3% Croat; 2% Serb; 1% Bosniak (Muslim); also Yugoslav and Hungarian
Religion:	69% Roman Catholic; 2% Uniate Catholic; 1% Muslim; 1% Lutheran; 4% atheist
Language:	91% Slovenian; 6% Serbo-Croatian
Literacy:	N/A
Exports:	manufactured goods, machinery, chemicals, food
Per capita GDP:	$16,000 (2001 estimate)
Unemployment:	11.5% (2001 estimate)
Percentage living in poverty:	N/A
Known for:	being confused with Slovakia

Always the richest of the Yugoslav bunch, ethnically homogenous Slovenia—not to be confused with Slovakia—slipped off in 1991 without much of a fuss. Ready to join up with the European Union, this former northern outpost pushed up against the Alps is happy to shake off its past. The arts are thriving in hipster outposts such as capital Ljubljana. The good-looking people produce many an internationally known model.

Croatia

FAST FACTS

Country:	Republic of Croatia
Capital:	Zagreb
Government:	parliamentary democracy
Independence:	25 June 1991 (from Yugoslavia)
Population:	4,391,000 (2002 estimate)
Leaders:	Head of Government: President Stjepan Mesic (February 2000); Head of State: Prime Minister Ivica Racan (January 2000)
Ethnicity:	78% Croat; 12% Serb; 1% Bosniak (1991 estimate)
Religion:	77% Roman Catholic; 11% Orthodox; 1% Muslim

Language:	96% Croatian
Literacy:	97% (99% men, 95% women; 1991 estimate)
Exports:	transport equipment, textiles, foodstuffs, fuels
Per capita GDP:	$8,300 (2001 estimate)
Unemployment:	23%
Percentage living in poverty	4%
Known for:	Diocletian's digs, Dalmatian Islands

Scouts for Roman Emperor Diocletian searched the empire over for the most beautiful place to build his personal retirement community in the fourth century A.D. After six years of looking they pointed the emperor here. Lapped by the mood-ring Adriatic, the land of forested hills and sparkling white coastal cities now looks like it fell out of a Roman history book. The country's visual splendor—evident in Split, Dubrovnik and the many Dalmatian Islands—made it a tourism hot spot even in the communist days. In fact, it was the money that Croatia added to the treasury—along with Slovenia, it was essentially subsidizing Yugoslavia—that prompted Croatia to declare independence in 1991. Ironically, by doing so Croatia helped launch the subsequent *Bosnian* War that trashed its all-important tourism industry. Slowly but surely travelers are venturing back and Croatia feels like a country in rehab, slowly learning to walk again. Young people are buying up theaters and opera houses, festivals banned under communists are celebrated again, the summer's one big party, and a feeling of hope fills the air as visitors discover that the emperor's scouts searching for the finest land in the empire weren't wrong.

Bosnia-Herzegovina

FAST FACTS

Country:	Bosnia and Herzegovina
Capital:	Sarajevo
Government:	emerging federal democratic republic
Independence:	1992 (from Yugoslavia); founded 1995
Population:	3,954,000 (2002 estimate)
Leader:	Chairman of the Presidency: Beriz Belkic
Ethnicity:	31% Serb; 44% Bosniak; 17% Croatian; 6% Yugoslav

Religion:	40% Muslim; 31% Orthodox; 15% Roman Catholic; 4% Protestant
Language:	Croatian, Serbian, Bosnian
Literacy:	N/A
Exports:	miscellaneous manufactures, crude materials
Per capita GDP:	$1,800 (2001 estimate)
Percentage living in poverty:	N/A
Unemployment	40% (2001 estimate)
Known for:	being site of nasty Bosnian War

Nationalism and ethnic chafing are nothing new here: the assassination of Austrian Archduke Franz Ferdinand by a Serb nationalist in 1914, after all, was what launched the First World War. And it was the ethnic tensions between Bosnia's mixed ethnicities—Serbs, Croats and Muslims—that blasted this country into the most brutal civil war of the 1990s, complete with genocide and rape camps, when it decided to break free of Yugoslavia in 1992. Serbs wanted Bosnians to become part of "Greater Serbia," Croats wanted Bosnia to be part of "Greater Croatia," and Muslims wanted it to be independent and the result was a bloody mess. Since the Dayton Agreement of 1995, it's been split into two republics—one Serbian, one Muslim-Croat. The groups still don't much get along, and the blood-soaked land where more than 250,000 died and thousands were raped during the Bosnian War is just limping along.

Serbia and Montenegro
(formerly Federal Republic of Yugoslavia)

FAST FACTS

Country:	Serbia and Montenegro
Capital:	Belgrade
Government:	republic
Population:	10,657,000 (2002)
Leaders:	Head of Government: President Vojislav Kostunica (October 2000); Head of State: Prime Minister Dragisa Pesic (July 2001)
Ethnicity:	63% Serb; 17% Albanian; 5% Montenegrin; 3.3% Hungarian (1991 estimate)

Religion:	65% Orthodox; 19% Muslim; 4% Roman Catholic
Language:	95% Serbian; 5% Albanian
Literacy:	93% (97% men, 89% women; 1991)
Exports:	manufactured goods, food and live animals
Per capita GDP:	$2,250 (2001 estimate)
Percentage lving in poverty:	30%
Unemployment	30% (2001 estimate)
Known for:	Kosovo, former President Slobodan Milosevic, Serbian nationalism

Former President Slobodan Milosevic is gone—sent to the Hague for a war crimes trial—and they gave it a new name in 2002, but the country that comprises Serbia, Montenegro and the autonomous province of Kosovo isn't exactly united. Montenegro wants to split off, and the historically symbolic region of Kosovo—filled with ethnic Albanians, mostly Muslim—wants independence as well. Plenty of horrible memories haunt the place—thousands of Muslims were killed in Kosovo in March 1999, which prompted a NATO attack on Serbia. That left a lingering legacy as well: depleted uranium from ammunition is leaching into the soil.

KOSOVO

Never mind the countryside's steeply folded green hills that look so enchanting. This piece of real estate has a twisted history: in 1389, an entire army of Serbs (and probably Croats and Muslims) was wiped out battling Ottoman Turks in the "Field of Blackbirds." Milosevic latched on to that battle to launch his Serbian nationalism campaign wherein contemporary Muslims (many Albanian) were viewed as fourteenth-century Ottomans. Albanians, who are the majority population, claim the territory as theirs too—and there's a chronic fear in this land where nationalism lives on that Kosovo will become part of Greater Albania.

THE BALKAN WAR

Ethnic strife in this land of Serb, Muslim and Croat may have been stomped out under dictator Tito, but when he died it gradually rose back to the surface. Serbian leader Slobodan Milosevic fueled the Balkan War, which broke out in 1992, with a hard-fiddled Serbian nationalism. Milosovic so convinced some Serbs that they were the superior bunch—who'd fought harder and sacrificed more than any other ethnic group—that it was somehow justified that Muslims in Bosnia were rounded up and slaughtered; in Srebrenica, which was sup-posed to be a UN-monitored safe haven, five thousand Muslims were massa-cred in one fell swoop. So important was the Serbian seed and the hope of establishing a "Greater Serbia" that rape camps were set up where women were kept until they became pregnant with Serbian offspring. Tens of thou-sands had died by the time the international community entered the scene in 1993, but even then Milosevic's "Serbia has arisen!" campaign wasn't over. In 1999, Milosevic unleashed his nationalist machine on Albanian Muslims in Kosovo, killing thousands, and prompting NATO to launch an offensive on Serbia. NATO accidentally bombed the Chinese embassy in Belgrade, and accidentally killed hundreds of civilians as it bombed bridges, but despite the clumsiness of the effort, they stopped Milosevic's dance of death. In 2001 the former leader was rounded up and tried in a UN war tribunal in the Hague, Netherlands. Milosevic denies the charges of genocide leveled against him and maintains he was merely trying to keep peace in Yugoslavia; as for the Srebrenica massacre, he says that was all a French plot. Whatever you say, Slobo.

Albania

FAST FACTS

Country:	Republic of Albania (Albania)
Capital:	Tirana
Government:	theoretical "emerging democracy"
Independence:	28 November 1912 (from the Ottoman Empire)
Population:	3,546,000 (2002 estimate)
Leaders:	President of the Republic Alfred Moisu; Prime Minister Fatos Nano
Ethnicity:	95% Albanians; 3% Greeks
Religion:	70% Muslim; 20% Albanian Orthodox; 10% Roman Catholic
Language:	Albanian, Greek
Literacy:	93% both sexes (1997 estimate)
Exports:	textiles, shoes, asphalt, metals, oil
Per capita GDP:	$3,800 both sexes (2001 estimate)
Unemployment	16 to 25% (2000 estimate)
Percentage living in poverty	30% (2001 estimate)
Known for:	slave trade, Mafia

The CIA optimistically calls Albania's government an "emerging democracy" now that its nutty Stalin-loving, xenophobic dictator Enver Hoxha is dead. But that may be overstating the case in the dirt-poor country, where everything is falling apart, the electricity often konks out, and there's no collection service to pick up the trash that heaps up in garbage mountains outside buildings. Filled with the ethnic group most hated by Christian Orthodox Serbs, Muslim Albania has never fully pulled itself together—ever—but the road was particularly rough in the 1990s: not only were Albanians targets of genocidal sweeps in Kosovo, but the whole economy almost collapsed over a pyramid scheme. The Mafia—Eastern European style—reigns in this gangland that serves as an illicit transit point to Western Europe. A frequent cargo: sex slaves, often young village girls from Moldova or Romania who are sold from owner to owner, their value increasing the closer they get to wealthy European capitals such as Amsterdam and Vienna. The corruption and woe has piled up higher than the trash: chronic crime and gang fighting prevent the government from having much of an effect on the place.

See www.armchairdiplomat.com for other important Balkan countries, including Macedonia and Greece.

UNITED KINGDOM

FAST FACTS

Country:	United Kingdom of Great Britain and Northern Ireland (United Kingdom)
Capital:	London
Government:	constitutional monarchy
Independence:	Unified 900
Population:	59,778,002 (2002)
Leaders:	Head of State: Queen Elizabeth II; Head of Government: Prime Minister Tony Blair (since 1997)
Ethnicity:	82% English; 10% Scottish; 24% Irish; 1.9% Welsh; 3% Indian, Pakistani, other
Religion:	45% Anglican; 15% Catholic; 1.6% Muslim; 1.4% Presbyterian; 1.4% Methodist; also Sikh, Hindu, Jewish
Language:	English (The Queen's Kind)
Literacy:	99% both sexes (2000 estimate)
Exports:	manufactured goods, fuels, chemicals, food
Per capita GDP:	$24,700 (2001 estimate)
Unemployment:	5.1%
Percentage living in poverty:	17%
Known for:	the Bard, the Beatles, Lady Di

Standout Qualities

Bloody history: the Tower of London, wars with Scotland
Bloody ban: no death penalty anymore
Bloody Yanks: the U.S. pulls them into military operations

Résumé

Never mind its checkered past of colonialism, opium wars, redrawing maps and exploiting countries such as India to benefit England's textile market and secure almighty tea. Ever since World War II, the U.K. has been the U.S.' best friend: linking arms in wars and pursuit of globalized corporate democracy, the two Western leaders are united in love of oil, arms sales and doing what is proper, especially if there's a quid or two to be made.

Quick Tour

So much of the U.K. is, well, charming, if overpriced and plagued by gray skies and rain. London's double-decker buses and huge black cabs, the quaint country villages ringed by pastures and lakes, Shakespearean treasures, the rolling green hills of Scotland and its mountaintop jewel Edinburgh Castle, the romantic inns and salty winds of

Northern Ireland and those funny British names—like Picadilly Circus—are but a few things that snagged tourists for centuries before the Harry Potter craze. The British Tourism Board is mighty thankful that J. K. Rowling's magic-infused childrens' novels put them back on the map: tourism was devastated several times since the 1990s from hoof-and-mouth disease and mad cow, both of which trampled the economy and resulted in unsightly pyres of flaming cattle.

BRITISH POISON PENS

Did they draw the map lines with toxic ink? Or were they simply selfish and/or thoughtless? Almost every border the British mapped out is a site of major wars and tension. Examples: Kashmir, Palestine, Iraq/Kuwait border, Iraq/Iran border.

UNITED KINGDOM V. GREAT BRITAIN V. IRELAND

The United Kingdom includes England, Wales, Scotland—which share the same island and are together Great Britain—as well as Northern Ireland, six counties from the island that sits a bit to the west. Although all of Ireland was once part of Great Britain, the bulk of Ireland became a separate, nonaffiliated country in 1921.

Politically, the monarchy—like the "Changing of the Guard" at Buckingham Palace—is mostly for show. Power resides with the House of Commons and rests most firmly on the shoulders of the prime minister—currently Tony Blair, whose relationship with President Bush is rather controversial. Shouldn't be a surprise, though. The Brits and the Yanks have had "a special relationship" for decades, particularly since the Churchill-Roosevelt alliance weathered World War II; Thatcher and Reagan kept the bonds strong as well.

Tony—as he prefers to be called by the masses—has backed President George W. Bush on almost everything except the latter's tariff on imported steel. In fact, Tony sometimes acts like a faux U.S. ambassador, an appearance that annoys his people and raises a collective eyebrow within the European Union, which is often more critical of American hawkish moves.

Tony's support for George was spoofed in a 2002 video by musician George Michael. In the video, "Shoot the Dog," President Bush continually tosses a bone to a disinterested dog. Prime Minister Blair, however, continually retrieves it.

Though a major player in the EU, the U.K. has yet to adopt the euro, though like other European countries it's feeling the strain of immigration. Its policy of offering political asylum to those who faced death penalties in their own countries brought many a thug to the fair land; asylum policies are now tightening.

Factoid: *Britain has a thriving arms industry: in 1986 under Prime Minister Margaret Thatcher, the so-called Al-Yamama Deal—a $32 billion arms sale to Saudi Arabia in 1985—was described as the biggest sale of anything to anyone ever.*

The long-running headache of the bomb-prone Irish Republican Army (IRA)—which wanted Northern Ireland to reunite with Ireland—has lessened since the "Good Friday Agreement of 1998" and arms burials in 2002. Offshoot groups, however, still sometimes set off car bombs and spark unrest in Belfast. The IRA, some say, actually developed the concept of the militant "cell." As a result, regardless of what the main branch does, some cells act independently and can't be controlled.

Despite a certain backwardness built into its legal system—pubs still close at 11 P.M. and taxis are legally bound to carry hay in their trunks (for horses)—the U.K. can also be extraordinarily progressive: a signatory of the Kyoto Protocol, it has reduced its greenhouse gas emissions by more than 12 percent well ahead of time goals. Although there are plenty of tabloids, much of the British media is remarkable: BBC News, the *Economist* magazine and the *Financial Times* are but three inspiring standouts.

MEDIA INSPIRATION

No wonder the Brits are so geopolitically savvy: with reporters everywhere, the noncommercial British Broadcasting Corporation provides the world's finest, most in-depth reporting. Funded by annual licensing fees—about $100 per year—from those who own TV sets, the BBC runs an amazing Internet site too.

Future Forecast

Tony will lose popular support if he continues to run after George's bones.

LANGUAGE LESSON

Brits toss in extra letters—as in favour, colour, programme, traveller and aluminium—and meanings of words are often different. When a Brit says he's "pissed," that means he's drunk; if he says he feels "giddy," he's about to faint.

Hot Spots

Belfast, Northern Ireland: Still site of tensions between IRA splinter groups and Ulster Boys; entire parts of town are segmented as Catholic or Protestant.

London, England: Some radical Muslims entrenched here.

Edinburgh, Scotland: Site of Europe's biggest arts festival every August.

Hot Shots

Tony Blair: Prime Minister since 1997, heading the "New Labour" Party, Tony promised that pubs would stay open longer if he was reelected in 2000. He apparently forgot his pub promise, but that's only one reason his people are getting ticked. His friendship with the U.S. is more of a concern, as are the growing numbers of poor in this pricey land. Some call him a poodle.

Queen Elizabeth II: Reigning monarch since 1952, she's survived her mother, her sister and her daughter-in-law Di in nominally overseeing the postwar boom. Crown Prince Charles waits in the wings.

Irish Republican Army (IRA): The original goal of the Catholic IRA and its political arm, Sinn Fein, was to force the British government to allow Northern Ireland reunite with Ireland. That goal has been at least temporarily abandoned, and the IRA actually issued apologies to the public in 2002 for its decades of violence.

Shootout: *With gun-related crime climbing, the U.K. is considering slapping a five-year jail sentence on those found possessing automatic weapons.*

WESTERN EUROPE

So what if for most of its history Western Europe was divided and united by battling empires and dynasties? Two world wars and globalization pushed the diverse countries together into the powerful European Union—which some call the U.S. of Europe—even though all the countries remain autonomous. Now they share a common currency, food quotas, high standards of living and a gnawing concern about immigration.

EU: *The EU unites most major Western European countries except Norway and Switzerland. The U.K., Sweden and Denmark don't use the Euro.*

Belgium

FAST FACTS

Country:	Kingdom of Belgium
Capital:	Brussels
Government:	parliamentary democracy under a constitutional monarch
Independence:	1830 (from the Netherlands)
Population:	10,275,000 (2002 estimate)
Leaders:	Head of State: King Albert II; Prime Minister: Guy Verhofstadt
Ethnicity:	58% Flemish; 31% Walloon; 11% other

Religion:	75% Roman Catholic; 25% Protestant/other
Language:	French, Flemish (Dutch)
Literacy:	98%
Exports:	machinery, chemicals, diamonds
Per capita GDP:	$26,100 (2001 estimate)
Unemployment:	6.8%
Percentage living in poverty:	4%
Known for:	chocolate, mussels, Hercule Poirot

Just about every European country has at one point or another occupied this strategic bit of land between France and Germany. Once part of the Netherlands, it broke off in 1830, but its history is still reflected in the present: residents of the southern half—Wallonia—speak French and those in the northern half—Flanders—speak Dutch, while capital Brussels is officially bilingual. The Walloons and the Flemish aren't the closest of friends, in part because the federal government currently favors economic development in the Flemish north. Nevertheless, the charming country is castle-dotted and culture-filled and it's a powerhouse given its small size: both NATO and the European Union are headquartered here. Brussels has been dubbed the "Capital of Europe," although few seem to know it outside of the city.

Parlay vous anglais?: A 2001 train crash that killed eight was caused because the signalmen—one Walloon, one Flemish—spoke different languages.

Factoid: Diamond center Antwerp is also a fashion hot spot. Newsweek named it one of the world's new, "cool cities" in 2002.

Germany

FAST FACTS

Country:	Federal Republic of Germany
Capital:	Berlin
Government:	Federal Republic
Independence:	1871 formation of unified Germany (Second German Reich); 1990 East and West reunified
Population:	83,252,000 (2000 estimate)
Leaders:	Chancellor Gerhard Schroeder; President Johannes Rau

Ethnicity:	91.5% German; 2.4% Turkish; 6.1% Serb, Croat, other
Religion:	36% Protestant; 34% Roman Catholic; 3.7% Muslim; 28.3% unaffiliated
Language:	German
Literacy:	99% (1997 estimate)
Exports:	machinery, cars, chemicals
Per capita GDP:	$26,200 (2001 estimate)
Unemployment:	9.4%
Percentage living in poverty:	N/A
Known for:	the crumbling Berlin Wall, Wiener schnitzel, Hitler

The EU land with the most people and, formerly, the fittest economy, Germany—the economic locomotive of Europe—seems to be losing steam: high unemployment and slowed growth are unintended side effects of reunification between West and East Germany. East Germany, communist for forty-four years following World War II, still lags behind in every way, from income to infrastructure, and with the jobless rate at 20 percent in the east, more and more youths are heading to the western part of the country.

Factoid: The Berlin Wall that split the eastern and western parts of the city was erected in 1961 and razed in 1989.

With Chancellor Gerhard Schroeder in the driver's seat, Germany also has had a few foreign policy wrecks. His run-ins with France's President Jacques Chirac over agricultural matters frayed what was until recently the German-French power duet of the EU. And while Schroeder sent German troops into Afghanistan after 9/11, his public criticisms of the U.S. "adventure" in Iraq raised bristles in the U.S., which has had friendly German relations for four decades. When his justice minister opined in late 2002 that the Iraq invasion was a move to keep the U.S. public from paying attention to domestic problems—and when she reportedly indirectly likened President Bush to Adolf Hitler—German-U.S. relations overnight became extremely chilly.

Factoid: Schroeder authorized payment of $5 billion to survivors of Nazi labor camps in Eastern Europe.

Influenced by a popular environment-friendly Green Party, Germany is heading toward a non-nuclear future: by 2021, all nuclear plants are to be shut down. Foreign Minister Joschka Fischer—of the Green Party—is widely considered Germany's most respected postwar politician.

Factoid: *The government is trying to ban the National Democratic Party—a small, but growing, neo-Nazi political group.*

France

FAST FACTS

Country:	French Republic
Capital:	Paris
Government:	republic
Independence:	1793 (from monarchy)
Population:	59,766,000 (2002 estimate)
Leader:	President Jacques Chirac
Ethnicity:	Celtic and Latin, with Teutonic, Slavic, North African, Indochinese and Basque minorities
Religion:	83% Roman Catholic; 10% Muslim; 2% Protestant; 1% Jewish
Language:	French (but of course)
Literacy:	95% (2001 estimate)
Exports:	machinery, cars, oil, aircraft
Per capita GDP:	$24,400
Unemployment:	10%
Percentage living in poverty:	N/A
Known for:	baguettes, berets, buttery accents

Europe's second largest economy, like Germany's, is plagued by unemployment. Unlike Germany, it relies heavily on agricultural subsidies from the European Union—which is why its feud with Germany started in the first place. Immigration woes caused an unforeseen swing to the conservative right in 2002, and saw right-wing Jean-Marie Le Pen in the final presidential runoff. Nobody really thought he would win, and power once again rests in the hands of President Jacques Chirac, who is sometimes the target of French complaints that he's overdeveloping the country, and tossing contracts to his friends.

Beyond its patisseries, bon bons and cafes, France has plenty of nuke plants including breeder reactors, but that doesn't stop tourists from flocking to Paris, "the City of Light," or to Provence in the south: France is the top travel destination in the world, not to mention the only place in the world where people say "Ooo la la" without laughing.

Many Algerians moved to France after Algeria won its independence from France in 1962.

Italy

FAST FACTS

Country:	Italian Republic
Capital:	Rome
Government:	republic
Independence:	1861
Population:	57,716,000 (2002 estimate)
Leaders:	Prime Minister Silvio Berlusconi; President Carlo Azeglio Ciampi
Ethnicity:	Italian
Religion:	Roman Catholic
Language:	Italian
Literacy:	98%
Exports:	engineering products, textiles, clothes, cars
Per capita GDP:	$24,300 (2001 estimate)
Unemployment:	10%; the south has a 20% unemployment rate (2001 estimate)
Percentage living in poverty:	N/A
Known for:	Michelangelo, Leonardo da Vinci, pasta

Italy is justly known for two things: a mind-blowing culture that among other things created (and preserved) Renaissance art and architecture, and a screwy government with dozens of parties and the occasional porn star senator. Things haven't changed with media mogul Silvio Berlusconi as prime minister: he's made several political gaffes and tried to gag the media that criticized him.

Whatsa Matter You? *In 2001, Berlusconi said that the September 11 attack proved that Western countries were superior to Islamic countries— and prompted an international scandal.*

With a young population that frequently lives at home into their forties or later—poor Mama is cooking and cleaning till she kicks—the birth rate is plummeting. Now immigrants—such as Africans and Chinese—are having more children than the Italians. Still heavily regionalized and heavy on the dialects, Italy has a hard time getting over grudges: for example, Florentines still consider the residents of Arezzo, some forty miles away, as foreigners due to some dispute several centuries back. Often provincial and sometimes racist, most Italians are open about their disdain for Sicilians, who are the lowest on the totem pole.

The country is also economically divided: the north (which includes Florence and Milan) is better educated and richer, and the south, except for Rome, has a 20 percent unemployment rate and is not as well developed. The Italian police and *carabinieri* have cracked several militant cells, including one that planned to pump cyanide gas into the U.S. Embassy in Rome.

Another cause for concern: Puglia. The heel of "the boot" boasts some of the finest cooking in the country, and a Mafia that is more brutal than most. Port city Bari is an entry point for smuggling from Albania, including Eastern European "sex slaves."

The Netherlands (aka Holland)

FAST FACTS

Country:	Kingdom of the Netherlands
Capital:	Amsterdam; government seat: the Hague
Government:	constitutional monarchy
Independence:	1579 (from Spain)
Population:	15,906,068 (2002)
Leaders:	Head of State: Queen Beatrix (since 1980); Prime Minister: Jan Peter Balkenende
Ethnicity:	83% Dutch; 9% Moroccan, Turk, Surinamese (1999 estimate)
Religion:	31% Roman Catholic; 21% Protestant; 4.4% Muslim; 40% unaffiliated (1998 estimate)
Language:	Dutch, Frisian
Literacy:	99% (2000 estimate)
Exports:	machinery, chemicals, fuels, food
Per capita GDP:	$25,800 (2001 estimate)
Unemployment:	2.6% (2000 estimate)
Percentage living in poverty:	N/A
Known for:	windmills, wooden shoes, Anne Frank

In many ways, the Netherlands is the most civilized of countries: the Dutch are more prone to ride on their bikes than drive in cars, they legalized euthanasia and prostitution, and tolerate marijuana and hashish while taking a hard line on hard drugs. Multilingual, well educated and generally well traveled, the Dutch typically are of the liberal persuasion and have an open mind on most matters—at least until recently.

Politician Pim Fortuyn—brazen, bald and openly gay—was the first to publicly point out in 2002 what before then was only whispered: most of the Turkish and Moroccan immigrants that the Dutch invited in during the 1980s to perform "menial labor" have stayed, many have not learned Dutch, many are now unemployed and many are leaning on the welfare system.

Dutch Treats: Holland is not the name of the country of windmills and canals: Holland is the name of a province, or rather two of them—one North Holland, one South Holland. To be proper, use "the Netherlands." But, then again, nobody does.

Fortuyn stirred up a huge national debate but he was shot down a few weeks before the election. His assassin was not a Muslim—a group at whom many of Fortuyn's comments were directed—but a young vegetarian Dutchman who was upset by the politician's views on animal rights. The issues he raised, however, live on: immigration regulations are getting tougher, and now everyone who wants to become a Dutch citizen must learn the language, which is no easy feat.

Factoid: The Hague is the headquarters for the International Criminal Court, where Serbian war criminal Slobodan Milosevic was tried.

EUROPEAN IMMIGRANTS

One reason for high populations of Turks, Moroccans and other foreigners in countries such as the Netherlands and France: "guest worker programs" of the 1970s and 1980s—during which non-nationals were invited in for a few years to perform "menial" jobs. Many of the temporary workers stayed.

Come on Down: In 2004, the EU will expand from fifteen to twenty-five countries. New entries: the Baltics—Lithuania, Latvia, Estonia—Poland, Hungary, the Czech Republic, the Slovak Republic, Slovenia, Malta and Greek-controlled Cyprus.

RWANDA

FAST FACTS

Country:	Rwandese Republic (Rwanda)
Capital:	Kigali
Government:	republic
Independence:	1962 (from Belgium)
Population:	7,398,000 (2002 estimate)
Leaders:	President Paul Kagame; Prime Minister Bernard Makuza
Ethnicity:	84% Hutu; 15% Tutsi; 1% Twa
Religion:	57% Roman Catholic; 26% Protestant
Language:	French, Kinyarwanda, English
Literacy:	48% (52% men, 45% women; 1995 estimate)
Exports:	coffee, tea, sorghum
Per capita GDP:	$1,000 (2001 estrimate)
Unemployment:	N/A
Percentage living in poverty:	70% (2000 estimate)
Known for:	Being ignored except for its gorillas and massacres

Standout Qualities

Cut off: landlocked, undeveloped
Cut off: little media connection to outside world
Cut off: bones scattered across country

Résumé

Most of Rwanda's 7 million people are peasants, tilling small plots of red dirt to grow sweet potatoes and sorghum and living simple lives complete with church on Sunday. But in the spring of 1994, farmers put down their hoes, grabbed their machetes and hacked up their neighbors and fellow Christians, even children in schools. The voice from the little box told them to.

Factoid: *Dian Fossey made Rwanda's gorillas famous.*

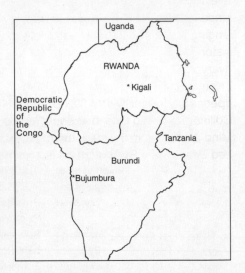

Quick Tour

Rwanda doesn't exactly jump out on a map. The landlocked central African country of small villages and grassy hills is one of Africa's most crowded and tiniest settlements—a geographical afterthought so small it could fit into Tennessee four times. Nevertheless it stands out for a brutal massacre so intense that on a killing-per-day basis it made the Nazis seem tame.

DANGEROUS FAVORITISM

Until 1962, Rwanda was a de facto colony of Germany and later Belgium. The Europeans favored the tall Tutsi tribe, while shunning the rounder, shorter Hutus. So important was the tribal distinction that Rwandans were forced to carry tribe-identifying ID cards.

But what happened in Rwanda is significant not just for its staggering numbers or the horrifying fact that the world crossed its arms, sighed and just let it happen. What is most peculiar about the horrible hundred days when Rwandans chopped up and bludgeoned 800,000 of their fellow Rwandans was that the mass murder was commandeered via radio.

MURDEROUS MEDIA MOGULS

Three men who owned Rwandan radio stations, TV stations and newspapers are currently being tried for inspiring genocide in what is known as "The Media Trial." Also being tried: propagandistic musicians.

In 1994, while Americans zapped on their TV for the latest on knee-whacking Tonya Harding and O. J. Simpson's white Bronco, the idea that voices could be heard from boxes was still magical in most of Rwanda. Commoners didn't have television, newspapers could be bought only in the capital. What did it matter since only half of the people could read? In lives marked by drudgery, where singing and music helped pass the time, the recent appearance of small transistor radios had radicalized rural life. Suddenly everyone had them, and everyone played them, blasting African folk songs as they hacked clods of dirt or sunk ankle-deep into mud pulling out weeds. In late 1993, the world had opened up further with a flick of the dial thanks to a new station, Radio Mille Colline—or Radio One Thousand Hills, a reference to Rwanda's rolling terrain. Mind-altering from the start, the radio station unleashed the Rolling Stones and Led Zeppelin on Rwanda, then fed them the Beatles and grunge.

HISTORIC RIVALS

The Tutsis, often herdsmen and sometimes kings, lorded over the vertically challenged Hutus, typically farmers, for centuries. That changed with independence in 1959, when Hutu governments became the norm. In the 1990s a new nationalistic movement was born called "Hutu Power."

And then, in between the songs, wise-cracking commentators began making jokes about Tutsis—the minority population in the Hutu majority country; soon they were calling Tutsis cockroaches and snakes. But by April 1994, the DJ's messages had accelerated beyond mere racial slurs.

When a plane carrying Rwandan President Juvénal Habyarimana and Burundi President Cyprien Ntaryamira—both Hutus—was shot by a surface-to-air missile and crashed in a fireball near the capital, Radio One Thousand Hills reported to its mostly Hutu listeners that their old rivals the Tutsis were behind it. That may have been true. But the rest of what the radio said was lies: the Tutsis were attacking Hutu villages, the DJs reported. The Tutsis had disguised themselves as peasants, they were in the markets, on the farms, they were going to exterminate each and every Hutu. In between broadcasting the names and addresses of Tutsis, the radio announcers urged the Hutu peasants to pick up their machetes and stop the Tutsi takeover.

There was no Tutsi takeover, but the Hutu peasants didn't know that. Besides, the centuries when Tutsis had ruled over them was part of Hutu history. Thousands upon thousands upon thousands of Hutus did what the radio said. They got their government-issued machetes they'd received the year before—

along with the radios, and they slashed and bludgeoned for three months and ten days, hacking their way into churches and chopping up parishioners, rooting out the huddled masses hiding in convents and setting them ablaze, tossing grenades into schools, bashing in the heads of babies and then their mothers. Corpses were pitched into ditches that literally "wiggled" as the still living tried in vain to get out. Streams were clogged with dead bodies. And at night the piles of bodies strewn in the streets were devoured by dogs.

PROPAGANDA PREZ

Some investigators believe deceased President Habyarimana was very much part of the Kill-the-Tutsi plot that appears to be part of the wider agenda of "Hutu Power."

GUILTY NUNS

Another disturbing element: some Hutu church leaders were implicated in the attempted genocide. Among them a mother superior—who told Hutus that Tutsis were hiding in her convent. Another nun gave the killers the gasoline they used to set the Tutsis on fire. One nun was sentenced to twelve years in prison—the other to fifteen—by a Belgian court.

Viewers around the world gasped and changed the channel. Leaders around the world did the same. Eighteen Americans had died in a Somalian peacekeeping mission the year before. The U.S. was wary, weary and Africa-ed out. The UN was also reluctant to reenter: the UN Security Council ignored both the warnings that the massacres would take place and the pleas from their peacekeepers to let them seize weapons from Hutus. Meanwhile, Tutsis with money paid Hutus to shoot them; chopping took too long.

After ten Belgian peacekeepers were killed at the onset, all Belgian and French troops pulled out. Left behind: troops with ammunition to last half an hour.

Three months later, a Tutsi armed force from Uganda put out the Hutu fire. Fearing revenge, Hutus fled—many running to the Democratic Republic of the Congo. Tutsis sought them out there, killing tens of thousands and helping stir up a civil war.

HUTU INVOLVEMENT

Not all Hutus were killers. To judge from numbers of the accused, perhaps one in fifty or so actively participated. Moderate Hutus who protested the massacre were often killed themselves; fearing for their lives, many just shut up.

Meanwhile, as the corpses rotted and were eaten by maggots, the massacre's death tolls shocked the world and international guilt spread like a blistering magma. The UN stood accused and ashamed, as did Belgium, France and the U.S.—all of whom knew what was happening and did nothing. The prime minister of Belgium flew in for a personal apology, as did President Clinton four years after the fact.

But for all the foreign powers that didn't intervene, it was Rwanda that did this to herself. Now Rwanda has a new flag, a new national anthem and a new peace treaty with the Democratic Republic of the Congo. More than one hundred thousand Hutus accused of aiding the mass murder await their trials in dirty jails, and hundreds have been sentenced to death; every few days the public can watch the convicted Hutus don black hoods before facing a firing squad.

Safety Valve? The government believed that by witnessing the executions, Tutsis would be less likely to go on a vengeful killing spree.

Future Forecast

The economy is slowly recovering, refugees are returning, international governments have given guilt-ridden billions in aid, and the World Bank is funding Rwandan projects. Nevertheless, the future of this tiny country isn't particularly bright. But the more quickly Rwanda can move away from the past, the better.

Hot Spots

Borders: Tutsi forces are headquartered in Uganda to the north; rebels and refugees make the Democratic Republic of the Congo to the west a minefield.

Hot Shots

Paul Kagame: President since 2000, serious, bright and a Tutsi, Kagame sent troops into the Democratic Republic of Congo when that country's government wouldn't help round up Hutu leaders hiding there. He's since negotiated a peace treaty. Stresses his nationality more than his tribe, and might be able to deflate future ethnic tensions.

Canadian Army General Romeo Dallaire: Left behind to witness the travesty, his frantic calls were ignored. The experience so devastated him that he quit the army, tried to kill himself, and now takes handfuls of medicine every day. He also wrote a book about the ordeal: *Shake Hands with the Devil.* Number of UN peacekeepers in Rwanda at time of massacre: 2,600, several hundred of them entirely unarmed.

Tutsis: The tall tribe preferred by colonial powers and for several centuries the dominant tribe in Rwanda.

Hutus: The shorter tribe who killed more than 800,000 Tutsis in 1994.

Twa: Only 1 percent of the population, this tribe is shorter than the Hutus: they're Pygmies.

THAILAND

FAST FACTS

Country:	Kingdom of Thailand (formerly Siam)
Capital:	Bangkok
Government:	constitutional monarchy
Independence:	founded 1350
Population:	62,354,000 (2002 estimate)
Leaders:	King Bhumibol Adulyadez; Prime Minister Thaksin Shinawata
Ethnicity:	75% Thai; 14% Chinese; 11% other
Religion:	95% Buddhist; 4% Muslim
Language:	Thai, English dialects
Literacy:	94% (96% men; 92% women)
Exports:	computers, textiles, rice
Per capita GDP:	$6,600 (2001 estimate)
Unemployment:	3.9% (2001 estimate)
Percentage living in poverty:	12.5% (1998 estimate)
Known for:	sex trade, beautiful beaches, cheap HIV drugs

Standout Qualities

Royal Highness: cool king
Rich leader: prime minister a billionaire
Religious tolerance: Buddhist style "live and let loose"

Résumé

Sex, drugs and elephants made Thailand stand out on the world tourist map, but it's the creative ways that its leaders confront problems that make Thailand stand out as a world inspiration. Doesn't hurt to have a benevolent king with a gift for inventing.

Quick Tour

It's hard to imagine when you're sitting in traffic-choked Bangkok—where taxis, rickshaws and sputtering three-wheeled "tuk-tuks" clog the streets alongside trumpeting pachyderms, and elevated trains whiz past ultramodern high-rises of glass—but not far away rice farmers live in forested villages of thatched open-air huts, wooden rafts replace cars, and entertainment may be as simple as launching a candle-carrying banana leaf downstream. It's also difficult to believe when you're standing mezmerized in a cloud of swirling incense, staring at an ancient jade Buddha, with the gut-vibrating chanting of orange-robed monks echoing through a temple, that around the corner neon lights flicker, house music pulses and go-go girls prance about in orange thongs. But Thailand, "The Land of Smiles," is a funny paradox of the modern and traditional, mayhem and ritual—a country where political parties have names like "Thais Love Thais" and governments are chronically accused of corruption, where the sex trade thrives but *The King and I* was banned, where there have been nineteen presidential overthrows since 1932, but where the monarch—kind King Bhumibol—is steadfastly adored.

So it makes perfect sense when politicians propose that prostitution be legalized and taxed, so that politicians can pump up their salaries and avoid taking bribes. It likewise make sense that urban-dwelling corporate hotshots keep flower-filled "ghost houses" outside their homes to give angry spirits a place to camp.

SPIRITS IN A MATERIAL WORLD

Thais are obsessed with ghosts: food, flowers, bottles of booze are left in mini-shrines for departed spirits, believed to live in trees.

Shimmering Thailand, once called Siam or "golden" for its gleaming bell-shaped temples, is an exotic wonder with its polished, pointy-headed Buddhas, its orchid farms, hermit caves, houses for ghosts, coconut groves and secluded beaches edged with turqouise waters. Its homogenous people who practice Theravada Buddhism—which regards the pursuit of enlightenment as holy—are usually among the world's most content, but recently the country has been wracked with problems: the once skyrocketing economy has fizzled out, 2 percent of the population is HIV-positive, and though opiates are on the wane, methamphetamine use is on the rise.

BOBBITING

One sign that not everyone's cheery: increasing numbers of women are trying to murder their men. To counter the rise of attempted husband-icide, the government is now encouraging divorce for unhappy spouses. Thailand is also site of the world's only clinic specializing in reconnecting severed members.

The scandal-prone government—despite never appearing to be entirely cohesive—is effectively addressing its woes. The foreign investment that triggered the Asian Financial Crisis is now held in check and the economy is steadily recovering as the baht regains strength; the HIV rate is rapidly declining after a condom campaign and education program that targeted prostitutes, tourists, students and the army.

Defying the wishes of American pharmaceutical companies, Thailand began producing its own HIV-fighting drugs, sold for a fraction of the Western price, and it is leading the world with its trials of AIDS vaccines. And to wipe out its poppy crops, which once flooded the world's heroin market, Thailand didn't resort to crop dusters and brute force. Instead, the king traveled into the mountains to talk with poppy growers. He asked them what they needed to grow other crops on their land. Now, as part of the "Royal Project," former poppy farmers are making far more money growing chrysanthemums and apricots.

PERSONAL TO COLOMBIA

President Uribe please take note: no less than the king of Thailand traveled into the mountains to sit down and talk with poppy growers, asking what they wanted and what else grew in the land. Starting up the so-called "Royal Project," he supplied them with seeds and a means to transport their goods to market. Poppy planting in Thailand has entirely dried up.

The once-revered elephants who no longer belong in the city, are being led to reserves, where at least two of them have become international acclaimed artists with their paintings going for thousands a pop.

ANIMAL RITES

Once the main form of transportation, whose image was on the Siamese flag, elephants not only can paint, they can make music as well, as evidenced by the 2000 CD release of an elephant band. Their likeness is so esteemed that Thailand holds an annual "Miss Elephant" contest—with hefty prizes for women who resemble the pachyderms. Even the the shape of the country—altered when Thailand offered Laos and Cambodia to the French so that it could stay colonialism-free—now greatly resembles an elephant's head.

Future Forecast

Problems still loom: tensions simmer at the Burmese borders, minority Muslims in the south are setting off bombs, and soupy-aired Bangkok is slowly sinking. But in Thailand, where the prime minister funded a treasure-hunting expedition in hope of paying off the country's $69.4 billion debt, there's no lack of exploring creative ways to cope.

Hot Spots

The southern border with Malaysia: Militant Muslims are believed to be behind occasional bombings and attacks on police.

The northwestern border with Burma: Refugees, skirmishes and land mines are just a few problems spilling over from Burma, aka Myanmar.

Hot Shots

King Bhumibol Adulyadez: Thai king since 1946, the world's longest-reigning monarch is a trained engineer and has devised more than one thousand programs and inventions to tackle Thailand's problems, including palm oil–based gasoline, for which he's won the equivalent of Asia's Nobel Prize. Mostly a beloved head of state, he is busy with his research projects and steps in whenever there's a political crisis.

Thaksin Shinawatra: Elected to lead Thailand while being tried for corruption—he was found innocent—self-made billionaire and leader of the Thais Love Thais party, Thaksin was elected prime minister in 2001 with hopes of fixing Thailand's ailing economy. He also promised if elected to pay $20,000 to every Thai village. Now nearly every grouping of more than three shacks is applying to be recognized as a village.

LATIN AMERICAN MEDLEY

Once home to sophisticated Amerindian civilizations and hundreds of tribes, Latin America encompasses Central America, the Caribbean islands and South America. Its name is derived from the Spanish and Portuguese who colonized it starting in the late fifteenth century. The languages the colonizers spoke are derived from Latin.

Brazil

Ethnicity:	55% white (Portuguese, German, Italian, Spanish, Polish); 38% mixed white/black; 6% black; 1% Japanese, Arab, Amerindian
Religion:	80% Roman Catholic (nominally)
Language:	Portuguese
Literacy:	83% both sexes (1995 estimate)
Exports:	manufactures, iron ore, soybeans, shoes, coffee
Per capita GDP:	$7,400 (2000 estimate)
Unemployment:	6.4% (2000 estimate)
Percentage living in poverty:	22% (1998 estimate)
Known for:	beauty, size, terrorist training grounds

Language Lesson: Brazilians speak Portuguese, because Portugal, not Spain, was the colonial power here.

The largest country in Latin America, Brazil is in a world of its own, not speaking Spanish, though it shares the tendency toward underdeveloped potential. The mouth-droppingly gorgeous land is folded with mountains and splashed with waterfalls, and the Amazon River gushes through it, creating the world's largest rain forest. Unfortunately, it is being cut down at an alarming rate that some believe will speed up global warming.

Factoid: Many Brazilians believe that the U.S. plans to conquer the Amazon. They're taught this in schools.

Overcrowded cities such as Rio de Janeiro and São Paulo hold the brightest business opportunities, but they're loaded with crime and circled by slums where anger levels are rising. Sometimes hundreds of the unemployed poor descend en masse into rich neighborhoods to loot them. Economically the class-stratified country hasn't yet hit it stride, although leaders are pushing to make it a global leader. Among the possible futures: Brazil might move heavily into the arms industry, a move that the U.S. does not want to see.

Factoid: With its economy destabilized by Argentina, Brazil took a $30 billion loan from the IMF in 2002.

What might lead the country to civil war, however, is its agricultural holdings outside the crowded cities. Since 1985, a movement of millions of peasants is a growing concern as they loudly demand agrarian reform and land redistribution. Called the Landless Workers Movement, the group often relocates thousands of farmer families onto plantations and public lands that they want the government to give them. Violence sometimes erupts, but the landless are dedicated to the cause and the government is forced to come up with some kind of solution or risk mass mayhem countrywide.

Hot Spots

Rio de Janeiro: Beautiful crime hot spot, the city was lampooned in an episode of *The Simpsons* and threatened to sue until producers wrote an apology.

Tri-border area and Paraguay border with Argentina: Hezbollah and other militants are believed to run training camps here.

Hot Shots

Luiz Inacio "Lula" da Silva: President since January 2003, the former factory worker's fourth stab at election proved successful, and he's on an anti-U.S. warpath, saying Brazil needs to steer clear of Uncle Sam's meddling (while borrowing billions nevertheless). Some fear he'll drive foreign investors away and financially ruin the country, but the masses are wowed by his charm.

Argentina

FAST FACTS

Country:	Argentine Republic
Capital:	Buenos Aires
Government:	republic
Independence:	9 July 1816 (from Spain)
Population:	37,813,000 (2002 estimate)
Leader:	President Eduardo Duhalde
Ethnicity:	97% white (Spanish, Italian); 3% mestizos, Amerindian, nonwhite
Religion:	92% Roman Catholic (less than 20% actively practice); 2% Jewish
Literacy:	96% both sexes
Language:	Spanish

Exports:	edible oils, fuels, cereals, cars
Per capita GDP:	$12,000 (2001 estimate)
Unemployment:	25% (2001 estimate)
Percentage living in poverty:	37% (2001 estimate)
Known for:	beef, beefs with banks, Eva Perón

THE DISAPPEARED: LOS DESAPARECIDOS

Argentina still lives under the shadow of "The Dirty War" of the late 1970s. More than thirty thousand Argentines vanished during the rule of a military junta from 1976 to 1982. The fates of most of "the disappeared" are still largely unknown, though it's suspected most were rounded up by the government and many were pushed out of planes into the ocean.

Plagued by political corruption and financial bad luck for decades, Argentina is Latin America's most modern country, its second largest and once its richest. Home to the tango, the gaucho (Argentine cowboy) and world-class beef, the highly literate nation is often described as "enigmatic." Part of the mystery is why this resource-rich, well-developed and cultured country that frequently has been poised to become a world leader instead has become a world-class screwup.

INTERNATIONAL EXPLOSIONS

During the 1990s, Buenos Aires was the site of two major bombings—one at the Israeli Embassy and another at the Israeli cultural center—which killed hundreds. Hezbollah is believed to have been the culprit. Ex-President Carlos Menem is accused of taking bribes from Iran to cover up Hezbollah's involvement.

For several decades prior to 1930, vibrant Argentina flaunted its status as one of the wealthiest countries on the planet and its capital, Buenos Aires, was regarded as "the Paris of South America"; filled with European immigrants, the country has always set itself apart from its neighbors. Argentina's early prosperity was due to the agricultural *pampas* and the British who built railroads and regarded the bountiful country as their own personal breadbasket: Argentina's meat, wheat and produce were the staples on many English tables until 1930, when the Great Depression derailed world economies. Brutal dictatorships, sticky-fingered politicians and economic experiments have since drained the country of its vitality. Now Argentina is reeling from a devalued peso and a $141 billion international debt that brought its banks to a close and its people rioting in the streets demanding their money. Some experts fear the imploding violence could lead to yet another takeover by a military government.

FISCAL NIGHTMARE

In recent decades Argentina financially overextended itself. Already saddled with international debt, the controversial Carlos Menem administration tried radical reform and pegged the Argentine peso to the dollar—giving it an inflated value—while selling off government-owned utilities to private companies. Initially it seemed to work, and world bankers hailed Menem and his financial advisor Domingo Cavallo as geniuses while they extended more credit. When the peso was unlinked to the dollar in 2002, its value plummeted. Argentina now doesn't have enough money to make even partial payments on its debt. And its credit rating is so bad, the IMF is dragging its feet about bailing out the country that it helped push into debt with huge loans in the first place. Meanwhile, two countries with whom Argentina traded in Mercosur—Brazil and Uruguay—are feeling the pinch and getting IMF loans.

Hot Spots

Buenos Aires: Never mind the lovely tree-lined boulevards and Italianate mansions, the capital could explode in anger. Argentines spend their lunch breaks banging on bank doors demanding return of money that they're unlikely to see.

The Falklands: The U.K. still claims the potentially oil-rich isles off the Argentine coast and Argentina still wants them back, despite their humiliating defeat in 1982.

Hot Potato: *When Argentina's economy collapsed in late 2001, it went through five presidents in a week.*

Hot Shots

Carlos Menem: Argentine president from 1989 to 1999. Once the darling of the international financial world, Menem helped push Argentina further into the mess it's now in. Now accused of gun running, bribe taking and general corruption.

MUCHAS GRACIAS

Menem sent Argentine troops to fight in Desert Storm in 1991, partly in thanks of all the credit the U.S. was extending.

Peru

FAST FACTS

Country:	Republic of Peru
Capital:	Lima
Government:	constitutional republic
Independence:	28 July 1821 (from Spain)
Population:	27,484,000 (2001 estimate)
Leader:	President Alejandro Toledo
Ethnicity:	45% Amerindian; 37% Mestizos and Amerindian-white; 15% white; 3% black, Japanese, Chinese
Religion:	Roman Catholic
Language:	Spanish and Quéchua
Literacy:	89% (95% men; 83% women)
Exports:	fish, copper, zinc, gold, oil, lead, coffee, sugar
Per capita GDP:	$4,550 (2000 estimate)
Unemployment:	7.7% (1997 estimate)
Percentage living in poverty:	49%
Known for:	Incas, Shining Path

In the former home of the Incan civilization, Peru's Amerindian population—unlike most other indigenous people in South America, who were nearly killed off—still thrives. The country now boasts its first Amerindian president—Alejandro Toledo—who stepped in after President-Dictator Alberto Fujimori fled to Japan—where he secretly held citizenship. The Pacific-hugging country is now being infiltrated by Colombia's FARC rebels—and former guerrilla groups Shining Path and Túpac Amaru seem to be making a comeback.

Factoid: In April 2001, Peruvian military shot down what it thought was a cocaine flight. Instead it carried missionaries.

Peru would prefer a return of wimpy Fujimori and his henchman Vladimiro Montesinos, both of whom are wanted on charges of corruption and mass murder. Coca growing, thought to be eradicated, may be experiencing a rebirth.

MILITARY LUSTING

The U.S. is trying to set up military operations in Peru, though those were at least temporarily derailed when the U.S. appeared to support the 2002 two-day coup in Venezuela, a move seen as politically incorrect.

Hot Shots

Vladimiro Montesinos: Former President Fujimori's intelligence chief, he was videotaped bribing a congressman. Also charged with a massacre, abductions, extortion and selling state secrets to the CIA, the man known as "Rasputin" trained at the U.S. Army School of the Americas.

Shining Path: Started up by a university professor in the 1960s, this Maoist group pushing agrarian reform was believed responsibile for the car bombs that exploded hours before President Bush's March 2002 visit. Brutality is a speciality: they're known to prefer murder by machete. Fujimori dealt them a blow, but apparently they're still kicking.

Túpac Amaru: Cuban-inspired Communist revolutionaries who want to overthrow the imperialist government and don't usually get along with Shining Path.

Haiti

FAST FACTS

Country:	Republic of Haiti
Capital:	Port-au-Prince
Government:	republic "elected government"
Independence:	1804 (from France)

Population:	6,965,000 (2001 estimate)
Leaders:	President Jean-Bertrand Aristide; Prime Minister Yvon Neptune
Ethnicity:	95% black; 5% mulatto and white
Religion:	80% Roman Catholic; 10% Baptist; 4% Pentecostal; 50% also practice Voodoo
Language:	Creole and French
Literacy:	45% (48% men, 42% women; 1995 estimate)
Exports:	coffee, mangoes
Per capita GDP:	$1,800 (2000 estimate)
Unemployment:	over 66% (1999 estimate)
Percentage living in poverty:	80%
Known for:	being a lovely cruise ship port of call

François Duvalier and his son Jean-Claude—better known as Papa Doc and Baby Doc—brutalized Haiti from 1957 to 1986. The dictators ruled through terror and bribery and plundered the treasury. Baby Doc's wife helped: in 1985, when many Haitians were starving, she flitted off to Paris and reportedly dropped $1.7 million buying new clothes.

The Western half of Hispaniola, Haiti is not doing well. Once a sugar colony, the half island on the Caribbean has suffered brutal dictatorships, constant poverty and is now losing much of its population due to AIDS: at least one in twenty is HIV positive. A high infant mortality, of 10 percent, and a low life expectancy, of forty-nine years, are only a few indicators of the heartache-filled life here. The presidency of Jean-Bertrand Aristide—first elected in 1990—has been plagued by a military takeover that prompted the U.S. to send out its military and a questionable 2000 reelection that brought international condemnation.

CUBA

FAST FACTS

Country:	Republic of Cuba
Capital:	Havana
Government:	communist state
Independence:	1898 (from Spain)
Population:	11,224,000 (2002 estimate)
Leader:	Fidel Castro since 1959
Ethnicity:	51% mulatto; 37% white; 11% black
Religion:	85% Catholic (prior to introduction of communism); also Protestant, Jewish, Santerían
Language:	Spanish
Literacy:	95% (estimated)
Exports:	sugar, tobacco, citrus fruits
Per capita GDP:	$2,300 (2001 estimate)
Unemployment:	4% estimate
Percentage living in poverty:	N/A
Known for:	failed U.S. assassination attempts on its leader

Standout Qualities

Booze: Rum!
Flooze: Models!
Blues: Sanctions!

Résumé

For over forty years the U.S. government has been trying to take Fidel Castro down—with sanctions, isolation and wacky assassination plots. Now, for the first time, Castro is stumbling, but mostly just from his own stubborn reluctance to change anything, including his clothes.

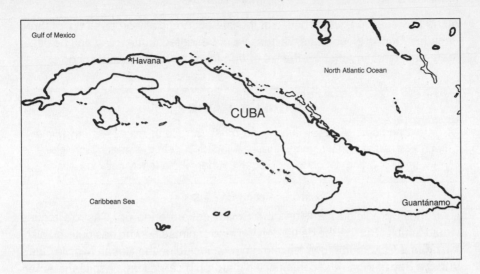

Quick Tour

With its old cars, hand-rolled cigars, color-splashed buildings and concoctions of rum, Cuba is certainly the zestiest of all communist countries right down to its life-loving locals who are quick to break into song and salsa, even though most make less than $15 a month.

Factoid: Only 4 percent of Cubans have phones.

Despite the country's chronic cash crunch—which increases the appeal of dollar-generating black markets and prostitution—and despite current food rations and Fidel Castro, who's never gotten around to that presidential vote he promised the people forty-four years ago, Cuba retains the tourist allure it had back in the 1950s when Americans flocked to the place.

Factoid: Moves to open Cuba for American travel were shot down by President Bush in 2002.

Not only does the peeling tropical getaway still look pretty much like it did back when Fidel moved in and corrupt dictator Batista fled for Florida—taking with him many of Havana's rich—it still attracts foreigners for the same reasons: too much drinking, too much dancing, too many beautiful Cubans who can be had for a song. Europeans, South Americans and especially Canadians have swamped Cuba since the 1990s, bringing in needed *dinero* after the collapse of the Soviet Union, which had kept the isle economically propped up for three decades. During those years, Cubans were better fed, better read and healthier than most in Latin America, thanks to free food, health care and schools.

MODEL BEHAVIOR

Untold numbers of Italian men—and other European males—return home with new Cuban brides, many former "models." Often the wealthy foreigners end up supporting not only the "model" but her whole family back in Havana.

Pundits predicted that when the Soviet coffers dried up, Castro's regime would tumble. But like the death-defying leader himself—who has outlived all of his enemies and numerous tense moments, including the Cuban Missile Crisis and the Bay of Pigs—the communist dictatorship carries on, despite the American economic sanctions in place since 1961, when Cuba first seized U.S. businesses and nationalized them.

Factoid: Castro, who claims he's been a target of more than six hundred assassination plots, opened up a museum showcasing the assorted attempts, including cigar bombs and toxic scuba diving gear.

However, the twenty-first century is proving more slippery for Castro, who is now pushing eighty. Not only have fellow Latin American countries condemned his human rights violations for the first time, thousands of his people have risen up against him with their pens. It may have taken four decades, but a group of dissidents behind the "Varela Project" presented Castro's government with a petition signed by eleven thousand Cubans. They asked not only that Cuba offer the free and open elections Castro promised back in 1959, but that the country move toward democracy, protect human rights and release political prisoners. The petition also requested that the U.S. lift its stifling economic sanctions on Cuba.

OVERSTEPPING?

The 1996 Helms-Burton Act—passed after Cuba shot down two American planes—underscored existing sanctions against U.S. firms doing business with Cuba; it also discouraged any country from doing business with Cuba, threatening lawsuits against those who dared try.

Castro countered with his own petition—which 8 million reportedly felt pressured to sign out of fear they'd lose their jobs—calling for the socialist government to continue running as it always had. Castro's petition was followed with marches, and even a parliamentary vote underscoring that even after he died the people wanted socialism to carry on. Pathetic though the government-orchestrated show of faith was, that Castro was forced to even go through with it indicates that the masses may finally be growing restless—as further evidenced by freedom seekers crashing a bus through the gates of the Mexican embassy and the thousands of Cubans who attempt to flee annually.

Factoid: Cubans pay as much as $8,000 for the ninety-mile trip across the Florida Straits.

Although Castro pretty much blames everything (the economy, condemnations by other countries, attacks on his political grip) on the U.S.—where President Bush is strongly influenced by powerful anti-Castro exiles in Miami—the cigar-puffing guerrilla shocked the world when he didn't even try to block American use of Guantánamo Bay. The naval base the U.S. has maintained since the Spanish-American War is now the site for internment of hundreds of members of Al Qaeda and Taliban rounded up during the American attack on Afghanistan.

Factoid: Castro never cashes the annual $4,000 check the U.S. sends to lease the base.

Also surprising: After Cuba was hit by Hurricane Michelle, Castro declined aid offered by the U.S. He did take advantage of briefly lifted sanctions to sign up to buy millions of dollar of U.S. food—the first such import in forty-two years. Although some predicted a thaw in U.S.-Cuban relations, they were wrong: the idea of easing economic sanctions was flushed in May 2002 when President Bush went out campaigning in Florida for his Miami-influenced brother Jeb.

SPANISH-AMERICAN WAR GRUDGE

When U.S. troops helped liberate Cuba from Spain in 1898, they refused to allow Cuban soldiers to march in the Victory Parade. That offense, often cited by Castro, helped power his rise in the 1950s.

Economic handcuffs would not be undone until Castro held "certifiably free and fair elections," proclaimed Bush, who added that "all elections in Castro's

Cuba have been a fraud." Those remarks—along with others calling Castro "a relic from another era" and noting that he "turned a beautiful island into a prison," caused a grumpy Castro spokesman to officially request that Bush simply "shut up."

Future Forecast

Cuba won't change a bit until Fidel drops and Miami real estate developers flood the place.

Factoid: A number of American presidents, including Thomas Jefferson, wanted to buy or otherwise wrestle Cuba from Spain.

Hot Spots

Guantánamo Bay: Controversial holding pen for Al Qaeda/Taliban prisoners from the U.S.-Afghan War. Several countries have demanded that foreign captives be sent back, but U.S. courts have shot down the idea.

Hot Shots

Fidel Castro: He wasn't even a full-fledged communist, and hadn't aligned with the Soviet Union until U.S. sanctions—snapped on when Castro seized and nationalized U.S. businesses—forced him to look for outside funding and food. Hasn't much changed his look, or his outlook, for four decades.

Raul Castro: Cuba's ever-patient number two man, Fidel's brother tricked a *New York Times* reporter back in the pre-revolution 1950s who wrote that the plotting rebel Castro controlled a huge army. In fact, he didn't: Raul just kept marching the same group of soldiers past the reporter.

Movimiento Cristiano de Liberación: The Christian Liberation Movement had the guts to question Castro with the "Varela Project."

Miami exiles: Powerful lobby of former Cubans who ensure President Bush will shut down every move to open up Cuba until Castro steps down.

LIBYA

Standout Qualities

Fashion makeover: from jumpsuits to caftans

Political makeover: from Arab world to African nation

Image makeover: hired PR firm to improve world standing

Résumé

Iraq has Saddam, Cuba has Fidel, Libya has Colonel Moammar Qaddafi—the Tom Jones of the oil world—and a quixotic personality blend of dictator, so-

cialist, revolutionary, thinker, playboy
and entertainer. Accused of backing
terrorist acts—the bombing of Pan
Am Flight 103 over Lockerbie, for
one—the colonel is putting on a
whole new song and dance as he
tries to unite Africa.

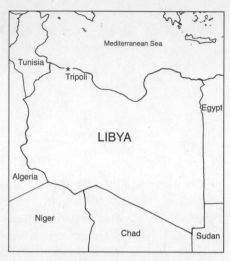

Quick Tour

From its land mine–dotted sands
that shift around Roman ruins and its
maze-like, covered towns that require
a torch even in daylight, Libya—a
country the UN stitched together from former Italian colonies in 1951—is a cu-
rious place. Home to the eighth wonder of the world—or at least that's how
Colonel Qaddafi described "The Great Man-Made River Project" his now leaking, corroding $30 billion pipe system to bring water from the desert—the North
African country that hugs Egypt is, well, confused.

> **Slippery Oil:** *Libya has the world's tenth largest oil reserves; due to as-
> sorted sanctions, American companies have had a hard time getting at
> oil rigs there since 1986.*

Nobody in Libya is sure what the date is anymore, since Qaddafi reinvented
the calendar, changing the year several times as well as renaming months. And
nobody is quite sure what to expect next from the eccentric, sometimes visionary military man who bloodlessly ousted King Idris in 1969, and ever since has
unveiled numerous plans for revamping his country (and saving the Arab and
African worlds) while prancing around in flashy jumpsuits (or traditional African
garb) and trying to seduce Western reporters. His people dare not question his
latest ideas and activities—be they his initial support for the "War on Terror," his
plan for a united Israel-Palestine called "Isratine" or his new vision for a united
Africa: dissidents have a way of disappearing or dying even when they're out of
the country.

BEWARE OF NUTS

After assorted coup attempts in the 1970s, Qaddafi went on a dissident reduction program across the world; his opponents became targets of assassinations

and attempts, including death by poison peanuts. In retaliation, the U.S. booted Libya out of its D.C. embassy in 1981.

Isratine: Qaddafi's idea for Middle East peace involved bringing back all the displaced Palestinians and relocating them in what is now Israel, a land that would be shared by Jews and Arabs. The Arab League refused to endorse the plan.

Once hoping to lead a united Arab world—hopes dashed by Arab leaders who viewed him as mentally iffy and a political question mark—in the 1970s, the colonel wrote the Green Book, his manifesto that introduced a "third way" to Libya. A cross between communism and socialism, Qaddafi's vision relied on people ruling, while he would be called "Brother Leader." So much for that: the colonel still dictates and most of the country's vast oil wealth doesn't make it to the people.

ARAB BROTHERS

Libya is a member of the oil-rich Arab League, where Qaddafi baffles members. Among his unusual ideas: allowing Israel to join. Furious that the Arab League wouldn't support his idea for Isratine, Qaddafi refused to endorse Saudi Arabia's 2002 plan for Mideast peace and threatened to quit. Although Qaddafi occasionally makes diplomatic moves toward Israel, he mostly concerns himself with the plight of Palestinians; ever since Israel shot down a Libyan commercial airline in 1973, Qaddafi has protested Mideast peace plans, from the Camp David to the Oslo Accords. Besides, he's much more interested in Africa these days.

The colonel and the U.S. have had rocky relations since 1980, worsened when President Reagan dubbed Qaddafi the "Mad Dog of the Middle East." After Libya was fingered in a Berlin bombing that killed three (including U.S. servicemen), the U.S. bombed Tripoli and Qaddafi's compound. Qaddafi allegedly upped the ante with an international bombing spree culminating in the 1988 Pan Am flight 103 bombing that killed 270 over Lockerbie, Scotland.

U.S. ALLEGATIONS

Why U.S. considers Libya a "rogue state":

Supported IRA, PLO, ETA
Ran militant training camps
Abetted Abu Nidal
Bombings:
    1986 Berlin disco (3 killed)
    1986 airport bombings in Rome, Vienna
    1988 Lockerbie bombing
Chemical plants

When Qaddafi refused to turn over the Libyan suspects, the UN hit Libya with sanctions in 1992. Although U.S. sanctions remain firmly in place, UN sanctions were suspended in 1999, when the colonel formally denounced terrorism and gave up the pair of Libyan intelligence men for the Lockerbie trial; one was found guilty and the other not.

Rumors: Some say that the 1988 Lockerbie bombing was actually funded by Iran, furious that the U.S. accidentally shot down an Iranian commercial plane in 1988, an act for which the U.S. never fully apologized.

Colonel Qaddafi: the Africa look. (Source: Associated Press)

Ever since, Qaddafi has been on a kick to prove he's a diplomat, peacemaker and statesman. Donning African tribal gowns, the colonel has been an oil-rich Santa Claus showering Zimbabwe, Ghana and Kenya with money, oil and food. He's sent out envoys to negotiate treaties between Uganda and Congo and peacekeepers to maintain order in places from the Central African Republic to Sierra Leone. His latest coup: becoming a founding father of the African Union, a new political-economic coalition that replaces the Organization of African States, and which is hoped to be more democratic than the group it replaced, dubbed the "African Dictators' Club."

DICTATING LIFE

Qaddafi's best-known works are the three volumes of his *Green Book,* but he has also published fiction: *Escape to Hell and Other Stories.*

In the Philippines, Malaysia and Afghanistan, Qaddafi helped negotiate hostage release. After 9/11, he was the first Arab leader to support the U.S. attack on Afghanistan as "self-defense."

WHAT PRICE FREEDOM?

Libya reportedly paid $1 million for each hostage held by the Philippines' Abu Sayyaf. The money in turn buys the kidnapper's flashy arms. Libya denies the charges, but has heeded President Gloria Arroyo's request to butt out of Philippines affairs.

When Qaddafi welcomed French diplomats and shared info on Al Qaeda, some speculated that he must be dying. Few doubt that behind all the hoopla, the colonel has but one intention: to shake loose remaining sanctions from the U.S. After all, he's lost many billions, while American oil fields lie idle. The U.S., however, won't lift the economic blocks until Qaddafi offers an apology and pays $2.7 billion to families of Lockerbie victims. While still maintaining that he had nothing to do with the 1988 in-flight bombing, Qaddafi is now leaning toward writing the hefty check. Lord knows how he'll date it.

Future Forecast

Sanctions will lift, oil will pump, the colonel will have time to pen a few more short stories.

Human Rights: Libya is scheduled to take over the rotating positions as head of the UN Human Rights Commission in 2003. The U.S. is loudly protesting.

TERMS TO KNOW

ILSA: Iran-Libya Sanctions Act. This 1996 law prohibits American companies—as well as international firms—from doing more than $40 million in business with Libya or Iran. Oil execs want to lift it—so they can get back to their Libyan pumps, which have been motionless for years. Families of Lockerbie victims help keep the act in place.

HUH WHAT?

Israel apparently hasn't noticed Libya's makeover. Prime Minister Ariel Sharon announced in September 2002 that Libya was developing weapons of mass destruction. Whether that's the case or whether that means Israel plans to turn its attention to battling Libya is anyone's guess.

Hot Spots

Qaddafi's tent: tries to lure female reporters there for a close, personal interview.

Hot Shots

Colonel Moammar Qaddafi: English writers still can't agree on how to spell his name or how to cast the mercurial leader who tossed the Libyan king in 1969 and took the power seat when he was a mere twenty-seven. A sufferer of deep depression, the man sometimes seems high on happy pills and definitely needs a stage. Too bad someone didn't offer him a recording contract or a talk show a few decades back; his country might have been spared his moods.

Seif al-Islam Qaddafi: The colonel's son, who may succeed him, has taken up painting and displayed his works in London's Kensington Gardens. The show was well attended and poorly reviewed.

VENEZUELA

FAST FACTS

Country:	Bolivarian Republic of Venezuela
Capital:	Caracas
Government:	federal republic
Independence:	5 July 1811 (from Spain)
Population:	24,288,000 (2002 estimate)
Leader:	President Hugo Chávez
Ethnicity:	Spanish, Italian, Portuguese, Arab, German, African, indigenous people
Religion:	96% Roman Catholic; 2% Protestant
Language:	Spanish
Literacy:	91% (92% men, 91% women; 1995 estimate)
Exports:	petroleum, bauxite, aluminum, steel
Per capita GDP:	$6,100 (2001 estimate)
Unemployment:	14% (2001 estimate)
Percentage living in poverty:	67% (1997 estimate)
Known for:	oil, proximity to Colombia and its rebels

Standout Qualities

Looks good: Amazon, Andes, Angel Falls
Good looks: beauty queen factory
Looks bad: four out of five are poor in the oil-rich country

Résumé

"The Devil's Excrement" was what the Spanish called that tarlike slime that oozed from Venezuela's ground. We know it as petroleum, and ever since it started gushing in 1928, we've been happy to know our li'l neighbor to the south. Until, that is, an iconoclastic talker named Hugo Chávez came along.

Trend Starter: Venezuela became
the Western Hemisphere's first petroleum exporter in 1928.

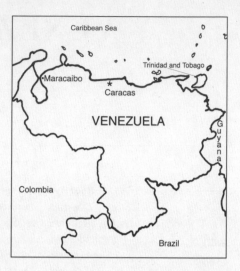

If Amerigo Vespucci sailed into
Lake Maracaibo today, he might have
called Venezuela "rigazuela" or "slickazuela" or maybe "chemazuela." But
five centuries ago the country's biggest
lake wasn't a rig-dotted toxic soup: it
was sparkling blue, filled with flamin-
goes and edged by small Indian huts
propped up on stilts that reminded
the Italian mapmaker of a miniature
Venice, hence the country's name.

NOT ALL BAD

Outside of oil areas and slum-encircled Caracas, which looks best hidden by
night, Venezuela, with its serrated landscape and dense Amazon, is still quite
a dazzler.

The Spanish who followed Vespucci may have been mesmerized by
Venezuela's misty jungles and waterfalls and the palm-fanned beaches along
the glistening Caribbean, but the place was pretty worthless by their standards
since they believed it held scant silver and gold. Little did they know that
Venezuela held the seeds to the Spanish demise: Simon Bolivar was born here
in 1783 and in 1811 spurred South America to independence.

WELL HELLO THERE, NEIGHBOR!

Venezuela holds more oil than anyplace else in the Western Hemisphere. It's
typically a top supplier to the U.S. Exports have gone down under President
Chávez. During December 2002, they stopped entirely.

What made the country a twentieth-century standout—besides its beauty
queens—was its plentiful crude, so much that Venezuela has the sixth largest
known oil reserves in the world.

BEAUTIFUL SPENDERS

Venezuela holds more Miss World and Miss Universe sashes that any other country: eight good-lookers have snagged the titles since 1979. The aggressive contest board actively scouts beauties and nudges natural beauty along: would-be winners are surgically nipped, tucked, sucked, plumped and trained in an intensive beauty queen "factory" that includes dermatology, dentistry, seaweed dieting and whatever else it takes to win. Venezuelan women also spend more on cosmetics than their compatriots in any other South American country.

The country had a history of corrupt politicians who greased their hands with oil money, but the U.S. didn't much seem to care: relations were fine and supply was guaranteed. At least until a charismatic paratrooper swaggered in and opened his mouth.

Until the mid 1980's, Venezuela was relatively well off, with a social welfare system in place. Dropping oil prices pushed it into a recession that it still hasn't shaken. Now 80 percent live on less than $2 a day.

President Hugo Chávez first caught the public eye during a 1992 coup. The takeover flopped: he was soon out on the street, but not before the would-have-been president snatched a mic and launched an impassioned anti-corruption speech on Venezuelan TV. The television-viewing masses liked what they saw, and in 1999 Chávez again entered the presidential palace—this time as a duly elected official, the highest in the land.

SKIN COLORS

In a world where the upper crust is white and the poor are darker-skinned, tawny Chávez, who grew up poor, was a symbol of hope to the masses.

His chattiness was evident the first night when he flung open the balcony doors—first singing an a cappella solo of the national anthem—and then giving a speech that dragged on until the sun peered over the square.

The U.S. soon grew antsy as President Chávez jetted off to meet with every one on their enemy list—Saddam Hussein, Moammar Qaddafi, Fidel Castro and Colombia's rebel group FARC. Mr. Loquacious loudly criticized Plan Colombia, encouraged OPEC leaders to cut supplies and announced that he might seek oil contracts with other countries.

LAST STRAW

While supporting the "War on Terror," Chávez blasted the Bush administration for the deaths of Afghan civilians. Holding up pictures of bloody corpses for the TV camera, he exclaimed, "These children were alive yesterday. They were eating with their parents when a bomb fell on them. . . ." The U.S. yanked back its ambassador the next day, prompting Chávez to launch a four-hour radio explanation/apology that brought the ambassador back.

Oil execs at the state-owned Petroleos de Venezuela twitched too, especially after he fired them and put his friends in their shoes. The upper class looked upon him as a leftist rabble-rouser, whose financial dabblings had caused the bolivar to plummet by 25 percent; the poor masses lost fondness for him too, as crime rates, especially in slums, soared.

Yikes: In Caracas alone, twelve murders on average occur every day.

Demonstrations for and against Chávez were almost daily events by 2002, but in April, unknown gunmen shot opposition protesters, killing at least nine. The military blamed Chávez, tossed him in jail, and well-to-do businessman Pedro Carmona was quickly sworn in, and announced he was dismantling their Congress and closing down the courts. Even if few supported Chávez, fewer could tolerate the illegal power grab: protesters flooded the streets, rioting until, two days later, Chávez was back.

LOST IDEALS

Uncle Sam diplomatically blundered and looked hypocritical when the Bush administration appeared to support the coup; some say the U.S. was very much behind it. Chávez has few friends, but Latin American leaders denounced the highly undemocratic act—as did the Venezuelan people. Peru was so steamed at President Bush that plans to set up a U.S. military program there were quickly shelved.

Chávez's hold is iffy: he says he'll ask voters if they want him around till 2007, when his term is scheduled to end. As much of a hot-air master as he may be, some worry that when the talker goes, Venezuelan democracy might follow.

Future Forecast

Venezuelans will soon be hearing a very long resignation speech, they hope.

Hot Spots

Venezuela-Colombian border: Caracas looks dreamy compared to Bogotá, and Colombians by the tens of thousands sneak in. The military also worries that Plan Colombia will lead to a war that will spread over the border.

Angel Falls: Highest waterfall in the world.

Hot Shots

Hugo Chávez: Former paratrooper whose dreams for new schools, libraries and hospitals didn't much come to fruition.

Stoppage: *A general strike that began in December 2002 with the intent of forcing Chávez to resign or call early election caused Venezuelan oil exports to dry up; in fact, the country has to import oil. As of January 2003 the stubborn leader was clinging to his post.*

President Chávez rattled U.S.-Venezuelan oil relations. (Source: Associated Press)

MEXICO

FAST FACTS

Country:	United Mexican States
Capital:	Mexico City (Distrito Federal)
Government:	federal republic
Independence:	16 September 1810 (from Spain)
Population:	103,400,000 (2002 estimate)
Leader:	President Vicente Fox Quesada
Ethnicity:	60% Mestizo (Amerindian-Spanish); 30% Amerindian; 9% white
Religion:	89% Roman Catholic; 6% Protestant
Language:	Spanish
Literacy:	90%; (92% men, 88% women; 1995 estimate))
Exports:	manufactured goods, oil, silver, produce, coffee
Per capita GDP:	$9,000
Unemployment:	3%
Percentage living in poverty	40%
Known for:	Frida Kahlo, cheap labor and Octavio Paz, who won the 1990 Nobel Prize for Literature

Standout Qualities

Muy enérgico: Big business is booming
Muy rico: rich in history, culture, resources
Muy pobre: 40 percent live in poverty

Résumé

There's more to Mexico than tequila, mariachi, Aztecs and tacos: Mexico is a major supplier of oil to the U.S. as well as this country's second biggest trading partner in the world. While over-the-border trade has tripled since 1994, the money isn't trickling down and millions are in dire straits.

HISTORY REVIEW

During the Mexican-American War that ended in 1848, the U.S. wrested California, Nevada, Utah and parts of Arizona, Wyoming, Colorado, Texas and New Mexico away from Mexico.

Quick Tour

From its lost Mayan cities on the Yucatan enveloped by jungle, to its huge, hustling, mural-splashed capital enveloped by smog, Mexico is a land of dreams and extremes. Hydroelectric dams tap the gushing waters in the southern mountains, while northern border towns are running dry. Millionaires live in palm-lined terraced *palacios* guarded by security men, while 14 million workers and peasants—about 15 percent of the population—live in tiny shacks with dirt floors and cardboard roofs.

The North American Free Trade Agreement (NAFTA) brought U.S. big business rolling in, but factory workers often pull down $2 an hour and loggers may make as little as $5 a day.

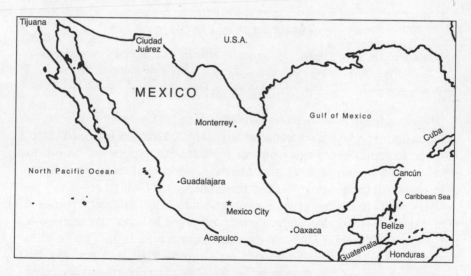

REVERSE ECONOMY

Since NAFTA went into effect in 1994, the number of Mexicans living in poverty has increased by 4 million.

This country of wondrous history (evident in numerous stepped pyramids and ancient stone writings) and heart-pounding beauty (emerald forests, cobalt waters, forgotten colonial towns blossoming amid mountains, tiny white churches perched on cliffs) is plagued with modern ugliness, from drug cartels that control highways, to police and politicians taking bribes, to the growing kidnapping industry.

Kidnapping was relatively infrequent until the 1990s, when police bragged that they'd finally caught the hostage-happy Arizmendi family, who made millions a year from nabbings. Previously unaware of the riches to be had, new kidnappers rushed into abduction adventure.

No one knows the potential and the problems better than Presidente Vicente Fox, who rode in during what were considered Mexico's first honest elections in seventy-one years. Taking office in 2001, the handsome six-foot-plus rancher and former Coca-Cola exec forced the U.S. to stop looking down on Mexico and instead meet its neighbor eye-to-eye.

Or at least that's how it seemed when Presidente Fox met with President Bush and started discussions on guest workers programs, water disputes and opening up borders. At present, nearly 8 million Mexicans live in the U.S., many illegally.

NEIGHBORLY RELATIONS

Mexico is President's Bush strong suit: he speaks a bit of Spanish, and Mexico was the only international country he'd visited before taking office.

Relations have gone south, so to speak, since 9/11, when the "War on Terror" took priority; relations worsened in August of 2002, when Texas executed a Mexican murderer over Fox's pleas for amnesty. Fox and others believe the rights of Mexico-born Javier Suarez Medina, convicted of killing a policeman, were breached because the Mexican consulate wasn't brought in.

Fox's hopes are fading at home too, particularly in the southern Chiapas region, the site of civil unrest. Brimming with coffee and banana plantations, electric plants and much of Mexico's oil reserves, the area is also home to the descendents of Mayans, most living in utter poverty. Villages of lean-tos don't have access to the electricity created not far away, most don't have running water, and dirt roads are so thick with mud only tractors can get through. Much of Mexico lacks basic infrastructure and sanitation services such as paved roads and sewage lines.

Since 1994, the group known as Zapatistas has demanded that the government hook the Chiapas region up to the world and grant them land rights.

Unlike his predecessors, Fox agreed that the Zapatistas had a point, and he developed a program of railways, economic development and limited autonomy. Legislators watered down Fox's plans, and deleted the clause on autonomy for the region, and the Zapatistas balked at the weakened program.

In July 2002, a group claiming to be Zapatistas held hostages to protest construction of a huge airport on farming land northeast of Mexico City. All were released when Fox promised to situate the airport elsewhere.

Fox has plenty of other migraines to contend with, among them boom towns created in the wake of NAFTA: more than a million Mexicans have moved to the northern border towns, where new *maquilladoras*—big factories run by Ford and Alcoa—pay most workers around $12 a day. Slums of workers' shacks ring the cities, where sewage lines and paved roads are luxuries and waves of murders are increasingly common. American companies are hacking down Mexico's luxuriant forests, and the country's oil reserves are projected to be sucked dry in the next twenty years. Despite arrests and crackdowns, corruption runs rampant. Mafia operations are expanding, kidnappers abduct thousands a year, urban air pollution is at life-threatening levels, tourism is down, water issues still loom, and even though the economy is humming along, three quarters still live in poverty. Well, at least Mexico's formerly booming population growth has slowed, which only goes to show: one thing at a time.

Factoid: With more than 18 million inhabitants, hilly Mexico City is the third most populous city in the world.

Future Forecast

Guest worker programs will soon bring tens of thousands of Mexican workers in to fill in gaps in the U.S. farm labor market, but U.S.-Mexican water wars will be breaking out soon if the Colorado River is further diverted for U.S. agriculture.

JUST AN IDEA

To simultaneously tackle unemployment and get the country up to modern standards, the Mexican government could create federally funded worker programs—like those in the U.S. during the Depression—to build roads.

Hot Spots

Chiapas: This southern state holds the country's greatest wealth and poverty, as well as indigenous populations who want out of the dark ages. The country's oil company—Pemex—which has oil wells a-pumping here, sure hasn't helped develop the place, though they're accused of polluting it. State where most of the country's coffee is grown and many trees are now felled.

Mexico's many Mayan and Aztec ruins are laden with mysteries, not the least of which is why the Mayans died out in A.D. 900. With hidden doorways and tunnels, the Indians' history-dripping temples bear names such as "Pyramid of the Magician" and "Moon God of Showers."

Juárez: Drug mobsters, mansions, factories and slums all in one border city where water will dry up by 2020.

Cancún: Resort paradise enjoyed by both vacationers and drug lords.

Mexico-U.S. border: Two thousand miles that divide the world's most affluent country from its impoverished neighbor. The good news is illegal border crossings are down; the bad news is the majority of cocaine destined for American nostrils still rolls across here.

As mandated by NAFTA, Mexican truckers will soon be rolling across American highways. U.S. Teamsters don't like the idea: they say, among other things, Mexican trucks are falling apart.

Hot Shots

Vicente Fox: Corruption-weary Mexicans considered it like the fall of the Berlin Wall, when pro-business, pro-U.S. rancher-exec Fox took over the reins in December 2000 after seventy-one years of corrupt one-party rule of the Institutional Revolutionary Party. Hopes are a bit dashed because he hasn't yet turned the country around, but geez the guy is trying.

Zapatistas: Formed the day NAFTA went into effect, this group aims to give Mexico's indigenous people their due, including a real roof over their heads. Mostly peaceful demonstrators—they walked (and bussed) to the capital in 2001 to present their demands—they could get rowdy if life in Chiapas doesn't improve: a 1994 uprising went on for twelve days, during which two hundred were killed after the army showed up. Named after Emiliano Zapata, who pushed for radical land reform during the Mexican Revolution, which killed some 2 million people between 1910 and 1920. Zapata wanted plantation owners to carve up their land for the peasants.

Subcomandante Marcos: Leader of the Zapatistas who is believed to be an urban intellectual, the masked subcomandante is a folk hero to many. Benetton offered the fatigue-wearing activist his own clothing line, but he declined.

NIGERIA

Standout Qualities

Oil rich: petroleum brings in billions
People poor: the people aren't seeing the wealth
People heavy: Huge population, high birth rate

Résumé

Africa's most populous country has plenty o' problems—a 28 percent unemployment rate among them—but at least one reason for hope: "Mama Power."

Quick Tour

Take a western African country of fishing villages, small farms, grass shacks, palm trees and 250 tribes (usually living peacefully) and discover that there's oil under the ground, and what do you have: Nigeria. The OPEC country—and sixth largest exporter in the world—has been plagued by military governments that plunder its wealth and oil companies that don't employ many locals. Outside of a few major cities—such as chaotic Lagos or glassily modern Abuja—towns are typically without electricity, roads and running water. But there is a space program, a huge military budget, not to mention steel plants and a host of other projects that seem ridiculous to a population where many survive on less than a dollar a day.

The land has been so poorly managed that the country that was once a food exporter now imports most of its food, and even though Nigeria pumps some 2 million barrels daily into the international energy pipeline—it's the fifth largest supplier to the U.S.—it has to import its energy. Crime—bank robberies, carjackings, kidnappings, counterfeiting—has gotten so out of control that northern states, which unlike the Christian south are mostly Muslim, have instituted Shariah law at its harshest. That doesn't seem to be deterring thieves, but it is putting Nigeria on the front page—for handing out death-by-stoning sentences to young mothers convicted of adultery. The spread of Shariah law has in fact only led to more violence, as Christians and Muslims battle it out; in one state, over two thousand died from religious battles in February 2000 alone. On top of this factor in AIDS: at least 5 percent of the population is HIV positive.

BEAUTY QUEEN PROTEST

Status-conscious Nigeria loves the international spotlight, so many were elated when Agbani Darego became the 2002 Miss World and Nigeria won a bid to stage the next Miss World competition. That dream blew up in November, when the pageant came to Nigeria and bloody protests broke out, killing a hundred. The reason: a newspaper editorial saying Muhammad would have taken a contestant for a bride. The pageant moved to London instead.

Bright spots were emerging on this depressing scene, though some have faded. Hope swirled around the administration of democratically elected President Olusegun Obasanjo, who stepped into the office in 1999 as the first civilian leader since 1984. Ironically, Obasanjo had himself once been a military leader, but he made the radical move of handing the power back to the people in the 1970s, and became such an outspoken critic of military rule that he was jailed for three years. Since taking office, he's kept the country geographically united—despite calls for secession in western areas—and has launched an anticorruption campaign. But problems quashed under military rule—including religious and ethnic conflicts and battles for land between farmers and herders—have emerged and have killed more than ten thousand since Obasanjo stepped into office. More disappointing: Obansanjo's promised "dividends of democracy" have mostly been to double the salaries of government employees, including the ever-present military, while nearly one of out three Nigerians remains unemployed. His value may simply be that his government may be more accountable than the entirely army-run administrations that blew through some $280 billion from oil after 1972.

Ken Saro-Wiwa became infamous for writing about oil companies' exploitation of Nigeria in the 1990s. The previous military government of General Sani Abacha was so alarmed at his works that they hung him.

Where the future of Nigeria may lie: its women. They have proven themselves to be an enterprising bunch. In the notoriously poor region of the Niger Delta—where most of the oil lies—companies such as Shell and Chevron are well versed in the tactics of some unemployed men who kidnap and extort for ransom. But the oil companies were taken aback when the local women barged into plants and introduced a new form of protest that thus far has proved the most effective. Starting in summer 2002, "The Mamas"—some of them eighty-year-olds, none carrying any weapons save for the occasional pot or pan—have taken over refineries to make demands that were not answered when they simply wrote letters. Their sit-ins—during which they threatened to strip—resulted in some oil companies, ChevronTexaco among them, promising to employ more of the village's local population and to bring electricity to the houses that are across the dirt road from the refinery. Stay tuned as to whether the oil giants make good on their promises.

Shell Tactics: Nigeria's largest oil exporter, Royal Dutch/Shell, refused to negotiate with protesting women, who were teargassed and dragged out after a peaceful August 2002 sit-in. Two women are missing and believed dead.

Future Forecast

As is the documented case with other developing countries, if investors fund small-scale businesses run by women, this country could economically improve from the grassroots level up. Politically, look for possible civil war, as religion and ethnicity divides a country made miserable by its chronic poverty.

Hot Spots

Niger Delta: Home of the oil companies, who are under fire for not sufficiently helping local economies and not cleaning up their oil spills and pipeline leaks. The air reeks of petroleum.

Kaduna and Kano: Two northern states where the implementation of Shariah law is causing Muslim-Christian conflicts.

Hot Shots

Amina Lawal: Convicted of adultery and sentenced to death by stoning, the thirty-year-old mother brought the issue before the world.

Olusegun Obasanjo: The president has made small progress whittling down Nigeria's mountain of woes.

The Mamas: Niger Delta women starting a small scale revolution with their nonviolent protests that force oil companies to become more accountable in the communities they exploit. Many are part of Niger Delta Women for Justice (www.NDWJ.kabissa.org).

AFRICAN ASSORTMENT

The African continent comprises more than fifty countries these days, many of which are struggling with widespread poverty, HIV, religious conflicts, famine and poor educational systems. A few standouts:

Algeria

FAST FACTS	
Country:	Democratic and Popular Republic of Algeria
Capital:	Algiers
Government:	republic
Independence:	5 July 1962 (from France)
Population:	31,736,100 (2001 estimate)
Leaders:	President Abdelaziz Bouteflika (1999); Prime Minister Ali Benflis (2000)
Ethnicity:	99% Arab-Berber
Religion:	99% Sunni Muslim (state religion)
Language:	Arabic and Berber, French
Literacy:	62% (74% men, 49% women; 1995 estimate)
Exports:	petroleum, natural gas
Per capita GDP:	$5,500 (2000 estimate)
Unemployment	30% (1999 estimate)
Percentage living in poverty:	23% (1999 estimate)
Known for:	anger, making mockery of democratic elections

A significant exporter of natural gas and oil, Algeria may be beautiful but it's no place for a vacation these days. A bloody war of independence with the

French raged on until 1962, but for the past twelve years religious violence has flared. Muslim militants are ticked: a 1991 election in which a Muslim fundamentalist party, the Islamic Salvation Front (FIS), was bound to win was abruptly canceled. The army came in, violence broke out, and the country still hasn't fully recovered. It was somewhat calmer after the government made an offer of amnesty, but the most fiery members of the Islamic Salvation Army (GIA)—the military wing of the Islamic Salvation Front—still show up in international operations, including some sponsored by Al Qaeda. They are also starting to kick back into action at home.

Morocco

FAST FACTS

Country:	Kingdom of Morocco
Capital:	Rabat
Government:	constitutional monarchy
Independence:	2 March 1956 (from France)
Population:	30,645,000 (2001 estimate)
Leaders:	King Mohamed VI; Prime Minister M. Abderrahmane Youssoufi
Ethnicity:	99% Arab-Berber
Religion:	99% Sunni Muslim
Language:	Arabic; Berber dialects
Literacy:	44% (57% men, 31% women; 1995 estimate)
Exports:	phosphates, fertilizer, food
Per capita GDP:	$3,500 (2000 estimate)
Unemployment:	23% (2000 estimate)
Percentage living in poverty:	19% (1999 estimate)
Known for:	markets, couscous, feisty king

The bad news is that only a third of Moroccan women can read and that less than a quarter of the population has access to clean drinking water. The good news is that maybe the exotic land of twisting alleys, souks and tapestries is improving under young King Mohamed VI—who is moving it toward democracy and definitely liberalizing the place, while standing out internationally as rather feisty. Morocco keeps butting heads with Spain over the latter's sardine-surrounded rock that Moroccans call Leila or "evening" and the Spanish call Isla de Perejil or "Parsley Island."

And U.S.-Moroccan relations are a bit iffy, too, ever since Secretary of State Colin Powell started off a 2002 trip to the Middle East with a stop in Rabat. The king kept him waiting for hours and then greeted the U.S. official by snippily asking why he didn't fly directly to Israel and Palestine. After the gruff reception, Powell may have been wondering the same.

Zimbabwe

FAST FACTS

Country:	Republic of Zimbabwe (formerly Rhodesia)
Capital:	Harare
Government:	parliamentary democracy in name—mostly a dictatorship
Independence:	18 April 1980 (from Britain)
Population:	11,365,000 (2001)
Leader:	Chief of State and Head of Government: Executive President Robert Mugabe
Ethnicity:	98% African (Shona, Ndebele tribes and others)
Religion:	50% Christian-indigenous blend; 25% Christian; 24% indigenous; 1% Muslim and other
Language:	English and many tribal dialects
Literacy:	85% (90% men, 80% women; 1995 estimate)
Exports:	tobacco, gold, cotton
Per capita GDP:	$2,500 (2000 estimate)
Unemployment:	50% (2000 estimate)
Percentage living in poverty:	60% (1999 estimate)
Known for:	hard-headed ruler, censorship, HIV
HIV/AIDS prevalence rate:	26%
People living with HIV/AIDS:	1.5 million (1999 estimate)

Landlocked Zimbabwe—tucked down in the southern cone of Africa—snags more than its fair share of press, and not just because Zimbabwe is fun to say. The name is about the only happy thing about this poor country where President Robert Mugabe, in power since 1980, has gone cuckoo, flipped his wig, stepped over the edge and is dragging his country through his personal insanity. Never mind, for the moment, that his 2002 reelection was allegedly fraudulent, that his promised democracy doesn't exist and that he has shut down the press and booted out international journalists. It's his ideas about land reform that are causing Zimbabwe to go down the drain: he's kicking out all white land owners in a maelstrom of violence, murder and lynching.

Land reform may indeed be required here, but Mugabe's methods of simply ordering white farmers out have brought famine, since nobody's effectively tending the land anymore. Mugabe looked like an idiot in summer 2002 when he rejected food from the U.S.: he didn't want the Americans' genetically modified corn, fearing his people would plant it. The point is legitimate—genetically modified plants, are sometimes called "terminators" because they overtake other strains—and American companies such as Monsanto seem to be trying to use Africa as their testing grounds. But the debate sure seems moot when millions are starving. A compromise was finally reached: all corn would be ground.

The bigger problem still remains: what to do with dictator Mugabe, whose behavior has caused the European Union, among other things, to ban him from visiting. Another woe: a quarter of the population is HIV positive.

South Africa

FAST FACTS

Country:	Republic of South Africa
Capital:	Pretoria (legislative center: Cape Town)
Government:	republic
Independence:	31 May 1910 (from Britain)
Population:	43,586,000 (2001 estimate)
Leader:	Chief of State and Head of Government: President Thabo Mbeki
Ethnicity:	75% black; 14% white; 9% "colored"; 3% Indian
Religion:	Christian 68%, 2% Muslim, 29% indigenous, 2% Hindu
Language:	11 official including Afrikaans, Xhosa, Zulu (1995 estimate)
Literacy:	82% both sexes (1995 estimate)
Exports:	gold, diamonds, metals
Per capita GDP:	$8,500 (2000 estimate)
Unemployment:	30% (2000 estimate)
Percentage living in poverty:	50% (2000 estimate)
Known for:	winning the war on apartheid, losing the war on AIDS
HIV/AIDs prevalence rate:	20% (1999 estimate)
People living with HIV/AIDS:	4.2 million (1999 estimate)

A former Dutch colony, South Africa became headline news when it threw off apartheid in the early 1990s and its majority black population was finally represented by a black government: visionary activist Nelson Mandela, elected in 1994, was released from prison and became the country's first black president. While South Africa was trying to put itself back together after years of white domination—and address issues such as poverty and education—another huge problem arose: AIDS. Now 20 percent of the population is HIV positive, 5 million are living with the disease, and AIDS orphans abound. For several years Mandela's successor President Thabo Mbeki steadfastly denied that HIV was transmitted through sex. Not only were education efforts stymied, but he also rejected offers for free medication for HIV-positive mothers. Mbeki came out of the dark in 2002 under international pressure—and now at least allows medical treatment for infected mothers.

Another huge problem: rape. According to some estimates, there are over three thousand cases of rape in South Africa every day. Women aren't the only targets of the crime that is mostly ignored by police: worried about exposure to HIV, rapists are turning to children and infants. Mandela best jump back in and do something about this heartbreaking mess.

Happy Fishing: The November 2002 sinking of the Prestige *off of Spain may have blackened the coastline of northwest Spain, but it improved that country's relations with Morocco. The Moroccan king invited fishermen whose livelihoods were ruined by the oil spill to drop their nets in Morocco's waters.*

SOUTHEAST ASIA SAMPLER

World of exotic delights, Southeast Asia lures international travelers with its island and jungles. A few attention getters:

Malaysia

FAST FACTS

Country:	Malaysia
Capital:	Kuala Lumpur
Government:	constitutional monarchy
Independence:	1957 (from Britain; Malaya, British Singapore, N. Borneo unified 1963)
Population:	22,662,000 (2002 estimate)
Leaders:	Prime Minister Mahathir bin Mohamed; Tuanku Syed Sirajuddin
Ethnicity:	58% Malay and other indigenous people; 24% Chinese; 8% Indian
Religion:	Islam, Buddhism, Daoism, Hinduism and others
Language:	Bahasa Melayu and others
Literacy:	84% (89% men; 78% women)
Exports:	electronics, petroleum, gas, chemicals, palm oil
Per capita GDP:	$9,000 (2001 estimate)
Unemployment:	3.7% (2001 estimate)
Percentage living in poverty:	8% (1998 estimate)
Known for:	musical travel ditty: "Malaysia: it's truly Asia."

You have to wonder if Malaysia means "country spread all over the place," because Malaysia is a patchwork pieced together from a little bit of this landmass and a little bit of that one. Part of it dangles off of Thailand, several parts are on northern Borneo, and at one point Malaysia also linked up with Singapore. Now it's home to the world's tallest buildings—the Petronas twin towers in Kuala Lumpur—and a wild ethnic mix. Politics are dramatic—aging Prime Minister Mahathir tearfully resigned in 2002, only to step back to the plate within an hour—and simmering in the background is militant Muslim anger. Hardcore Muslims have car bombed Thailand several times and some governments are issuing warnings to travelers not to go there. Some worry that Kuala Lumpur's towers will go the way of New York's.

Burma

FAST FACTS

Country:	Union of Myanmar
Capital:	Rangoon
Government:	military regime
Independence:	4 January 1948 (from U.K.)
Population:	42,238,000 (2002 estimate)
Leader:	Prime Minister and Chairman of the State Peace and Development Council/dictator Than Shwe (1992)
Ethnicity:	68% Burmese; 9% Shan; 7% Karen; 3% Chinese; others
Religion:	89% Buddhist; 4% Muslim; 4% Christian
Language:	Burmese
Literacy:	30% both sexes (1999 estimate)
Exports:	apparel, shoes, wood products, precious stones
Per capita GDP:	$1,500 (2001 estimate)
Unemployment:	5% (2001 estimate)
Percentage living in poverty:	23% (2000 estimate)
Known for:	Nobel Peace Prize winner, wacky twins

Thickly forested, mountainous and malaria-plagued, Burma, or Myanmar as the ruling military junta renamed it, is forgotten on the world power map. Rising up next to Thailand, this major opium grower has plenty to ponder—let's start with the fact that few governments challenge its dictatorship, even though the junta refused to step down in 1990 when Nobel Prize winner Aung San Suu Kyi and her party—National League for Democracy—won 82 percent of the vote. Since then Aung has mostly been locked up under house arrest, but international pressure in 2002 worked to get her out of the prison house, if not into her deserved office.

The Burmese military is known for its brutality and massacres, and when U.S. oil giant UNOCAL—which runs a pipeline through Burma to Thailand— hired them for security, they allegedly ravaged villages—including killing at least one baby by tossing it in a bonfire. UNOCAL, which rejected offers for human rights monitors to supervise the army, now stands accused of human rights violations in a California Superior Court.

Wilder and weirder are the fifteen-year-old Htoo twins, who are believed to have magical powers and run a rebel group of Karen villagers against Burma's army. They've been commanding grown men since they were nine—after they almost single-handedly drove off the vicious government military when it attacked their village. Sometimes "God's army" make runs into Thailand—once holding a hospital under siege while they ransacked the place for supplies.

Nepal

FAST FACTS

Country:	Kingdom of Nepal
Capital:	Kathmandu
Government:	parliamentary democracy/constitutional monarchy
Independence:	1768 (unified by Prithvi Shah)
Population:	25,285,000 (2001)
Leaders:	King Gyandera Bir Bikram Shah; Prime Minister Sher Bahadur Deuba
Ethnicity:	Brahman, Chetr, Newar and others
Religion:	87% Hindu; 8% Buddhist; 4% Islam
Language:	Nepali and a dozen other languages
Literacy:	28% (40% men; 14% women)
Exports:	carpets, clothing
Per capita GDP:	$1,400 (2001 estimate)
Unemployment:	47% (2001 estimate)
Percentage living in poverty:	42% (1995 estimate)
Known for:	stunning mountains that beckon climbers, being the only official Hindu State in world

Smashed between India and China, Nepal is a standout, from the towering Himalayas to the hideously low literacy rate and the $100 or so the Nepalese make a month, mostly from farming. But what seized the world's attention in 2001 was the bloody murder of the royal family, an act committed by the crown prince, who after turning a gun on himself became king for a few short hours on his deathbed. The reason Prince Dipendra committed famili-cide appears to be twisted in astrology: years before, a stargazer had warned beloved King Birendra not to allow the prince to marry until the prince was thirty-five—or the king would be killed. It may have been a case of self-fulfilling prophecy: when the king refused to let the twenty-five-year-old prince wed his fiancée for another ten years, the son flipped out and killed the whole family. At least that's one version of what happened during the ghastly royal dinner. Conspiracists point to the new King Gyanendra—the former king's brother, who just happened to be out of the country that night. Whatever his story is, King Gyanendra inherited a nightmare: Maoist guerrilla violence is raging at his door.

Sri Lanka

FAST FACTS

Country:	Democratic Socialist Republic of Sri Lanka (formerly Ceylon)
Capital:	Colombo
Government:	republic
Independence:	February 1948 (from U.K. as Ceylon)
Population:	19,577,000 (2002 estimate)
Leaders:	President Chandrika Bandaranaike Kumaratunga; Prime Minister Ranil Wickremesighe
Ethnicity:	74% Sinhalese; 18% Tamil; 7% Moor; others
Religion:	70% Buddhist; 15% Hindu; 8% Christian; 7% Muslim (1999 estimate)
Language:	Sinhala, Tamil, Moor
Literacy:	90% (93% men; 87% women)
Exports:	textiles, tea, diamonds
Per capita GDP:	$3,250
Unemployment:	8.8%
Percentage living in poverty:	22%
Known for:	Ceylonese tea

The Tamil Tigers sound cuddly but they're not: during the seventeen-year militant separatist movement they've spearheaded a drive to acquire a home for minority Tamils, more than sixty-five thousand have died. After meeting with peacemakers from Norway, the Tigers have changed their tune and now say they are pushing only for autonomy, and they're conducting peace talks with the government. Everyone hopes the Tigers aren't lions. In the meantime, the government, now headed by female President Kumaratunga, has done a fine job extending medical services and raising literacy levels. Got to start somewhere.

Cambodia

FAST FACTS

Country:	Cambodia
Capital:	Phnom Penh
Government:	multiple democracy under a constitutional monarchy
Independence:	November 1953 (from France); 1979 (from Khmer Rouge)
Population:	12,775,000 (2002 estimate)
Leaders:	King Norodom Sihanouk (Sept. 1993); Prime Minister Hun Sen (Nov 1998)
Ethnicity:	90% Khmer; 5% Vietnamese; 1% Chinese
Religion:	95% Theravada Buddhist
Language:	Khmer
Literacy:	35% (42% men, 22% women; 1990 estimate)
Exports:	timber, garments, rubber, rice, fish
Per capita GDP:	$1,300 (2001 estimate)
Unemployment:	3% (1999 estimate)
Percentage living in poverty:	36% (1997 estimate)
Known for:	country dotted with land mines and skulls

Tourists are slowly returning to this land of ancient domed temples and thick jungles, but many Cambodians who endured the bizarre and horrifying regime of madman Pol Pot (and the two decades of civil war that followed it) are still suffering psychological traumas. How does one forget that four-year nightmare that began in 1975—when cities were suddenly shut down, money, religion and education were banished, and everyone was forced to slash jungle and farm in the so-called "Killing Fields"? Nearly 2 million died—many executed for such things as looking intelligent or wearing glasses—and the UN is working with the Cambodian government to bring leaders of the Khmer Rouge regime to trial for genocide.

King Sihanouk is now back in power and Prime Minister Hun Sen is attracting hefty international aid, some of which funds thousands of new schools in the country where only one out of three can read. A folksy sort who likes to write songs, Sen is also being pressured to crack down on the sex slave trade that's emerged in Cambodia, ensnaring some two hundred thousand—mostly young girls—every year.

FUNDED GENOCIDE

The U.S. government supported and economically aided the Khmer Rouge regime (1975–1979) headed by Maoist dreamer Pol Pot. The reason: the Cambodians hated the American foe of that hour—the Vietnamese.

CANADA

FAST FACTS

Country:	Canada
Capital:	Ottawa
Government:	confederation with parliamentary democracy
Independence:	1 July 1867 (but still has ties to U.K.)
Population:	31,902,000 (2002 estimate);
Leaders:	Sovereign Queen Elizabeth II; Governor-General Adrienne Clarkson; Prime Minister Jean Chrétien
Ethnicity:	28% British origin; 23% French origin; 15% other European origin; 2% Amerindian
Religion:	46% Roman Catholic; 36% Protestant; 18% other
Language:	English and French
Literacy:	97% (1986 estimate)
Exports:	cars, newsprint, timber, petroleum
Per capita GDP:	$27,700 (2001 estimate)
Unemployment:	7.2% (2001 estimate)
Percentage living in poverty:	N/A
Known for:	Neil Young, Joni Mitchell, Paul Schaeffer and others who left

Standout Qualities

Northern Lights: visible from upper reaches
North Pole: moving from Canada to Russia
South Park: ouch!

Résumé

To say that Canada is America's number one trading partner illustrates the problem. First, most U.S. citizens don't know this fact. Secondly, Canada is America too.

Quick Tour

Still tied to the British crown—Queen Elizabeth II adorns their money and is nominally head of state—the world's second largest country, Canada, unfurls from the jagged, glacier-packed Canadian Rockies through oil fields and wheat plains across European-style cities and stunning modern metropolises to storm-blasted coasts and fishing towns socked in by fog. The stunning, nature-happy chunk of land, half of which is woods and forests, is largely undeveloped, since most residents live within two hundred miles of the U.S.-Canada border.

CANADA, NOT KANSAS!

A recent poll illustrates how clueless U.S. citizens are about the Great White North: nearly one-third of those polled didn't know that Canada was a country: they thought it was part of the U.S.

Canada has its problems: the French-speaking province of Québec may still secede; unemployment hovers around 7 percent; and Canada is experiencing a "brain drain"—as some Canadians look for higher-paying jobs in the U.S. Such woes aren't important to U.S. citizens.

DOUBLE OUCH!

Canadians who regard U.S. as best friend and ally: 60%
U.S. citizens who regard Canada as U.S. best friend and ally: 18%

What makes the U.S. gaze at its neighbor with dollar signs in its eyes is Canada's abundant natural resources: lumber, minerals, oil and natural gas are four major reasons why the U.S. not only deigns to speak to Canada, but has created trade-enhancing agreements such as the North American Free Trade Agreement (NAFTA).

WAR OF WOODS

Canada typically supplies one-third of the U.S.' "softwood"—pine, fir and spruce used for frames in house building. The Bush administration slapped harsh duties on Canadian wood—with 32 percent tariff. The U.S. says that Canadian lumber, less expensive because most comes from federal lands, is subsidized by the Canadian government. Canada disagrees; the World Trade Organization sides with Canada, saying U.S. tariffs are unfair.

End result: when the U.S. slaps huge tariffs on Canadian lumber—which it has done four times since 1940, twice under Bush—Canadian mills are forced to lay off. Some say 30,000 jobs have been axed due to recent U.S. tariffs. Since many small towns are dependent solely upon their mills, entire towns are turning out their lights.

Another reason the U.S. government doesn't totally ignore Canada: security. Since World War II—when Canada jumped into battle after Japan's attack on Pearl Harbor—the two countries have grown ever more entwined militarily. Both countries are founding members of the world's strongest military alliance, NATO. Both countries partake in NORAD (North American Air Defense Command)— its super-deluxe subterranean command control near Cheyenne Mountain—that since 1958 has monitored the seas and skies; originally designed to counter the "cold war threat," it remains the heart of North American security. Canada joined the U.S.-led Persian Gulf War against Iraq in 1991 and Canada was there at the U.S.' side for the Afghanistan invasion of 2001.

The movie *South Park: Bigger, Longer & Uncut* spoofs an inept Canadian attack on the U.S., but the two countries have in fact battled it out before. Most recent: the War of 1812.

Now the U.S. is pushing Canada to join in on its latest security scheme: the $60 billion national missile defense shield. Already under construction in Alaska, the program will surround North America (or at least the U.S.) with intercept missiles that would theoretically knock enemy missiles out of the sky. Canada, however, doesn't want to join in on this military money sucker that hasn't been proven to work. Besides, Canadians are worried it will trigger an arms race, and that's exactly what Canada is trying to prevent.

GREEN NEIGHBOR

A major force behind the international Land Mine Treaty and signatory of the Kyoto Protocol, Canada also signed the Nuclear Nonproliferation Treaty that is supposed to reduce the number of nuclear weapons. Canada has destroyed much of its nuclear arsenal and challenges the world leadership to eradicate their nukes and quit encouraging arms buildup around the world.

Canada may be bullied into it anyway. Canadians fear that if they don't sign on with the missile shield—even if the pricey project doesn't work—the U.S. will retaliate with more tariffs. Another concern: Canada would probably have to leave NORAD.

Factoid: Percent of Canada exports to U.S.: 86 percent.

Since 9/11, relations with Canada have become even touchier. The porous borders between the U.S. and Canada are cause for concern, as is Canada's immigration policy, which Washington legitimately criticizes as lax. Prime Minister Chrétien's government—embroiled in scandal over missing millions—is turning chilly toward the Bush administration and won't support an Iraq invasion unless approved by the UN Security Council. Chrétien labeling Bush as "naive" didn't help matters when he also said that Western arrogance was an underlying cause of the 9/11 attack. Never mind that he was probably right; the politically incorrect statement was taken by Washington as a slap.

FROST BUILDUP

On top of all the other tensions—lumber, Iraq and the National Missile Defense—an episode of friendly fire in Afghanistan, when U.S. pilots bombed Canadian troops and killed four Canadians, did not play well up north. Underscoring the seriousness of the situation: the U.S. military is trying the pilots for aggravated assault and dereliction of duty.

ENERGIZING EFFECTS

Canada, the world's tenth largest oil exporter, not only supplies its southern U.S. neighbor with petroleum and natural gas, through an elaborate power grid system, Canada also supplies 10 percent of U.S. electricity.

Future Forecast

An arctic wind may blast down from Canada if the U.S. doesn't start treating its neighbor a bit more like kin.

UP IN SMOKE

Canada never did partake in the U.S. boycott of Cuba, and north of the border one can buy Havana's finest cigars. Also annoying to DC: Canada legalized commercial harvesting of hemp—and is experimenting with using the plant to make paper. Downright scary to the U.S.: Canada is considering legalizing marijuana.

Hot Spots

U.S.-Canada border: 90 percent of Canadians live within two hours' drive of it; several suspected terrorists have been caught crossing it; massive six-hour delays are common at it since 9/11. Most alarming: the gaping "security holes" along coastlines.

IN TIMES OF NEED

The U.S. isn't always a jerk to Canada. In 1917, when an explosive gas-carrying ship in Halifax's harbor wrecked and let off a nuclear bomb–sized blast that killed more than seventeen hundred and blinded thousands more, Boston doctors rushed to the scene. In thanks, every year Canada sends a fifty-foot Christmas tree to Boston, which is illuminated in front of the famous Prudential Building.

British Columbia: The westernmost province, along the U.S.-Canadian border, supplies most of Canada's lumber.
Alberta: Source of Canada's gas and oil wealth and home of the Calgary Stampede.
Rodeo Roast: Prairie oysters are a delicacy around Calgary: Mmm, sautéed bull testicles!

Ontario: Home of the capital Ottawa and modern megalopolis Toronto.

Québec: They speak French (that the French don't understand); they live in old French-style towns (Québec City and Montreal), so why is anyone surprised they act whiny and fickle like the French and some days want to secede? Scandalous millions—an alleged gift from the Chrétien government—may have been paid out here to keep Québec part of the Canadian family.

Nunavut: Region chopped off of Arctic-hugging Northwest Territories and handed over to Inuit and other "first nations" following the official establishment of the new territory on April 1, 1999.

CULTURAL GENOCIDE?

During the so-called "Sixties Scoop"—that continued into the 1970s—government welfare agencies placed thousands of indigenous children in European-Canadian homes or sent them to religious schools. The social experiment backfired: many of the adoptees ran away and now suffer a wide range of mental problems. The "first nations" in general are not doing well: Canada's most impoverished population, they have high rates of suicide and alcoholism.

Hot Shots

Jean Chrétien: Canadian prime minister since 1993, elected to counter corruption, he's accused of political bribery in the name of keeping Canada united. Criticized for most everything, including his inarticulate manner of speaking—he's said to speak both French and English like a foreigner—he has nevertheless kept Canada united as one and has voiced some of Canada's typically mumbled concerns about its neighbor.

Africa . . . Asia . . . Europe . . .
Latin America . . . North America
Oceania **PART FOUR** Issues:
A Very Brief Overview . . . Africa . . .
Asia . . . Europe . . . Latin America
. . . North America . . .

. . . The Big Picture . . .

. . . Asia . . . Europe . . . Latin
America . . . North America. . . Oceania
. . . Issues: A Very Brief Overview . . .
Africa . . . Asia . . . Europe . . .
Latin America . . . North America
. . . Oceania . . . Issues: A Very Brief
Overview . . . Africa . . . Asia . . .
Europe . . . Latin America . . . North
America . . . Oceania . . .
Issues: A Very Brief Overview
. . . Africa . . . Asia . . . Europe . . .
Latin America . . . North America
. . . Oceania. . . Issues: A Very Brief
Overview . . . Africa . . . Asia . . .

AFRICA

Home to more than fifty countries, many of which are fond of frequently changing their names, Africa is huge, stunning, culturally complex, and chronically
lagging behind the rest of the world in its development and quality of life. The
vast continent of savannahs and plains is the world's most untouched, and outside its urban centers, wild animals still run free, lending more of an unsettled
feel to its austere beauty. Home to the Nile, the world's largest river, ancient
wonders such as the Egyptian pyramids, and mineral resources from oil to diamonds, Africa is also site of many of the worst global tragedies, particularly in
its sub-Saharan region, which suffers more than any other.

WE'LL TAKE THAT

The 1884 Berlin Conference divvied up Africa—and its resources—to European countries. Some African countries, such as Algeria, were still European
colonies until the 1960s.

Of all of Africa's current woes, HIV is the most horrific: the disease plagues
the continent, with more than 28 million cases of people suffering from it, and
leaving the legacy of millions of AIDS orphans. Part of the tragedy is that prevention efforts have been hampered both by leaders such as South Africa's
President Mbeki, who until recently denied HIV was transmitted by sex, and by
the Catholic HIV clinics, which typically refuse to counsel about the use of condoms to halt spread of the disease. But the tragedies of HIV don't stop there: it
is frequently passed on by rape, not only of women in countries ravaged by civil
wars such as Democratic Republic of the Congo, but also of children and infants, particularly in South Africa, the most heavily hit by HIV.

TERRORIST ACTS

Al Qaeda and other militant Muslim groups first demonstrated their ire in
Africa, which is no surprise since Sudan was Al Qaeda's first headquarters
and many of the group's higher-ups came from Egypt. Not only did Egypt's
militant Muslim group Gama'a Islamiya massacre fifty-eight at the Temple of
Luxor in Egypt in 1997, Al Qaeda bombed the U.S. embassies in Tanzania and
Kenya. Al Qaeda is believed to have been linked to the 1993 "Black Hawk
Down" incident in Somalia as well as the 2002 hotel bombing in Kenya.

Although the situation seems to be improving, Africa is still ravaged by frequent famine. Drought and flooding are two factors in the food shortages that
put millions at risk of starvation in 2002, but so is agricultural mismanagement,
such as in Zimbabwe, where President Robert Mugabe's government is seizing lands from white farmers and giving them to black farmers who have not
been trained on how to work such huge tracts. Another problem: new international trade agreements that force African countries to import American
and European food. Since American and European agriculture is heavily subsidized, the imported food sells at prices far less than what African farmers
need to charge to keep their land. As a result, some Africans are losing their
farms.

LITERACY PROBLEMS

If you can read this, you're probably not a resident of Niger (literacy rate 14
percent), Burkina Faso (19 percent), Mali (31 percent), Sierra Leone (31 percent) or Guinea (36 percent). Of all the African countries, the residents are
most likely to be able to read in Zimbabwe (85 percent), Mauritius (83 percent), and Libya (76 percent).

Civil wars haunt the land, such as the one in Sudan, where the fighting has
been going on for decades and Democratic Republic of the Congo is involved
in a particularly brutal struggle that has killed millions. Tribal rivalries play out
not only in wars, but massacres, as evidenced by the bloody attack of Tutsis by
Hutus in Rwanda. Of all the tensions, however, the one that seems to be most
on the increase is that between Muslims and non-Muslims or between Muslim
fundamentalists and moderates: Sudan, Nigeria and Algeria are three hot
spots for those religious struggles.

Factoid: Belgium's King Leopold II, whose men ravaged the Congo for its rubber during the late 1800s, working villagers to death and hacking off their hands, is held responsible for the death of over 10 million.

Politically the continent is moving toward democracy, but elections are often rigged, leaders dip into the coffers, and even when the country has resources, the money never seems to trickle down to the people. On a positive note: Chad is a new oil hot spot, the continent's problems are increasingly being pondered by international agencies, and rock star Bono of U2 dragged U.S. Secretary of the Treasury Paul O'Neill on a tour of Africa to illustrate that the place is full of potential and just needs some help. Some analysts are hopeful as well about the new fifty-three-country African Union, brought together by Libya's Moammar Qaddafi, which seeks to further solve Africa's problems and promote economic development and democratic government. That the AU is headed by South Africa's President Mbeke, however, doesn't bode well, particularly for a continent crippled by AIDS.

MAJOR ISSUES

HIV: prevention hindered by ignorant leaders who deny HIV is transmitted by sex and Catholic AIDS clinics that refuse to discuss condoms

Famine: chronic issue that threatens, and sometimes kills, millions a year; the problem is worsened by international trade agreement

Agricultural reform: Zimbabwe is seizing large tracts from white farmers, but the inexperienced black farmers have never planted on such wide scales; exacerbated by trade agreements that require that African countries import subsidized American and European food at prices less than African farmers can charge and stay in business

Poverty: even in oil rich countries such as Nigeria, corruption and mismanagement prevent the country from ever getting ahead; cacao and coffee, two of Africa's main exports, are also subject to great fluctuations in price; currently both products are selling low

Religious/ethnic struggles: problems between Muslims and non-Muslims and between different tribes lead to constant wars

Chronic victimization: despite providing food aid and humanitarian supplies, Western countries tend to continue their history of exploiting Africa; economic deals often include requirements not necessarily beneficial to the African countries, such as privatization of water by questionable international companies and international imports that devastate local farmers; if they're not getting ripped off from the outside world, Africans often suffer from within—many leaders are notoriously corrupt

ASIA

Embracing more cultures, religions and ethnic groups than anywhere else on the planet, Asia—that landmass that stretches from Japan to Israel, unrolling across Russia, China, Afghanistan, the 'Stans, Iran and Saudi Arabia along the way—contains most of the world's oil treasures: 66 percent of the known reserves are buried in the Middle East alone (mostly in Saudi Arabia and Iraq), but there's plenty of black gold gurgling up in Russia, Kazakhstan and Azerbaijan as well. Home to the most people on the planet and the fastest growing populations, Asia is also site of the most intractable armed conflicts, which have been going so long that they just seem a fact of life. But lately they've gotten worse, as if a tectonic plate was shifting and setting off all of Asia's fragile points.

FLASH POINTS

Wars have been raging on and off for decades across Asia. A few places where the rage and violence never seems to die down:

Kashmir
Israel/Palestine
Afghanistan
Chechnya

Also potentially problematic: Indonesia, North Korea, Malaysia, Taiwan and new conflicts between Israel and the Lebanon-Syria duo. And it's anyone's guess what will happen in Iraq—and environs—if the U.S. sends in troops.

Across the continent, regions seems hell-bent on redrawing their country lines: Taiwan, Tibet and the farthest western reaches of China (Xinchiang)—all want independence from the motherland; Chechnya wants to shake off from Russia, Kashmir is pulled between India and Pakistan, the southern parts of the Philippines want to be free, and assorted parts of Indonesia want to break off. Part of what is fueling the secessionist desire is religion: most of these regions are Muslim-dominated areas, which want to install Islamic governments. Tibet is wrapped in the Buddhism that makes the mountainous area so different than Beijing. Taiwan is simply economically, politically and socially different from China, which tries to boss it around and has kept it in the fray.

MAJOR ISSUES

Religious divisions	Shortage of water
Ethnic gratings	Too many nukes
Constant power plays	Dislike of U.S. bases

The other factor that divides the land is ethnicity—Afghanistan being the finest example. They may all look like Afghans to us, but within that world they're Pashtuns, Tajiks, Uzbeks and Hazaras, and except when an invading outsider stumbles in, they've been fighting among themselves since a little after the sun was born. The Kurds are so ethnically different that they mostly live in separate parts of Turkey and Iraq—an area they call Kurdistan, and which the British promised them back when the dust from the breakup of the Ottoman Empire was settled. The central governments of both Turkey and Iraq have clamped down hard on the group that refuses to fit in: Turks tried to strip away their identity, right down to the language, and Iraq gassed them.

When not busy fighting outsiders, the people of these countries tend to squabble among themselves. And Israel and Palestine blend both the religious divisions and the ethnic edginess that define the whole continent in an endless saga that simply seems unresolvable.

Layered on top of that is a battle for resources, in this case particularly water. The random location of oil wealth has created financial inequality throughout the Middle East. But water is just as important: a huge factor in the feuds between Israel and its neighbors, it's also straining relations between Arab countries, particularly Turkey—at the headwaters of the Tigris and Euphrates, which it's madly damming—and Syria and Iraq downstream.

Despite all the problems, experts predict that the twenty-first century will belong to Asia. China's surging productivity—it has the world's second largest GDP—new oil and gas discoveries in Russia and central Asia, and India's diversified economy that's increasingly computer-linked certainly point to potential financial dominance. But the region's ethnic, religious, resource and political battles keep bogging it down. Factor in the fact that at least five countries in Asia are nuclear powers (China, Russia, India, Pakistan and Israel—and probably North Korea and Japan) and you may have the most likely spot for World War III.

EUROPE

They may all fall under the heading European Union one day, but European countries—even those bonded by use of the common euro—remain ethnically homogenous within and distinct from one another, right down to the language that they cling to much more firmly than their currency. Rarely does a French man marry a Dutch woman or a Spaniard wed a German, and even countries are divided into slightly different ethnic regions. The previous hatred and animosities between Western European countries are now hidden mostly in jokes. "Typically Dutch!" say the Belgians of bad driving, bad service or bad weather in the country that once dominated them, until the nineteenth century. "Typically Belgian," say the Dutch about bad service, bad architecture or bad attitude, in the country that used to dangle in the most nether regions of the Netherlands. Not so for Eastern Europe, where there's still plenty of real tension, especially between Serbs and Albanians.

Long divided by empires and bloody wars, Europe knocked itself out during World War II—literally. In the course of putting itself back together after that debacle that killed millions and ravaged its cities and towns, Europe embarked on an intra-country cooperation that defines its political atmosphere today. While each country retains independence, its own language and history, fifteen countries of Western Europe altered the course of the continent when they forged the European Union in 1992. The umbrella government is still battling things out—issues such as agricultural subsidies benefit some countries more than others, and smaller countries fear that their voices will be shut out by more powerful ones. Nevertheless, support for the union is high—and their adoption of a common currency, the euro, has made life a lot easier.

MAJOR ISSUES

Unification: the West and the East
Immigration: in many countries immigrants are having far more children than the original ethnic groups

Racism: subtle though it may be, a class system exists within Europe: native Europeans don't socialize with the immigrants, who are many rungs down on the economic ladder

LESS GAS, FEWER CARS

Although the U.K. has some oil reserves in the North Sea, Europe as a whole is extremely dependent on imported oil, a factor that has led to the development of sophisticated train networks and public transportation systems. Another factor that makes driving cars less attractive: the price of oil—which unlike in the U.S. is not largely subsidized. In the EU, one can pay $3 or more per gallon of gas.

After Eastern Europe emerged from communism in 1991, many of the countries wanted to establish stronger links with Western Europe. Starting in 2003, more and more are coming on board, changing policies and joining arms in the EU. By 2005, when two dozen individual countries will make up the heavily bureaucratic EU system, the bugs may have been worked out. Some, however, fear the union will sink under the weight of so many countries united only by location—and divided by incomes, languages, economic potential and almost everything else. Whether Europe can pull off the daunting task of truly uniting West with East remains to be seen.

IMMIGRATION

During 2001, many European countries witnessed a shift to the political right. One reason: "guest workers" and other immigrants—many from Africa, many Muslim, some from Eastern Europe—who came to the countries seeking menial labor. Once welcomed, during the 1970s and 1980s, because they filled the jobs many Western Europeans didn't want, they are viewed more harshly lately. Many immigrants have not really assimilated into the society: they often don't speak the language and in some countries are the group that most requires social welfare. They also tend to be the group with the highest population rate. All these factors were hammered in by right-wing politicians.

Brrr!: Icy feelings blast across EU as Europeans debate their stances on U.S. policies, particularly in war. U.K. and Spanish leaders signed on for Iraqi war; France and Germany said no. The majority of European residents are against the U.S.-led war in Iraq.

LATIN AMERICA

THE NAME

Central America, South America and often the Caribbean Islands are lumped together under the heading "Latin America." The very name illustrates one of the main issues here: "Latin" refers to the Spanish and Portuguese who ran the place as their own from the 1500s into the 1800s, leaving behind lasting imprints such as their languages and the Catholic religion. The term ignores the complex cultures of the Aztecs, Mayas and Incas—and hundreds of other indigenous people—who thrived here long before the conquistadors showed up and changed all the rules.

The land that sits at our back door might as well be in a different solar system: most U.S. citizens don't travel there—it's always appeared politically shaky, potentially violent and possibly upsetting to the stomach—and we don't follow the politics. U.S. businesses, however, are much more savvy: lured by its fertile, resource-rich lands and cheap labor since the late 1800s, North American enterprises have set up businesses there, from banana plantations and logging operations to copper mines and manufacturing plants. The U.S. government has also been dialed in to the point of being interventionist: waving the Monroe Doctrine, the U.S. has had no qualms about helping toss elected leaders deemed harmful to American business interests—even if that means backing military juntas and dictators. We've armed guerrillas, we've trained the military officers who have overseen the most brutal, dirty wars, and we've funded drug eradication programs—such as Plan Colombia—that deaden the land and make peasants ever poorer. Consequently, an anti-Yankee sentiment is on the rise in the region.

BONAPARTE'S LEGACY

Napoleon indirectly caused the independence movements of the 1800s: when he took over Spain for three years, Latin Americans saw an opening to rebel against the dispirited and weakened Spanish.

Whether you're talking about the Amerindians or the landless peasants or the illegal drug industry, most of Latin America's problems are locked in two simple facts: 10 percent of the people hold 40 percent of the land and wealth (and almost all the power) and most of those rich are white. The social caste system created by the colonial Europeans remains, and blatant racism is nearly systemized: white descendents of the Europeans top the power pyramid, followed by mestizos—white and Indian ancestry—then blacks, then the indigenous tribes who once ruled here, many of whom are pushed into the jungle and backlands. Little opportunity exists for those who aren't the upper crust, but that is slowly changing: indigenous people (Aztecs, Mayas, Incas and more), whose ancient cities are still being discovered in jungles from Mexico to Peru, are sick of suffering the low-man-on-the-totem-pole status that they've endured since the Spaniards moved in during the 1500s and stayed for three centuries.

Most Amerindians are peasants, but they sure aren't the only ones hurting in these countries where typically between 20 and 50 percent live in poverty: they're joined by landless farmers and the urban poor, who number in the tens of millions. Separately or united, throughout Latin America, they're rising up and demanding the government give them land. Between job shortages and poverty, general restiveness is the mood in many countries where you're either very rich or very poor: kidnapping is increasingly common, bands of the poor are ganging together looting neighborhoods of the rich, and crime in some places has gotten so bad, bandits demand the shoes off victims' feet. Foreign investors are skipping over Latin America and instead heading to Asia, and companies that are already there are closing up shop, fueling more unemployment and continuing the downward spiral.

MAJOR ISSUES

Poverty: Rising unemployment and shamefully low wages have created a surge in crime, kidnapping and bands of poor who loot the rich.

Land reform: Plantation and ranch owners have most of the land; landless peasants would like some of it.

Agricultural reform: In drug-producing countries such as Colombia, coca farmers don't have anything else that's profitable to plant.

Infrastructure: Outlying areas in most Latin American countries have few roads, little electricity and shortages of clean drinking water.

Financial woes: Argentina's economic ills, created in part by international lenders extending too many loans to questionable leaders, are spreading.

The underground drug industry and its mafia thugs are likewise triggering violence, from the volatile triangle where Colombia, Peru and Ecuador meet, to Central America and the Caribbean, through which cocaine and heroin travel toward their North American markets. Latin American leaders keep pointing out that the U.S. creates the drug trade problems with its vociferous appetite for the illicit substances; the U.S. keeps trying to stomp drugs out by supplying guns, military equipment and herbicides, which further fuels violence.

DIRTY FIGHTING

Argentina wasn't the only country during the 1970s that experienced a subversive "Dirty War" in which the military abducted and killed suspected dissidents. Across Latin America, many countries experienced the phenomenon of "the disappeared."

But amid all the social mayhem and unhappiness, there is a ray of light: currently all Latin American governments are democracies with elected heads of state. The way things are going, though, it's hard to believe that rule by military junta will remain a thing of the past.

NORTH AMERICA

"We are the champions, my friends."—Queen

Hang around long enough—as in a few millennia—and everybody has their time to rule: Spain, France, England, China, the Romans, the Ottoman Empire, the Abbasid Dynasty, the Mongols, the Incas and the Mayas are but a few who've taken their turn as the dominant society on the planet, or at least as much as had then been discovered. The past century, particularly since World War II, has belonged to North America, especially the U.S., with Canada geographically along for the ride. With a per capita income of $36,300 and Canada following right behind at $27,700, we're the richest continent on the globe. And it's true: some people are jealous, although they're not usually the militant types.

MAJOR ISSUES	
Car and oil dependence	Overeating
Racism	International illiteracy
Depression	Economy that depends on cars, oil
Arming the world	and arms sales

To much of the world, North America has everything: freedom, beautiful land, clean water, a dependable economy, and lots of American style and know-how, evident in slick media, trendsetting culture and amazing marketing skills. Women have more rights than anywhere else in the world, there's still a Horatio Alger possibility, albeit lessened if one is Indian, Mexican or black—or Muslim. Racism still abounds, though it isn't KKK style much anymore—although given the vast ethnic diversity of North America, for decades now, we've more or less gotten along surprisingly well. Where North America, particularly the U.S., most goes awry is its settlement patterns, plans pushed by the auto and tire industries that ripped up trolley tracks. In most of the world, the periphery neighborhoods that ring a city are the least desirable places to live. In

North America, the suburbs were marketed as the place to be. And many Americans live there, requiring that to go to work, to the store or the bank, they have to drive their car. That design flaw alone has made the U.S. both vulnerable and defensive: we rely on foreign oil, we pollute the air, we get fat—and we don't want to change. Ask an American to carpool and he or she starts sputtering. Go for a walk in the suburbs, and people stop to offer you a ride, thinking your auto is on the blink or that you're a prostitute. Cars fuel the American economy—as does oil—and you might not be able to get a loan to go to school, but you can probably land one for an SUV.

LESSONS FROM THE CHINESE

The powerful and advanced Chinese empire began to crumble in the fifteenth century when it ceased to look outward, focused only on itself, shrugged off the rest of the world and stopped discovering foreign lands. Although international travel is at an all-time high, only 10 percent of Americans own passports, few speak foreign languages and few have mastered the intricacies of the world map.

Armchair Diplomat Says: Spend more time on geography in schools and give more specials on the news, taking viewers by the hand instead of slamming them with tidbits of information forgotten by the commercial break.

Slowly that's changing: more and more people are moving into the city, more and more planned "urban villages" are sprouting up where you can walk to the store, work and the bank, more and more people are working at home. But the form of transportation that defines North America keeps getting the U.S. in trouble: if we didn't so love Saudi crude, we might never have encountered the likes of Osama bin Laden. And if Americans weren't so addicted to oil, we might not be spending billions to go into Iraq, as seems likely to be the case as of fall 2002. The other flaw, at least as seen from an international perspective, in the land of plenty, where so many in the world long to live, is what powers the American economy: sales of arms, cars, oil and drugs. Not to mention that we always ignore our geographical sibling, the Great White North.

OCEANIA

The faraway Southern Hemisphere region that contains New Zealand, the Cook Islands and the tropical islands of Micronesia is mostly defined by behemoth Australia—the only country in the world that takes up an entire continent. A former British colony that's still linked to the monarchy—a bond that many Aussies want to hack—white-dominated, well-to-do Australia keeps coming under international fire for its immigration policy: ships of Afghans and Kurds, among others, have been refused port entry, even when those on board were famished. If they're allowed to disembark, wanna-be immigrants who don't arrive with their papers already in order usually wait in detention centers for years before their case it heard.

NATIVE CONCERN

Known for their telepathic powers and painting, the Aborigines who once had the place pretty much to themselves are not well-integrated into modern Australian society. Making up 2 percent of the population, Aborigines are the poorest Australians and have lost their tribal ways as they settle into the ghettos, where they suffer from extremely high rates of alcoholism.

Developed mostly on its east coast—with most Aussies living in the southeast—Australia is bursting with resources: most of the planet's diamonds, bauxite and offshore oil can be found here. The land also has more uranium than anywhere else—and its sale keeps the world nuclear-powered. Since World War II, when the U.S. helped Aussies fight the Japanese in the Battle of the Coral Sea, Australia and the U.S. have been militarily allied. A signatory of the postwar ANZUS (Australia, New Zealand, U.S.) security treaty, Australia ever since has been a site of several controversial military bases and installations, including super-secret Pine Gap, an eerily modern construction in the midst of the desert that's said to be a major U.S. intelligence center. Aussies are perpetually intrigued with what really happens at the base, which more and more is the site of protests.

LI'L SIS

That broken finger of land lying to Australia's southeast, gorgeous New Zealand is liberal, feisty and populated mostly by Europeans, although the Maori are still abundant, and not quite so ticked off, since after 150 years of waiting they finally received compensation for the land the Britons snatched from them in 1840. Still loyal to the British crown, the country boasts a woman prime minister, Helen Clark, and the government has been getting the U.S. military's cold shoulder, since banning American ships containing nuclear devices from docking in its ports.

MAJOR ISSUES

Down Under syndrome: Hard to get to from the U.S. and Europe, Australia et al. often aren't major players in world politics, although they often send troops to help out in conflicts

Dethroning: Movement under way to cut Australia's ties to Britain

ISSUES

A Very Brief Overview

Arms

Love doesn't make the world go round, arms sales do. World leaders are addicted to both buying and selling the nifty war toys which become flashier every year: in 2002, more than $700 billion was shucked out for tanks, fighter planes, helicopters, missiles, bombs, land mines, automatic weapons and all the fixins—making arms sales the top legal moneymaker in the world.

Wishful thinking: when the Cold War heaved a final sigh in the early 1990s with the breakup of the Soviet Union, experts predicted major weapons slashing and defense budget cuts. Dream on: instead arms sales shot through the roof. Saudi Arabia and the United Arab Emirates seriously spiffed up their military after Desert Storm, purchasing billions of dollars of shiny new equipment a year, pumping up the American economy in the process. Another huge arms junkie: Taiwan.

Fingers wag at rogue North Korea for its missile sales, but the U.S. is by far the number one dealer of lethal weaponry, selling $11 billion of arms in 2001; Britain, France, Russia, China and Israel also cash in on the highly profitable arms peddling game. The billion-dollar figures for the amounts being *sold,* however, are only part of the world picture: nearly as much is simply handed out as presents from the arms-happy Santa Clauses, who now grease the wheels of diplomacy with promises of fighter planes instead of gifts of fine scotch. And it's not as though older model weapons, planes and tanks just disappear: they just get passed down the arms food chain. Colombian rebels use guns the U.S. gave to Central American freedom fighters in the 1980s, Afghan warlords still cling to arms the U.S. supplied them with to fight Soviets, and most small-scale civil wars rely on weaponry passed out during the Cold War.

What started as a defense mechanism to fight communism has turned into such a lucrative biz—and such an easy way to boost the economy—that arms sellers are just as hooked on selling as the buyers are on buying. But while the

U.S. is mightily arming the world, assuming that none of the weapons it sells will be turned against the U.S., it's also outpacing the world: the budget request for arms purchase in 2003 is $396 billion—more than the total combined military purchases of the next twenty countries on the arms buyer list.

Also cause for concern: the new weaponry used in "conventional war" by countries such as the U.S. and Britain. Armor-piercing depleted uranium (DU) now tips missiles and ammunition that has left the ground, water and air radioactive in southern Iraq, Kosovo, Serbia and most likely Afghanistan, where many believe it was used. If such radiological devices were used in the U.S., we'd be calling them dirty bombs—particularly if they also contained deadly plutonium, an ingredient that reportedly spikes American weapons made with DU. The Defense Department maintains that DU isn't hazardous, but cancer rates in Iraq, say physicians there, are seven times higher in some parts near Desert Storm battlefields. Some war veterans are also raising a big stink, believing that DU may be responsible for "Gulf War Syndrome," and some physicians in the international community are wondering if GWS isn't really radiation sickness. NATO and the EU won't use weapons made with depleted uranium until the verdict is in, and the World Health Organization, which is supposed to be looking into the effects of DU in Iraq, has been suspiciously silent.

Here Comes Santa Claus: The top three recipients of free U.S. military aid: Israel, Egypt and Colombia—together they receive more than $6 billion in giveaways.

Defense manufacturers aren't the only ones hawking military wares: the big deals are often pushed by U.S. presidents, secretaries of state, secretaries of defense—and people who have formerly held those important posts. Between intensive lobbying efforts, hefty political donations and promises dangled before today's politicians of future jobs in the industry, so many politicos feed from the defense contractor trough that the whole thing smacks of conflict of interest.

A FEW INTERESTING EXAMPLES

Lynne Cheney, wife of the vice president, until 2001 was director of Lockheed Martin, the number one U.S. manufacturer of arms and a major benefactor in the missile shield defense contracts; George Bush, Sr., and former Secretary of State James Baker are consultants for the Carlyle Group, an "investment firm" started by former Secretary of Defense Frank Carlucci that, among other things, brokers arms deals.

Countries such as North Korea, Iraq and Iran are accused of trying to develop weapons of mass destruction, but the biological and chemical legacy of the Cold War still haunts: even though the U.S. and Russia have both officially shut their bio-chem programs, the nasty stuff they produced—anthrax, the plague, smallpox and more—is still floating around.

Unilateralism

The U.S. is getting a bad reputation for often going it alone and disregarding what the international community thinks. On the one hand, the U.S. is now the lone superpower—and can get away it. On the other hand, such moves ultimately alienate the U.S. in the eyes of the world and cause the country to be more of a target, as it seems that America is out to hog the planet.

SIGNED IN INVISIBLE INK?

The U.S. refused to sign or ratify—or "unsigned"—the following international agreements and treaties, which were signed and ratified by all or almost all of the other world players:

Kyoto Protocol (to reduce greenhouse emissions)
The International Criminal Court (to establish the UN worldwide court for prosecuting war crimes and crimes against humanity)
The Comprehensive Nuclear Test Ban (limits nuclear testing)
Land Mine Treaty (bans use of anti-personnel land mines)

Nuclear Matters

The good news: nuclear energy doesn't produce visible air pollution. The bad news: it produces just about everything else. Nuclear plants are terrorist targets—Al Qaeda, for one, has plans to blow them up. We still have no idea how to safely store nuclear wastes that remain extremely radioactive for millions of years: Yucca Flats in Nevada is the current storage spot, but it's earthquake-prone. The global transportation of nuclear material, whether it's via ships from Japan to England or via trains and trucks across the U.S., is fraught with hazards—from wrecks to hijacking. And despite the 1950s campaign pushing the "peaceful use of the atom," the plutonium that nuclear plants were created in large part to produce is the deadly ticker in nuclear bombs: often countries that have nuclear plants have nuclear weapons—or want to build them.

Chernobyl and Three Mile Island notwithstanding, the nuclear energy business is still humming along, with new plants going on line from Finland to Taiwan. Germany is the only country trying to completely wash its hands of them: all nuclear reactors are scheduled to be shut down by 2020.

Countries that admit to having nuclear weapons: U.S., Russia, China, U.K., France, India, Pakistan
Others that don't admit it: Israel, probably North Korea and Japan
Countries that could make them: anyone who has or had a nuclear plant—33 countries in all
Number of operating nuclear plants in the world: 448
   Top ten:
      U.S.: 104 (additional 25 shut down)
      France: 58
      Japan: 54
      U.K.: 35
      Russia: 30
      Germany: 19 (additional 14 shut down)
      Ukraine: 15
      Canada: 14
      South Korea: 13 (plus 5 under construction)
      Sweden: 12

Meanwhile the U.S. and Russia are slashing their nuclear arms to some two thousand each. While Russia is planning to destroy its weapons, the U.S. is merely disassembling and mothballing its retired nukes, which can be called back into play if required.

Water

The world is running out of clean drinking water. Already 20 percent of the population doesn't have access to the substance that is still often viewed in industrialized countries as an endless resource. Dams, irrigation, overpumping are draining supplies so quickly they can't be replenished. There is so much friction in the Middle East and Africa over water rights that experts predict we'll soon be looking at major water wars. In the U.S. too there are plenty of water worries—from California to Tennessee, and including the chronic shortages in western Florida that require desalination plants in Tampa Bay.

THE NEXT SPLASH

Desalination may be the wave of the future, and thousands of plants world-wide already take salt out of seawater. The downside is that the process—a form of reverse osmosis—is costly and it's not energy efficient: huge amounts of oil or natural gas are needed to run the plants.

While the value of the resource is overlooked by many household con-sumers, it hasn't been ignored by corporations: with numerous countries suf-fering from old, leaking pipes, companies such as Bechtel and Vivendi have galloped in offering to put in new systems. Within months of taking over opera-tions, they've so jacked up the price—doubling and tripling monthly rates in poor areas of Argentina and Bolivia for instance—that the masses have rioted in the streets, sending the companies fleeing.

Water Waster: Nearly three-quarters of water in the U.S. is used in the bathroom.

Cars and Oil

The slimy stuff is fueling more than our cars: it's driving the U.S. into wars. We Americans may be loath to confront our addiction to the stuff, but the rest of the world is very aware of the fact that with 4 percent of the population, the U.S. uses 25 percent of the world's oil, and we're willing to sacrifice global sta-bility to ensure that we have unhindered access at prices we like. What further damages the American image abroad: the U.S. refusal to sign treaties, such as the Kyoto Protocol, that aim to reduce air pollution from fossil fuels.

DIRTY POLITICS

In a 2002 Pentagon briefing, Rand think tank thinker Laurent Murawiec por-trayed Saudi Arabia as "the kernel of all evil" and recommended that the U.S. seize Saudi oil fields. Many pundits believe any war in Iraq goes far beyond the fear of Saddam developing weapons of mass destruction and is mostly a way for the U.S. to gain control of Iraqi oil and establish a presence in the Middle East to ensure cheap unfettered oil for the Western world, particularly the U.S.

Food

Who'd have guessed that food would become such a complicated, controversial issue in the twenty-first century? The most disturbing issue surrounding it is that despite there being plenty of food in the world, millions starved to death over the past decade because they couldn't get to it or vice versa. The debate over genetically modified corn and soy rages from England to Africa, and some American chefs are boycotting environmentally engineered fish. Mad cow disease and hoof and mouth nearly slaughtered Europe's beef industry over the past decade and raised serious questions about the safety of meat. Overfishing of oceans is wiping out species since small fry are caught before they reproduce. Heavily subsidized agribusiness in the U.S. and Europe is pushing out the world's small farmers—who can't compete with big business prices and are selling their farms, a situation that only perpetuates famine in developing countries. The number of obese people in the world—1.1 billion—now equals the number of underfed. American cattle and pigs are pumped up with hormones and antibiotics, fruit is often dyed, sprayed and waxed, hybrid strains emphasize improved shelf life over taste. Overcrowded conditions for farm animals have animal rights activists screaming, and vegetarianism is growing, with non–meat eaters pointing out that the grain that feeds a herd of cattle could feed millions of people instead. What can one say except "What's for dessert?"

HOW SAFE?

Monsanto, Dow and the U.S. Food and Drug Administration would like you to know that they consider genetically modified (GM) plants and food to be 100 percent safe, and there haven't appeared to be adverse health effects since the GM products began flooding the markets in the mid 1990s. Others aren't so sure and believe that the products are being rushed onto American food shelves. After mass protests, Europe won't accept some GM food from the U.S.; African countries initially rejected GM corn in fall 2002 out of fears that its kernels would be planted and permanently alter African crops. Whatever the health effects, the truth is GM plants and their seeds don't stay put; cases where they've contaminated nearby farmers' crops have ironically resulted in GM seed producers bringing the farmers to trial for not paying them for the genetically altered seeds. Developed to resist predators, GM crops instead often require more herbicides than normal crops, not to mention chemical releasers that allow them to grow. Some wonder if GM food is mostly a grand marketing plan: not only does one buy seeds from producers such as Monsanto, but farmers are also required to buy specialized chemicals and pesticides from them as well.

Drugs

Whether you're talking about illegal drugs that bring in between $400 and $800 billion a year, or you're referring to the sanitized capsules and pills pushed by MDs, the drug business is typically the world's second biggest and most lucrative, a fact that seems to indicate that many people are sick, in pain, unable to cope, and perhaps that humans have a need to alter consciousness and cop a buzz.

The illegal drug biz poses plenty of problems from convincing poppy and coca farmers to change crops, to the violence that accompanies drug production and delivery to markets, to the addictive qualities of the substances and the prison system clogged up with minor drug offenders who might benefit more from counseling. Issues swirl around legal drugs too—from the ethics of wooing physicians to peddle possibly unneeded drugs, to the overuse of antibiotics that create treatment-resistant strains, to the fact that American pharmaceuticals are the most profitable businesses in the world and Americans pay far higher prices than anybody else for their medicine. The ethics of charging exorbitant amounts for HIV drugs have caused international rifts: when American drug companies refused to lower their prices for HIV treatments, Asian companies began producing their own, which led to American firms screaming about trade agreements and violation of copyrights.

Another matter for concern: industrialized societies—with their painkillers, sleeping pills, antidepressants and anxiety meds—are becoming heavily drugged and increasingly complacent.

FLOWER POWER

The U.S. takes an aggressive approach to cultivation of drug crops: in Colombia, for example, we financially back fumigation of crops (and peasants), shooting drug planes out of the sky and heavily arming the military to battle farmers. Such actions haven't produced much besides violence: after two years of strong-arm tactics, Colombia's cocaine production is higher than it was before the spraying, shooting and arming began. More effective: crop substitution such as that pushed by the king of Thailand. Now former poppy farmers in Thailand are making far more from growing apricots and chrysanthemums, and poppy production is essentially wiped out.

Population

WORLD'S TOP TEN HIGHEST POPULATION GROWTH RATES

1.	Marshall Islands	3.88%
2.	Eritrea	3.84%
3.	Sierra Leone	3.61%
4.	Singapore	3.5%
5.	Afghanistan	3.48%
6.	Somalia	3.48%
7.	West Bank	3.45%
8.	Oman	3.43%
9.	Kuwait	3.38%
10.	Yemen	3.38%

Doubling Time: To figure out how many years will be required before a country's population doubles, divide seventy by the birthrates. For instance, a country with a 2 percent birthrate will double its population in thirty-five years.

The world may feel plenty crowded already with its current population of 6 billion, but just wait until 2050 when global populations may be 9 billion or more. Asia and Africa are the regions where population is surging—typically in poorer areas least able to cope with the growth—but the U.S. population is climbing as well, being five times greater than that of Western Europe.

Babies Galore: The world population rises by over 100 million each year—twice the number of people who died during the Second World War.

What it all means if population continues galloping ahead at today's rate: more grappling for land, food and water, more divisions between rich and poor. What could slow the growth: more education and family planning.

Factoid: In 2002, the Bush administration withdrew its pledged $400 million from the UN Population Fund.

Treatment of Women

The sight of Afghan women covered in burkas became the symbol of their oppressed life under the Taliban, who forced them to quit school and quit working and who placed white flags over the houses of unmarried women to signal availability to marauding by Taliban forces. The brutal treatment of women is almost ritualistic in parts of the world: female slaves are bought and sold in Eastern Europe and forced into prostitution in European capitals; Sudan runs a slave trade of Dinka women from the south. Rape camps were the trademark of Serbian soldiers in Bosnia, and gang rapes by armies are common in India as well as Africa, where they are linked to the spread of HIV. In some Muslim societies, including Egypt, women are forced to undergo female genital mutilation, and in Pakistan group rape is meted out as a punishment.

In general, Western Europe holds a much more egalitarian view of females, but by far the best place to be a woman is the U.S.

A Few More Issues by the Numbers

People with HIV and AIDS: 40 million worldwide, about 28 million in Africa
HIV clinics in Africa that refuse to mention condoms: about 25%
World's population living in poverty according to the World Bank: 50%
Number of people who live on less than $1 a day: 1.2 billion
Adult population in downtown Detroit that is functionally illiterate: 47%
Amazon rain forest that could be hacked down by 2020: 42%
Number of refugees worldwide in 2002: 20 million

While this ain't a pretty picture, it is *our* reality, the one we *all* live in—not just "them" over there.

Afterword:
Ten Things You Can Do

The biggest dangers facing the U.S. right now are not terrorists who are out to get us, but American complacency and ignorance, two factors that have helped to fuel the rise of militant sorts. The worst thing, I believe, that you can do after finishing this book is to think "Wow, the world is really a mess!" and then go on living your life exactly as you had before. As an American you are one of the most empowered people on the planet, and I hope that you use that power to write letters and make phone calls and follow issues and developments in countries. A few things that you can do:

1. Buy a world map. It's the best way to get a sense of the world picture and follow along with the news. I have one hanging on the wall: you'd think it was a priceless work of art for all the attention it receives from visitors.

2. Plug into the world media: www.news.bbc.co.uk—the Internet site of the British Broadcasting Corporation—gives a far broader view of the world than much of the American media, follows international issues extensively with detailed reports, and also boasts helpful country profiles on its site; you can access the entire archives for free and you could get lost on the site for days. The weekly London-based magazine *The Economist* is a lively and informed political read despite its name. Through the subscription service thePaperboy.com you can get papers from all over the world via the Internet; another great research tool for accessing articles from the U.S. and abroad is elibrary.com—you can try it free for a week. Want to know what the international media are saying about the U.S.? Check out the U.S. State Department's site at www.usinfo.state.gov/homepage.htm. Their International Information Programs' Office of Research provides "Foreign Media on the U.S.," a very insightful summary of how the U.S. is viewed in the world press.

3. Check out Internet sites—and print out the articles for later study. World-watch.com brings you up to date on many pressing international issues, particularly of an environmental nature. Foreign Policy Association spotlights contemporary issues at fpa.org, where you can also order their short, easy-to-read books. PBS runs a fabulous site at pbs.org, where you can watch or print out shows, from *Frontline* to *The Jim Lehrer Newshour.* Alternet.org, TomPaine.com and Commondreams.org turn you on to the alternative news: you can read about issues here weeks or months before they hit the mainstream press; one of Alternet's many stars to follow is Jim Lobe. The Council on Foreign Relations maintains a site on world militancy: www.terrorismanswers.com. Mother Jones has an eye-opening though slightly outdated site about arms at www.motherjones.com/arms and you can find lots about weaponry and arms sales at the Center for Defense Information (www.cdi.org/issues/wme).

4. Learn more about foreign policy. The Bulletin of Atomic Scientists gives news about nuclear matters at www.bullatomsci.org. The World Policy Institute offers insights into foreign relations at www.worldpolicy.org. Influential journal *Foreign Affairs* posts articles and excerpts and www.foreignaffairs.com and *Foreign Policy in Focus* (www.foreignpolicy-infocus.org) runs articles about global to-dos. Numerous think tanks publish their reports online, among them the Brookings Institute at www.brook.edu. The Library of Congress offers detailed reports on countries online, as does Country Watch at countrywatch.com. Human Rights Watch gives an overview of human rights abuses at www.hrw.org. And for a feel for what's going on behind the scenes across the world, and what places look like, check out travel book publisher Lonely Planet's site at lonelyplanet.com; their newsletter "Scoop" gives great behind-the-scenes info.

5. Write letters. Want to change the world? Start by picking up your pen or sending a personal email. I don't trust that those email chain letters ever make it to where they're going, and besides it's much more impressive to open up the day's mail and find that hundreds of people are concerned enough to send individual letters, than to find one letter with five hundred names on it. Write to our government leaders, write to embassies, write foreign governments, write to corporations, write voicing your support, concern or opposition. Just write.

6. Talk politics. There's long been a taboo against it in the U.S., but that may be lifting in the post–9/11 society. Organize a study group—and assign countries to members.

7. Stock your library. One of the handiest books for quick facts about countries is *The Oxford Handbook of the World* by Peter Stalker. Another helpful if slightly complicated reference book: *The Penguin Dictionary of International Relations* by Graham Evans and Jeffrey Newnham. Anyone who wants a feel for what's happening in the Middle East—from Sudan to Saudi Arabia, Lebanon to Israel—should delve into Judith Miller's wonderfully insightful *God Has Ninety-Nine Names.* Also fantastic for transporting you to foreign worlds are Mary Anne Weaver's *A Portrait of Egypt* and Robert Kaplan's *The End of the Earth. New York Times* columnist Nicholas Kristof pens fascinating books about Asia with Sheryl Wu Dunn, including *Thunder from the East;* they also wrote the Pulitzer Prize–winning *China Wakes: The Struggle for the Soul of Rising Power.* Yossef Bodanksy's complex *Bin Laden: The Man Who Declared War on America* might have warned Americans what lay ahead if only more of us had read it in 1999 when it came out. For alarming insight on questionable Western world power plays check out John Pilger, particularly *The New Rulers of the World,* as well as William Blum's *Rogue State.* These are but a few of the eye-opening books available that can change your worldview.

8. Travel abroad. The most enjoyable form of continuing education is to see what life is like in a foreign country and to hear the perspectives of foreigners. Likewise, learning a foreign language is another way to open more doors.

9. Walk more, drive less. Lessen the U.S. demand for foreign oil.

10. Take advantage of public broadcasting while it's still there: National Public Radio and the Public Broadcasting System offer a much more thorough exploration of international events than mainstream media.

Glossary

ABM (Anti-Ballistic Missile) Treaty: Considered the keystone of U.S.-Soviet relations during the Cold War, this 1972 treaty prohibited both countries from building extensive anti-ballistic missile systems. The idea was that if neither country had a defensive "missile intercept" system, then neither would be likely to launch an attack—knowing that they'd be vulnerable to a return attack. President George W. Bush withdrew from the treaty with Russia so that the U.S. could pursue its National Missile Defense system.

Alawite: Religious sect that blends elements of Christianity with Shia Islam, the Alawite control Syria's socialist-leaning Ba'ath party.

Allah: Muslim word for God.

Al-naqba: Arabic for holocaust, "al-naqba" is used by Arabs to refer to the creation of Israel and the 1948 war that began the day afterward.

Amazon: World's largest river, it gushes four thousand miles through South America, running from the Andes mountains in Peru through Brazil to the Atlantic. Lush flora sprouts up along it, creating the world's largest tropical rain forest.

Anatolia: Old-fashioned name for land that today is mostly Turkey.

Anti-ballistic missiles: Defensive intercept missiles that aim to hit an enemy's incoming missiles, theoretically exploding them in midair before they reach their land target.

Apostate: Person who defects from the faith. Under Islamic law (Shariah), an apostate Muslim can be sentenced to death.

Arab: There's some debate on what an Arab is ethnically; what most defines an Arab is that he or she speaks Arabic. Arabs typically live on the Arabian Peninsula or in North Africa.

Arabia: The oil-gushing deserts popularized to the Western world by T. E. Lawrence, Arabia was the name of Saudi Arabia before Ibn Saud came along and stamped his family name on it.

Arabic money lending: A complex system of credits and balances among shopkeepers that leaves no paper trail. See Hawala.

Arabic names: Studded with "ibn" (son of) and "al" (of the tribe), Arab names often map out family trees. Take the case of Abdul-aziz ibn Abdul-Rahman ibn Abdullah ibn Mohammad al-Saud, which means "I am Abdul-aziz, son of Abdul Rahman, son of Abdullah, the son of Mohammad of the esteemed family Saud." Foreigners just called him—Saudi Arabia's first king—Ibn Saud.

Aramco (Arabian-American Oil Company): Petroleum company that in the 1930s first brought Saudi sweet gurgling up from the sands, ARAMCO ushered in sweeping changes—from radios to roads—unleashing the modernity that the Wahhab sect of Islam abhorred. Initially American-owned, the company (a subsidiary of Standard of California) bought its oil for pennies, but the royal family eventually wised up and bought the company. Aramco's purchase along with OPEC price hikes led to Saudi Arabia's first major wealth in the 1970s.

Article 5, NATO: Clause in charter of North American Treaty Organization that says in the case of an attack on a member country, other members will treat it as an attack upon themselves. Invoked for first time after 9/11 attack.

Asian Financial Crisis: Too much credit and too much foreign speculation are what are generally seen as the causes for this financial horror that began in Thailand in May 1997 with the devalued baht and domino-style devastated the economies of Indonesia, Malaysia and the Philippines over the next year.

AWACS (Airborne Warning and Control System): Known as the "eyes in the skies," these large, slow-moving planes lug advanced radar systems to monitor air traffic over potential targets such as nuclear plants, sports stadiums and bustling urban areas.

Axis of Evil: Controversial term unveiled in January 2002 during President George W. Bush's first State of the Union address, the "Axis of Evil" listed countries believed to be trying to acquire weapons of mass destruction or to already have them. Although at least a dozen countries—including the U.S., U.K. and Israel—also have weapons of mass destruction, Bush singled out North Korea, Iraq and Iran as the world's great evildoers.

Ayatollah: Honorific bestowed upon esteemed Shia scholars, ayatollah means "miraculous sign of Allah." Iran's leaders Khomeini and Khamenei are actually "grand ayatollahs."

Ba'ath party: Created in the 1940s, this political party wanted to unite Arabs everywhere regardless of their religion or territorial boundaries. The ideology-heavy Ba'ath split up: in Iraq it became the party of Saddam Hussein; in Syria it became the party of his enemy President Hafez al-Assad.

Balfour Declaration: This ambiguous 1917 document, written by British Foreign Secretary Arthur James Balfour, is where the Israeli-Palestinian issue starts. In the declaration—actually a letter to Lord Walter Rothschild, a Jewish leader in Britain—Balfour writes:

"His Majesty's Government view with favour the establishment in Palestine of a national home for the Jewish people, and will use their best endeavors to facilitate the achievement of this object, it being clearly understood that nothing shall be done which may prejudice the civil and religious rights of existing non-Jewish communities in Palestine, or the rights and political status enjoyed by Jews in any other country."

What exactly Balfour was saying has been a matter of debate ever since: Zionists interpreted it as guaranteeing a homeland for Jews, while Palestinians believed it guaranteed that a Jewish homeland would not be created without Palestinian endorsement.

Balkanization: Process whereby one large entity or region—such as the former Yugoslavia—fractures, often along religious and ethnic lines, into smaller independent factions or countries that are hostile to one another.

The Balkans: Eastern European countries that rise up between the Black and Adriatic Seas, the Balkans include countries that were part of the former Yugoslavia, several former Soviet republics and technically Greece and sometimes Turkey. The general list includes: Slovenia, Croatia, Bosnia-Herzegovina, Montenegro and Serbia (and autonomous region Kosovo), Macedonia, Albania, Greece, Romania, Bulgaria and Moldova.

Beards: Mandated under strict interpretations of Islamic law; beards that were too short were cause for arrest or flogging under Afghanistan's Taliban regime.

Bedouins: Dying breed of nomads who trek deserts with camels and herds, mostly on the Arabian Peninsula.

Bhopal, India: Site of biggest chemical disaster in human history in December 1984, when a toxic cloud was released from a Union Carbide pesticide plant, killing an estimated sixteen thousand.

Bin Ladin Construction Company: Company of Osama bin Ladin's kin that made billions constructing and renovating palaces and mosques across Saudi Arabia, including the Grand Mosque in Mecca.

Blood Diamonds: All that glitters may not be good: the sparkly gems may fund underground operations. Diamonds from Africa's Sierra Leone in particular have been banned by the United Nations, which believes that they fund rebel groups. Also suspect: diamonds from Liberia and India. The U.S. sees an Al Qaeda link.

Blowback: CIA term for a situation that a government or its agents create that comes back to haunt them. Examples: Saddam Hussein, whom the U.S. supported in the 1980s, and Osama bin Laden, whom the U.S. backed during the Soviet-Afghan War.

Bretton Woods: 1944 economic agreement between United States and the United Kingdom that established the International Monetary Fund and World Bank.

Buddhism: Created some twenty-five hundred years ago in India, Buddhism encourages followers to free themselves from worldly suffering and seek Nirvana. Meditation plays heavily in most forms of this religion; the Theravada school emphasizes pursuit of happiness. Found in Thailand, Sri Lanka, Nepal, Taiwan, China, Tibet, Japan and other parts of the Far East, as well as throughout the West.

Burka: Mandated by the Taliban as the only acceptable fashion for women in Afghanistan, the burka veil cloaks the entire body, including the face; a patch of netting covers the eyes.

Bush Doctrine: Essentially an international ultimatum, the so-called "Bush Doctrine" made its appearance during President Bush's first speech after the September 11 attacks. Bush created reverberations around the world when he announced, "Either you are with us or you are with the terrorists." Most countries quickly lined up on the "with us" side—at least initially.

Calendar, Islamic: The Islamic calendar dates its beginning at A.D. 622—when the Prophet Muhammad led his followers from Mecca to Medina, a trek called the *hijra.* Thus, what is year A.D. 2001 in the Gregorian calendar is 1379 in the Islamic version.

Camp David Accords: President Jimmy Carter brokered this earth-shattering 1978 land-for-peace agreement between Israel and Egypt, in which Israel agreed to return the Sinai region taken from Egypt during the 1967 Arab-Israeli War and Egypt agreed to recognize Israel's right to exist. Another part of the agreement concerned granting autonomy to Palestinians, but has largely been ignored. The U.S. gives Israel and Egypt billions of dollars of military equipment annually for upholding the agreement—at least $1.3 billion a year for Egypt and over $2 billion a year for Israel.

Caspian Sea: New hot spot for Central Asian oil, the resource-rich sea in Central Asia is the source of territorial bickerings between Iran, Russia, Azerbaijan, Kazakhstan and Turkmenistan.

Caucasus: The name of the spectacular mountain range that splits Europe and Asia, this term also refer to countries that spill down from its hills. The northern Caucasus include volatile Chechnya, Dagestan and other regions that are still part of Russia. The southern Transcaucasus are basically Azerbaijan, Georgia and Armenia.

Cells, terrorist (aka sleepers): Small groups of militants, typically with three to five members, planted around the world, often performing normal jobs while they plan attacks and await word to take action. Al-Qaeda cells have been uncovered in numerous cities, including Milan, London, Amsterdam, Brooklyn, Jersey City, Hamburg and Madrid.

Chernobyl: Worst nuclear accident in human history, this 1986 explosion in Russia released radioactive gases that killed 41 and are believed to have caused 2,000 cases of thyroid cancer. Some watchdog groups believe the number of deaths and illnesses is underreported.

Chop-Chop Square: The nickname given to the main square in downtown Riyadh, Saudi Arabia, which every Friday is the site of hand choppings and beheadings—punishments meted out by practitioners of strict Shariah law.

Collateral damages: An antiseptic way of saying war-related deaths and injuries of civilians and destruction of nonintended civilian targets.

Constitutional monarchy: Royals are heads of state but must mind the constitution and laws; a prime minister usually runs the government.

Crusade: A word President Bush naively used when describing his "War on Terror," crusade literally refers to the bloody marches of Christians to reclaim Jerusalem from Muslims, during the Crusades—commissioned by assorted popes from 1095 to 1291. Thousands of Muslims were massacred.

Daisy cutter: A fifteen-thousand-pound bomb that explodes several feet aboveground, forms a mushroom cloud and causes extensive damage for several hundred yards in all directions.

Dayton Agreement: November 1995 peace plan that among other things split Bosnia-Herzegovina into two parts—one controlled by Serbs, the other controlled by Bosniaks and Croats.

Dearborn, Michigan: Home to the most Arab immigrants in the U.S.

Depleted uranium: The dense, armor-piercing element left over when uranium is enriched for power plants, depleted uranium or U-238 was used in missiles and bullets during the 2001 campaign in Afghanistan, the 1999 bombings in Kosovo and Desert Storm. Depleted uranium is under fire because it leaves ground, water and air radioactive, and is reportedly linked to increased rates of cancers in areas where it's been used; some soldiers who used DU are also developing cancers and their babies have a much higher incidence of birth defects. The Defense Department denies it's a health risk, but NATO and the EU have issued a ban on using DU in weapons.

Desert Storm: Popular name for the 1991 Persian Gulf War that resulted when Iraq invaded Kuwait and a U.S.-led coalition forced the Iraqis out.

Diaspora: Fragmented ethnic or religious communities scattered over different lands. Classically used to describe Jews, especially before Israel was created, the word now best lends itself to Palestinians.

Dirty bombs: Explosive radiological devices made with low-grade radioactive material, such as strontium-190 or cesium-137, dirty bombs don't pack the wallop of a full nuclear bomb: few may die from an exploded dirty bomb, but they can ruin the land and make an area uninhabitable for centuries. The greatest risk is the mass panic these devices could produce. Some regard the depleted uranium missiles the U.S. uses as dirty bombs, particularly when they contain plutonium, as they sometimes do.

Dishdash: Arab slang for the white flowing robes worn by men; name comes from the sound the robes make when they move.

Dove: A leader who tries to make peace through negotiations. Example: former Israeli Prime Minister Ehud Barak.

Drugs: Whether you're talking about Afghanistan's opium that bankrolled the Taliban or the "super-heroin" that Osama bin Laden hoped to develop as a new form of "narco-terrorism" to make Western countries even more drug-crazed, or you're commenting on the run on Cipro or the anti-anxiety pills Americans are gulping by the handful, or you're merely pointing out that pharmaceutical companies with their antibiotics and vaccines are the only beneficiaries of bioterrorism or that Donald Rumsfeld used to be the CEO of Searle, drugs seem to turn up around every bend of this war.

Eisenhower Doctrine: Formulated at the onset of the Cold War, the Eisenhower Doctrine provided economic and military support to any country fighting against communism.

Fallaqa: Painful beating of the bottom of the feet which leaves no telltale bruises, sometimes used in Saudi Arabia.

Fatwa: Arabic word for a ruling or call to action from a respected Islamic leader or scholar. Ayatollah Khomeini issued a fatwa to kill Salman Rushdie.

Fedayeen: Arabic for guerrilla fighters—particularly anti-Israeli Palestinians, such as Hamas and factions of PLO.

Five Pillars of Islam: The most important acts of worship of the Islam religion:
1. *Shahada:* The important profession of faith: "There is no god but God, and Muhammad is a messenger of God."
2. *Salah:* Believers must pray five times a day—facing the direction of Mecca (in Saudi Arabia)—and recite the above credo.
3. *Zakat:* Followers must give to charity.
4. *Sawn:* Followers must fast during daylight of the holiday Ramadan.
5. *Hajj:* If possible, followers must make a pilgrimage to Mecca at least once.

Foreign aid, U.S.: Typically grants—i.e., gifts—to foreign countries to help rebuild and strengthen economies and fortify militaries. Often requires that the money is used buying U.S. goods.

Freedom fighter: President Reagan tossed this term around referring to anyone fighting communism; now used by some fighting whatever they see as oppression.

Fundamentalists: The factions of a religion that rely on the original tenets and typically interpret holy texts at their most literal. In Islam, fundamentalists are usually called "Islamists" or "revivalists."

Genetically Modified (GM): Plants or food where the original genes have been altered, often to increase production or fight off natural predators.

Geneva Conventions: A series of conventions starting in the nineteenth century and updated several times since, the Geneva Conventions govern treatment of war prisoners. Among other things, they ban torture, require that prisoners be treated humanely and state that prisoners must reveal only name and rank.

Genocide: Attempted annihation of a specific ethnic group.

Geographically challenged: Derogatory term used to describe U.S. citizens, who in years following World War II have ceased to know the physical lay of the world, a situation resulting in part because geography is scarcely covered in schools.

Globalization: Interconnectedness between countries, particularly economic. One sign: increasing numbers of corporations setting up operations around the world, typically opening up where labor costs are lowest.

Golan Heights: Water-rich hills rising up in the southwest corner of Syria, the coveted Golan Heights were captured by Israel in 1967 during the Six Day War. Israel has since "occupied" the territory and, ignoring UN resolutions and U.S. chastisements, has built housing settlements in the area.

Guantánamo Bay: The U.S. naval base acquired as a result of the Spanish-American War finally came in handy: Camp X-Ray is being renovated as a prison and is now home to hundreds of suspected Al Qaeda and Taliban fighters shipped here from the war in Afghanistan. Pictures of the blindfolded men in chain-link cages caused some to criticize that the U.S. was violating the Geneva Conventions. The U.S. responded by saying the incarcerated men weren't really "prisoners of war" thus the Conventions didn't apply.

Hajj: Arabic for the important pilgrimage to Mecca, Saudi Arabia, birthplace of the Prophet Muhammad and the most sacred site in the world for Muslims. So important is the journey that pilgrims can add the word *hajj* to their name; some paint a plane or car on their house showing the method of transport they used to get to the holy site.

Hawala: Popular form of money transfer among Arabs, *hawala* doesn't leave a paper trail and is difficult to trace since it's essentially a method of credit between money dealers across the world. Example: a man in Chicago wants to send $1,000 to Islamabad. He forks over $1,000 to a *hawala* dealer in Chicago, who calls a dealer in Islamabad who doles out the cash to the person waiting for the money in Pakistan. The $1,000 debt held by the Islamabad dealer is eventually worked out when someone in Islamabad sends money back to Chicago.

Hawk: Term for a leader or politician with a reputation for pushing military action. Examples: Donald Rumsfeld and Ariel Sharon.

Hazmat: Term for hazardous materials, including biological agents such as anthrax, toxic chemicals and radioactive substances that require special care in handling.

Hegemony (note the "g" is like in "gem"): Power, domination and/or authority over others.

Hinduism: World's oldest religion, and the majority faith in India. Worships numerous gods.

Holland: Two provinces—North Holland and South Holland—of the country known as the Netherlands.

Homeland Security: Not to be confused with the Civil Defense System of the 1950s and '60s, which had bomb shelters and sirens and warnings galore—Homeland Security hasn't seemed to do anything tangible since it was formed in the face of the 9/11 attacks, except to occasionally issue heightened color-coded security alerts, having utterly failed to inform the masses on what to do or where to go in the case of attacks. Soon to be a multiagency bureaucracy.

ICBM: Short for intercontinental ballistic missile, ICBMs are long-range missiles that can deliver nuclear payloads thousands of miles away. The U.S., Russia, China and North Korea have them.

Ikhwan: Arabic for "brotherhood," Ikhwan usually refers to the Muslim Brotherhood—an Egyptian Islamic group that was the granddaddy of modern-day Islamist movements. May also refer to the Bedouin warriors who fought for Ibn Saud.

Imam: Prayer leader in a Muslim mosque.

Infidel (aka keffir): A term Osama bin Laden slapped on Americans in Saudi Arabia, infidel means a nonbeliever or unfaithful follower, whom he felt sullied the holy Saudi soil.

International Criminal Court: Headquartered in the Hague—political seat of the Netherlands—this UN-established international court prosecutes government leaders and power players accused of perpetrating war crimes, human rights abuses and genocide. Former Serbian president Slobodan Milosovic was tried in a separate UN war criminal tribunal in the Hague in 2002. President Clinton signed the treaty creating the court, but the Bush administration doesn't like it and threatened to pull peacekeeping troops out of Bosnia if the U.S. wasn't given immunity. A compromise was struck: the U.S. was offered immunity for the first year of the court—or until summer 2003. Now the U.S. refuses to give out military or financial aid to any country until that country certifies that it won't prosecute any U.S. leaders or military men in the court that meant to stand for global justice. While the U.S. can be faulted for never playing by the same rules it imposes on everybody else, you can't blame them for being afraid of fierce prosecutors like Carla Del Ponte.

International Monetary Fund (IMF): Like its lending partner, the World Bank, the IMF was born out of the international banking spirit that emerged after World War II. Supposed to help countries through rough times, the IMF and its loans increasingly are accused of worsening situations. For instance, developing countries getting IMF aid must open up trade and their small farmers can't compete with subsidized food from the U.S. and EU; the developing farmers may be forced to give up their farms. With Argentina in a total economic crisis—after the IMF loaned billions to iffy leaders—some are pressuring the institution to drop debt repayment for countries that can't pay.

Intifada: Arabic for "uprising," it typically refers to Palestinian insurrections against Israel. The most violent one began in October 2000 and is marked by suicide bombers who blow themselves up in Israeli stores, buses and clubs.

Iran-Iraq War (1980–1988): With the internal confusion surrounding Iran's Islamic Revolution of 1979, Iraq's Saddam Hussein seized the vulnerable moment to lodge a territorial dispute against Iran and send his troops over their borders. Eight bloody years later, when the UN negotiated a truce between the two countries, nothing had been gained, and a million lives and billions of dollars had been lost. The U.S. supported Saddam.

Islam: Monotheistic religion "popularized" by Muhammad in the seventh century A.D. and based on the holy book the Koran. First taking root in Arabia, where Mecca (Muhammad's birthplace) and Medina (Muhammad's burial site) are its two holiest places, Islam has two main branches—Sunni and Shiite—and numerous sects within those divisions. Followers are called Muslims, and there is theoretically no religious hierarchy since all Muslims are created equal. The fastest growing religion in the world, with 1.2 billion practitioners, Islam has more followers in Indonesia than any other country. The religion's basic tenets are "The Five Pillars of Islam."

Islamist: A person who wants traditional Islam to be reflected in everyday life, often with a religious government and Shariah law as part of the package. Not all Islamists are militant, but most militant Muslims are Islamists.

Jihad: Arabic for "struggles," jihads are Muslims' personal attempts to improve themselves and thus become closer to Allah. Quitting smoking or being a patient parent (especially trying to do both at the same time) are examples of jihad as classically used. A less common meaning is used commonly of late: jihad as Muslim "holy war," typically against non-Muslims. Osama bin Laden was using the latter meaning when, on several occasions, he called for a jihad against Americans and Israelis. While a true jihad would include the mandate not to harm innocents—civilians, women and children—bin Laden urged followers to kill any and all infidels. Suicide bombers are not part of a traditional jihad, since Islam also forbids taking one's own life.

Judaism: Originating around 1700 B.C., Judaism was the first monotheistic religion. The outgrowth of the tribes of Jacob—aka Israel—the religion holds that God (aka Yahweh) dictated the Ten Commandments to Moses, as well as the first five books of the Bible (aka the Torah). Rife with stories of plagues, parting seas, pregnant maids, smashed tablets, sacrificial calves, marked doors and banishment, Jewish religious history also holds that God promised historical Canaan—the area that is today Israel, Palestine and Jordan—to the Jews and that King David gave them Jerusalem. While most Jews live in the U.S., some 6 million live in Israel, the country for Jews that came into being in 1948.

Koran: The holy book of Islam that holds what are believed to be the exact words of God to the prophet Muhammad via the angel Gabriel.

Kyoto Protocol: International treaty, resulting from 1997 Kyoto conference on climactic change, which holds most of world's countries legally responsible for reducing greenhouse gas emissions—believed responsible for global warming—by nearly 15 percent by the year 2015; by the year 2050, emissions are to be 50 percent less. President George W. Bush refused to sign the treaty that every other industrialized nation has committed to.

Landmine Treaty: International treaty of 1999 than bans use of antipersonnel land mines. U.S. government ultimately refused to sign.

Maastricht Treaty: 1992 economic/political agreement signed in Maastricht, the Netherlands, it resulted in the common currency the euro and made the governments of the European Union countries even more intertwined.

Mad cow: Disease transmitted by eating infected beef that causes brain to go all mushy.

Madrassas: Muslim religious schools for the poor originally designed to teach children to read. Now in places such as Pakistan they're mostly Koran-memorization schools, where the young 'uns are also taught how to fight holy wars and learn how to fire high-powered weapons. Often funded by Saudi Arabian charitable groups, the thousands of madrassas that dot Central Asia have been called "Islamic West Points." Pakistan's President

Musharraf is trying to shut down the hundreds that operate in his country, but good luck: madrassas, like those that produced the Taliban, are entrenched in the system.

Material witness: Someone believed to have information relevant to investigations. Under Justice Department statutes, material witnesses can be arrested and kept in custody until their testimony is obtained. Of the 1,147 detainees picked up in the first six weeks after the September 11 attacks, at least 180 were believed to be material witnesses.

Mecca: Located in southwestern Saudi Arabia, Mecca—where the Prophet Muhammad was born around A.D. 570—is the holiest place in the world for Muslims, and the direction they face when praying five times a day. One of the requirements of being a good Muslim is to make a pilgrimage to Mecca at least once, and millions travel each year to the Grand Mosque—a spectacular Muslim temple—that was renovated by Osama bin Laden's family.

Medina: The second holiest place for Muslims, this site in Saudi Arabia is where the Prophet Muhammad was buried, after he led his followers there when they were kicked out of Mecca.

Missile Shield Defense: See National Missile Defense—NMD.

Monroe Doctrine: Single defining event of President James Monroe's administration—(1817–1825), the 1823 Monroe Doctrine cordoned off the Americas North, South and Central—from any country's meddling or "future colonization" and warned that any attempts to do so would prompt U.S. military retaliation. Ironically, the "hands off American lands" threat—issued to protect Latin America from Europe—soon became the basis for the U.S. to intervene in Latin American political affairs.

Mossad: Israeli intelligence agency that admits to aggressively seeking and killing known enemies of the state.

Muezzin: The crier whose voice echoes through Islamic cities as he calls Muslims to prayer five times a day. Job security is dicey: the calls are now sometimes prerecorded and played as garbled tapes; calls to prayer are also sent as text messages on cell phones.

Mufti: Powerful religious official who has the right to interpret Muslim law, mete out punishment and issue edicts in Islamic countries, particularly Saudi Arabia. The highest ranking there is the Grand Mufti.

Mujahideen (aka Arab-Afghan): An Arab word meaning "holy warrior" defending the religion of Islam and the security of Muslim countries, mujahideen have fought through the centuries. The term usually refers to Muslims who came to Afghanistan in the 1980s to drive back atheist Soviets.

Muslim: A practitioner of Islam.

NAFTA (North American Free Trade Agreement): 1999 act between the U.S., Canada and Mexico that lifted tariffs and subsidies to promote greater trade between the countries, NAFTA has benefited all three on paper. In practice, it's created slummish factory towns on the Mexican border, brought Mexican trucks barreling across U.S. interstates and led to showdowns with the Canadian lumber companies who accuse the U.S. of unfair practices.

National Missile Defense: This idea to protect North America with an extensive anti-ballistic missile system is ultramodern and super-pricey, and it may not work; nevertheless construction for the $60 billion NMD began in 2002 and will just lead to another arms race.

Near East: Turkey and environs. As with Far East and Middle East, this description was placed upon parts of Asia from the European perspective: Turkey was near, Arabia was middle, India and beyond was far.

Operation Noble Eagle: The domestic air defense operation that began minutes after the September 11 attacks on the World Trade Center and Pentagon. AWACS and F16 fighter planes now constantly patrol the skies over the U.S., monitoring flights near critical sights, including nuclear power plants.

Oslo Accords: Initiated as a poli sci class project in Norway, these 1993 accords resulted from secret meetings between Palestinian leader Yasser Arafat and Israeli leader Shimon Peres. They ultimately created a temporary self-governing Palestinian Authority in the West Bank and Gaza Strip.

Ottoman Empire: Vast Turkish empire that once extended through the Arabian Peninsula and into northern Africa, as far east as the Caspian Sea and as well west as the Balkans. A world presence starting in the thirteenth century, the Ottoman Empire had conked out by the twentieth century, and was formally disbanded in 1920, after World War I.

People of the book: Muslim term for Jews and Christians emphasizing that Judaism, Christianity and Islam all have the same roots. Islam recognizes the teachings of some Jewish prophets as well as those of Jesus.

Persia: Land that is now Iran.

Plan Colombia: Super-pricey Plan Colombia, initiated in 2000, aims to eradicate the coca plant that shoots roots in Colombia's mountains. A few problems in the program, to which the U.S. is tossing over $1.5 billion: sprayed pesticide is deadening the land for all future agricultural uses, the villagers are getting sick, and cocaine production has somehow increased. Plan Colombia's goals are also widening: it is now used by the Colombian government to battle rebels, and the U.S. is using it to protect its oil interests in the region as well.

Radical Triangle: The northwestern corner of South America, where Colombia, Venezuela and Ecuador meet, is called the Radical Triangle due to a preponderance of heavily armed guerrillas, rebellious Indians, drugs and general discontent. This tri-country area, central to drug production and trafficking, has been the most resistant to assertions of U.S. power in Latin America.

Ramadan: The holiest Muslim holiday of fasting which takes place on the ninth month of the Muslim calendar (around November for the U.S.). Its observance is one of the "Five Pillars of Islam"—the five most important acts for Muslims—and during the month-long holiday of meditative thought, Muslims assess their lives and initiate acts of forgiveness. U.S. troops traditionally have stopped fighting in Muslim countries during Ramadan, although during 2001 such wasn't the case, as fighting continued in Afghanistan.

Rapprochement: Literally meaning "to approach" with the intent of establishing friendly relations, rapprochement is usually used these days to mean "re-approach"—as in "Yes, things went screwy before, but let's try it again."

Right to exist, Israel's: In a nutshell, this loaded phrase—Israel's right to exist—lies at the heart of most Arab-Israeli conflicts. Israel is officially recognized by Egypt, Jordan and by the PLO, but most Arab countries do not acknowledge that the Jewish nation has a legitimate claim to the land that it occupies—even the original land delineated in 1948.

Rogue states: Catchy term for Uncle Sam's enemy list, "rogue states" are those countries that the U.S. believes sponsor terrorism. The rogue roster varies but Iraq, Iran and North Korea are all roundtable members; Libya, Syria, Cuba and Sudan are sometime rogues. The term originated during the Clinton administration, but was later changed to the more politically correct "states of concern." The Bush administration, however, has brought the term "rogue" back in vogue.

Satanic Verses: "The Satanic Verses" is more than the name of Salman Rushdie's book that so enraged Iran's Ayatollah Khomeini that he issued a fatwa calling for Rushdie's death. It actually refers to a devil-inspired entry penned by Muhammad when he was writing the Muslim holy book, the Koran. The false entries concerned worshiping multiple gods, and were hastily deleted, when the angel Gabriel informed Muhammad that the devil had dictated those lines.

Saudi Peace Plan: Put forth by Saudi Arabia's Crown Prince Abdullah, this 2002 plan adopted by the Arab League essentially stated that Arab-Israeli relations would be normalized—and Arab countries would acknowledge Israel's right to exist—if Israel pulled back to its boundaries prior to the 1967 Six Day War. Palestinians embraced the idea; Israeli response was lukewarm, and the plan apparently got lost in another wave of Israeli-Palestinian conflicts.

Scandinavia: The lovely, affluent, and brutally cold countries of northern Europe—(plus Danish territory Greenland), these lands are united by little except their shared history of Vikings. Finland, once part of the Soviet Union, was until 1991 really out of the loop. Specifically: Norway, Sweden, Finland, Denmark and Greenland.

Sectarian: Religious.

Secular: Worldly or nonreligious—particularly with regards to government.

Settlements: Typically refers to Israeli residential and agricultural areas in occupied territories of the West Bank or Syria.

Shah: Honorific used to describe Persian leaders, later borrowed by Iran's two secular dictators.

Shariah law (Islamic law): Shariah or "the path that leads to God," is the basis for law in some Muslim countries, though the extent to which its harsh punishments are carried out varies. Saudi Arabia, Sudan and Afghanistan under the Taliban hold (or held) a strict interpretation of Shariah, or Islamic, law, which includes amputations and beheadings. The secular government of Egypt now includes some religious courts that rely on Shariah: they have banned books and movies deemed offensive. Some countries with many Muslim residents, such as Jordan and Indonesia, do not heavily base their laws or punishments on Shariah; other countries, such as Qatar and the United Arab Emirates, have both Shariah and civil courts.

Shariah is based on four sources: the Koran, the sunna—containing the writings of Muhammad—and the hadith, outside observations of his life. Existing laws as well as writings of Muslim scholars are all factored in when Islamic judgment is passed.

Shia: minority branch of Islam, mostly practiced in Iran. See Shiites.

Shiites: Muslims who follow the Shia branch of Islam, Shiites believe that the caliphs (leaders of Islam) who ruled after the prophet Muhammad were not valid leaders unless they were blood relatives of Muhammad. Shiites make up 10 percent of the Muslim population. Most Arabs are Sunni Muslims. Relations between the two branches of Islam range from tense to hateful; some Shiites say they are treated like second-class citizens by Sunnis.

Sick Man of Europe: The term the "Sick Man of Europe" was used to describe the last days of the once-grand Ottoman Empire, which hobbled into the twentieth century greatly weakened.

Smart bombs: Self-guiding bombs which can be preprogrammed or directed by laser points. May also be led by heat sensors.

Stealth bomber: Kite-shaped B-2 plane designed to be nearly imperceptible on radar screens.

Steganography: The use of embedded or hidden messages in otherwise normal-looking pictures, pieces of text or files on the Internet. Messages may be revealed when they are decoded, enlarged or changed to different computer fonts such as "Wing Dings."

Stress: A reason cited by some research teams as cause for increased cancer rates in areas exposed to radioactive leaks or weapons, including Three Mile Island.

Stupid American: Ouch! Widely held international view of U.S. citizens that portrays us as ignorant about the world. The condition is caused by geography-deficient educations, media that are increasingly "info-tainment" and a general sense of being overwhelmed.

Sufism: A mystical sect of Shia Islam, Sufis believe that death and life have been confused with each other, and they seek to tap elevated states of wisdom—including telepathy—through meditation, breathing, poetry and dance. As whirling dervishes, Sufis spin themselves silly seeking enlightenment. Practiced mostly in Turkey and Iran, Sufism also has a following among Kurds.

Sunni: One of the two major branches of Islam, which holds that religious leaders did not have to be a blood relative of the prophet Muhammad.

Sunshine Policy: South Korea's policy—extended by President Kim Dae Jong—of engaging North Korea, with whom it has been separated since 1953.

Sykes-Picot Agreement: One of those back-room agreements that haunt civilization long after the ink has dried on paper, the secret Sykes-Picot Agreement—named for the Brit and Frenchman who signed it—a secret plan between the British and French drawn up during World War I that outlined plans to segment the Ottoman Empire after the war and place them temporarily under British or French mandate. The plan went into effect in 1919, ultimately carving five new states out of Arab lands: reconfigured Palestine, Transjordan and Iraq (formerly Mesopotamia) were British mandates, while the French redrew the boundaries of Syria and created Lebanon. The agreement negated other agreements the British had made with Arabs. The Hashemite clan, for instance, who had helped fight the Ottomans in the Arab Revolt, had been promised that they would be made rulers of one large Arab nation. The Europeans' partitioning of the Middle Eastern lands once under Ottoman rule also countered attempts by the residents of those regions to organize as they wished.

Theater Missile Defense: A system of missiles that aim to take out incoming enemy missiles, but have a tighter arena. TMD focuses on short-range and medium-range missiles, not those flying in from another continent.

Ulama: Arabic term for mosque leaders and other religious VIPs.

Umma: Arabic word for the Muslim community.

Unmanned aerial vehicle (UAV): Straight out of Hollywood, these small aircraft carrying video cameras silently hover through the night spying on enemies. Some varieties, called drones, carry Hellfire missiles.

Unilateral: Generally refers to international actions taken alone, with apparent disregard to what the world thinks.

Wahhabism: The strict translation of Islam in Saudi Arabia, Wahhabism bans mixing of the sexes in social groups, requires that women be covered and bans music.

UN Resolutions 242 and 338: Issued in response to the Arab-Israeli wars of 1967 and 1973, these resolutions recognize Israel's right to exist and call for Israel to pull out from "occupied territories" acquired during the wars.

USA Patriot Act (The Uniting and Strengthening America by Providing Appropriate Tools Required to Intercept and Obstruct Terrorism Act of 2001): Hastily passed anti-terrorism law that greatly increased U.S. government powers to search, hold prisoners, wiretap and spy. Prompted by 9/11, the act resulted in thousands being detained without being charged, Internet companies being forced to allow the government to spy on their navigations and letters of customers and bookstores being forced to turn over the details of who bought what books. Civil rights groups are going nuts. In 2002, Canada's legislature tossed out its equivalent anti-terrorist law.

Weapons of mass destruction: Term used for nuclear, chemical and biological weapons in hands of enemy states. When WMD such as nuclear bombs are in the hands of the U.S. or allies, they're just called needed defense.

West Bank: Palestinian territory along the West Bank of the Jordan River. Suicide bombers usually come out of here, and Israeli tanks come rolling in. Also site of the Palestinian Authority's headquarters.

Wobbly warheads: Poorly designed missiles that miss their targets and are hard to shoot down because their path is essentially undetermined. Come up in discussions of the Anti-Ballistic Missile Shield.

Yucca Mountain: Earthquake-prone site in Nevada slated to become the repository for the U.S.' nuclear waste.

Zionism: Movement to establish a homeland for Jews—preferably in Palestine—that was revived during the late 1800s.

Power Players and Elitist Groups

Abu Sayyaf: Gang of vicious jungle thugs who've made millions from kidnapping in the Philippines, Abu Sayyaf was the reason U.S. special forces trained the Philippines military in 2002, but the boys are still ticking. See Philippines.

Al Aqsa Brigade: Associated with the Fatah branch of the PLO, this West Bank group is known for its suicide bombers. See Israel and Palestine.

Al-Jazeera: Twenty-four-hour news station running out of Qatar, Al-Jazeera is the Middle East's first uncensored TV. Likened to CNN, but with its controversial and dramatic content, al-Jazeera may be closer in style to alarmist Fox News. See Qatar.

Al-Jihad (aka Egyptian Islamic Jihad and variants): Deadly, dedicated, sneaky Egyptian Islamists blamed for President Sadat's assassination and 1995 bombing of Egyptian embassy in Pakistan, among other deeds. Al-Jihad leaders joined forces with Osama bin Laden to create Al-Qaeda. See Egypt.

Al Qaeda ("The Base"): The umbrella organization of multinational militant Islamists affiliated with Saudi-born millionaire Osama bin Laden is one of the most dangerous, dedicated groups in the world, especially to U.S. citizens, whom they savagely targeted in the September 11 attacks. Rising up against the dominant U.S. role in Middle Eastern affairs, Al Qaeda denounced the American military presence in the Persian Gulf region as well as U.S. support of Israel and its role in the economic sanctions on Iraq. Working in cells, Al Qaeda members are mostly from Egypt and Saudi Arabia—both countries which the U.S. has sold or given billions of arms; Algeria, Yemen, Lebanon, Syria and other Arab and Muslim countries are represented by mujahideen who fought with bin Laden in the 1980s during the Soviet-Afghan War or later trained in his Afghanistan camps. Still lurking around the world despite the "War on Terror," estimates of their number range from a few hundred to thirty thousand. Said to be heading back to their spawning grounds: the caves of Afghanistan.

Arab League: If you want the official Arab perspective, look at the Arab League, the most powerful forum for Middle East policy. A political, economic and defense organization of Arab-speaking countries started up in 1945, the Arab League never recognized Israel and took numerous actions against it, including economic boycotts and starting up the Palestine Liberation Organization (PLO) in 1964. The League also booted out founding member Egypt when Sadat made peace with Israel in 1979, but let Egypt rejoin a decade later. It was a major to-do when the Arab League accepted the Saudi Peace Plan in March 2002 and offered to recognize Israel's right to exist if the latter pulled back to pre-1967 boundaries; the proposal was shelved in a wave of increasing Palestinian-Israeli violence.

Members: Egypt, Saudi Arabia, Iraq, Jordan, Lebanon, North Yemen, Kuwait, Algeria, Bahrain, Comoros, Djibouti, Kuwait, Libya, Morocco, Syria, Tunisia, Oman, Qatar, United Arab Emirates, Mauritania, PLO, Somalia, Sudan, Yemen.

Note: Iran is not included in the Arab League because Iranians are Persian, not Arab.

Atef, Mohammed: Tall, thin and scraggly, Egyptian Mohammed Atef—a former policeman in Cairo—was Al Qaeda's main military planner. Involved in the 1993 attacks on American Marines in Somalia, he's believed to have helped plan the 1998 embassy bombings in Kenya and Tanzania. Also bin Laden's security man, Atef was the first of Al Qaeda's elite to die during the 2001 Afghan campaign.

Bin Laden, Osama: Founder of Al Qaeda and sponsor of the September 11 attacks, millionaire militant Osama bin Laden was once hailed a hero by Saudi Arabia and the U.S. for training mujahideen to fight Soviets in Afghanistan during the 1980s. His warm relationship with the Saudi government frosted after the royal family denied his request to fight Iraq with his mujahideen warriors in 1990; bin Laden's loud criticism of the Saudi's reliance on the U.S. Army prompted his being asked to leave the country and he was stripped of Saudi citizenship in 1994.

In Sudan, he linked arms with Islamist Egyptians Ayman al-Zawahiri and Mohammed Atef, formed what eventually became Al Qaeda and first began issuing calls for Muslims to attack Americans and Israelis in 1996. Booted from Sudan later that year, he returned to Afghanistan, where he set up more militant training camps and plotted diabolical schemes while sometimes living in caves. Bin Laden's stated beefs with the U.S. in 2001: the American military presence in Saudi Arabia; economic sanctions against Iraq; and U.S. support for Israel. Just as significant: his wounded male ego. Bin Laden was never rabidly anti-American until the Saudis rejected his fighting offers and instead brought in the U.S. to fight Desert Storm.

An aside: bin Laden cultivated many loyal fighters during the Soviet-Afghan War by sending generous checks to the families of the wounded and dead. Building housing and guerrilla training camps, he also picked up airfare to Pakistan and successfully urged the Saudi government to fund and, with the U.S., arm the mujahideen.

ELN: Colombian left wing rebels who specialize in kidnapping and attacking oil pipelines. See Colombia.

ETA: Spanish militants who want the northern Basque region to secede from Spain. See Spain.

European Union (EU): Since 1950 assorted European countries have been growing more interdependent economically and politically and adopting a number of names, but the European Union created in 1992 gave this supernational organization more power and the new EU name. Now an umbrella government representing fifteen independent European member countries, the EU comprises most of Western Europe (except Switzerland and Norway) and unites the region economically, judicially and politically, imposing universal standards on everything from bakeries and budgets to farms. Creating the common currency euro (used by all except the U.K., Sweden and Denmark since 2002) was its most significant achievement; border checkpoints between countries also came down. Headquartered in Brussels, this multi-armed bureaucracy is forcing Europe to pursue common goals and function more or less as one united entity for the first time in its history. When the poorer countries of Eastern Europe come in starting in 2004, the whole thing may implode. Alternately, the EU could become a world superpower.

FARC: Armed left wing Colombian rebels who tax the drug trade while theoretically pushing for peasant rights and crop substitution for coca farmers, FARC—or rather its ongoing war with the Colombian government—is a main factor in why the U.S. is engaging in Plan Colombia. See Colombia.

G-8: The Group of Eight Leading Industrial Nations, the G-8 are the Big Boys of the global economy—namely the U.S., Britain, France, Germany, Italy, Japan, Canada and Russia—whose countries claim over half of the world's economic output. Loosely organized, it's nearly a Gentlemen's Club and not just anyone can join: member countries have to be democracies, for one thing, which is why China isn't on the roster. Beside economic matters, the G-8 discusses such issues as terrorism, poverty, drugs and unemployment between multicourse dinners and lunches.

Hamas: Islamic resistance movement that has one main objective—eliminate Israel—and is behind much anti-Israeli violence coming out of the West Bank. Started by the Muslim Brotherhood, the militant group also has humanitarian goals: it runs food and medical programs and gives out scholarships for Palestinians studying to be doctors. Known for also attacking Muslims whom they regard as too closely aligned with Israelis, the group also despises Palestine Authority leader Yasser Arafat. See Israel and Palestine.

Hezbollah: Backed by Iran, this Lebanese group of Shiites started up in 1982 when Israel invaded southern Lebanon. An anti-Israeli resistance group, they also run clinics, own TV and radio stations and hold seats in the Lebanese parliament.

IRA: Irish Republican Army. Said to be the originators of the militant "cell," the Irish Republican Army's original goal was to free Northern Ireland from the British government. American George Mitchell helped bring about "Good Friday Agreement," a peace treaty between the IRA and the British government, but peace is tenuous. Their political arm is Sinn Fein.

ISI: Pakistan's secret service that trained mujahideen, adored Osama bin Laden and sent mujahideen to stir up discord, the shady ISI wasn't pleased when Pakistan's president decided to help the U.S. with its "War on Terror." Can put in and take out leaders.

Kurds: Ethnically different from the majority populations in Turkey and Iraq, where most live, Kurds saw their culture repressed in Turkey and were gassed by Saddam Hussein. Promised their own land after World War I by the Brits, they never got it; starting in the 1980s PKK (Kurdistan Workers' Party) fought for an independent Kurdistan in Turkey, with some thirty thousand dying in a sixteen-year struggle. Promised U.S. support if they rose up against Saddam Hussein in 1991, Kurds were massacred by the Iraqi Army when the U.S. didn't show up. Turkey fears that Kurds in Iraq will establish an independent country in a post-Saddam era, and has promised military action if they do. See Turkey, Iraq.

Labor party (Israel): More moderate than right wing Likud, Israel's Labor party is more willing to engage in peace negotiations. The party of Shimon Peres and Ehud Barak.

Landless Farmers: Millions of Brazilian peasants who are pressuring the government to give them land, by illegally setting up homes and farms on large plantations.

Likud: Right-wing Israeli party that pushes security over peace and favors settlements in Palestine and Syria. The party of Ariel Sharon and Benjamin Netanyahu will never go down in history for being peacemakers.

Mossad: Israel's secret service that aims to assassinate enemies of Israel.

Muslim Brotherhood: Godfather of all modern Islamist movements, this Egyptian group was born in the 1920s and aimed to clear Egypt of Western influence and put a religious government in power. They haven't been really successful in either aim, but greatly influenced many militant Muslim groups around today, from Al Qaeda to Hamas. Technically outlawed, the now violence-shunning (or so they claim) Muslim Brotherhood nevertheless operates in the open, running clinics, ambulances and other social services; its members occupy seats in Egypt's Parliament too.

National Security Council: Not to be confused with the UN Security Council, this influential group of special advisors—among them weighty Condoleezza Rice—help guide the U.S. President and form foreign policy.

NATO (North Atlantic Treaty Organization): This world's mightiest military alliance, this Western European–North American organization was created in 1949 to counter the Soviet threat of communism in Europe. They were so effective that despite the trillions sunk into weaponry, they never were called out to fight during the Cold War. Since the downfall of the Soviet Union in 1991, NATO has been trying to figure out what its purpose is anymore. When it finally did go out to fight—in the 1999 Kosovo campaign—NATO actions were blunder-filled, including the accidental bombing of the Chinese embassy in Belgrade. Now the group that rose to battle the communists has new members, including Russia. Members: Belgium, the Czech Republic, Denmark, France, Germany, Greece, Hungary, Iceland, Italy, Luxembourg, the Netherlands, Norway, Poland, Portugal, Russia, Spain, Turkey, the U.S. and the U.K.

Organization of American States (OAS): Formed in 1948, this association of governments includes all Latin American countries and the U.S.

Organization of Islamic Conferences (OIC): With fifty-seven members from four continents, the Organization of Islamic Conferences is the largest organization of Muslim countries in the world. Founded in 1969, OIC is mostly an arena for discussion, and the group often sends requests to the UN for action. At its meeting in October, OIC condemned the September 11 attacks on the U.S. and tiptoed around the U.S. retaliatory bombing of Aghanistan, neither supporting nor condemning it.

Organization of Petroleum Exporting Countries (OPEC): The name may not have been widely known until 1973—when OPEC raised international prices and embargoed their oil to the U.S., but the cartel has been controlling much of the world's petroleum supplies—and thus the prices—since 1960, when it was formed by Saudi Arabia, Iran, Iraq, Kuwait and Venezuela. Current members also include Nigeria, Algeria, Libya, Indonesia, United Arab Emirates, Qatar and Gabon.

Peres, Shimon: Israeli statesman who's been prime minister twice and is handtied foreign minister under Ariel Sharon (2001–present), Peres shared the 1994 Nobel Peace Prize with Israeli Prime Minister Yitzhak Rabin and the PLO chairman Yasser Arafat for his work on the Oslo Accords the previous year. Appearing sincerely dedicated to negotiating peace with Palestinians, Peres is now a spry eighty.

SAVAK: Iran's secret service which under the Shah was believed to have killed thousands in the 1970s.

United Nations (UN): The first international organization of such a vast scale, the United Nations was formed by fifty-one countries in October 1945; currently its members represent 189 countries. Seeking to "maintain international peace and security," "develop friendly relations," "cooperate in international problems" while "harmonizing" international relations, the association is best known for its General Assembly (representing all nations) and its high-profile Security Council. With a mind-boggling array of goals— from fostering economic development to aiding refugees—the UN is often accused of being too strongly linked to the U.S., which is often behind in paying its UN dues.

United Nations Security Council: The major power players of the UN, the fifteen-member Security Council is responsible for trying to maintain international peace and security: they're the ones who send out peacekeepers, call for cease-fires, slap on economic sanctions and try to negotiate international disputes. China, France, Russia, the U.K. and the U.S. hold permanent seats— and all of their "yeas" are required on big matters. Other seats rotate every two years between UN member countries, which are selected by region.

World Health Organization (WHO): This specialized agency affiliated with the UN eradicated smallpox, helps control malaria and is the last word on

global health. Accused of bias in recent years: they all but hid a study find-
ing that secondhand smoke did not cause cancer and they've been under
fire by antinuclear organizations for their affiliation with the International
Atomic Energy Agency; some think the bond has interfered with studies,
such as those showing an unexpectedly low rate of cancer in groups exposed to Chernobyl radioactive fallout. WHO never conducted anticipated
studies about the use of depleted uranium in Iraq.

World Trade Organization (WTO): Referee board for the big global traders, the
weighty World Trade Organization makes rulings on government tariffs and
policies. Their opinion helped resolve the "banana war" between the U.S. and
the European Union; they've also ruled on such matters as the U.S. tariffs on
Canada lumber.

Yousef, Ramzi Ahmed: Bomb maker, follower of the "Blind Sheik" and militant
Muslim, Yousef was the mastermind of the first bombing of the World Trade
Center, in February 1993, which killed six and injured hundreds, at that time
the deadliest attack on U.S. soil. Yousef had other devious ideas, including
a plan to simultaneously blow up eleven American commercial jets flying
over the Pacific. In 1998, the deadly dreamer was found guilty and sentenced to life imprisonment in the U.S.

Al-Zawahiri, Ayman Mohammed (aka Dr. Abdel Moez): Al Qaeda's number two
man and the group's philosophical guru, Egyptian physician Ayman al-
Zawahiri has been seething since the 1970s, when he took ideas he'd picked
up from the Muslim Brotherhood—foremost that Egypt's secular government should be Islamic—and organized a younger more radical group, Al-
Jihad. When Egyptian President Anwar Sadat made peace with Israel in
1979, Al-Jihad plotted to kill him, a fait accompli two years later. Rounded
up in the subsequent sweeps, al-Zawahiri served three years in Egyptian
prison for illegal possession of weapons; upon release in 1984, he headed
to Pakistan, where he may have first met bin Laden during the Soviet-
Afghan War. What's for sure: the Egyptian and the Saudi aligned in Sudan
to form what would become Al Qaeda. Indicted in the 1998 U.S. embassy
bombings and sentenced to death in absentia for the 1995 bombing of the
Egyptian embassy in Pakistan's capital, al-Zawahiri is skilled at multitask-
ing: between plotting government overthrows, writing books (most recently
his memoirs), raising money and (some believe) tending to bin Laden's reported kidney maladies, he's served as philosophical leader of, brains behind and most recently spokesman for Al Qaeda. Al-Zawahiri's initial gripes
included that the U.S. helped keep Islamists out of power in Egypt, backed
Israel and had an overreaching presence in the Middle East. Now he has far
more to be furious about: his wife and children were killed in a bombing dur-

ing the Afghanistan campaign, and during an October 2002 video—in which he promised more devastation to the U.S.—the bespectacled Islamist looked terribly ill; his thick speech and eyes rolling back in his head made one wonder if he'd been gassed. Then again, perhaps he was high on heroin and simply "on the nod."

Bibliography

Bard, Mitchell, Ph.D. *The Complete Idiot's Guide to the Middle East Conflict.* Indianapolis: Alpha Books, 1999.*

Berhardson, Wayne. *Argentina, Uruguay, Paraguay.* Oakland, CA: Lonely Planet, 1996.

Blum, Howard. *The Gold of Exodus: The Discovery of the Most Sacred Place on Earth.* London: Hodder and Stoughton, 1998.

Blum, William. *Rogue State: A Guide to the World's Only Superpower.* London: Zed Books Limited, 2000.

Bodansky, Yossef. *Bin Laden: The Man Who Declared War on America.* New York: Random House, 2001.

Brosnahan, Tom. *Turkey: A Travel Survival Kit.* Berkeley, CA: Lonely Planet, 1993.

Buckley, Michael. *Bangkok Handbook.* Chico, CA: Moon Publications, 1992.

Bunge, Frederica M. *Philippines: A Country Study.* Washington, DC: Foreign Area Studies, The American University, 1984.

———. *South Korea: A Country Study.* Washington, DC: Foreign Area Studies, The American University, 1982.

Bunge, Frederica M., and Nena Vreeland. *Indonesia: A Country Study.* Washington, DC: Foreign Area Studies, The American University, 1983.

Bunge, Frederica M., and Donald P. Whitaker. *Japan: A Country Study.* Washington, DC: Federal Research Division, Library of Congress, 1990.

Chomsky, Noam. *The Fateful Triangle: The United States, Israel and Palestine.* Boston: South End Press, 1983.

———. *A New Generation Draws the Line: Kosovo, East Timor and the Standards of the West.* London: Verso, 2000.

———. *Propaganda and the Public Mind.* London: Pluto Press, 2001.

Collier, Simon, and Harold Blakemore, eds. *The Cambridge Encyclopedia of Latin America and the Caribbean.* New York: Cambridge University Press, 1989.

Crassweller, Robert. *Peron and the Enigmas of Argentina.* New York: W.W. Norton, 1987.

Crossette, Barbara. *India: Old Civilization in a New World.* New York: Foreign Policy Association, 2000.

*Professor Bard's book is chock-full of great information about the Israeli-Palestinian situation and entirely biased toward Israel.

Crow, John A. *Spain: The Root and the Flower.* Berkeley: University of California Press, Ltd., 1985.

Curtis, Glenn E. *Kazakstan, Kyrgyzstan, Tajikistan, Turkmenistan and Uzbekistan: Country Studies.* Federal Research Division, Library of Congress, 1997.

———. *Yugoslavia: A Country Study.* Washington, DC: Federal Research Division, Library of Congress, 1992.

Davison, Michael Worth, ed. *When, Where, Why and How It Happened.* New York: Reader's Digest Association Ltd, 1993.

Dudley, William, ed. *The Middle East: Opposing Viewpoints.* Greenhaven Press, 1992.

De Blij, H. J., and Peter O. Muller. *Geography: Realms, Regions and Concepts.* New York: John Wiley & Sons, 1997.

Ebrey, Patricia Buckley. *Cambridge Illustrated History China.* Cambridge: Cambridge University Press: 2001.

Evans, Graham, and Jeffrey Newman. *The Penguin Dictionary of International Relations.* New York: Penguin Putnam Inc., 1998.

Evans, Richard. *Deng Xiaoping and the Making of Modern China.* London: Penguin, 1997.

Feitlowitz, Marguerite. *A Lexicon of Terror: Argentina and the Legacies of Torture.* New York: Oxford University Press, 1998.

Fisk, Robert. *Pity the Nation: Lebanon at War.* Oxford: Oxford University Press, 2001.

Fletcher, Richard. *Moorish Spain.* New York: Henry Holt and Co., 1992.

Franklin, Fay, ed. *History's Timeline.* New York: Crescent Books/Crown, 1981.

Friedman, Thomas L. *From Beirut to Jerusalem.* New York: Anchor Press, 1995.

Geyer, Georgie Anne. *Buying the Night Flight.* New York: Delacorte Press, 1983.

Glenny, Misha. *The Balkans: Nationalism, War, and the Great Powers: 1804–1999.* New York: Penguin, 2001.

Gresh, Alain, and Dominique Vidal. *A to Z of the Middle East.* Atlantic Highlands, NJ: Zed Publishing, 1990.

Haggerty, Richard A. *Venezuela: A Country Study.* Washington, DC: Federal Research Division, Library of Congress, 1993.

Hertz, Noreena. *The Silent Takeover: Global Capitalism and the Death of Democracy.* London: William Heinemann, the Random House Group, 2001.

Hooper, John. *The New Spaniards.* London: Penguin, 1995.

Guillermoprieto, Alma. *Looking for History: Dispatches from Latin America.* New York: Vintage, 2002.

Harris, Joseph E., Ph.D. *Africans and Their History.* New York: Penguin, 1998.

Hopkins, Adam, and Gabrielle MacPhedran. *Fodor's Exploring Spain.* New York: Fodor's Travel Publications, 1996.

Hourani, Albert. *A History of the Arab People.* New York: Warner Books, 1992.

Huntington, Samuel P. *The Clash of Civilizations and the Remaking of World Order.* New York: Touchstone, 1996.

Inman, Nick. *Spain.* New York: DK Publishing, 1999.

Jennings, Peter, and Todd Brewster. *The Century.* New York: Doubleday, 1998.

Kaplan, Robert. *The Ends of the Earth: A Journey to the Frontiers of Anarchy.* New York: Vintage, 1996.

Keefe, Eugene K. *Spain: A Country Study.* Washington, DC: Foreign Area Studies, The American University, 1985.

Kirk, John M. *José Martí: Mentor of the Cuban Nation.* Tampa: University Presses of Florida, 1983.

Knight, Franklin W. *The Caribbean: The Genesis of a Fragmented Nationalism.* New York: Oxford University Press, 1990.

Kristof, Nicholas D., and Sheryl Wudunn. *Thunder from the East.* New York: Vintage, 2000.

Kux, Dennis. *Pakistan: Flawed Not Failed State.* New York: Foreign Policy Association, 2001.

Lapidus, Ira M. *A History of Islamic Societies.* New York: Cambridge University Press, 1988.

Laqueur, Walter. *The New Terrorism: Fanaticism and the Arms of Mass Destruction.* London: Phoenix Press, 2002.

LePoer, Barbara Leitch. *Singapore: A Country Study.* Washington, DC: Federal Research Division, Library of Congress, 1991.

———. *Thailand: A Country Study.* Washington, DC: Federal Research Division, Library of Congress, 1989.

Lewis, Bernard. *The Middle East: A Brief History of the Last 2,000 Years.* New York: Touchstone, 1995.

Lewis, Jon E. *The Mammoth Book of Eye-Witness History.* New York: Carroll and Graf, 1998.

Malcolm, Noel. *Bosnia: A Short History.* New York: New York University Press, 1994.

———. *Kosovo: A Short History.* New York: HarperCollins, 1999.

Marshall, Bruce, ed. *The Real World: Understanding the Modern World through the New Geography.* Boston: Houghton Mifflin Company, 1991.

McLean, Iain. *Oxford Concise Dictionary of Politics.* New York: Oxford University Press, 1996.

Metz, Helen Chapin. *Iran: A Country Study.* Washington, DC: Federal Research Division, Library of Congress, 1989.

Michener, James. *Iberia: Spanish Travels and Reflections.* New York: Random House, 1968.

Miller, Judith. *God Has Ninety-Nine Names: Reporting from a Militant Middle East.* New York: Touchstone, 1997.

Milton, Giles. *Nathaniel's Nutmeg.* New York: Farrar, Straus and Giroux, 1999.

Naipaul, V.S. *Beyond Belief: Islamic Excursions among the Converted People.* New York: Vintage, 1999.

O'Connor, Geoffrey. *Amazon Journal: Dispatches from a Vanishing Frontier.* New York: Plume, 1998.

Pilger, John. *The New Rulers of the World.* London: Verso, 2002.

Pinder, John. *The European Union: A Very Short Introduction.* Oxford: Oxford University Press, 2001.

Potter, Lawrence G. *The Persian Gulf in Transition.* New York: Foreign Policy Association, 1998.

Rashid, Ahmed. *The Taliban: Militant Islam, Oil and Fundamentalism in Central Asia.* New Haven: Yale University Press, 2001.

Reeve, Simon. *The New Jackals: Ramzi Yousef, Osama bin Laden and the Future of Terrorism.* London: Andre Deutsch, 1999.

Rogozinski, Jan. *A Brief History of the Caribbean: From the Arawak and Carib to the Present.* New York: Plume, 2000.

Rohr, Janelle, ed. *The Third World: Opposing Viewpoints.* San Diego: Greenhaven Press, 1989.

Roosevelt, Kermit. *Arabs, Oil and History.* New York: Harper and Brothers, 1949.

Rothfeder, Jeffrey. *Every Drop for Sale: Our Desperate Battle over Water in a World About to Run Out.* New York: Putnam, 2001.

Rutherford, Scott, ed. *Bangkok Insight Guide.* London: APA, 1996.

———. *Burma, Myanmar Insight Guide.* London: APA, 1996.

———. *Japan Insight Guide.* London: APA, 1998.

———. *Malaysia Insight Guide.* London: APA, 1999.

———. *Philippines Insight Guide.* London: APA, 1998.

———. *Taiwan Insight Guide.* London: APA, 2000.

Ruthven, Louise. *Cairo.* Amsterdam: Time-Life International, 1980.

Said, Edward. *The End of the Peace Process: Oslo and After.* New York: Vintage, 2001.

Schlosser, Eric. *Fast Food Nation.* London: Penguin, 2002.

Scobie, James. *Argentina: A City and a Nation.* New York: Oxford University Press, 1971.

Silber, Laura, and Allan Little. *Yugoslavia: Death of a Nation.* New York: TV Books/ Penguin USA (dist), 1996.

Skidmore, Thomas E., and Peter H. Smith. *Modern Latin America.* Oxford: Oxford University Press, 2001.

Smith, Wayne S. *Portrait of Cuba.* Atlanta: Turner Publishing, 1991.

Stalker, Peter. *Handbook of the World.* New York: Oxford University Press, 2000.

Tarallo, Pietro. *Asia: Between History and Legend.* New York: White Star.

Viorst, Milton. *Sandcastles: The Arabs in Search of the Modern World.* New York: Knopf, 1994.

Weaver, Mary Anne. *A Portrait of Egypt: A Journey Through the World of Militant Islam.* New York: Farrar, Straus and Giroux, 2000.

Wheeler, Tony. *Southeast Asia on a Shoestring.* Berkeley, CA: Lonely Planet, 1992.

Williamson, Edwin. *The Penguin History of Latin America.* London: The Penguin Press, 1992.

Wyatt, David K. *Thailand: A Short History.* New Haven: Yale University Press, 1984.

Yergin, Daniel. *The Prize: The Epic Quest for Oil, Money and Power.* New York: Touchstone, 1993.

Resources

Magazines, Newspapers, Online Publications and Websites

"All Things Considered" (NPR)

alternet.org

The Atlantic

BBC online
news.bbc.co.uk

Brookings Institute
www.brook.edu

Bulletin of Atomic Scientists
www.bullatomsci.org

The Cairo Times (Cairo)

Center for Defense Information
www.cdi.org

cnn.com

www.commondreams.org

www.countrywatch.com

The Daily Telegraph (London)

The Economist (London)

Department of Energy
www.eia.doe.gov

Financial Times (London)

Foreign Affairs
www.foreignaffairs.org

Foreign Policy Association
fpa.org

Foreign Policy in Focus
foreignpolicy-infocus.com

Frontline (PBS)
www.pbs.org/wgbh/pages/frontline

Great Decisions Series
www.fpa.org

The Guardian (London)
www.guardian.co.uk

Harpers

Human Rights Watch
www.hrw.org

The Independent (London)

International Herald Tribune

Jane's Defense Weekly

The Jerusalem Post

www.lonelyplanet.com

Los Angeles Times

McCleans

Mother Jones
www.motherjones.com

msnbc.com

National Public Radio
npr.org

The New Republic

News Hour with Jim Lehrer
www.pbs.org/newshour

Newsweek and Newsweek
International

The New York Times
www.nytimes.com

The New Yorker

Nightline with Ted Koppel (ABC)

pbs.org

60 Minutes (CBS)

www.terrorismanswers.com

Time

tompaine.com

U.S. CIA World Factbook
www.cia.gov/cia/publications/factbook

U.S. Library of Congress
www.loc.gov

U.S. State Department
www.usinfo.state.gov

The Washington Post
www.washingtonpost.com

Washington Times

www.worldpolicy.org

Notes

In researching this project, I read thousands of articles, watched numerous shows, read dozens of books, contacted everyone I could and was continually amazed by the work of so many thoughtful, plugged-in and talented people—and those were only the ones whose language I could read. The following are but a few of the helpful resources I encountered, but ones that made a difference. I'm emphasizing Internet sources where possible and focusing mostly on information in "Tickers" and "Slow Tickers." In all sections, the Fast Facts sources were the *CIA 2001 World Factbook* and the *CIA 2002 World Factbook*. Additional notes, links and updates will be posted on the Internet site www.armchairdiplomat.com.

Iraq

As of this writing, the United Nations Security Council had unanimously authorized a resolution demanding that Iraq comply with international mandates, acknowledge and turn over all its biological, chemical and nuclear weapons and allow United Nations weapons inspectors to return; nevertheless a U.S.-led attack on Iraq still appears highly probable during early 2003.

p. 4 [Some] *believe the country's oil riches are the real attraction* Sources include Youssef M. Ibrahim, "Bush's Iraq Adventure Is Bound to Backfire," *International Herald Tribune,* 11/1/02; U.S. Representative Cynthia McKinney, "Another Oil War," *Counterpunch,* 9/23/02, www.counterpunch.org/mckinney0922.html; Dan Morgan and David B. Ottaway, "In Iraqi War Scenario, Oil Is Key Issue," *Washington Post,* 9/15/02, www.washingtonpost.com; Michael Kinsley, "Oil and Israel," MSNBC, 10/24/02, www.msnbc.com/news/825517.asp; "All About Oil," Nightline, ABC News, 10/2/02; "Spoils of War," ABC News.com, 10/4/02, www.abcnews.com; Michael Moran, "Oil, War and the Future of Iraq," 10/10/02, www.msnbc.com/news/819220.asp; James Ridgeway, "The Spoils of War," *Village Voice,* 10/11/02, www.alternet.org.

p. 6 *Chemical Warfare* (U.S. supported Saddam after gassing) Sources include J. F. O. McAllister, "Diplomacy: The Lessons of Iraq," *Time,* 11/02/02; Michael Albert, "Chomsky on Iraq, U.S., Weapons—A Preview," an excerpt from *Z* magazine, *Scoop,* 9/9/02, ww.scoop.co.nz/mason/stories/HL0209/ S00041.htm; Patrick Tyler, "Officers Say U.S. Aided Iraq Despite Use of Gas," *New York Times,* 8/17/02.

p. 7 *Mixed Signals or Green Light?* Graham Evans and Jeffrey Newnham, *Penguin Dictionary of International Relations,* London: Penguin Group, 1998, p. 432. Excerpts of meeting: http://achilles.net/~sal/greenlight.htm.

p. 7 *Was He or Wasn't He?* Sources include Howard Blum, *The Gold of Exodus: The Discovery of the Most Sacred Place on Earth,* London: Hodder and Stoughton, 1998, p. 327 (note: Blum is a former *New York Times* reporter, twice nominated for the Pulitzer Prize); letter to Senator Jesse Helms from columnist Jude Wanniski, "Where Did Saddam Come From, Part II," 2/19/98, www.polycomics.com/searchbase/02-19-98.html.

p. 8 *. . . President Bush, Sr., encouraged the Kurds . . .* Sources include Peter W. Galbraith, "There's a Price for Kurdish Help Against Saddam," *International Herald Tribune,* 8/12/02; "Overthrowing Saddam Hussein: Testimony of Ahmad Chalabi, President of the Executive Council of the Iraqi Congress to the Senate Foreign Relations Committee," 3/2/98; Howard G. Chua-Eoan, "WORLD: Iraq Defeat and Flight," *Time,* 4/15/91.

p. 8 *Nukes Lite* Scott Peterson, "A Rare Visit to Iraq's Radioactive Battlefield," *Christian Science Monitor,* 4/29/99; www.csmonitor.com/durable/1999/04/29/p13s1.htm; Scott Peterson, "Pentagon Stance on DU a Moving Target," *Christian Science Monitor,* 4/30/99, www.csmonitor.com/atcsmonitor/specials/uranium; "International: Defiance and Death: Iraq," *The Economist,* 9/14/02; Alex Kirby, "Depleted Uranium: The Lingering Poison," BBC News, World Edition, 6/7/99, http://news.bbc.co.uk/2/hi/in_depth/362484.stm; Ramsey Clark, "An International Appeal to Ban the Use of Depleted Uranium Weapons," www.iacenter.org/depleted/appeal.htm; speech by Dr. Doug Rokke, Ph.D. presented at UNESCO International Conference, 5/24/01, "The Scourge of Depleted Uranium," www.nirs.org/intl/depleteduranium.htm; press release of United States Department of Defense, 12/19/00, "Gulf War Depleted Uranium Environmental Exposure Report Update," www.defenselink.mil/news/b12192000_bt753-00.html; Department of Defense Briefing—Mr. Kenneth H. Bacon, ASD PA, 1/4/01, www.defenselink.mil/news/Jan2001/t01042001_t0104asd.html.

p. 12 [Saddam] *has a gentle side . . .* Sources include "Alleged Mistress Describes Saddam," Associated Press Online, 9/10/02.

Israel and Palestine

Helpful info: See "Israel and Palestinians" Key Maps, http://news.bbc.co.uk/hi/english/static/in_depth/world/2001/israel_and_palestinians; "Middle East Conflict," News Hour with Jim Lehrer www.pbs.org/newshour/bb/middle_east/conflict.

p. 15 *Arms for Peace* Sources include Mitchell Bard, "U.S. Aid to Israel," Jewish Virtual Library, www.us-israel.org/jsource/US-Israel/foreign_aid.html; "Issues-Foreign Aid-The Budget for 2001," www.yannone.org/NewFiles/foreign-aid-costs.html; "Israel USAID," www.usaid.gov/regions/ane/newpages/one_

pagers/israel01a.htm; "A High Price, but Worth It," *Denver Rocky Mountain News,* 1/5/00; Shirl McArthur, "U.S. Tax Dollars at Work: Calculating Foreign Aid to Israel," policy brief, The Center for Policy Analysis on Palestine, www.hotpolitics.com/tax4israel.htm.

p. 18 *Bloody History* Alain Gresh and Dominique Vidal, *A to Z of the Middle East,* London: Zed Books, 1990. Also see: www.unitedjerusalem.com/HIS-TORICAL_PERSPECTIVES/Israel_Wars_Maps_History/israel_war_maps_history.asp#anchor1_map1947 and www.jajz-ed.org.il/100/maps/refuge.html.

p. 19 *Oslo Accords* More info: www.cnn.com/SPECIALS/2001/mideast/stories/palestinian.government; www.acpr.org.il/resources/oslo1.html; www.acpr.org.il/maps/index.html.

p. 21 *The ratio of dead Palestinians to Israelis . . .* For latest figures from both sides, see www.miftah.org and www.btselem.org.

Indonesia

p. 29 *Starting in May 1997 . . .* See timeline at www.fas.org/man/crs/crs-asia2.htm.

p. 29 *Riots broke out, dictator Suharto was tossed . . .* Suharto officially resigned in May 1998.

p. 29 *. . . the Dayak hacked up—and ate—their enemies . . .* Simon Elegant, "The Darkest Season" *Time,* www.time.com/time/asia/news/magazine/0,9754,101389,00.html.

p. 29 *. . . even on relatively modernized Java, villagers decapitated each other . . .* Nicholas Kristof, *Thunder from the East,* New York: Vintage, 2001, pp. 1–17.

p. 29 *Bali Blast* Sources include R. Nolan, "Global Q&A—Indonesia and the Bali Blast Investigation," 11/21/02, Foreign Policy Association, www.fpa.org/topics_info2414/topics_info_show.htm?doc_id=134295.

p. 29 *Meanwhile, fringe Muslim groups . . .* Rajiv Chandrsekaran, "Radical Muslim Groups Assail Indonesia's Ties with US," *Washington Post,* 10/9/01; "Indonesian Clerics Warn of Jihad," CNN.com, 9/25/01, www.cnn.com/2001/WORLD/asiapcf/southeast/09/25/ret.indonesia.jihad/index.html; Melinda Liu and Joe Cochrane, "Battle of the Greens," *Newsweek International,* 7/1/02.

p. 31 *Semi-Slave Labor?* John Pilger, *The New Rulers of the World,* London: Verso, 2002, pp. 15–44.

Kashmir/India/Pakistan

p. 37 *Division didn't end the hostility . . . two more major wars in 1965 and 1971.* Note: the 1971 war started as a civil war between West Pakistan and East Pakistan.

p. 38 *Revved up and recently trained . . . sent in by Pakistan's questionable secret Inter-Services Intelligence . . .* Assorted sources, including Yossef Bodansky, *Bin Laden: The Man Who Declared War on America,* Roseville, CA: Prima Publishing, 1999, p. 320.

p. 38 *The mujahideen splashed violence . . .* See Luke Harding, "Valley of the

Vanishing Women," *The Guardian,* 9/4/01, www.guardian.co.uk/Kashmir/ Story/0,2763,546762,00.html. General Kashmir info: *The Guardian* and BBC both offer insightful overviews with maps. See "Jammu and Kashmir" at www.guardian.co.uk/flash/0,5860,627234,00.html, "India-Pakistan Troubled Relations" at http://news.bbc.co.uk/hi/english/static/in_depth/south_asia/2002/india_pakistan and "Kashmir Flashpoint" at http://news.bbc.co.uk/hi/english/in_depth/south_asia/2002/kashmir_flashpoint/.

p. 39   *If India and Pakistan Nuke It Out*   Assorted sources, estimates vary. See www.guardian.co.uk/kashmir/Story/0,2763,723512,00.html and www.nrdc.org/nuclear/southasia.asp.

p. 42   *Sir Cyril Radcliffe . . . unfamiliar with the country he was carving up . . .* Tim McGirk, "Making the Final Cut: An Able but Unprepared Barrister, Sir Cyril Radcliffe, Took a Heedless Knife to India in the Raj's Hectic Last Days," *Time International,* 8/11/97.

p. 46   *Bhopal*   Assorted sources, numbers vary. A few sources: Claude Salhani, "Bhopal: An Atomic Bomb About to Explode," UPI, 6/13/02. Also see www.bhopal.net/backdam.html and Union Carbide's www.bhopal.com.

p. 47   *Deobandism*   Celia Dugger, "Indian Town's Seed Grew into the Taliban's Code," *New York Times,* 2/23/02. Also see www.darululoom-deoband.com.

p. 48   *In the first country created specifically for Muslims . . .*   Note: however, Pakistan was created as a secular, nonreligious state, which it remains today.

p. 49   *madrassas*   Sources include Rick Bragg, "Nurturing Young Islamic Hearts and Hatred," *New York Times,* 10/14/01.

p. 49   *Along Afghan borders tribal elders mete out such gruesome punishments . . .*   See "Gang-Rape Trial Begins in Pakistan," BBC News, 7/26/02, http://news.bbc.co.uk/2/hi/world/south_asia/2153370.stm.

p. 50   *General Musharraf*   Pakistan's prez is looking iffier by the second, especially since it was revealed that he helped North Korea's nuclear program; David Sanger, "In North Korea and Pakistan, Deep Roots of Nuclear Barter," *New York Times,* 11/24/02.

North Korea

p. 54   *Skeletal Bodies*   North Korea suffered seven years of famine due to drought and shortages of fertilizer and energy supplies.

p. 54   *Long before North Korea snagged . . . missiles that could blast Seattle . . .* North Korea Advisory Group Report to the Speaker, U.S. House of Representatives, November 1999, www.house.gov/international_relations/nkag/report.htm.

p. 55   *So flick-crazy . . . kidnapping of his favorite South Korean actress . . .*   Assorted sources, including CNN in-Depth: "Korea at 50," www.cnn.com/SPECIALS/2000/korea/story.

p. 55   *Dear Leader may be stripping . . . pet projects include ostrich farms . . .* "Free Market Stirrings in North Korea," *The Economist,* 7/25/02.

p. 56   *"If the U.S. imperialists know that we do not have rice . . ."*   Speech by Kim Jong-il on the fiftieth anniversary of Kim il-Sung University, www.kimsoft.com/korea/kji-kisu.htm.

p. 58   *Among Dear Leader's alleged accomplishments . . .*   North Korea: Chronology of Provocations, 1950–2000, CRS Report for Congress.

p. 60   *Sunshine Policy*   The South Korean proengagement stance could cloud over the moment President Kim Dae Jung steps down.

Colombia

p. 61   *A murder rate thirteen times higher than the U.S.'!*   U.S. Government Travel Warnings, http://travel.state.gov/Colombia.html.

p. 63   *The reason: Plan Colombia . . .*   As of 2002, the United States had committed more than $2 billion to the project. Sources include Juan Forero, "Rightist's Hard Line Appeals to War-Weary Colombians," *New York Times,* 5/19/02; Narco-War: With Colombia Under a New Regime: The U.S. Must Avoid Getting Embroiled in Its Civil War," *Newsday,* 8/8/02; Garry Leech, "Washington Targets Colombia's Rebels," *Colombia Report,* 7/29/02, www.colombiareport.org/colombia124.htm; "Toxic Effects on Villagers: Herbicide Problems," *60 Minutes,* 1/14/02, www.cbsnews.com/stories/2002/01/10/60minutes/main323944.shtml. For an interesting range of comments on effects see "Colombia Policy Briefs: Fumigation," www.colombiapolicy.org/fumigation.htm.

p. 64   *Meanwhile, the real objective . . . over $98 million is earmarked . . .* Sources include Letta Taylor, "Oil a Key to U.S. Role in Colombia," *Newsday,* 3/4/02.

p. 66   *Pity the Peasant*   Sue Brandford, "Farmer Losing Colombia's Drugs War," BBC News, 1/17/02, http://news.bbc.co.uk/hi/english/world/from_our_correspondent/newsid_1765000/1765.

p. 67   *FARC's bad PR*   Jeremy McDermott, "Colombia Rebels Kill Cancer Boy's Father," BBC News, 4/7/02, http://news.bbc.co.uk/hi/english/world/americas/newsid_1915000/1915456.stm.

p. 68   [Pipeline] *leaked eleven times more crude oil than the* Exxon Valdez. . . . Amazon Watch, www.amazonwatch.org/megaprojects/020418_uwafacts.pdf.

p. 68   [Occidental Petroleum] *heavily lobbied Congress to authorize funding.* Sam Lowenberg, "Well-Financed US Lobby Seeks Relief from Drug Wars," *Legal Times,* 2/23/00.

p. 69   *The plan is a public relations nightmare . . .*   Assorted sources, including Senator Patrick Leahy, "The Colombia Quandary," *Los Angeles Times,* 5/5/02, www.leahy.senate.gov/issues/foreign%20policy/latimes%20op-ed.html; www.amazonwatch.org/megaprohects/plancol.html.

Russia

p. 74   *Broken Machine*   The World Bank Group, "The Impact on Poverty," 2002, www.worldbank.org.ru/eng/group/strategy3/strategy034.htm; Marielle Eudes, "Poverty Maintains Grip on Russia's New Poor," Agence France-Presse, 7/11/01, www.globalpolicy.org/socecon/develop/2001/0711russia.htm.

p. 77   *Oil Twitchings*   Multiple sources, including Edward Morse and James Richard, "The New Oil War," *Foreign Affairs,* 3–4/02.

p. 78   *To deflect criticism, Putin clamped down on the media . . .*   Assorted sources, including Romesh Ratnesar, "Putin's Media Blitz," *Time,* 4/30/01, www.time.com/time/europe/eu/magazine/0,9868,107338,00.html;   Emma Gray, "Putin's Media War," Committee for Protection of Journalists, Press Freedom Reports, 3/27/00, www.cpj.org.

Saudi Arabia

Great general information about Saudi Arabia: "Inside the Kingdom," News Hour with Jim Lehrer, 2/14–15/02, www.pbs.org/newshour. "Saudi Time Bomb?," *Frontline,* 10/20/01, www.pbs.org/wgbh/pages/shows/saudi/. Also helpful: www.saudiembassy.net.

p. 83   *Koran penned . . .*   Officially the Koran was revealed to Muhammad, whose hand was divinely guided as he wrote.

p. 85   *Average Per Capita Income for Saudis*   Neil MacFarquhar, "Leisure Class to Working Class in Saudi Arabia," *New York Times,* 8/26/01. See also "Palpitations at the Kingdom's Heart," *The Economist,* 8/24/02. Note: *The Economist* says it dropped from $24,000 to $7,000 "in less than a generation."

p. 86   *Scandal!*   Judith Miller, *God Has Ninety Names,* New York: Touchstone, 1996.

p. 87   *Ibn Saud actually wanted the geologists to look for water.*   Daniel Yergin, *The Prize,* New York: Touchstone, 1992.

p. 87   *Conquering a Desert*   Sources include "Saudi-U.S. Relations: Seven Decades of Friendship" and other articles from the Saudi Arabian Embassy magazine,   www.saudiembassy.net/publications/Magazines-Fall-2001/SA-US-Relations.htm; Judith Miller, *God Has Ninety Names,* New York: Touchstone, 1996.

p. 89   *Twelve of the September 11 hijackers . . .*   Charles M. Sennott, "Why bin Laden Relied on Saudi Hijackers," *Boston Globe,* 3/3/02, www.boston.com/news/packages/underattack/news/driving_a_wedge/part1.shtml.

p. 89   *Bin Laden's Smashed Dreams*   Sources include Yossef Bodansky, *Bin Laden: The Man Who Declared War on America,* Roseville, CA: Prima, 1999, pp. 28–32; Douglas Jehl, "Holy War Lured Saudis as Rulers Looked Away," *New York Times,* 12/27/01, www.pulitzer.org/year/2002/explanatory-reporting/works/122701.html; Patrick Tyler, "Feeling Secure, U.S. Failed to Grasp bin Laden Threat," *New York Times,* 9/8/02, www.mtholyoke.edu/acad/intrel/bush/tyler.htm.

p. 92   *Almost Last Supper*   "Missed Hit by Saudis?" UPI, 2/17/01, www.newsmax.com/archives/articles/2001/2/17/222240.shtml; Ian Bruce, "CIA Paid Saudi to Poison bin Laden," *The Herald,* 9/25/01, www.theherald.co.uk/news/archive/25-9-19101-1-4-59.html.

Egypt

General information: The *Cairo Times* (in English) gives a great insider's peek at Egyptian issues and politics, including censorship (www.cairotimes.com). Mary Anne Weaver's fascinating *A Portrait of Egypt* (New York: Farrar, Straus and Giroux, 2000) also provides an overview of VIPs, including the Muslim Brotherhood.

p. 93 *U.S. has given $40 billion . . .*   Following the money trail is tricky: since 1979 Egypt has received around $1.3 billion in military aid annually, as well as $700 million in nonmilitary aid yearly. An additional $14 billion of Egyptian international debt was also forgiven in exchange for Egypt supporting the 1991 Persian Gulf War (Desert Storm). USAID reports a total of $24.3 billion given to Egypt between 1975 and 2000; see www.usaid-eg.org/detail.asp?id=5. Note that most of the military aid must be spent buying U.S.-made military equipment: it's like the U.S. government issues a gift certificate for shopping at American military stores, so it helps boost the U.S. economy. Other sources include Susan Sachs, "The Despair Beneath the Arab World's Growing Rage," *New York Times,* 10/14/01.

p. 95 *Behind the Reappearing Veil*   Based on interviews.

p. 95 *Egyptians—notoriously passive—are loudly whispering . . .*   Sources include National Public Radio interview in which Geneive Abdo discusses how an Islamist movement has really taken over Egyptian society, *All Things Considered,* 10/20/00.

p. 97 *Changing History*   For all the great hoorah about this 1978 peace accord, it has resulted in a very cold peace: Egyptian-Israeli economic-political relations are often frosty and the whole facade continues mostly because of the annual U.S. financial bribe to both parties, which rarely gets mentioned.

p. 99 *This Won't Hurt a Bit!*   U.S. Department of State, Egypt: Report on FGM, 2001, www.state.gov/g/wi/rls/rep/crfgm/10096.htm.

p. 100 *. . . the Grand Mufti. . . . FGM as a Muslim woman's duty.*   United Nations Population Network, *Populi,* 23.1, 3/96, www.un.org/popin/unfpa/populi/popu9603.html. For more on population, see Mona Khalifa et al., "Population Growth in Egypt," Rand Issue Paper, www.rand.org/publications/IP/IP183/.

p. 100 *Shaking Loyalties*   Sources include Mary Anne Weaver, *A Portrait of Egypt,* New York: Farrar, Straus and Giroux, 2000, p. 162.

p. 101 *Gamal Mubarak*   Sources include "Egyptian Elections Bring Mubarak's Son into Spotlight," Associated Press, 10/27/00, www.cnn.com/2000/WORLD/meast/10/27/egypt.mubarak.son.ap/.

Iran

Helpful overview of Iran-U.S. relations: "Terror and Tehran," *Frontline,* www.pbs.org/wgbh/pages/frontline/shows/tehran.

p. 105 *They rounded up fifty-two hostages . . .*   Initially ninety hostages were taken, but some were released.

p. 105 *Taking Sides*   Iraq is Sunni-dominant, although about half of the population is Shiite.

p. 107 *. . . more than three hundred thousand chastity gals work Tehran alone.*   Nazila Fathi, "To Regulate Prostitution, Iran Ponders Brothels," *New York Times,* 8/28/02.

p. 107 *. . . the signs of change are everywhere . . .*   Sources include "Police on Guard in Tehran's Streets," Associated Press, 11/10/01.

p. 109 *Pointing Fingers?*   No one is sure how far along Iran may be in any nuclear weapons program, but Russia is in hot water over supplying them with reactors. See www.cdi.org/russia/217-3-pr.cfm, and Michael Donovan, "Iran, Israel and Nuclear Weapons," Center for Defense Information, 2/14/02, www. cdi.org/terrorism/menukes.cfm. For more on Iran's alleged terrorism links see www.terrorismfiles.org/countries/iran.html and www.terrorismanswers.com.

China

Great info: BBC online has specials sections, including "China: 50 Years of Communism," (http://news.bbc.co.uk). For a chronology of U.S.-China relations, see http://news.bbc.co.uk/hi/english/world/asia-pacific/newsid_1258000/1258054.stm.

p. 112   *The Chairman v. the Führer*   Matthew White's death stat site: http://users.erols.com/mwhite28/warstat1.htm.

p. 113   *1999: Chinese embassy . . .*   Sources include John Leicester, "China Demands Fuller U.S. Apology," Associated Press Online, 5/11/99.

p. 114   *Communiqué-tion*   Former U.S. ambassador to the United Nations Richard Holbrooke, "A Defining Moment with China," *Washington Post,* 1/1/02, www.cfr.org/public/resource.cgi?pub!4264. Also www.taiwandocuments.org; www.china-embassy.org/english.

p. 115   *Re: Arms*   "Concerns in U.S. About Israel-China Arms Deals," Reuters, 4/30/02; China-Taiwan arms, CNN.com asia, http://asia.cnn.com/SPECIALS/2001/us.china/includes/index.html; "Pentagon Warns of China Threat," CNN, 7/13/02, www.cnn.com/2002/WORLD/asiapcf/east/07/13/china.taiwan/index.html.

p. 115   *U.S. Worry List*   Jim Lobe and Tom Barry, "The Yellow Peril Revisited," *Foreign Policy in Focus,* 7/12/02, www.foreignpolicy-infocus.org/commentary/2002/0207china_body.html.

p. 118   *The Dalai Lama*   See www.tibet.comDL/biography.html.

p. 118   *Falun Gong*   See http://faluninfo.net.

Taiwan

Helpful overview: BBC's Timeline Taiwan at http://news.bbc.co.uk/hi/english/world/asia-pacific/newsid_1286000/1286033.stm.

p. 121   *Hundreds of China's missiles . . .*   Sources include Gerald Segal, "China's Options Against Taiwan Are Limited," 8/19/99, www.taiwandc.org/wsj-9909.htm.

p. 123   *The Road Less Decided*   See Nisid Hajari and Melinda Liu, "Chen Run," *Newsweek International,* 5/20/02.

Sudan

For great info about Hassan al-Turabi's conferences, see Yossef Bodansky, *Bin Laden: The Man Who Declared War on America,* Roseville, CA: Prima, 1999. Also see the Sudan section of Judith Miller, *God Has Ninety Names,* New York: Touchstone, 1996; Mary Anne Weaver, *A Portrait of Egypt,* New York: Farrar, Straus and Giroux, 2000.

p. 127   *Make That a Triple*   Sources include U.S. Committee for Refugees, www.refugees.org/news/crisis/sudan.htm; UNICEF, www.unicef.org/newsline/00prslpa.htm; Christian Solidarity International, www.csi-int.ch/; www.child-soldiers.org/report2001/countries/sudan.html.

p. 128   *The Prob*   Sources include "Sudan's Troubles," News Hour with Jim Lehrer, 7/25/01, www.pbs.org/newshour/bb/africa/july-dec01/sudan_7-25.html; "Sudan Oil Attacks to Continue," BBC, Business, 3/26/02, http://news.bbc.co.uk/hi/english/business/newsid_1894000/1894648.stm; Peter Wanbali, "In Khartoum's Oil Pipelines Flow Blood," *The Nation,* 5/21/02, http://allafrica.com/stories/printable/200205200647.html.

p. 130   *Invitation List*   Yossef Bodansky, *Bin Laden: The Man Who Declared War on America,* Roseville, CA: Prima, 1999.

p. 132   *Hassan al-Turabi*   For more info see Austin Cline "Islamic Extremism," http://atheism.about.com/library/islam/blfaq_islam_turabi.htm; Hannah Wettig, "More Equal Than Others," *Cairo Times,* 1/7/99, www.cairotimes.com/content/region/turabi.html.

Afghanistan

For a great overview, see Ahmed Rashid, *Taliban: Militant Islam, Oil and Fundamentalism in Central Asia,* New Haven, CT: Yale University Press, 2000.

p. 134   *Pipeline Scoop?*   Sources include Mary Pat Flaherty, "How Afghanistan Went Unlisted as Terrorist Sponsor," *Washington Post,* 11/05/01; "Central Asia Gas Deal Signed," BBC News, 5/30/02, http://news.bbc.co.uk/2/hi/world/south_asia/2016340.stm.

p. 137   *Turki Shoots*   Sources include Ahmed Rashid, *Taliban: Militant Islam, Oil and Fundamentalism in Central Asia,* New Haven, CT: Yale University Press, 2000, p. 48.

p. 139   *Cave Crumblers*   U.S. Department of Defense spokesman Colonel Dave LaPan, during an 11/6/02 interview, denied U.S. use of depleted uranium during campaign in Afghanistan.

p. 139   *Hamid Karzai*   Sources include Ilene R. Prusher et al., "Afghan Power Brokers," *Christian Science Monitor,* 6/10/02.

p. 140   *Eeeney Meeney Miney Mo*   Sources include Ilene R. Prusher et al., "Afghan Power Brokers," *Christian Science Monitor,* 6/10/02.

Somalia

p. 145   *Hey, Mr. Warlord, Where'd Ya Get That Gun?*   Dan Connell, "War Clouds over Somalia," *Common Dreams,* 3/26/02, www.commondreams.org/views02/0326-01.htm.

p. 146   *Will the Real Radio Mogadishu . . .*   BBC Country Profile, Somalia, http://news.bbc.co.uk.

p. 146   *Hussein Aideed*   Sources include "Fractured Leadership in a Fractured State," abcnews.com, abcnews.go.com/sections/world/DailyNews/Somalia.who.html.

Japan

p. 150   *Girls*   Sources include Nicholas D. Kristof, "Japanese Men Fawn Over High School Girls: Fantasies are Fulfilled in Mock Environment in Sex Club 'Classrooms,'" *Rocky Mountain News,* 4/20/97. More info at www.iastate.edu/~rhetoric/105H17/nnguyen/cof.html.

p. 150   *Checkbook Apologies   CIA World Factbook 2001.*

p. 151   *Japan's longtime anti-nuclear stance is also looking shaky*   Robin Lim, "Nuclear Temptation in Japan: No More American Umbrella?," *International Herald Tribune,* 4/15/02.

p. 152   *Japan bought a hefty $22 billion of U.S. arms . . .*   Monica Mehta, "The Best Defense Is a Good Offense," Mother Jones' Mojo Wire, www.motherjones.com/arms/japan.html.

p. 154   *Aum Shinri Kyo*   For more info see www.terrorismanswers.com.

Turkey

p. 161   *Battles between Kurds . . .*   See http://kurdistan.org; www.fas.org/asmp/profiles/turkey_background_kurds.htm.

p. 161   *Bone-chilling evidence*   See www.onwar.com/aced/data/alpha/armenia1915.htm.

p. 162   *Recep Tayyip Erdogan*   The troublemaking poem was religious; Erdogan was convicted of Islamist sedition.

Caucasus Combo

p. 163   *Caspian Considerations*   Sources include "The Next Middle East?" abcnews.com, 4/24/02; "The Quest for Caspian Crude," www.abcnews.go.com/sections/caspianoil930/index.html.

p. 167   *Pipeline Power*   Caspian Sea Region, Energy Information Administration, 7/02, www.eia.doe.gov/emeu/cabs/caspian.html.

p. 168   *Festive Religion*   Scott Simon, "Profile: Ancient Philosophical Practice of Kebzeh," National Public Radio, Weekend Edition, 7/6/02.

The 'Stans

p. 173   *Kazakhstan . . . nearly five hundred nuclear tests conducted there . . .*   Peter Stalker, *Oxford Handbook of the World,* New York: Oxford University Press, 2000. More energy info: www.eia.doe.gov/emeu/cabs/caspgrph.html#TAB1.

Philippines

p. 177   *Breeding Grounds*   Two percent of the population own over a third of the land. Source: Peter Stalker, *Oxford Handbook of the World,* New York: Oxford University Press, 2000.

p. 180   [Abu Sayyaf] . . . *grossed over $20 million . . .*   Sources include Emily Clark, "In the Spotlight: Abu Sayyaf," Center for Defense Information, 3/5/02, www.cdi.org/terrorism/sayyaf.cfm.

Syria

p. 184   *Few dared defy Assad . . .*   Sources include Scott Peterson, "How Syria's Brutal Past Colors Its Future," *Christian Science Monitor,* 6/20/00, www.csmonitor.com/durable/2000/06/20/pls3.htm.

p. 185   *Golan Heights*   Israel has considered purchasing the plateau from Syria. Associated Press, "Sheetrit: Buy Golan Heights from Syria," *Jerusalem Post,* 2/20/02.

Spain

p. 192   *Another factor that lures . . .*   Tourism dollars make up over half of the Spanish economy: July 2002 interview with Spanish tourism board.

p. 196   *ETA . . .*   Sources include Jo Episcopo, "ETA's Bloody Record," BBC News, 12/2/99, http://bbc.co.uk/hi/english/world/europe/newsid_547000/547130.stm; Daniel Schweimier, "Proud Basques Defend Ancient Culture," BBC, 12/6/99, http://news.bbc.co.uk/hi/english/world/europe/newsid_548000/548545.stm.

Jordan

p. 197   *Close calls*   Sources include "The Hashemite Dynasty," *The Sunday Telegraph,* 2/27/99.

p. 197   *Close connections*   Sources include Mary Beth Warner, "The Balancing Act That Is Jordan," *National Journal,* 10/6/01.

Mideast Medley

p. 207   *. . . a collective case of post-traumatic stress disorder . . .*   Brian Whitaker, "The Day Kuwait Wants to Forget," *The Observer,* 7/30/02, www.al-bab.com/arab/countries/kuwait/forget.htm.

p. 207   *A Happy Image*   Jeff Stein, "When Things Turn Weird, the Weird Turn Pro," TomPaine.common sense, 2/26/2002, http://tompaine.com/feature.cfm/ID/5188.

p. 212   *. . . Qataris the world's richest citizens by 2020.*   Peter Stalker, *Oxford Handbook of the World,* New York: Oxford University Press, 2000, confirmed with Qatari embassy.

Balkan Bunch

p. 213   *Problems still lurk in the shadows . . .*   Sources include David Binder and Preston Mendenhall, "Sex, Drugs and Guns in the Balkans," msnbc.com, 11/18/02, www.msnbc.com/news/667790 and personal interviews.

p. 220   *That left a lingering . . . depleted uranium . . .*   Sources include Marlise Simons, "Montenegro Cleaning up Radioactive Legacy of War," *New York Times,* 9/2/02.

p. 220   *Ethnic strife in this land of Serb, Muslim and Croat . . .*   Sources include David Lawday, "Doomed by an Ancient Disease," *U.S. News and World Report,* 5/17/93.

p. 222   *A frequent cargo: sex slaves ...*   Sources include Tom Hagler, "Trafficking: A Human Tragedy," BBC, 6/19/2000, http://news.bbc.co.uk/hi/english/world/europe/newsid_797000/797366.stm; Michael Voss, "Slave Trade Thrives in Bosnia, BBC, 3/8/01, http://news.bbc.co.uk/hi/english/world/europe/newsid_1209000/1209085.stm.

United Kingdom

p. 225   *... Tony sometimes acts like a faux U.S. ambassador ...*   Sources include Roy Denman, "Britain Plods along a Lonely Road," *International Herald Tribune,* 3/22/02; William Pfaff, "Britain Should Give up on EU and Rely on the U.S.," *International Herald Tribune,* 3/23/02.

p. 225   *Tony's support for George*   Sources include Stryker McGuire, "Oil Meets Oxbridge," *Newsweek International,* 10/14/02.

p. 226   *Britain has a thriving arms industry ...*   Sources include Will Self, "Addicted to Arms," BBC, 4/28/02, http://news.bbc.co.uk/2/low/programmes/correspondent/1939250.stm.

Western Europe

p. 228   *... powerful European Union ...*   Sources include John Pinder, *The European Union: A Very Short Introduction,* Oxford: Oxford University Press, 2001. For information on lovely Ireland—the only one of the European Union countries that put EU entry to the people as a vote—and peace-promoting Norway, see www.armchairdiplomat.com.

p. 228   *... a gnawing concern about immigration.*   Sources include Peter Finn, "A Turn from Tolerance: Anti-immigrant Movement in Europe Reflects Post–September 11 Views on Muslims," *Washington Post* Foreign Service Edition, 3/29/02; "Europe: Here We Come ... Anti-immigrant Politicians," *The Economist,* 3/16/02.

p. 228   *EU*   The twelve European Union countries using the Euro as of 2002 are Austria, Belgium, Finland, France, Germany, Greece, Ireland, Italy, Luxembourg, the Netherlands (aka Holland), Portugal and Spain. The three EU countries not using the Euro in 2002: Denmark, Sweden and the United Kingdom.

p. 230   *... German-U.S. relations overnight became extremely chilly.*   Sources include Jim Hoagland, "German Vote Exposes Global Fault Lines," *Washington Post,* 9/26/02.

Rwanda

p. 236   *The voice from the little box told them to.*   Sources include Bill Berkeley, "Sounds of Violence: Rwanda's Killer Radio," *The New Republic,* 8/22/94.

p. 236   *Dangerous Favoritism*   Sources include "Rwanda: How the Genocide Happened," BBC, 6/7/01, http://news.bbc.co.uk/2/hi/world/africa/1288230.stm. Tutsis and Hutus also duked it out during a low-grade civil war from 1990 to 1992. Peacekeepers were deployed in 1993 to help keep the calm.

p. 236   *Murderous Media Moguls*   Sources include Marlise Simons, "Trial Centers on Role of Press During Rwanda Massacre," *New York Times,* 3/3/02.

p. 237   *. . . "Hutu Power."*   Sources include George Packer, "Rwanda's Machete Rule," *The Nation,* 11/16/98.

p. 240   *. . . Romeo Dallaire*   Sources include Ken Ringle, "The Haunting; He Couldn't Stop the Slaughter in Rwanda," *Washington Post,* 6/15/02.

Thailand

p. 243   *Spirits in a Material World*   Sources include Wadee Kheourai, "Thai Studies through Games," www.thailandlife.com/spirithouses.htm.

p. 243   *. . . the HIV rate is rapidly declining . . .*   "Thailand Achieves Sustained Reduction in HIV Infection Rates," WHO report, www.who.int/inf-new/aids1.htm.

p. 243   *And to wipe out its poppy crops . . .*   Sources include *Thailand: International Narcotics Control Strategy Report-2001,* the Bureau for International Narcotics and Law Enforcement Affairs, U.S. Department of State, March 2002, www.usa.or.th/services/docs/reports/nr02thai.htm.

Latin American Medley

p. 247   *Many Brazilians believe that the U.S. plans to conquer the Amazon.*   Larry Rohter, "Deep in Brazil, a Flight of Paranoid Fancy," *New York Times,* 6/23/02.

p. 250   *Fiscal Nightmare*   See   www.guardian.co.uk/argentina/story/0.11439.687692,00.html.

p. 252   *Shining Path*   Sources include Robert Plummer, "Peru's Shining Path— Who Are They?," BBC, 7/15/99, http://news.bbc.co.uk/hi/english/world/americas/newsid_395000/395370.stm.

p. 253   *Baby Doc's wife helped . . .*   Jan Rogozinski, *A Brief History of the Caribbean,* New York: Plume, 2000, p. 270.

Cuba

p. 255   *Moves to open Cuba for American travel were shot down . . .*   Sources include Thomas Omestad, "So What's Castro Smoking," *U.S. News and World Report,* 4/29/02.

p. 256   *Model Behavior*   Based on personal interviews with European men.

p. 256   *Castro, who claims he's been a target of more than six hundred assassination plots . . .*   "Government Museum in Cuba Dedicated to Assassination Attempts on Fidel Castro," National Public Radio, 6/5/01.

Libya

Great info: Judith Miller, *God Has Ninety Names,* New York: Touchstone, 1996. You can't find a funnier profile of Qaddafi, including his amorous intentions with reporters.

p. 260   *. . . a whole new song and dance . . .*   Sources include Lawrence F. Kaplan, "The Quiet Coalition to Rehabilitate Qaddafi," *The New Republic,* 7/24/00.

p. 260 *Nobody in Libya . . .*   Sources include Neil Macfarquhar, "Libya Under Qaddafi: Disarray is the Norm," *New York Times,* 2/14/01.

p. 262 *U.S. Allegations*   Sources include Terrorism Q&A, Council on Foreign Relations, www.terrorismanswers.com/sponsors/libya.

Venezuela

p. 265 *Good looks*   Sources include Thomas Omestad, "In the Land of Mirror, Mirror on the Wall . . . ," *U.S. News and World Report,* 7/23/01.

p. 266 *If Amerigo Vespucci . . . "slickazuela" or maybe "chemazuela."*   Sources include Christina Hoag, "A Great Lake Fills with Filth . . . As Salt Seeps in from the Sea," *Business Week International,* 12/18/00, www.businessweek. com/2000/00_51/c3712238.htm.

p. 268 *Yikes*   Serge F. Kovaleski, "Violence Heightens Despair . . . ," *Washington Post,* Foreign Service Edition, 2/27/2000.

Mexico

p. 271 *Reverse Economy*   CorpWatch Corporate Globalization Fact Sheet, www. corpwatch.org.

p. 272 *Fox and others believe the rights of Mexico-born . . .*   Sources include "Mexico's Fox Cancels Texas Trip," BBC, 8/15/02, http://news.bbc.co.uk/2/ hi/world/americas/2194566.stm.

p. 273 *. . . border towns, where new* maquilladoras *. . .*   Sources include Ginger Thompson, "Chasing Mexico's Dream into Squalor," *New York Times,* 2/11/01.

Nigeria

p. 277 *. . . a space program . . .*   Jeff Koinange, "Inside Africa," CNN Traveller, spring/summer 2002.

p. 277 *. . . have instituted Shariah law at its harshest.*   Sources include "Sharia Compromise for Nigerian State," BBC, 11/2/2001, http://news.bbc.co.uk/hi/ english/world/africa/newsid_1634000/1634403.stm.

p. 279 *Amina Lawal*   Sources include Simon Robinson, "Casting Stones," *Time International,* 9/2/02.

African Assortment

p. 280 *. . . famine . . .*   Sources include Simon Robinson, "Scarred," *Time,* 8/5/02.

p. 283 *. . . [Mugabe is] kicking out all white land owners . . .*   Sources include "Mugabe Orders White Farmers to Leave," BBC, 8/12/02, www.news. bbc.co.uk/1/hi/world/africa/2187453.stm.

Southeast Asia Sampler

p. 288 *. . . a case of self-fulfilling prophecy . . .*   Sources include Susannah Price, "Royal Tragedy Seen in the Stars," BBC, 6/4/01, http://news.bbc. co.uk/hi/english/world/south_asia/newsid_1369000/1369375.stm.

p. 289   *Nearly 2 million died . . .*   Sources include "Cambodia to Resume UN Tribunal Talks," BBC, 8/27/02, http://news.bbc.co.uk/2/hi/world/asia-pacific/
2209063.stm.

Canada

p. 291   *North Pole: moving from Canada to Russia*   The North Magnetic Pole is
migrating and may bid Canada adieu by 2004. See www.cnn.com/2002/
TECH/space/03/20/north.pole.

p. 292   *Canada, Not Kansas!*   "While 60% of Canadians Consider U.S.A.
Canada's Closest Friend and Ally, Only 18% of Americans Name Canada
As Same—56% Instead Name Britain," Ipsos-Reid press release, 5/7/2002,
www.ipsos-reid.com/media/dsp_pre_more_cdn.cfm.

The Big Picture: Africa

p. 300   *Literary Problems . . .*   UNESCO, "Adult Literacy Rates . . . Africa,"
www.uis.unesco.org/en/stats/statistics/indicators/I_pages/literacyreg\litreg
19000.asp?.

p. 301   *Belgium's King Leopold II, whose men ravaged the Congo . . .*   "King
Leopold's Ghost," Fresh Air, National Public Radio, 9/9/98.

The Big Picture: Europe

p. 304   *Unification: the West and the East*   Current European Union countries are
Austria, Belgium, Denmark, Finland, France, Germany, Greece, Ireland,
Italy, Luxemburg, the Netherlands (aka Holland), Portugal, Spain, Sweden
and the United Kingdom (aka Britain). Ten new potential members (including the two Mediterranean islands of Cyprus and Malta) have been given
the initial okay to enter the EU in 2004: the Baltic states—Estonia, Latvia
and Lithuania—Cyprus, Czech Republic, Hungary, Malta, Poland, Slovakia
and Slovenia. See Paul Hazebroek, "Europe's Big Bang," Radio Netherlands, 10/9/02, www.rnw.nl/hotspots/htmal/eu021009.html. Turkey also wants
to get into the European club.

The Big Picture: Latin America

p. 307   *Whether you're talking about . . .*   The problem of land holdings is even
more extreme when one talks about fertile ground: 17 percent of Latin America's landowners have 90 percent of arable land according to some studies.
"Inequalities in the Third World," Oxfam, www.caa.org.au/publications/iid/
WATW/WATW4.html. In Ecuador, less than 3 percent own 44 percent of the
land; in Paraguay, 1 percent of landowners have 88 percent of the land; in
Brazil, 2 percent own half of the cultivatable land. Sources include "Development and Peace," www.devp.org/anglais/america.html; news.bbc.co.uk/
2/low/Americas.735225.stm; unesco.org/courier/2001-01/UK/doss21.htm.

The Big Picture: North America

p. 310   *Armchair Diplomat Says*   According to a 2002 Roper survey sponsored by *National Geographic,* young Americans are essentially geographically illiterate. Survey results indicate that of the eighteen-to-twenty-four-year-old crowd: 87 percent could not find Iraq; 83 percent could not find Afghanistan; 49 percent could not find New York state; and geez louise, 11 percent could not find the United States on a map. See "Global Goofs: U.S. Youth Can't Find Iraq," cnn.com, 11/20/02, www.cnn/2002/EDUCATION/11/20/geography.quiz/index.html. Take the quiz at www.nationalgeographic.com/geosurvey.

The Big Picture: Issues

For a fantastic overview of numerous environmental and geopolitical issues, check out the intriguing site of the Worldwatch Institute: www.worldwatch.org.

p. 313   *. . . in 2002, more than $700 billion was shucked out . . .*   Lawrence Korb, "Arms Spending Instead of Basic Aid," *International Herald Tribune,* 8/22/02.

p. 314   *. . . $396 billion—more than the total combined military purchases of the next twenty countries on the arms buyer list.*   CDI Center for Defense Information, "World Military Expenditures," www.cdi.org/issues/wme.

p. 314   *Armor-piercing depleted uranium*   The U.S. Department of Defense emphatically denies that depleted uranium (DU) was used in Afghanistan, although my research, including interviews with those fighting in Afghanistan, contradicts that. The Department of Defense does not consider DU harmful or a radiological weapon. For more info on the DOD's point of view, see www.deploymentlink.osd.mil/du_library. Others do consider DU harmful and to be the equivalent of dirty bombs. See Notes, Iraq, *Nukes Lite.* Also see John LaForge, "U.S. Dirty Bombs: Radioactive Shells Spiked with Plutonium," Common Dreams Center, 7/9/02, www.commondreams.org/views02/0709-07.htm. For more info from both sides of this controversial issue, see www.armchairdiplomat.com.

p. 316   *Others that don't admit it*   See cnn.com/SPECIAL/cold.war/experience/the.bomb/deployment.

p. 316   *Number of operating nuclear plants*   International Atomic Energy Agency. See www.insc.anl.gov/pwrmaps/map/world_map.php; "Nuclear Power Plants Information," International Atomic Agency Commission," http://www.iaea.org/cgi-bin/db.page.pl/pris.oprconst.htm and www.nucleartourist.com.

p. 317   *Water Waster*   Jeffrey Rothfeder, *Every Drop for Sale,* New York: Jeremy P. Tarcher, 2001, p. 189.

p. 320   *World's Top Ten Highest Population Growth Rates*   CIA World Factbook 2001.

Glossary

pp. 325–347   Also see the remarkable *Encylopaedia of the Orient* at http://lexicorient.com/e.o./index.htm and the *Middle East Israeli-Arab Glossary* at www.mideastweb.org/glossary.htm.

Index